EL DORADO CANYON

EL DORADO CANYON

Reagan's Undeclared War with Qaddafi

Joseph T. Stanik

Naval Institute Press
Annapolis, Maryland

Naval Institute Press
291 Wood Road
Annapolis, MD 21402

Library of Congress Cataloging-in-Publication Data

Stanik, Joseph T.
  El Dorado Canyon : Reagan's undeclared war with Qaddafi/ Joseph T. Stanik.
  p. cm.
  Includes bibliographical references and index.
  ISBN 1-55750-983-2 (alk. paper)
  1. United States—Foreign relations—Libya. 2. Libya—Foreign relations—United States. 3. United States—Foreign relations—1981-1989. 4. United States—Military relations—Libya. 5. Libya—Military relations—United States. 6. Reagan, Ronald. 7. Qaddafi, Muammar. I. Title.
  E183.8.L75 S726 2002
  327.730612—dc21

2002016520

Printed in the United States of America on acid-free paper ⊗
10 09 08 07 06 05 04 03   9 8 7 6 5 4 3 2
First printing

For my father, Joseph Stanik,
and in memory of my mother,
Maxine Slaven Stanik

Contents

Preface

In the dead of night on 15 April 1986, U.S. Air Force fighter-bombers and U.S. Navy attack aircraft struck terrorist headquarters and support facilities in and near the Libyan cities of Tripoli and Benghazi. President Ronald Reagan had ordered the operation—code named "El Dorado Canyon"—in retaliation for Libyan leader Muammar al-Qaddafi's involvement in a terrorist bombing in West Berlin that had claimed the life of one U.S. serviceman, mortally wounded a second, and injured several other Americans. The raid's purpose was three-fold: to punish Qaddafi for the West Berlin attack, to disrupt Libyan terrorist operations by crippling the country's terrorist infrastructure, and to dissuade Qaddafi from sponsoring or supporting further acts of terrorism. The American public overwhelmingly supported Reagan's decision to use force against Qaddafi, though many believed that Reagan should have acted much sooner against the agents and sponsors of international terrorism.

When Ronald Reagan took office as the fortieth president of the United States on 20 January 1981, the country was under assault from the forces of international terrorism. American citizens were the primary targets of terrorist violence and, on the day Reagan began his presidency, fifty-two American hostages were freed after 444 days of captivity in Iran. The hostage crisis was a humiliating experience for the United States, and it played no small role in driving Reagan's predecessor, Jimmy Carter, from office. A week later, at a public ceremony celebrating the homecoming of the hostages, Reagan pledged that his administration would respond to acts of terrorism with "swift and effective retribution." Over the next five years terrorist aggression against Americans became increasingly violent, and after each incident Reagan stated that the responsible party would be held accountable for its deed. Yet he did not act. He did not avenge the bombing of the U.S. embassy in Beirut in April 1983, the destruction of the U.S. Marine Corps barracks in Beirut six months later, the murder of off-duty Marine embassy guards in El Salvador in June 1985, the hijacking of TWA Flight 847 that same month, or the massacres of innocent travelers at the Rome and Vienna airports in December 1985. With each new and more horrifying act of violence the American people felt more vulnerable, became increasingly angry and frustrated, and began to believe that Reagan's war against terrorism consisted of powerful rhetoric but not much else. By early 1986 it seemed likely that Reagan's presidency would fall victim to terrorism, just as Carter's had years before. Then, in mid-April 1986, the president gave a convincing response to a specific terrorist incident by ordering Operation El Dorado Canyon.

Why did it take Reagan so long to retaliate? The likely answer is that it was much easier for him to promise military action than to carry it out. It was difficult to locate the perpetrators of a terrorist act. State sponsors, if their involvement could be established, were often immune from attack because of unique political or strategic circumstances. One of Reagan's most important advisers was opposed to using military force except under strict criteria. At the same time America's European allies were staunchly opposed to military action due to their own political and economic concerns.

Once Reagan committed his administration to a campaign against terrorism in January 1981, his policymakers trained their focus on Qaddafi's radical regime in Tripoli. They did so for several practical reasons: Qaddafi was the most open advocate of international terrorism, many leaders in Africa and the Middle East reviled his regime, and Libya was the weakest militarily of the leading state supporters of terrorism (a list of states that included Syria and Iran).

America's difficulties with Qaddafi did not begin with Reagan's presidency. In 1973 Qaddafi declared the entire Gulf of Sidra an integral part of Libyan territory. His unlawful claim violated international conventions governing territorial waters and spurned the right of the U.S. Sixth Fleet and other navies serving in the Mediterranean to conduct naval exercises in international waters and airspace. Furthermore, during the 1970s Qaddafi became a leading practitioner of state-sponsored terrorism, which he considered a practical means of achieving his foreign policy objectives. He instigated acts of subversion against moderate governments in the Middle East and Africa, he aided "liberation" movements in countries all over the world, and he provided training, arms, and funding for a disparate collection of terrorist organizations. By the end of the decade the United States and other Western governments considered Qaddafi the world's most notorious champion of terrorism.

The Reagan administration set out to develop a multifaceted strategy to challenge Qaddafi's illegal claim over the Gulf of Sidra, to contain his subversive activities, and to confront his reprehensible involvement with terrorism. The strategy consisted of diplomatic and economic sanctions, covert operations, and demonstrations of military power. During the first five years of Reagan's presidency certain elements of the strategy became stricter, bolder, and more assertive. In 1981 the Central Intelligence Agency (CIA) launched a covert operation in Chad designed to challenge indirectly Qaddafi's hold on power. In 1985 the CIA planned to provide lethal aid to Libyan dissident groups in the hope that they would abolish the Qaddafi regime, and the National Security Council (NSC) actively encouraged an Egyptian attack on Libya. In 1982 Reagan ordered an embargo on imported Libyan oil and in 1986 he severed all economic ties between the two countries. During his first year in office Reagan directed the U.S. Sixth Fleet to conduct a large naval exercise near Libya; five years later he ordered the fleet to carry out a series of progressively larger and more complex demonstrations, which eventually culminated in major surface and air operations in the Gulf of Sidra.

The Sixth Fleet exercises vigorously challenged Libya's claim over the Gulf of Sidra and forcefully demonstrated the will of the American people in the struggle against Libyan terrorism. In August 1981 and March 1986 Qaddafi attempted to strengthen his illegal claim to the gulf with military force. In each instance the fleet defended itself and answered Qaddafi's challenge with a stern rebuke. To avenge his humiliating defeat in March 1986 Qaddafi ordered several terrorist operations against American citizens and interests overseas. In early April his agents carried out the deadly attack on La Belle discothèque in West Berlin.

Ironically, for about two years Reagan's Libya strategy seemed to have a quieting effect on Qaddafi but, by 1984, the Libyan dictator was linked to several notorious acts of subversion, terrorism, and dangerous mischief. Reagan's strategy had failed to induce Qaddafi to renounce terrorism and subversion largely because America's European allies had given the policy little support and rejected certain portions of it outright. Reagan had sought the closure of all Libyan embassies and a total ban on the purchase of Libyan oil, but the Europeans for the most part were unwilling to take those steps. They feared Libyan reprisals and wanted to avoid any action that might threaten their lucrative commercial relationships with Libya. When U.S.-Libyan relations reached a crisis in early 1986, the United States found itself virtually alone in confronting Qaddafi. After the West Berlin bombing Reagan realized that other steps that fell short of military force—diplomatic measures, economic sanctions, and large naval demonstrations—had not produced a noticeable change in Qaddafi's behavior. Knowing full well that few allies would support his decision, Reagan nevertheless proceeded with Operation El Dorado Canyon. Most of them later criticized his action.

Yet the air strike profoundly affected both Colonel Qaddafi and America's allies. Qaddafi received the unambiguous message that he could no longer attack Americans with impunity. The allies, on the other hand, sought to forestall further U.S. military action by implementing stronger counterterrorism measures and pledging to cooperate more closely with the United States in the fight against international terrorism.

Several years have passed since American bombs fell on Libya, and the events leading up to Operation El Dorado Canyon and the raid itself have faded from public memory. By 1991 the air strike was eclipsed by several important foreign affairs developments, such as the Iran-Contra affair, a large U.S military commitment in the Persian Gulf during the later stages of the Iran-Iraq War, U.S.-Chinese relations following the massacre at Tiananmen Square, the collapse of Soviet communism, the U.S. invasion of Panama, and Operations Desert Shield and Desert Storm. Moreover, it is worth noting that two well-known biographies of Ronald Reagan—*President Reagan: The Role of a Lifetime* by Lou Cannon, originally published in 1991, and *Dutch: A Memoir of Ronald Reagan* by Edmund Morris, published in 1999—each devote only a few paragraphs to the U.S.-Libyan showdown of the 1980s.

Nevertheless, the story of Operation El Dorado Canyon and the events and circumstances leading up to it deserve to be told. On a number of occasions the dispute between Reagan and Qaddafi dominated U.S. foreign policy and, during the first three and a half months of 1986, it was a full-fledged crisis. This book presents a political-military history of relations between the United States and Libya from the beginning of Reagan's presidency through the aftermath of the air strike, including the development of Reagan administration policies regarding international terrorism and its most prominent advocate, Muammar al-Qaddafi, and the political and economic strategies, diplomatic initiatives, covert actions, and military operations aimed at the Qaddafi regime. During Reagan's presidency hostilities erupted between U.S. and Libyan forces on four occasions. Therefore, considerable space here is devoted to operational planning, descriptions of military equipment and tactics, and a portrayal of the combat actions that took place.

In recounting the turbulent relationship between Reagan and Qaddafi I have emphasized a number of points. First, developing a comprehensive U.S. strategy toward Libya was a long and difficult process. Many policy decisions took months to achieve because of bureaucratic infighting, disagreements between senior officials, conflicting interpretations of intelligence, and the need to assuage allies' concerns. Second, despite having a reputation among his critics as a "trigger-happy cowboy," Reagan refrained from using force in response to Libyan terrorism until he could reliably attribute responsibility for a specific terrorist incident to the Qaddafi regime and until other measures had been given a reasonable chance to modify Qaddafi's behavior. Third, the U.S. Navy and U.S. Air Force planned and trained for operations against Libya with exceptional skill and precision—often facing short deadlines and working under intense political pressure—and carried them out with extraordinary heroism. Fourth, the Sixth Fleet played an indispensable role in the prolonged confrontation with Libya by demonstrating the advantages of using naval power to achieve and maintain foreign policy objectives without resorting to all-out war or the long-term deployment of military forces. Finally, the air strike of 15 April 1986 was a devastating political and psychological defeat for Qaddafi. It undercut his ability to carry out or support further acts of terrorism, and it convinced him that he could no longer harm Americans without paying a terrible price. After Operation El Dorado Canyon Qaddafi was haunted by the prospect that the next terrorist incident that bore his fingerprints could trigger another armed riposte from the United States. While he did not forswear the use of terrorism, he was forced to adjust his operational methods, which in turn significantly reduced his involvement in the deadly practice. Moreover, the effect of the air strike on Qaddafi, namely the effective employment of military force against his regime, was not lost on other practitioners and supporters of global terrorism.

Certain portions of this book reveal a particular bias of the author. As a retired naval officer I take great pride in describing the extraordinary professionalism and heroic actions of Navy, Marine Corps, and Air Force servicemen who risked their lives in combat against Libyan air, naval, and air defense forces. I have the highest admiration of and deepest respect for the courage of our servicemen and, in the case of two airmen, their supreme sacrifice. On the other hand, I am not blind to the faults of the Reagan administration and the U.S. military, especially regarding policies that did not serve the interests of the American people and tactical decisions that placed American forces in exceptional danger.

The body of this work begins and ends with a look at Libya. Chapter one contains an overview of Libyan history, an account of Qaddafi's rise to power, and a description of revolutionary Libya. Portions of chapter seven examine the impact of El Dorado Canyon on Libya's leader and describe Qaddafi's attempts to end his country's isolation in the years immediately following the air strike. The epilogue recounts the Lockerbie incident, its lasting impact on U.S.-Libyan relations, and Qaddafi's succeeding efforts to rejuvenate his prestige in Africa, the Middle East, and the West. The final pages of this work contain an assessment of the legacy of El Dorado Canyon, an overview of the terrible events of 11 September 2001 and President George W. Bush's call for a global war to eradicate terrorism, and a glimpse at the prospects for U.S.-Libyan relations in the wake of the September 2001 terrorist attacks.

Editorial Note: Concerning the transliteration of Arabic words into English, I followed the system practiced by the *Middle East Journal,* with the following exceptions: first, I assimilated the definite article "al-" when it precedes "sun" letters of the Arabic alphabet (for example, Anwar as-Sadat, not Anwar al-Sadat); second, to avoid confusion I retained the widely accepted spellings of well-known people and places (such as Gamal Abdul Nasser, not Jamal abd an-Nasir, and Tripoli, not Tarabulus); and third, to maintain consistency with regard to geographic names, I adopted the system used by the editor of *Libya: A Country Study,* an area studies handbook published by the U.S. government in 1989.

Another thought on this subject: There are literally hundreds of English renderings of the last name of the leader of Libya. Qaddafi, Qadhafi, Qadhdhafi, Gadhafi, Gaddafi, Gadaffi, and Kaddafi are some of the more common spellings. "Qaddafi" is used throughout the body of this work because it is less cumbersome than "Qadhdhafi," which is the most accurate transliteration. The reader can gain some appreciation of the range of alternate spellings of the name Qaddafi by browsing through the titles of books, articles, and documents shown in the bibliography.

Acknowledgments

I wish to recognize the assistance and support of several individuals and groups who aided me in the preparation of this work. I am particularly grateful to four accomplished historians, valued colleagues, and dear friends: Professor Craig L. Symonds of the Department of History at the U.S. Naval Academy, whose invaluable lessons on researching and writing history (which I learned as a midshipman) greatly influenced this endeavor; Dr. Edward J. Marolda, senior historian at the Naval Historical Center, who entrusted me with writing an illustrated history of the confrontation between the United States and Libya and provided valuable advice and direction during the preparation of that work (which is titled *"Swift and Effective Retribution": The U.S. Sixth Fleet and the Confrontation with Qaddafi*); Lt. Comdr. Thomas J. Cutler, USN (Ret.), my former colleague at the U.S. Naval Academy and Walbrook Maritime Academy, who encouraged me to follow up the earlier work with a book-length history; and Professor Earnest S. Tucker of the Department of History at the U.S. Naval Academy, who greatly enhanced my knowledge and understanding of the history of the Middle East and who on several occasions has graciously allowed me to share my work on Libya with his midshipmen.

I owe a special debt of gratitude to several friends and colleagues who reviewed the manuscript and offered constructive criticism and helpful suggestions. They include Professors David F. Appleby, Thomas E. Brennan, Nancy W. Ellenberger, John G. Kolp, David P. Peeler, Thomas Sanders, Brian VanDeMark, Lt. Kylan Jones-Hoffman, USN, and Capt. Chris Morton, USMC, all of the Department of History at the U.S. Naval Academy; Ms. Barbara M. Manville of the Nimitz Library, U.S. Naval Academy; Comdr. Richard J. Cassara, USN (Ret.) and Mr. John Morrow, both of Walbrook High School–Uniform Services Academy; Professor James C. Bradford of the Department of History, Texas A&M University; Mr. Roy A. Grossnick and Comdr. Michael S. Lipari, USN (Ret.), both of the Aviation History Branch at the Naval Historical Center; and Dr. William Armstrong of the Naval Air Systems Command.

Since I began studying U.S. military operations against Libya, the dedicated professionals at the Naval Historical Center have provided me with a steady supply of information, materials, and support. These individuals include Dr. Dean

C. Allard and Dr. William S. Dudley, successive directors of naval history; Dr. Robert J. Schneller, Mr. Robert J. Cressman, and Mr. Curtis A. Utz of the Contemporary History Branch; Mr. Todd Baker, Mr. Steven D. Hill, Ms. Gwendolyn J. Rich, and Ms. Judith A. Walters of the Aviation History Branch; Comdr. Diana Cangelosi, USN, Ms. Sandra Russell, Mr. Morgan I. Wilbur, Ms. Wendy Leland, Mr. Charles C. Cooney, and JO1 Eric S. Sesit, USN, of the *Naval Aviation News* Branch; Mr. Bernard F. Cavalcante, Ms. Kathy Lloyd, Ms. Judith Short, Mr. John Hodges, Ms. Regina T. Akers, and Ms. Ariana A. Jacob of the Operational Archives Branch; OSCS Rashad W. Shakir, USNR, FOIA coordinator; Ms. Ella W. Nargele, information security specialist; Mr. John C. Reilly and Mr. Ray Mann of the Ships' History Branch; and Ms. Tonya Montgomery of the Navy Department Library.

The following individuals and organizations furnished important information and materials: Adm. Frank B. Kelso II, USN (Ret.); Ms. Cate Sewell of the Ronald Reagan Library; the information and privacy coordinator at the Central Intelligence Agency; the Archives Section of the Marine Corps Historical Center; headquarters, U.S. Air Forces in Europe; the Nimitz Library at the U.S. Naval Academy; the Albin O. Kuhn Library at the University of Maryland, Baltimore County; the McKeldin Library at the University of Maryland, College Park; Mr. Bob Lawson of the Tailhook Photo Service; Mr. Hill Goodspeed of the National Museum of Naval Aviation; the Photo Archives Department at the U.S. Naval Institute; the Department of Defense Still Media Records Center; the Still News Photo Division at the Navy Office of Information; and the National Archives Still Pictures Branch.

Most important I wish to thank my wife, Julie, and sons, Michael and William. Without their encouragement, patience, love, and support I could not have completed this significant undertaking.

EL DORADO CANYON

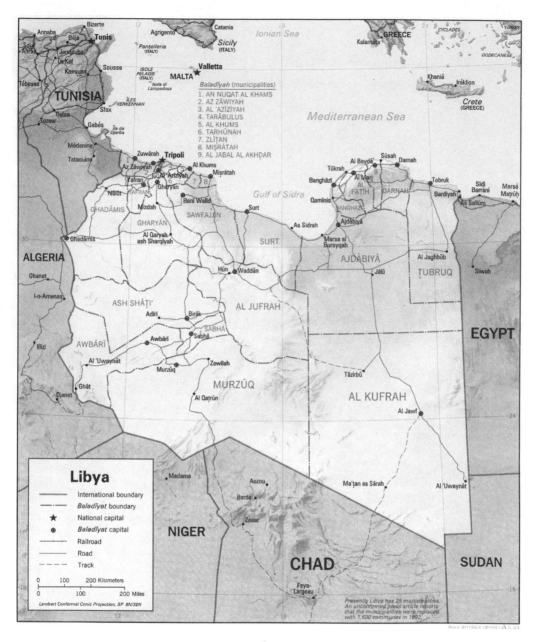

Baladīyah (municipalities)
1. AN NUQAT AL KHAMS
2. AZ ZĀWIYAH
3. AL 'AZĪZIYAH
4. TARĀBULUS
5. AL KHUMS
6. TARHŪNAH
7. ZLĪTAN
8. MIṢRĀTAH
9. AL JABAL AL AKHḌAR

Libya

International boundary
Baladīyat boundary
★ National capital
◉ Baladīyat capital
Railroad
Road
Track

0   100   200 Kilometers
0   100   200 Miles
Lambert Conformal Conic Projection, SP 8N/32N

Presently Libya has 25 municipalities.
An unconfirmed press article reports
that the municipalities were replaced
with 1,500 communes in 1992.

Libya
Central Intelligence Agency

Prologue: The Air Battle
Near Tobruk

"Bogeys have jinked back at me for the fifth time. They're on my nose now, inside of twenty miles."[1]

"Master arm on. Master arm on. Centering up on the T."

"Bogeys have jinked back into me again. Sixteen miles. Centering the dot."[2]

"Fourteen miles. 'Fox one'! Fox one!"[3]

"Aw, Jesus!"

"Ten miles. He's back on my nose! Fox one again!"

"Six miles. Six miles."

"'Talley two'! Talley two! Eleven o'clock high. They're turning into me!"[4]

"Five miles. Four miles."

"Okay . . . Got a missile off."

"Good hit! Good hit on one!"

"Roger that. Good kill! Good kill!"

"I've got the other one."

"Select 'Fox two'! Select Fox two!"[5]

"All right, Fox two!" . . .

"Shoot him!"

"I don't got a tone!"[6]

"Lock him up! Lock him up!"

"Shoot him! Fox two!"

"I can't! I don't have a fucking tone!"

"Good kill! Good kill!"

"Good kill!"

"Pilot ejected."

"Okay. Let's head north. Head north."

"Let's go down low, on the deck. Unload, five hundred knots. Let's get out of here!"

"We're showing two good chutes in the air here."

"Roger that. Two Floggers. Two Floggers splashed."[7]

THIS FRENETIC DIALOGUE between American airmen was captured by the recording equipment in their fighter aircraft. It describes vividly the air battle that took place between two U.S. Navy F-14 Tomcats and a pair of Libyan MiG-23 Floggers on 4 January 1989 in the noonday sky over the central Mediterranean Sea. The entire engagement—from the moment the Floggers left their base in Libya until the Tomcats shot them down—lasted about seven and a half minutes. The combat occurred just sixteen days before the end of Ronald Reagan's presidency.

At the start of the new year 1989, Ronald Reagan and Muammar al-Qaddafi were engaged in a process that had become all too familiar during the previous eight years. Typically it involved the following progression: first an underlying controversy, then an escalating war of words, and finally a demonstration of American military power. On three previous occasions the process had culminated in hostilities. There were important differences between this confrontation and those of 1981 and 1986, however. This time the controversy did not involve an illegal territorial claim, subversion, or terrorism.[8] It concerned the likelihood that Libya was developing the capacity to produce chemical weapons. This time the military action did not take place in the Gulf of Sidra or in the skies over Tripoli and Benghazi. It happened north of Tobruk, an historic city in northeast Libya. This time the battle between U.S. and Libyan forces was for the most part unexpected (whereas in 1981 and 1986 the United States had determined when and where it would challenge Qaddafi militarily). This time Qaddafi called the shot by deciding to confront a U.S. naval task force as it steamed through the central Mediterranean several miles from the Libyan shoreline. Nevertheless, the outcome of this clash was the same as the others before it: for the fourth and final time in eight years Ronald Reagan's military had trounced the armed forces of Muammar al-Qaddafi.

1

Muammar al-Qaddafi and the Libyan Jamahiriyya

History of Early Libya

Libya, whose name derives from the appellation given a Berber tribe by the ancient Egyptians, did not become an independent and unified state until the middle of the twentieth century. Since antiquity the three regions that comprise modern Libya—Tripolitania in the northwest, Cyrenaica in the east, and Fezzan in the southwest—have maintained relations with different parts of the outside world and developed unique histories and identities due to the harsh deserts that kept them separate. This internal disunity combined with Libya's history of foreign domination had a profound impact on its modern political development and the ideology of its mercurial leader, Colonel Muammar al-Qaddafi.[1]

Greek settlers founded Cyrene and four other city-states in Cyrenaica between the seventh and fifth centuries B.C. Phoenicians from Carthage established several commercial settlements in Tripolitania by the fifth century B.C. From about 1,000 B.C. Fezzan was loosely governed by the Garamentes tribe, which controlled major caravan routes in the Sahara Desert. The native Berbers, especially those of the hinterland, maintained their autonomy and preserved their distinct culture despite the influence of Greek and Carthaginian settlers and domination by several foreign masters including, by the time of the Arab conquest of the seventh century, the Egyptians, the Persians, the forces of Alexander the Great, the Ptolemies of Egypt, the Romans, the Vandals, and the Byzantines.

Already well developed, the cultural and historical differences between Tripolitania and Cyrenaica intensified during nearly five hundred years of Roman governorship. The two regions maintained their distinct Carthaginian and Greek cultures and, after the partition of the Roman Empire in 395, Tripolitania was attached to the western empire and Cyrenaica was assigned to the eastern. In the fifth century Rome recognized the mastery of the Vandals (a Germanic tribe) over much of North Africa including Tripolitania. Belasarius, a general serving the Byzantine Empire—the successor to the Eastern Roman Empire—recaptured Tripolitania in 533 but, by the time of the Arab invasion, the once prosperous cities of Tripolitania and Cyrenaica were racked by political decay and religious strife and resembled bleak military outposts.[2]

Ten years after the death of the Prophet Muhammad in 632, an Arab general by the name of Amr ibn al-As conquered Cyrenaica. Spirited Berber resistance, however, delayed al-As's conquest of Tripolitania until 649. Another Arab general, Uqba ibn Nafi, subdued Fezzan in 663. By 715 the Arabs had spread across North Africa and had captured all but the extreme northern portion of the Iberian Peninsula.

Over the next few centuries waves of Arab armies and settlers transmitted Islam, the Arabic language, and Arab culture to the indigenous populations of North Africa. City dwellers and farmers there converted to Islam and adopted Arab culture somewhat readily, but the Berbers of the interior, while professing Islam, remained linguistically and culturally separate from the Arabs. As part of the *umma* or community of Muslims, Tripolitania and Cyrenaica were ruled by the *caliph* (the successor to the Prophet Muhammad) from Damascus and, later, from Baghdad, and were governed according to *sharia,* the Islamic legal code.[3]

From the early tenth to the sixteenth centuries Tripolitania and Cyrenaica suffered widespread intraconfessional violence and political instability. Consequently, the regions were dominated by a series of Islamic dynasties, tribes, and Christian governments, which included the Fatimids of Egypt, the Berber Zurids, the Hilalian Bedouins from Arabia, the Normans from Sicily, the Almohads of Morocco, the Hafsids of Tunis, the Mamluks of Egypt, the Hapsburgs of Spain, and the Knights of St. John of Malta. During this very turbulent period corsairs operating from North African ports harassed commercial shipping in the Mediterranean.[4]

In the sixteenth century the Ottoman Turks captured the entire North African coast except Morocco, and the sultan, the Ottoman ruler in Constantinople, established regencies in Algiers, Tunis, and Tripoli, the principal city of Tripolitania. In Tripoli the political authority was conferred upon a pasha or regent, who represented the sultan there. In the early seventeenth century Tripoli lapsed into political chaos as coup followed upon coup, and few military dictators survived a year in power. In 1711 Ahmad Qaramanli, a Turkish-Arab cavalry officer, seized power in Tripoli and founded an independent ruling dynasty while acknowledging the Ottoman sultan as his suzerain. Politically savvy and ruthless, Ahmad Pasha recognized piracy as a valuable source of revenue.[5] During the reign of one of Ahmad's successors, Yusuf ibn Ali Qaramanli, Tripoli's program of state-sponsored piracy led to a naval war with the newly independent United States.

Mr. Jefferson's War

For centuries the seizure of merchant ships and the imprisonment of their crews by North African corsairs prompted several European countries, and later the United States, to pay tribute or "protection money" to the potentates of Morocco, Algiers, Tunis, and Tripoli—the so-called "Barbary states"—to ensure the safe passage of their merchant ships in the Mediterranean. The capture of several American merchantmen by Algerine corsairs spurred Congress to pass the Navy Act of 27 March 1794, which authorized the construction or purchase of six frigates to protect American commerce. Furthermore, in 1799 President John Adams began paying annual tribute to the rulers of the Barbary states. The share allotted to the pasha of Tripoli was eighteen thousand dollars. In exchange for the payment Yusuf Pasha promised that the corsairs based in his country would not harass American shipping.

In 1801 President Thomas Jefferson rejected Yusuf's demand for a huge increase in annual tribute and in response the pasha declared war on the United States. Unaware of the pasha's actions, Jefferson had already dispatched a naval squadron to the Mediterranean to protect American merchantmen and to dissuade the Tripolitan government from demanding additional tribute.[6]

The lackluster performances of the first two U.S. squadron commanders, Capt. Richard Dale and Capt. Richard V. Morris, did not make much of an impression on the pasha. The deployment of the third squadron, commanded by Capt. Edward Preble, got off to a disastrous start when the frigate *Philadelphia* ran aground on a reef outside Tripoli harbor, resulting in the capture of the ship and the imprisonment of her crew. Despite the stunning loss, Preble displayed a relentless fighting spirit during his yearlong command of the Mediterranean Squadron. His first order of business was to destroy the U.S. frigate to prevent Yusuf from adding her to the Tripolitan fleet. In February 1804 Lt. Stephen Decatur led a raiding party that boarded and burned the *Philadelphia* directly beneath the guns of the citadel that protected the harbor.

On five occasions in late summer Preble shelled Tripoli with two bomb ketches borrowed from the Kingdom of Naples. Meanwhile, boarding parties led by Decatur captured or sank several Tripolitan gunboats after vicious hand-to-hand fighting. Despite the furious assaults Yusuf rejected Preble's offer of ransom for the crewmen of the captured frigate. In early September Preble's men loaded the ketch *Intrepid* with one hundred barrels of black powder and 150 rounds of shot and planned to detonate her inside Tripoli harbor. Preble hoped the explosion would stun the pasha, destroy the remainder of the pasha's fleet, and blast a hole in the city wall near his castle. The plan failed when the *Intrepid* blew up prematurely, killing Lt. Richard Somers and his volunteer crew of two midshipmen and ten men. A week later Preble's plucky squadron was relieved by a larger naval force commanded by Capt. Samuel Barron. Preble returned to the United States, where he received a hero's welcome and accolades from Jefferson and the Congress.

While Preble had relied on naval power to confront Yusuf, Barron supported a political scheme to remove the Tripolitan despot from power. William Eaton, the American naval agent in North Africa, located Yusuf's older brother, Ahmad ibn Ali Qaramanli, in Alexandria and persuaded Ahmad to join him in a march on Tripolitan territory. Ahmad's promised reward for participating in the expedition was the regency of Tripoli, which Yusuf had snatched from him in a bloodless coup in 1796. Eaton's "army" included Lt. Presley N. O'Bannon of the Marine Corps, seven enlisted Marines, a midshipman, a sailor, several Greek mercenaries, and hundreds of desert tribesmen and camp followers. In April 1805 the irregular force, supported by cannon fire from the brig *Argus,* schooner *Nautilus,* and sloop *Hornet,* captured the Cyrenaican city of Darnah. When Yusuf learned of the loss of Darnah he quickly sued for peace. Yusuf dropped all demands for tribute and ransomed the imprisoned Americans for sixty thousand dollars. In return the United States abandoned support of Ahmad and evacuated Darnah. On 10 June 1805 the United States and Tripoli signed the Treaty of Peace and Amity, which ended the four-year Tripolitan War.[7]

Ottoman Rule, the Sanusis, and Italian Colonization

In the years following the defeat of Napoleon at Waterloo in 1815, the European powers forcefully eradicated Mediterranean piracy and put an end to the system of paying tribute to the Barbary states.[8] Deprived of the revenue derived from piracy, Tripoli's economy declined and the country slipped into civil war. In 1835 the Ottomans forced the Qaramanli ruler, Ali II, into exile and reestablished direct rule over Tripoli. The Ottomans combined the three regions of the country into one *vilayet* or province—Tripolitania—ruled by an Ottoman *wali* (governor general) who was appointed by the sultan. In 1879 Cyrenaica became a separate province. Ottoman rule in the two provinces was for the most part turbulent, repressive, and corrupt.[9]

In the early nineteenth century Muhammad ibn Ali as-Sanusi, a highly respected Islamic scholar and *marabout* (holy man) from present-day Algeria, preached a message of Islamic revival based on the purity and simplicity of the early faith. He won many followers among Cyrenaican Bedouins who were attracted to his message of personal austerity and moral regeneration. In 1843 the Grand Sanusi, as he came to be known, founded the first of many lodges in Cyrenaica, which became the center of the new religious order. By the end of the nineteenth century virtually all of the Bedouin tribes in the region had pledged their allegiance to the Sanusi brotherhood. In the next century the Sanusis spearheaded the nascent Libyan nationalist movement.[10]

A late starter among European powers in the race for overseas colonies, Italy coveted the Ottoman provinces of Tripolitania and Cyrenaica. In 1911 the Italian government sent an ultimatum to the sultan, demanding to occupy the two provinces to protect Italy's growing commercial interests. When Constantinople ignored the demand, Rome declared war. Italian forces invaded and captured Tripoli and occupied several coastal cities in Cyrenaica. Libyan tribesmen fought alongside Ottoman troops to resist the Christian invaders, but with war looming in the Balkans the Ottoman government had no choice but to sue for peace. Under the ambiguous terms of the Treaty of Lausanne signed in 1912, the sultan gave up his political dominion in Tripolitania and Cyrenaica but retained the right to supervise Libya's religious affairs. Rome's annexation of the provinces, recognized by the other European powers, marked the start of a colonial war that lasted off and on for two decades.[11]

Fighting for both Islam and their independence, Sanusi tribesmen prevented the Italians from expanding beyond their enclaves on the Cyrenaican coast. By contrast, in Tripolitania the Italians had greater success subduing and controlling large portions of the region because many local leaders lacked the will to continue armed resistance. After Italy's entry into the First World War on the side of the Allies, Sanusi leader Ahmad ash-Sharif sided with the Central Powers. Following a disastrous raid into British-occupied Egypt in 1916, ash-Sharif turned the leadership of the movement over to the young, pro-British Muhammad Idris as-Sanusi. In 1917 Idris negotiated a truce with the Allies whereby Italy and Great Britain recognized him as the ruler over the interior of Cyrenaica, while he agreed to halt attacks on Italian-held coastal cities and Egypt.[12]

After the war Italy attempted to govern the country with a colonial policy that was both moderate and accommodating. The Italians recognized the autonomous Tripolitanian Republic and accepted Idris's hereditary rule in Cyrenaica.[13] Nevertheless, in 1922 when Idris reluctantly accepted Tripolitania's suggestion that he become the ruler over all of Libya, the fascist leader Benito Mussolini responded by launching a brutal campaign of military conquest. The Second Italo-Sanusi War began later that year, and by the end of 1924 the Italians had subdued northern Tripolitania and most of coastal Cyrenaica. Southern Tripolitania was pacified in 1928, Fezzan in 1930. The fiercest action took place in the interior of Cyrenaica where the aged but vigorous Shaykh Umar al-Mukhtar led Sanusi tribesmen in a relentless guerrilla campaign against the larger and technologically superior Italian forces. The Italians completed the conquest of Libya in 1931 when they captured Mukhtar in the Green Mountains of northern Cyrenaica and defeated the remnant of his rebel army at al-Kufrah Oasis in southern Cyrenaica. During the last stages of the war the Italians executed more than twenty-four thousand Cyrenaicans, herded most of the civilian population into concentration camps, and forced the remaining population to flee into the desert.[14]

In 1934 Mussolini formally established the Italian colony of Libya, which was comprised of four provinces—Tripoli, Misratah, Benghazi, and Darnah—in addition to a military district in Fezzan. In 1939 Libya became part of metropolitan Italy. During the 1930s the Italians invested large amounts of capital and launched several public works projects to modernize Libya's economy, especially the agricultural sector. They set out to improve the country's irrigation systems, roads, and port facilities. Significant progress was made, but the improvements primarily benefited the Italian colonists (who numbered over 110,000 by 1940) and a few upper-class Libyans, not the vast majority of Libya's population. In many respects the Libyans suffered under Italian rule. Tribal grazing lands were transferred to Italian settlers, tribal government was abolished, the Sanusis were repressed, education and training programs were not established, and Libyans were excluded from the administration of their country.[15]

World War II and the United Nations

When Italy entered the Second World War in June 1940, Idris and other Libyan leaders declared their support for the Allies and began consulting with British military authorities. Idris pressed the British to endorse Libyan independence, but the government responded that it could not make a commitment while the war was still in progress. Idris accepted the British position, urged his followers to be patient, and continued the program of military cooperation. The British raised five Libyan battalions largely from Cyrenaica. The Libyan Arab Force (or "Sanusi Army," as the Libyan contingent was popularly known) served under British command during the epic desert battles that raged between the German Afrika Korps of Gen. Erwin Rommel and the British Eighth Army of Gen. Claude Auchinleck and his successor, Gen. Bernard L. Montgomery. In November 1942 British forces liberated Cyrenaica from Axis control. By February 1943 all of Libya was free of Axis troops.[16]

The war was a traumatic experience for many Libyans, who found themselves mere pawns in a major conflict between colossal military powers. Lillian Craig Harris, an analyst with the U.S. Department of State, pointed out that for Qaddafi and many of his countrymen, "World War II is no mere historical event but a living reality that must be remembered and used. Thousands of Libyan Arabs, out of a population of less than one million were killed. The country's economic structure, such as it had been, was devastated. Qaddafi, whose sense of history is infused with the Bedouin idea of blood debt, to this day frequently repeats his demand that Italy and Britain pay reparations for damage to Libya during World War II."

During the war the British established military governments in Cyrenaica and Tripolitania, and Free French forces from the French colony of Chad set up a military administration in Fezzan. After the war conflicting interests among the victorious powers, conflicts that were exacerbated by the onset of the Cold War, prevented agreement among the Allies on the form and administration of a trusteeship for Libya. Consequently, the issue was referred to the United Nations for a solution. In November 1949 the General Assembly passed a resolution that called for the establishment by January 1952 of a sovereign Libyan state comprised of all three regions. The UN created a special council to supervise the transition to independence and to assist in drafting a constitution.[17]

United Nations officials faced extraordinary challenges as they prepared Libya for independence. About 90 percent of the population was illiterate and the country's economy was extremely weak. In 1950 per capita income was about fifty dollars per year, and the largest source of revenue was the sale of scrap metal salvaged from World War II battlefields. Politically the Libyans could not agree on the structure of their new government. The Cyrenaicans favored a loose federation, while the Tripolitanians advocated a strong central government. Nevertheless, the Libyan Constituent Assembly, which met for the first time in November 1950, agreed unanimously that Libya would be established as a democratic, federal, and sovereign state; that the government would be a constitutional monarchy; that Tripolitania, Cyrenaica, and Fezzan would be provinces in the new kingdom; and that Idris would be the new nation's first head of state. The proposed national government, in addition to the monarchy, would consist of a cabinet and a bicameral legislature, and each province would have a governor appointed by the king, a cabinet, and a legislature. In October 1951 the assembly approved the constitution and, on 24 December 1951, King Idris I proclaimed the independence of the United Kingdom of Libya.[18]

Independent Libya

Newly independent Libya was friendly toward the West and identified with the bloc of conservative Arab states. In the mid-1950s Libya signed treaties with Britain and the United States, whereby the two Western powers provided Libya with economic and military aid in return for military base rights. The United States continued to operate Wheelus Air Base, located just outside Tripoli. The U.S. airfield, built during World War II, was ideally situated near desert bombing ranges and strategically positioned on the southern flank of the U.S. Sixth Fleet in the Mediterranean. Over the next two decades Sixth Fleet ships made frequent port visits to Tripoli. In 1957 Libya accepted the terms of the Eisenhower Doctrine, a U.S. economic and military aid program designed to counter Soviet influence in the Middle East and North Africa. Through the program Libya acquired a substantial increase in American economic assistance and additional military equipment.[19]

In the 1950s and 1960s Libya supported Arab causes but played a minor role in the Arab-Israeli conflict and the turbulent arena of inter-Arab politics. The radical Arab nationalism espoused by Egypt's Gamal Abdul Nasser threatened conservative monarchs like Idris and galvanized millions of young Arabs who shared Nasser's vision of Arab unity, nonalignment, and social justice.

Despite the infusion of economic and technical assistance from the United States, Great Britain, and the United Nations, Libya remained a very poor and underdeveloped country throughout the 1950s. This situation changed unexpectedly and dramatically in June 1959 when the American oil company Esso discovered a major oil field in Cyrenaica. Commercial development followed and, with foreign companies paying royalties of 50 percent to the Libyan government, the country experienced unprecedented affluence. The government financed several major public works projects, expanded educational and health services throughout the country, and supported the development of low-cost housing, small businesses, and industries. Within a decade the Libyan per capita income had increased to about fifteen hundred dollars per year.[20]

The oil boom of the 1960s created social and economic problems that the weak national government was neither able nor willing to address. Tripolitanians resented the priority Idris gave to Cyrenaican affairs, while the growing urban middle class felt excluded from the political process and younger Libyans objected to his pro-Western foreign policy and his affiliation with conservative Arab leaders. Furthermore, many Libyans were outraged by widespread government inefficiency and corruption and protested the inequitable distribution of oil revenues, which enriched prominent families over poorer elements of the population. The group most dissatisfied with Idris, however, was the junior officer corps of the armed forces. They were inspired by Nasser's message of Arab nationalism and were determined to restore Arab honor in the wake of the devastating Arab defeat in the June 1967 Arab-Israeli War. As the disaffection of the population intensified, the king became increasingly estranged from the Libyan people and spent most of his time secluded in his palace in Darnah.

The Libyan Revolution

On 1 September 1969, while Idris was out of the country for rest and medical treatment, a group of junior army officers calling themselves the Free Unionist Officers boldly took control of the Libyan government and overthrew the monarchy. The bloodless coup was enthusiastically supported throughout the country, especially by young city dwellers. The Free Officers, who modeled their coup after Nasser's 1952 takeover of Egypt, named a twelve-member directorate, the Revolutionary Command Council (RCC), to serve as the supreme governing authority.[21] The RCC proclaimed that "Libya is deemed a free, sovereign republic under the name of the Libyan Arab Republic—ascending with God's help to exalted heights, proceeding in the path of freedom, unity, and social justice, guaranteeing the right of equality to its citizens, and opening before them the doors of honorable work."[22]

The Nixon administration heeded the advice of State Department officers who had served in Libya and five days after the coup recognized the new government. The administration believed that the Free Officers might provide a bulwark against the spread of Soviet influence in the Arab world. In the years immediately following the revolution the decision seemed vindicated by the volume of anti-Soviet and anticommunist statements issued by the RCC. For example, the new government frequently referred to the Soviet Union as an atheistic society, and it condemned Soviet involvement in the 1971 war between India and Pakistan because the conflict signaled "Soviet imperialist designs in the area."[23]

Within weeks the RCC transformed Libya from a conservative monarchy into a revolutionary republic devoted to Islamic principles and dedicated to Arab nationalism. The new government embarked on a campaign to cleanse the country of corruption; it initiated important social, economic, and political reforms; it rejected colonialism and foreign values; it declared its neutrality in the struggle between the Western and Eastern blocs while denouncing both communism and imperialism; it sought the immediate evacuation of the American and British bases; and it affirmed Libya's dedication to Arab unity and the liberation of Palestine. The young officers immediately issued decrees that banned the sale and consumption of alcohol beverages, they closed nightclubs, and they ordered all public signs to be written in Arabic.

It soon became apparent to international observers that the most influential member of the RCC—and the de facto leader of the new republic—was a twenty-seven-year-old army captain by the name of Muammar al-Qaddafi, a deeply pious and ascetic Signal Corps officer whose revolutionary views on Arab nationalism were patterned after those of his hero, Gamal Abdul Nasser. Shortly after the coup the RCC named an eight-member cabinet to govern the country, appointed Qaddafi commander in chief of the Libyan Armed Forces, and promoted him to the rank of colonel. Qaddafi attained widespread support and popularity by pledging to end foreign political, economic, and cultural domination of the country and by extending the benefits of prosperity to all Libyans through a considerable expansion of free social services. He believed that as long as he maintained a high standard of living for the Libyan people he could purchase support and legitimacy for the regime.[24] Qaddafi was certainly a revolutionary, but there was no denying the pragmatism that enhanced his chances for survival.

Muammar al-Qaddafi

Muammar al-Qaddafi was born in 1942 to a Bedouin family in Sirtica, the barren territory that separates Tripolitania and Cyrenaica. His family belonged to a tribe of Berber-Arab livestock herders, al-Qaddafa. As a youth Qaddafi was profoundly influenced by stories of Italian atrocities committed against his country during the colonial period, the devastation wrought by World War II, the shocking Arab defeat in Palestine in 1948–49, and events in Nasser's Egypt of the 1950s. It was during his early adolescence that he began listening to Nasser's fiery speeches on the "Voice of the Arabs" radio program and started formulating his political ideology. Qaddafi attended a Quranic elementary school in Surt and began secondary school in Sabha in Fezzan. While at Sabha he surrounded himself with similar-minded classmates who wanted to "liberate" Libya by overthrowing their king. He formed a "central committee" and held secret meetings to discuss Nasser's political ideas. He was expelled for leading a pro-Nasser student demonstration and completed his secondary education under a tutor in Misratah in Tripolitania. From his Islamic upbringing and Bedouin background Qaddafi cultivated a deep religious consciousness, a strict set of personal ethics, and a strong sense of egalitarianism.

For Libyans of humble origins, a military career provided the best means of obtaining an advanced education and achieving higher economic and social status. Furthermore, for Qaddafi and other devotees of Nasser, the military offered the best vehicle for producing revolutionary change within the political establishment. In 1963, at the first general meeting of his movement (which was attended by followers from Sabha, Misratah, and Tripoli), the conspirators decided that Qaddafi and two other young men would enroll in the Libyan Royal Military Academy in Benghazi in Cyrenaica. After entering the academy Qaddafi began recruiting other officer-cadets into his revolutionary organization, which he named the Free Unionist Officers. After receiving his army commission in 1965 Qaddafi studied communications at the Royal Military Academy at Sandhurst in Great Britain. Then came the devastating Six-Day War, which the Libyan armed forces observed from the sidelines. Just as Nasser had vowed to act against his king after Egypt's humiliating defeat in 1948, after Israel's stunning victory over Egypt, Syria, and Jordan in June 1967 several young Libyan officers pledged to rescue Arab esteem and deepen Libya's commitment to Arab causes by abolishing the corrupt, pro-Western monarchy.

Revolutionary Libya

Within months of the coup the RCC consolidated its control over Libyan society and Qaddafi increased his power within the ruling apparatus. Qaddafi assumed the posts of prime minister and minister of defense while maintaining his leadership of the RCC. The regime brought more than two hundred former government officials to trial before "people's courts" on charges of treason and malfeasance. Several individuals received death sentences or long prison terms. Former King Idris was tried and convicted in absentia and sentenced to death, but the sentence was never carried out. The RCC undermined the power and prestige of the Sanusis and assailed tribal distinctions as impediments to unity and social progress. The legal code was brought into compliance with sharia, and all political parties, except the RCC-sponsored Arab Socialist Union (ASU), were abolished. The ASU, which was modeled after Nasser's party of the same name, was established to stimulate political participation, promote revolutionary fervor, and stoke enthusiasm for the regime. All trade unions were incorporated into the ASU, intellectuals were publicly repudiated, newspapers were shut down or taken over by the government, and all Italians and Jews were expelled from the country.[25]

In the mid-1960s the independence afforded by oil income and the growing popular appeal of Arab nationalism prompted the Libyan government to negotiate an end to the basing agreements it held with the United States and Great Britain. Both countries decided before the coup to evacuate their bases and hastened their departures after the RCC assumed power. The Nixon administration decided that Wheelus field was of marginal value and believed that a confrontation over the base could harm relations with the new leaders in Tripoli and could threaten America's very lucrative oil interests. In the summer of 1970 the United States transferred control of Wheelus Air Base to the Libyan government.

After the closure of the American and British bases, Tripoli sought new sources for the country's military equipment. To remain dependent on the United States and Great Britain for modern weaponry would have generated protest at home and criticism throughout the Arab world, since both countries were viewed as supportive of Israel and hostile to Arab interests. France, which had become increasingly dependent on imported Libyan oil and had developed an even-handed policy toward the Arab-Israeli conflict, agreed in 1970 to sell Libya a weapons package valued at four hundred million dollars. Although the contract included 110 Mirage fighter aircraft, France refused to sell Tripoli a fleet of medium tanks. That same year Qaddafi approached the Soviet bloc for arms, all the while maintaining his staunch opposition to communism and asserting his country's status as a nonaligned state. He subsequently negotiated a deal with Moscow for the purchase of thirty tanks and one hundred armored personnel carriers.[26] By the time Libya and the Soviet Union concluded their first major arms deal in 1974 both countries had come to realize that the immediate benefits of their tentative relationship outweighed their ideological differences and long-term disagreements. Tripoli relied on the Soviet Union for huge quantities of modern military equipment and technical assistance. Moscow appreciated Libya's anti-Western policies, shared its goal of fostering radical elements in the Arab world and Africa, and valued its hard currency. Nonetheless, Qaddafi remained steadfastly opposed to communism, which he equated with slavery, and the Kremlin carefully avoided support for or identification with Qaddafi's controversial theories and causes.[27] A senior State Department official described the burgeoning Libyan-Soviet relationship as a "marriage of convenience."[28]

By the mid-1970s Libya's foreign policy had tilted dramatically toward increased cooperation with the Soviet Union, although the regime still maintained the facade of nonalignment. Furthermore, shortly after the United States evacuated Wheelus field the RCC informed the Nixon administration that Washington would not be able to achieve good relations with Tripoli so long as it supported Israel. In light of these developments, relations between the United States and Libya cooled rapidly. In 1973 the United States recalled its ambassador to Libya and did not dispatch a replacement.[29]

The Cultural Revolution

In 1972 Qaddafi relinquished his duties as prime minister and dedicated himself to articulating his revolutionary ideology, which he named the Third International Theory. According to the theory both capitalism and communism are false ideologies, because the former emphasizes worker exploitation while the latter stresses class warfare. Qaddafi's theory, on the other hand, eliminates class distinctions and provides for direct popular participation at all levels of government. The Third International Theory also champions the concept of positive neutrality by which Third World nations can coexist with the United States and the Soviet Union and can conclude agreements with them for their own interests but will not fall under the domination of either superpower.[30]

By 1973 Qaddafi realized that the ASU was not going to generate the "tumultuous popular revolution" that he had envisioned.[31] Consequently, in April he launched a new revolution based on the following five-point program:

1. All existing laws must be repealed and replaced by revolutionary enactments designed to produce the necessary revolutionary change.

2. All feeble minds must be weeded out of society by taking appropriate measures toward perverts and deviationists.

3. An administrative revolution must be staged in order to eliminate all forms of bourgeoisie and bureaucracy.

4. Arms must be distributed to the people who will point them at the chests of anyone who challenges the revolution.

5. A cultural revolution must be initiated to get rid of all imported poisonous ideas and to fuse the people's genuine moral and material potentialities.[32]

Over the next five years Qaddafi outlined his revolutionary political, economic, and social ideas in his three-volume work, *The Green Book,* which he called "the gospel of the new era, the era of the masses."[33] The CIA called the work "a blueprint for reshaping human society."[34] With the publication of *The Green Book* Qaddafi's program to indoctrinate the masses became more thorough and organized.[35]

During the Libyan Cultural Revolution Qaddafi instituted several reforms to overhaul the political order of the country. Hoping to kindle a revolutionary passion among the people and believing that direct democracy was the true form of democracy, he urged his countrymen to take charge of the government and run it themselves through a system of "people's committees." Within a few months thousands of committees were established throughout Libya. They were organized both on a geographical basis and within diverse organizations, such as universities, businesses, and government bureaucracies. Eventually the committees assumed responsibility for local and regional administration and operated basic services in fields such as education, agriculture, housing, and public utilities. The concept of direct democracy or "people's power," which Qaddafi espoused in *The Green Book* and which the people's committees embodied, provided the basis for a new political structure: the "people's congresses." In September 1975 the General People's Congress (GPC) was instituted as the umbrella organization for the people's committees. The GPC replaced the RCC as the highest legislative and executive body in the country and supplanted the ASU as the national political organization.

The GPC designated Qaddafi as its general secretary and transferred most of its authority to him. At Qaddafi's urging, on 2 March 1977 it approved the "Declaration of the Establishment of the People's Authority" and proclaimed the birth of the Socialist People's Libyan Arab *Jamahiriyya*. The difficult-to-translate term *jamahiriyya* is generally rendered as "peopledom" or "state of the masses." Under the system of "people's congresses" all adults participated in the deliberations of their local Basic People's Congress (BPC), whose decisions were passed to the GPC for consideration and possible implementation. In theory the BPCs were the ultimate source of government authority and decision-making power, thus illustrating Qaddafi's belief that the people were capable of governing themselves.

Qaddafi also established a system of "revolutionary committees" staffed by young political zealots that were meant to supervise the people's committees and congresses, to increase the population's devotion to the revolution, and to protect the *Jamahiriyya* against opposition to and deviation from the official ideology. The systems of committees and congresses succeeded in producing higher levels of public participation. In March 1979 the GPC announced that power had been successfully transferred to the people. Soon after that Qaddafi abdicated his position as general secretary and adopted the title of "Leader of the Revolution" or, more simply, "the Leader."[36] All official claims to the contrary, the Libyan political system had become more authoritarian with Qaddafi exercising supreme power with the aid of a small coterie of trusted advisers. "Theoretically, this is genuine democracy," wrote the Leader. "But realistically, the strong always rule."[37]

Qaddafi's remaking of the Libyan economy paralleled his efforts to reform the political structure. According to *The Green Book*, private enterprise, rent, and wages were forms of exploitation that had to be abolished.[38] He urged Libyan workers to liberate themselves from the slavery imposed by the "wage owners" and to become full "partners, not wage earners" in the economy by taking control of "the public and private means of production."[39] Under his radical economic reforms workers formed self-management committees, and employees seized control of agricultural enterprises, service organizations, and private companies (except those in the oil and banking sectors). The ownership of private property was severely restricted, since Qaddafi believed that the accumulation of personal wealth in excess of one's basic necessities could only be done at the expense of others. Owning more than one dwelling was prohibited, private retail stores were replaced by state-run discount "people's supermarkets," and access to individual bank accounts was restricted to provide funds for public projects. Qaddafi declared that all Libyans should have their basic needs satisfied and by 1980 virtually no citizen lacked food, clothing, education, medical care, housing, or transportation.[40] "I have created a Utopia here in Libya," he declared. "Not an imaginary one that people write about in books, but a concrete Utopia."[41]

Qaddafi's economic measures benefited the poor but created deep resentment among members of the enterprising and educated middle class, who began leaving the country in large numbers. By 1982 as many as one hundred thousand Libyans had emigrated, resulting in a critical shortage of skilled managers and experienced technicians. Some exiles formed highly visible groups opposed to Qaddafi's increasingly autocratic regime and, in early 1980, Qaddafi launched a concerted effort to assassinate expatriate dissidents. Over the course of the year Libyan assassins carried out fourteen attacks in seven countries, resulting in the murder of eleven dissidents and the wounding of one.[42] In a speech on 2 March 1981 Qaddafi called for the elimination of all opposition to his regime. "It is the duty of the Libyan people constantly to liquidate their opponents," he declared. "The physical and final liquidation of the opponents of popular authority must continue at home and abroad, everywhere."[43]

Inside Libya Qaddafi faced several disaffected groups. The property-owning middle class opposed his economic reforms; intellectuals castigated his ideology; and Islamic leaders denounced his nationalization of endowed Islamic properties, they condemned his rejection of the *hadith*—the sayings and teachings of the Prophet Muhammad—as a source of sharia, and they denied his assertions that *The Green Book* was compatible with and based upon Islamic principles. The most serious threat to Qaddafi, however, came from the military and the RCC. In 1975 the ministers of foreign affairs and planning (both members of the RCC) with the help of about thirty army officers tried unsuccessfully to overthrow the regime. The two senior government officials vehemently disagreed with Qaddafi over the way in which the oil revenues were being spent. They sought to reduce spending for military equipment and foreign ventures in favor of internal development. In a severe crackdown on dissent the regime executed twenty-two of the accused army conspirators in 1977. After the attempted coup Qaddafi surrounded himself with a tight circle of loyalists and became increasingly isolated from the people, rarely mingling with crowds as once was his habit. He became so obsessed with his personal security that, for a time, he employed a cadre of female bodyguards because he believed that an Arab gunman would have difficulty firing at women.[44]

Qaddafi's Foreign Policy

In the area of foreign affairs Qaddafi struggled ceaselessly to elevate Libya's status from a relatively insignificant actor on the stage of Arab politics to a major force in the affairs of the Arab world and the Middle East. His foreign policy was preoccupied with Arab unity, support for the Palestinians and the need for front-line Arab states to confront Israel, the removal of outside influences from the Middle East and Africa, and support for liberation movements in all parts of the world.

After Nasser's death in 1970 Qaddafi became the most outspoken proponent of Arab unity. He believed that the Arab nation was one homogeneous entity and that Arab power could only be attained through complete union. Furthermore, he was convinced that a unified Arab nation could not be achieved until Israel was destroyed and the Palestinian people returned to their homes in historic Palestine. He considered the creation of Israel the ultimate indignity wrought by the West upon the Arab nation. It is important to note, however, that he considered Zionism—the political movement born in Europe in the late nineteenth century—the real enemy of the Arabs, not the Jewish people as such. Nevertheless, under Qaddafi Libyan Jews suffered greatly, having been forced to leave the country shortly after the coup.

Over the years Qaddafi attempted unsuccessfully to merge Libya with a number of Arab countries, including Egypt, Sudan, Tunisia, Algeria, Syria, and Morocco. He argued that the unification process should start immediately and rejected the view of most Arab leaders that a union between two or more countries could only be attained through a long, gradual process. In April 1971 Anwar as-Sadat (Nasser's successor), Qaddafi, and Syrian president Hafiz al-Asad proclaimed a union between Libya, Egypt, and Syria which they named the Federation of Arab Republics (FAR). Regarding the FAR as only the first step toward comprehensive Arab unity, Qaddafi proposed a full political merger between Sadat's Egypt and Libya. Qaddafi believed that the combination of Libyan petroleum wealth and Egyptian military strength would make him the dominant leader in the Arab world and would invigorate the struggle against Israel. Sadat agreed to the proposal in principle but disagreed with Qaddafi over the pace of unification. Qaddafi pushed for immediate union, but Sadat urged an incremental approach. The Egyptian president realized that unification would be difficult to achieve considering the profound political, economic, and social differences between their two countries.

During the October 1973 Arab-Israeli War the relationship between Qaddafi and Sadat took an unexpected turn. Qaddafi was furious that his FAR partners —Sadat and Asad—had excluded him from their prewar planning and had devised a stunning, two-pronged attack on Israel. He was further outraged that Sadat agreed to a cease-fire while Egyptian troops were still fighting on the east bank of the Suez Canal. He went so far as to call the Egyptian president a coward. In the years following the war their relationship deteriorated into a series of accusations and counter-accusations that effectively ended any possibility of a merger. In July 1977 mutual suspicion between the two leaders and Egyptian charges of Libyan subversion led to a series of violent border clashes in which the Egyptian military prevailed over Qaddafi's armed forces. The final break between the two countries came when Sadat launched his peace initiative in late 1977, an effort that culminated in the Israeli-Egyptian peace treaty of March 1979. Tripoli severed diplomatic relations with Cairo, and Qaddafi played a leading role in rallying the radical Arab states—Algeria, Libya, South Yemen, and Syria—and the Palestine Liberation Organization (PLO) in vehement opposition to Sadat's separate peace with Israel.[45]

Convinced of the righteousness of his causes, Qaddafi employed a number of unconventional tactics to achieve his foreign policy objectives. In particular he used petroleum as a political weapon, he targeted moderate Arab and African governments for subversion, and he supported and sponsored international terrorism. Qaddafi realized that his country's vast petroleum resources could finance huge internal development projects and the purchase of sophisticated weaponry. In 1970 and 1971 he demanded and won large increases in the price that foreign oil companies paid for Libyan crude oil, raising the per barrel price from $2.23 to $3.45. Within two years the government had acquired a controlling interest in all oil companies operating in Libya, and by early 1974 the level of control had risen to approximately 60 percent. During the October 1973 Arab-Israeli War Qaddafi joined other Arab oil producers in imposing an embargo against the countries that supported Israel, an embargo that chiefly was aimed at the United States.[46]

Qaddafi targeted moderate Arab governments for their opposition to his vision of a united Arab nation under Libyan leadership, their positive relations with the West, and, for some, their willingness to discuss peace with the Zionist enemy. He also sought the overthrow of moderate governments in sub-

Saharan Africa as the precursor to the establishment of a Libya-dominated league of radical, anti-Western, and anti-Zionist states.[47] In the 1970s Qaddafi's growing isolation within the Arab world and in Africa flamed his penchant for subversion, which included instigating coups, supporting opposition groups, aiding insurrections, and planning assassinations. Qaddafi's subversive activities not only disturbed Western governments but led to extremely poor relations with three of his African neighbors: Tunisia, Chad, and Sudan.

In 1974 President Habib Bourguiba of Tunisia first accepted but then canceled a proposed union with Libya. He later accused Qaddafi of carrying out several acts of subversion, including plots to assassinate Tunisian officials and incite armed rebellion. The most spectacular accusation came in 1980 when Libya was charged with fomenting a guerrilla uprising. At Qaddafi's direction several Tunisian insurgents attempted unsuccessfully to capture the town of Gafsa in central Tunisia. To counter Qaddafi's aggression the United States increased its military assistance to the Bourguiba government.[48]

Libya's interest in Chad was based on ethnic and religious ties, which gave rise to longstanding territorial claims. Qaddafi coveted a portion of Chadian territory bordering Libya—the Aouzou Strip—and in 1973 dispatched troops to occupy the area, which was reputed to be rich in mineral deposits. In 1975 Libya annexed the Aouzou Strip and, from this base, Qaddafi supported northern Muslim tribesmen in their protracted rebellion against the predominantly non-Muslim Chadian government. In early 1979 fighting reached N'Djamena, the capital, and, with Libyan backing, the rebel leader Goukouni Oueddei was installed as the head of the Transitional National Unity Government (GUNT). Oueddei became, in effect, the president of Chad. Qaddafi supported Oueddei and his private army, the People's Armed Forces (FAP), which was locked in a struggle against the Armed Forces of the North (FAN), a competing rebel army commanded by Hissene Habré, Oueddei's fellow tribesman and a former prime minister. By 1980 Habré's troops, who were backed by France, Egypt, and Sudan, controlled most of N'Djamena and several important towns in the northern half of the country.[49] In October of that year Qaddafi ordered his armed forces into the fray and sent shock waves across most of Africa when he publicly declared that Libya considered "Niger second in line to Chad."[50] By the end of the year approximately sixty-five hundred Libyan troops were serving in Chad. Buttressed by the Libyan intervention, Oueddei's forces launched a major offensive that resulted in the capture of N'Djamena in December. In a fateful decision Oueddei and his Libyan allies decided not to pursue the remnants of Habré's army, which managed to escape to Sudan.

After the victory Qaddafi announced the merger of Libya and Chad. His statement generated such a negative reaction among African heads of state that an ad hoc committee of the Organization of African Unity (OAU) met in emergency session in January 1981. The OAU issued a communiqué that condemned the merger and called on Qaddafi to withdraw his troops from Chad immediately.[51] After months of intense diplomatic pressure Qaddafi canceled plans for the merger and redeployed his troops to the Aouzou Strip.

Throughout the 1970s and early 1980s President Jafar an-Numayri of Sudan accused Qaddafi of subverting his regime by instigating several coup attempts, by sponsoring acts of sabotage (including the bombing of the Chadian embassy in Khartoum), by fomenting unrest in the western province of Darfur, and by supporting the rebellion in southern Sudan. The two leaders also sparred bitterly over foreign affairs. Qaddafi condemned Numayri for failing to denounce Sadat's peace initiative and, in 1980, Numayri reproved Libya's incursion into Chad. The following year, in the aftermath of the bombing of the Chadian embassy in Khartoum, the Sudanese government expelled all Libyan diplomats.[52] Numayri was thoroughly obsessed with what he perceived as a genuine Libyan threat to his regime. In response he strengthened his ties with Egypt; he provided weapons and logistical support to Chadian rebel Hissene Habré and several anti-Qaddafi exile groups; he negotiated a military aid package with the United States valued at over one hundred million dollars; and he offered Washington the use of Sudanese military bases in the event Sudan was threatened by an outside force.

Qaddafi was also accused of meddling in the affairs of several other African countries, particularly the nations of the Sahel (the huge grassland region south of the Sahara Desert). Presidents Moussa Traoré of Mali and Seyni Kountché of Niger charged Qaddafi with plotting to overthrow their governments. The popularly elected government of Ghana expelled Libyan diplomats, accusing them of subversive activities. The governments of Senegal and Gambia severed diplomatic relations with Libya, accusing the Qaddafi regime of imprisoning their citizens and forcing them into military training against their will. They reported that Libyan agents hired Muslim tribesmen from drought-battered areas to work in the Libyan oil fields and then forced them to serve in Qaddafi's "Islamic Legion." After completing their basic training these "legionnaires" often slipped back to their native countries and performed acts of sabotage and insurrection.[53] The widely respected former president of Senegal, Leopold Senghor, stated that Qaddafi's campaign of aggression was "designed to destroy Africa south of the Sahara and create a vast Libyan empire."[54] Similarly, the U.S. State Department called Qaddafi's announcement of a merger with Chad a valid expression of his "expansionist goals to absorb his Arab and Muslim neighbors in a Libyan-dominated state."[55]

Exacerbating his estrangement from his fellow African leaders, Qaddafi came to the aid of two of the world's most reviled dictators—Jean-Bedel Bokassa of the Central African Empire and Uganda's Idi Amin Dada—during their struggles to remain in power. When Bokassa was overthrown in 1979 two hundred Libyan soldiers were serving in his army. In late 1978 and early 1979 Qaddafi airlifted more than two thousand soldiers and a substantial amount of sophisticated military equipment to Uganda in a vain attempt to help Amin defeat a combined invasion force of Tanzanian troops and Ugandan exiles. After escaping from the capital at Kampala (which was soon captured by the invading army), the deposed "President for Life" found temporary asylum in Tripoli. Approximately six hundred Libyans were killed and most of their equipment lost during the Ugandan operation—an unmitigated military debacle.[56]

Many African countries reacted strongly to Qaddafi's record of aggression. Equatorial Guinea, Gambia, and Senegal severed diplomatic relations with Libya in 1980. That same year Ghana, Mali, Mauritania, Niger, and Nigeria vigorously protested the conversion of Libyan embassies into "people's bureaus" staffed by revolutionary zealots instead of professional diplomats. Each country responded by expelling the Libyan delegations from their countries. Furthermore, Kenya and Upper Volta (renamed Burkina Faso in 1984) refused to permit Libya to establish people's bureaus in their countries. By 1981 a total of twelve African countries had either broken diplomatic relations with Libya, expelled Libyan diplomats, or closed Libyan people's bureaus. Political analyst Ronald B. St. John very aptly noted that "Sub-Saharan Africa was beginning to show the unity which Qaddafi had long advocated, the common bond being opposition to Libyan policy."[57]

Qaddafi and Terrorism

By the late 1970s Western leaders regarded Qaddafi as one of the world's most notorious practitioners of international terrorism. They accused him of using it to attain foreign policy objectives that he could not achieve through conventional diplomatic or military means. According to the CIA Qaddafi's role in international terrorism included the funding of terrorist activities, the procurement of arms and other supplies for terrorist organizations, the use of

Libyan camps and advisers for guerrilla training, and the use of Libyan diplomatic posts as bases for terrorist operations.[58] The CIA also reported that Qaddafi frequently used Libya's United African Airlines (UAA) to support terrorist operations, subversion, and armed intervention. Ostensibly a nonscheduled passenger and cargo air carrier, UAA was staffed by several Libyan intelligence operatives and provided transport services for the Libyan armed forces and the Libyan intelligence service. In August 1981 Qaddafi directed the airline to open eighteen new offices in Africa, thus expanding and strengthening his intelligence network on the continent. When Qaddafi dispatched his troops to Chad, UAA airlifted weapons, ammunition, and military vehicles into the country.[59]

Within a few years of seizing power Qaddafi had established his reputation as a major supporter of international terrorism because of his involvement in a series of sensational terrorist acts. He provided extensive logistical support, funding, weapons, and training for the Palestinian terrorist group Black September. The organization was best known for the brutal massacre of Israeli athletes at the 1972 Olympic Games in Munich, West Germany. Libya was linked to another deadly Black September operation: the attack on the Embassy of Saudi Arabia in Khartoum in March 1973. The assault claimed the lives of Cleo A. Noel Jr., the U.S. ambassador to Sudan, and his chargé d'affaires, George C. Moore. That same month the Irish navy intercepted the SS *Claudia* near the coast of Ireland and, upon inspection, discovered it was transporting weapons to the Irish Republican Army. Qaddafi readily admitted that the arms were from Libya. In December 1973 Palestinian terrorists assaulted a Pan Am airliner at Rome's Fiumicino Airport, murdering thirty-one passengers. Italian investigators learned that the terrorists had traveled from Tripoli to conduct the attack and that Libya had provided them with money and arms. Qaddafi also developed a close working relationship with Ilich Ramirez Sanchez, the notorious Venezuelan terrorist known as "Carlos," whose group carried out the spectacular 1975 kidnapping of oil ministers attending a meeting of the Organization of Petroleum Exporting Countries (OPEC) in Vienna.[60]

In 1981 the State Department reported that Qaddafi spent hundreds of millions of dollars each year on terrorist activities and operated more than a dozen training camps where terrorist organizations, radical groups, and guerrilla movements received instruction in hijacking, assassination, commando tactics, and the use of explosives.[61] By the early 1980s Qaddafi was providing funds, training, and logistical support to insurgent movements, opposition groups, and terrorist elements in more than thirty countries, from South America to the Philippines.[62] "Libya runs twenty-five terrorist training camps," observed William J. Casey, President Ronald Reagan's first CIA director. "[Terrorism is] their second largest export, after oil."[63] Casey may have exaggerated the number of training camps but there was no denying Libya's huge role in the world of terrorism.

Qaddafi unabashedly defended his use of terrorism and subversion as a matter of principle, regarding it as a powerful way to avenge every injustice committed against Libya. Political scientist René Lemarchand noted that Qaddafi's "violently anti-Western disposition and his passionate commitment to a reconstruction of the Arab nation are the product of a uniquely cruel and frustrating historical experience."[64] Similarly, a CIA analyst pointed out that Qaddafi seems "to be motivated by a strong desire to take revenge . . . not so much for what we did to him last year or two weeks ago but for the humiliation of Islam, for the cultural and actual conquest of the Middle East."[65] According to the CIA, "He publicly portrays attacks by groups anywhere in the world as spontaneous events in an ongoing war against colonialism and Zionism and paints himself as a leading player in this war whose revolutionary ideals are shared by the 'oppressed' worldwide."[66] A State Department special report concluded that Qaddafi "fancies himself a leader and agent of historic forces that will reorder Third World politics to his taste. His vision provides both a motive and a rationale for providing military and financial aid to radical regimes and for undermining moderate governments by creating or supporting subversive groups and abetting terrorists." Furthermore, "Qaddafi's aggressive policies increasingly have focused on undermining U.S. and other Western interests in the Third World, as he sees these as the main barrier to his radical and expansionist goals."[67]

Qaddafi's involvement with international terrorism defined his country's relationship with the United States. According to Ronald B. St. John, "What Libya saw as justifiable support for national liberation movements, the United States viewed as blatant interference in the domestic affairs of other states, if not active support for international terrorists."[68] During the early and mid-1980s relations between Washington and Tripoli dramatically worsened and eventually led to a series of violent confrontations.

2

"Swift and Effective Retribution"

Qaddafi's Claim over the Gulf of Sidra

In 1970 the Libyan Arab Republic demanded and received a substantially higher price for the crude oil it sold to foreign petroleum companies, becoming the first oil-producing country in the world to do so. Over the next five years Libya's annual oil earnings jumped from $1.35 billion to $6 billion, and with this huge revenue windfall Colonel Qaddafi procured foreign military equipment —mostly from the Soviet Union—at a rate that soon outpaced his country's security needs and the ability of his armed forces to operate it efficiently. The CIA ascribed Qaddafi's extravagant arms purchases to megalomania. According to the agency the Libyan leader believed that his huge arsenal, the country's considerable oil earnings, and his revolutionary ideology would make him the leader of the Arab struggle against Zionism and Western influence in the region. Between 1970 and 1985 Qaddafi spent more than $20 billion on Soviet-made armaments, making Libya one of the largest customers of Soviet military hardware and technical assistance in the world.[1]

By the mid-1980s Qaddafi's country of 3.6 million people possessed one of the best-equipped armed forces in the Middle East. The Libyan military boasted 2,800 tanks (including top-of-the-line, Soviet-built T-72s), 2,300 armored vehicles, 535 combat aircraft (including sophisticated French-built Mirages and high-performance, Soviet-built MiG-23s and MiG-25s), 6 Soviet-built *Foxtrot* diesel-electric submarines, 65 surface combatants (most of which were capable of firing deadly antiship cruise missiles), and one of the most modern air defense networks in the world. In reality, however, Libya's military strength was considerably more formidable on paper than in fact. Hundreds of battle tanks and combat aircraft remained packed in their shipping crates, and a general lack of technical expertise and operational know-how hampered the effectiveness of the regular military, which numbered seventy-three thousand men in 1985. The Libyans relied heavily on advisers and technicians from the Soviet bloc for the installation, maintenance, and operation of the modern equipment in their large arsenal. In the early 1980s approximately twenty-five hundred Soviet military advisers served in Libya. Furthermore, it was widely reported that pilots from the Soviet Union, Eastern Europe, Syria, Pakistan, and North Korea as well as some Palestinian groups flew missions for the Libyan Arab Air Force (LAAF) because the quantity of available operational aircraft exceeded the number of qualified Libyan pilots. The normal ratio, by comparison, was two pilots per aircraft.[2]

The Nixon administration was concerned about the accumulation of French- and Soviet-made arms on the southern littoral of the Mediterranean and, in 1972, commenced aerial reconnaissance to monitor Libya's importation of military equipment. U.S. flight operations were conducted well outside Libyan airspace. Nevertheless, on 21 March 1973 two Libyan Mirage fighters attacked a U.S. Air Force RC-130 reconnaissance plane that was operating more than eighty miles off the coast of Libya. Fortunately the unarmed plane was not hit. Not surprisingly, Qaddafi ignored the protest note sent from Washington.

In retaliation for President Nixon's decision to resupply Israel during the October 1973 Arab-Israeli War and in an attempt to make aerial surveillance of his country more difficult, Qaddafi made a fateful announcement on 11 October 1973.[3] He said that the entire Gulf of Sidra is "located within the territory of the Libyan Arab Republic . . . extending north offshore to latitude 32 degrees and 30 minutes, constitutes an integral part of the territory of the Libyan Arab Republic[,] and is under its complete sovereignty."[4] By proclaiming the huge gulf to be Libyan internal waters Qaddafi blatantly repudiated several long-standing international conventions. To support Libya's claim he advanced his own interpretation of international law. First he argued that the Gulf of Sidra was a bay, although its 250-mile-wide opening far exceeded the 24-mile-wide maximum size allowed to enclose internal waters by Article 7 of the 1958 Geneva Convention on the Territorial Sea and Contiguous Zone. Second

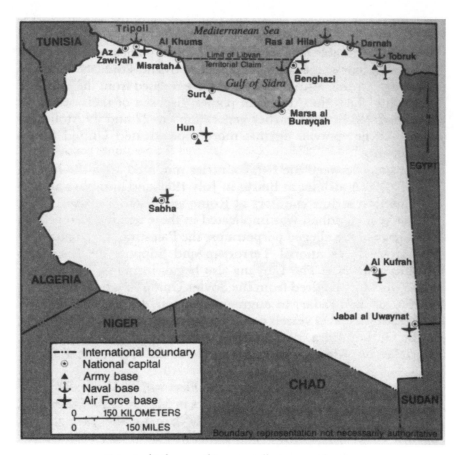

Principal Libyan military installations, mid-1980s

Libya: A Country Study, ed. Helen C. Metz, 1989

he stated that Libya's claim over the Gulf of Sidra was historic, but W. Hays Parks, an authority on international law, explained that "such a claim must be long-standing, open, and notorious—with effective and continuous exercise of authority by the claimant—and one to which other states acquiesce." Qaddafi's declaration of sovereignty over the Gulf of Sidra dated from 1973, hardly a long-standing claim. Furthermore, by the mid-1980s only two countries—the post-Numayri regime in Sudan and Burkina Faso—had recognized Qaddafi's claim.[5]

On 11 February 1974 the U.S. Department of State issued a démarche that called Libya's claim of sovereignty over the Gulf of Sidra "unacceptable as a violation of international law." The note made a further declaration: "The

United States Government views the Libyan action as an attempt to appropriate a large area of the high seas by unilateral action, thereby encroaching upon the long-established principle of freedom of the seas. . . . The United States Government reserves its rights and the rights of its nationals in the area of the Gulf of Sidra affected by the action of the Government of Libya."[6] Similar protests were issued by the Soviet Union and several other nations.[7]

The United States and other maritime powers enjoyed a long history of operating in the international waters of the Gulf of Sidra and were understandably concerned about Qaddafi's assertion of sovereignty over the gulf for two important reasons. First, the gulf forms a large indentation—120 miles at its deepest—in the North African coastline and is therefore a convenient location for naval forces to conduct surface and air exercises free of commercial fishing zones and away from the busy shipping lanes and air routes of the central Mediterranean. Acquiescence to Libyan sovereignty would have severely complicated and restricted training opportunities for the U.S. Sixth Fleet and other navies operating in the Mediterranean. Second, if left unchallenged Qaddafi's claim would have encouraged other nations to advance their own unreasonable claims of extended territorial seas, creating, in the words of Parks, "the danger of international maritime anarchy." At the Third United Nations Conference on the Law of the Sea, held from 1973 to 1982, the U.S. delegation fought vigorously to maintain maximum operational mobility for its naval forces worldwide. The 1982 UN Convention on the Law of the Sea extended territorial sea limits from three to twelve nautical miles but also reaffirmed important sections of the 1958 Convention on the Territorial Sea and Contiguous Zone including the definition of what constitutes a bay. The convention denied any recognition whatsoever of Libya's claim over the Gulf of Sidra.[8] Although the United States did not sign the 1982 convention, it accepted the convention's twelve-mile limit for denoting territorial waters.[9]

President Carter's Libya Policy

On three occasions between 1973 and 1979 the United States challenged Qaddafi's illegal claim of sovereignty over the Gulf of Sidra by conducting routine naval exercises in the disputed waters. In late 1979 Zbigniew Brzezinski, President Jimmy Carter's national security adviser, and Adm. Thomas B. Hayward, the chief of naval operations, proposed a large-scale freedom of navigation (FON) exercise designed to assert U.S. rights in the gulf and underscore Qaddafi's inability to back up his claim with military force. Carter's Libya policy, however, was influenced by his desire to maintain economic relations, avoid military confrontation, and prevent closer cooperation between Tripoli and Moscow. Carter rejected the FON plan out of a concern that a bold challenge to Qaddafi might provoke a military incident, endanger Americans living and working in Libya, or embarrass Arab and other Muslim leaders who were trying to negotiate the release of American hostages being held since 4 November 1979 by radical Iranian students at the U.S. embassy in Tehran.[10]

Despite Carter's cautious policy toward Libya, relations between Washington and Tripoli rapidly deteriorated. On 2 December 1979 a large mob gathered outside the U.S. embassy in Tripoli, demonstrating against the United States and shouting pro-Iranian slogans. Before long the crowd overran, sacked, and burned the embassy while a single Libyan policeman looked on. The Carter administration immediately lodged a stern protest with the Libyan government. The United States demanded that Libya admit responsibility for the attack and destruction of the embassy, since it had not provided adequate protection for the facility. The Libyans responded with expressions of regret for the incident but denied any responsibility. After the Carter administration threatened to suspend operation of the U.S. mission in Tripoli the Libyan government agreed to compensate the United States for the damages. In April and May 1980 the Carter administration expelled six Libyan diplomats because they were engaged in a "campaign of intimidation" against Libyan exiles living in the United States. In May the administration finally closed the American diplomatic mission in Tripoli.[11]

On 16 September two Libyan MiG-23 Floggers allegedly fired missiles at an unarmed U.S. Air Force RC-135 reconnaissance plane flying in international airspace. The American plane escaped unharmed. Since the evidence surrounding the incident was not conclusive, the Carter administration neither acknowledged the suspected attack nor sent a formal protest to Tripoli. Five days later another confrontation took place when eight Libyan fighters flown by Syrian pilots attempted to intercept an RC-135 operating two hundred miles off the Libyan coast. This time, however, the electronic surveillance plane was accompanied by a trio of F-14 Tomcat fighters from the aircraft carrier USS *John F. Kennedy* (CV-67). The Tomcats immediately challenged the aggressors, who wisely broke off the engagement and returned to base. Once again the administration did not publicly acknowledge the incident. Carter did not want to escalate tensions between the United States and Libya during his reelection campaign.[12]

On 22 October the Libyan people's bureau in Washington purchased advertising space in the *Washington Post* and reprinted a letter from "Brother Leader" Qaddafi to Carter and his Republican opponent in the election, former California governor Ronald Reagan. Qaddafi claimed that "several aggressive measures have been taken by America against Libya, as represented in . . . the taking of very hostile political and media attitudes." He stressed that an armed conflict between the United States and the Arabs could "only be avoided if America stops the military steps it has taken which threaten the independence of the Arab homeland." He warned that if the United States persisted in its aggressive policies toward the Arab nation, the Arabs would be entitled to exercise the right of self-defense to protect their homeland. Finally, in regard to his own country, Qaddafi demanded that the United States stop its "surveillance planes from spying across Libyan borders."[13] In light of the recent Libyan attack on U.S. aircraft and the nearly identical one in 1973, administration officials were convinced that Qaddafi was prepared to use force to defend his airspace and obstruct American intelligence-gathering activities.

In the fall of 1980 the Pentagon again proposed a FON exercise for the Gulf of Sidra, but Carter could not risk another crisis in the Middle East. He was fighting for reelection and his attention was consumed by the Iran hostage crisis and the Soviet occupation of Afghanistan. He ordered the Sixth Fleet to operate north of 32° 30', and by doing so he granted implicit recognition to Qaddafi's claim over the Gulf of Sidra.[14]

The Election of 1980

In the November election Ronald Reagan won the presidency in a landslide, capturing forty-four states and 51 percent of the popular vote. Jimmy Carter won only six states and the District of Columbia and 41 percent of the popular vote. A master of modern media politics and a champion of the conservative values of Middle America, Reagan campaigned against big government. He advocated lower taxes, fewer regulations, and less interference by government in business and everyday life. Radiating an unwavering faith in the abilities of the American people and in the potential of the free enterprise system, Reagan preached that all Americans could achieve unprecedented prosperity if only government would "get off their backs." In the area of foreign affairs he called for a stronger national defense, the restoration of U.S. prestige around the world, and a tougher stance toward the Soviet Union (which he decried as an unrelenting enemy of American values and a threat to world peace). He also spoke out on the problem of international terrorism: "We must take a stand against terrorism in the world and combat it with firmness, for it is a most cowardly and savage violation of peace."[15]

Carter suffered one of the worst electoral defeats by an incumbent president in U.S. history. Many Americans viewed the magnitude of the loss as a repudiation of his leadership. Others, including Carter himself, believed that the landslide was more an indication of the nation's frustration over a set of circumstances that no president could have handled to the satisfaction of the public. In the latter half of his term these circumstances included rising gasoline prices, double-digit inflation, high unemployment, the Soviet occupation of Afghanistan, and, most frustrating of all, the long captivity of the American hostages in Tehran. As a final insult to Carter and his presidency, the Iranian government did not release the hostages until moments after Reagan took the oath of office on 20 January 1981.

Reagan Grapples with the Terrorism Issue

President Reagan wasted no time making good on his promises to increase defense spending by huge amounts, to develop a tougher policy toward the Soviet Union, and to combat international terrorism. Since fighting terrorism would certainly involve Libya, that country was briefly discussed at the first meeting of the National Security Council on 21 January 1981. The new president and his chief advisers considered Qaddafi a genuine threat to American interests in the Middle East and Africa and were determined to thwart his efforts to destabilize friendly governments in the region. According to political scientist Lisa Anderson, the Libyan dictator "was selected for special attention by the United States as the symbol of all the United States finds repugnant in international affairs—support for international terrorism, opposition to a peaceful solution of the Arab-Israeli conflict, and support for a diminished U.S. role in the world."[16]

Five days later, on 26 January, Reagan and his top national security advisers —Vice President George Bush, Secretary of State Alexander M. Haig Jr., Secretary of Defense Caspar W. Weinberger, National Security Adviser Richard V. Allen, FBI Director William H. Webster, and CIA Director William J. Casey— gathered to discuss state-sponsored and state-supported terrorism. This deadly phenomenon continued to claim more innocent victims with each passing year. Since 1968 when the CIA began compiling statistics on terrorism, the year just completed was in fact the bloodiest one on record. Particularly alarming was the rate at which Americans were becoming vulnerable to terrorist attacks. In 1980 nearly 40 percent of all terrorist incidents involved American citizens or property. Of the 278 attacks on U.S. citizens, ten people were murdered and ninety-four injured.

Reagan and his advisers regarded international terrorism as an issue of vital national importance, and combating it became one of the new administration's highest foreign policy priorities. They reviewed the federal government's programs and resources devoted to countering terrorism. They evaluated everything, from the secret antiterrorist Delta Force to the various interagency working groups and task forces responsible for carrying out U.S. policy on terrorism. They concluded that more had to be done, but they quickly realized that before they could develop new policies for confronting terrorism, they had to learn as much as possible about the nature of the enemy. They determined that greater emphasis had to be placed on the collection of intelligence on the terrorist threat. Casey immediately ordered all CIA stations to elevate terrorism on their list of intelligence collection priorities, known as the "essential elements of intelligence" in the intelligence trade. At some stations, especially those in Europe and the Middle East, collecting intelligence on terrorism became the number one priority.[17]

The next day, 27 January, at a ceremony held on the White House lawn Reagan welcomed home the Americans who were held captive in Iran for 444 days. Reagan was intensely concerned about the well-being of the former hostages, and his anger over their captivity had not yet subsided. Furthermore, the American people were overjoyed that the hostages were returned safe and sound, but they were still angry and frustrated that Iran had been able to humiliate the United States virtually without consequence. Speaking before the former hostages and their families and with the world as his audience, Reagan proclaimed that the time had come to retaliate against terrorism.[18] He proclaimed: "Let terrorists beware that when the rules of international behavior are violated, our policy will be one of swift and effective retribution. We hear that we live in an era of limits to our power. Well, let it be understood that there are limits to our patience."[19]

Reagan's rhetorical bombshell took some of his closest advisers and several career officials by surprise. Kenneth Adelman, a former member of Reagan's transition team and at the time working at the State Department, had drafted the phrase "swift and effective retribution." Adelman had traveled with former

President Carter to West Germany to greet the former hostages on their journey home from Iran and learned firsthand how badly the Iranians had treated their captives. When Adelman briefed Reagan on their condition the president became "very disturbed" by what he heard. The hostages had been treated far worse than anyone suspected. Following his meeting with Reagan, Adelman composed the powerful phrase, believing it was appropriate for the moment. He had no doubt that Reagan would follow through on the tough statement.

Reagan's declaration effectively committed his administration to a war against international terrorism even before it had developed a strategy or even knew with certainty what it was confronting.[20] Nevertheless, Haig became the first administration official to take up the call to arms against terrorism. At his first news conference as secretary of state, held one day after Reagan's remarkable statement, the former chief of staff in the Nixon White House and former NATO supreme commander asserted that "international terrorism will take the place of human rights [in] our concern, because it is the ultimate abuse of human rights."[21] In an attempt to clarify his remark Haig explained that the campaign against terrorism by the Reagan administration would have the same priority that the battle for human rights had held in the Carter administration. Nevertheless, Haig refused to speculate about actions the administration might take following a future terrorist incident. He stated that Reagan's pledge of "swift and effective retribution" was "consciously ambiguous."[22]

Haig also expressed his belief that the Soviet Union played a significant role in international terrorism. He claimed that the Soviets were actively "training, funding, and equipping" terrorists, and he accused them of "conscious policies . . . which foster, support, and expand this activity which is hemorrhaging in many respects throughout the world today."[23] Haig was convinced that Moscow controlled a vast terrorist network and used the terror weapon to undermine Western interests. His view was buttressed by the writings of American journalist Claire Sterling. In her book *The Terror Network* Sterling claimed that an existing international syndicate of disparate terrorist organizations helped one another and obtained support from "not altogether disinterested outsiders," most significantly the Soviet Union and its allies. The outside assistance included training, weapons, funding, diplomatic cover, and logistical support. Although Sterling did not agree with Haig's belief that the Soviet Union directed the day-to-day operations of terrorist groups, she emphasized that the Soviets were quite eager to benefit from the actions of the terrorist groups they supported. Sterling labeled it "terror by proxy."[24]

Ronald I. Spiers, the chief of the State Department's intelligence branch, informed Haig privately that current intelligence did not support his public statements. Unconvinced, Haig requested from William Casey a formal intelligence report—a National Intelligence Estimate (NIE)—to analyze the role of the Soviet Union in international terrorism. Since terrorism was not a topic routinely covered by NIEs, Casey ordered the Office of Soviet Analysis (SOVA) to draft a special NIE (SNIE) on Moscow's involvement in terrorism. Although Casey's gut instincts told him that Haig's thinking was correct, Casey believed that the best way to prove Haig's point was through good analysis of the available intelligence.[25] While the SNIE was being written Casey held a meeting with Sterling, who lambasted the CIA for not thoroughly investigating the Soviet role in international terrorism. Casey came away from the meeting impressed by the strength and passion of her arguments. "God damn it. . . . I've got this woman who's written a pretty persuasive book faulting us," he fumed. "Just because nobody heard a tree fall in the forest doesn't mean it didn't fall."[26]

The first draft of the SNIE did not support Haig's perception of the Soviet role. It concluded that the Soviets did not organize or direct terrorist activity and argued that the Soviets did not approve of it. The estimate made a careful distinction between the actions of national liberation movements and other insurgent groups that were supported by Moscow versus the activities of terrorist organizations that were not. The SOVA analysts also stressed that no conclusive evidence of Soviet or Eastern European involvement in international terrorism existed. In late March Casey reviewed the draft and stated that he was "greatly disappointed" with its conclusions and "he would not be willing to put his name on it." He accused SOVA of trying to prove Soviet involvement in terrorism beyond a shadow of a doubt and relying too heavily on Moscow's own pronouncements on terrorism. Rather than ask SOVA to rethink its conclusions, Casey directed the Defense Intelligence Agency (DIA) to prepare a new draft analysis. Casey favored the DIA's version which, in contrast to the SOVA analysis, stated that current intelligence reporting supported the existence of terrorist training camps in Eastern Europe. Over the next few weeks a senior CIA analyst supervised the preparation of a compromise draft analysis, which SOVA and DIA accepted with few reservations.[27] In May the SNIE, titled *Soviet Support for International Terrorism and Revolutionary Violence,* was signed by Casey and forwarded to Haig and other senior administration officials.[28]

The estimate contained a number of key judgments and conclusions:

> the Soviet Union was deeply involved in the support of revolutionary violence for the purpose of "weakening unfriendly societies, destabilizing hostile regimes, and advancing Soviet interests";

the Soviets were ambivalent about the use of terrorist tactics in the performance of revolutionary violence, but they were deeply concerned that terrorist violence would promote or harm their interests in specific situations;

strong evidence existed that the Soviets directly or indirectly supported several national insurgencies and liberation movements that used terrorism in their programs of revolutionary violence;

evidence of Soviet support for nihilistic terrorist organizations—groups whose only purpose was to attack symbols of the status quo—was weak and contradictory since some members of nihilistic groups were trained and supported by Soviet friends and allies while the Soviets occasionally characterized nihilistic terrorism as "criminal";

some revolutionary organizations supported by the Soviets accepted a degree of control and direction from Moscow, while others did not;

the Soviets provided extensive military and paramilitary training to members of revolutionary organizations in camps located in the Soviet Union, Eastern Europe, Cuba, and the Middle East, and they supplied weapons and other forms of assistance to a wide spectrum of revolutionary groups around the world;

the Soviets backed many countries or organizations that in turn supported the terrorist activities of revolutionary groups, including Libya, South Yemen, Palestinian groups, Eastern bloc nations, and Cuba;

Moscow accepted the support that its allies and friends gave to revolutionary groups because these actions either advanced its interests or were "the price to be paid" for maintaining and strengthening its influence with its friends and allies; and

the Soviet Union's policy of supporting various forms of revolutionary violence was likely to continue because it enhanced Soviet interests at minimal cost and with little damage to Soviet prestige.[29]

The SNIE made it clear that the Soviets were responsible to a significant degree for the phenomenon of modern international terrorism. The Soviets became involved in the deadly movement after Israel's stunning victory in the June 1967 Arab-Israeli War. After the war the Palestinians had concluded that conventional Arab military forces could not defeat Israel and decided to mount a protracted guerrilla war against Israel just as the Vietcong guerrillas were doing against the United States in South Vietnam. This change in Palestinian strategy coincided with Moscow's determination to play a more prominent role in the affairs of the Middle East. The Palestinians believed that effective use of terrorism would demonstrate their national strength and would prompt Israel to respond with repressive measures that would turn international public opinion against them and encourage many Palestinians living in exile to join the armed struggle against Zionism. The Soviet Union and its allies in Eastern Europe developed the Palestinian insurgent movement into an effective fighting force and, in the process, trained several guerrillas in the complex workings of international terrorism.

In the late 1960s Soviet, Czech, and East German instructors trained a large number of PLO commandos in camps located in Czechoslovakia. The Palestinians then established their own training facilities in several countries throughout the Middle East and North Africa. By the early 1970s the Palestinians were training not only their own guerrillas but also members of several nihilist terrorist groups such as the West German Baader-Meinhoff Gang, the Italian Red Brigades, and the Japanese Red Army. In return the PLO received political and logistical support from several nihilist groups in Europe. By 1970 the Soviets had very little direct involvement in terrorist training yet, according to Reagan's deputy CIA director Adm. Bobby Inman, little doubt remained that the Soviets were "the grandparents" of modern international terrorism. "They built the original training camps and gave the PLO the capability to train their own," Inman said.[30]

The impact of the new Palestinian strategy was felt immediately. In the eighteen months following the June 1967 Arab-Israeli War the Israeli government reported more than twelve hundred terrorist attacks within the country's borders. Furthermore, radical factions of the PLO, such as the Marxist Popular Front for the Liberation of Palestine (PFLP), refused to limit their guerrilla war to Israel. The PFLP vowed to attack Zionism and its supporters anywhere in the world.

Two essential conclusions can be drawn about Moscow's involvement in international terrorism. First, although the Soviets were deeply engaged in supporting acts of revolutionary violence, their support was largely opportunistic. They hoped to advance their interests simply by creating trouble for their opponents. There was no centralized program for terrorism in Moscow but, if a revolutionary group sought assistance, the Soviets rarely turned it down. Second, international terrorism became self-sustaining largely through the efforts of the Soviet Union. Moscow conducted the initial terrorist training in the late 1960s and, by the end of the decade, its graduates were operating their own camps and carrying out their own terrorist operations. Therefore, since terrorism was operating independently of the Soviet Union, being able to persuade Moscow to disavow support for revolutionary or terrorist groups would not end the problem of terrorism. The SNIE did not support Haig's view that the Soviet Union controlled day-to-day terrorist operations. The Soviets supported terrorism when the opportunity presented itself, but they did not call the shots.[31]

A decade later, after the collapse of Soviet communism in Eastern Europe, the former communist governments disclosed the true nature of the terror network. The Eastern Europeans, most notably East Germany, provided extensive support to several nihilist groups and freelance terrorist organizations. For example, the East German intelligence service, the Stasi, supplied the West Germany–based Red Army Faction with weapons, false documents, training, and funds. The East Germans also allowed Palestinian terrorists to use their country as an operating base and provided sanctuary to the notorious freelance terrorist Carlos. Hungary gave safe harbor to Carlos, Czechoslovakia operated a major terrorist training program, and Yugoslavia served as a major base of operations for the Palestinians. Sterling's controversial hypothesis about a functioning terrorist network supported by interested outsiders, such as the Soviet Union, and Casey's belief that the Soviet Union and its allies were extensively involved in international terrorism were both vindicated.[32]

The Reagan Administration Develops a Libya Policy

For senior policymakers in the State Department, the CIA, and the NSC there was no better target for Reagan's advocacy of "swift and effective retribution" against terrorism than Qaddafi's Libya. In a 1981 research paper titled *Patterns of International Terrorism: 1980*, the CIA identified Libya as "the most prominent state sponsor of and participant in international terrorism."[33] Whereas Admiral Inman referred to the Soviets as the "grandparents" of international terrorism, Claire Sterling labeled Qaddafi as "the Daddy Warbucks of terrorism."[34] Haig pointed out that Qaddafi's oil revenue was "almost exclusively diverted to the purchase of armaments, the training of international terrorists, and the conduct of direct intervention in neighboring states of Northern Africa."[35] The CIA reported that Libya's support for terrorism included "financing for terrorist operations, weapons procurement and supply, the use of training camps and Libyan advisers for guerrilla training, and the use of Libyan diplomatic facilities abroad as support bases for terrorist operations."[36]

The Reagan administration immediately began crafting a systematic, comprehensive, and multifaceted strategy aimed at exerting extraordinary pressure on the Qaddafi regime. The strategy would consist of covert operations, diplomatic actions, economic sanctions, and demonstrations of military power.[37] According to one official the plan would, as a minimum, "make life uncomfortable" for the Libyan dictator, whom many Reagan appointees erroneously perceived as a Soviet surrogate bent on spreading mischief throughout the Middle East and Africa.[38] Administration officials hoped that an aggressive Libya policy would damage Qaddafi's reputation as an Arab leader, isolate him diplomatically, dissuade him from new foreign adventures, and deprive him of international support in the event of a confrontation with the United States or one of its allies in the Middle East, namely Egypt. They wanted to weaken Qaddafi's domestic authority and increase the likelihood that he would be removed from power. They sought the support of U.S. allies in Europe but were determined to carry out their plan with or without the help of the Europeans, who did not share their view of Qaddafi as a crazed terrorist and international menace.[39]

This dramatic change in U.S. policy toward Libya did not occur overnight. For a number of departments and agencies of the U.S. government—particularly the State Department, the Pentagon, and the CIA—producing a complicated strategy required several months of intense discussion and negotiation.[40] Nevertheless, some of the components of the strategy were ready for implementation within a few months.

Planning covert operations against Libya began immediately. During his first week at the CIA Casey reviewed an SNIE titled *Libya: Aims and Vulnerabilities*. The secret study, which the Carter administration initiated following the attempted assassination in October 1980 of an exiled Libyan dissident living in Colorado, was completed only a few days before Casey took office. It contained a number of conclusions that piqued the director's interest in taking direct action against Qaddafi.[41] First, after his recent success in Chad, Qaddafi was likely to undertake other foreign ventures that would challenge U.S. and Western interests in the Middle East and Africa.[42] Second, the number of recent coup attempts suggested that Qaddafi's grip on power might be loosening. Unfortunately, the exile and internal opposition to Qaddafi was fragmented, disorganized, and largely ineffective. The activities of Libyan exile groups consisted mainly of publishing anti-Qaddafi materials and smuggling them into the country. To enhance the opposition's chances of effectively challenging the Qaddafi regime the CIA had to play a more direct, hands-on role. Merely supplying funds and arms would not be enough.[43] Third, although Qaddafi was not a Soviet pawn, his relationship with the Soviet Union was "based on common short-term interests rather than on a shared world view." The Libyans purchased Soviet military equipment in huge quantities and the Soviets benefited from the hard currency generated by the arms sales—estimated at $1 billion per year—as well as from Qaddafi's anti-Western policies.[44] Fourth, Qaddafi had ordered his armed forces to attack any U.S. ship or aircraft entering the Gulf of Sidra, which made the chance of an incident occurring between U.S. and Libyan forces extremely high.[45] Finally, Qaddafi was to a large extent a "traditional Arab street politician" who derived his political legitimacy from his charisma and the public's perception of his invincibility. If the aura of Qaddafi's personality could be irreparably damaged then his inept domestic and foreign policies might overtake him and prove to be his undoing.[46] Consequently, some of Qaddafi's regional opponents, most notably President Sadat of Egypt and President Numayri of Sudan, focused "their resources on quietly bleeding Qaddafi at his most vulnerable point—his overextension in Chad and the danger this [posed] for him at home."[47]

The strategy of undermining Qaddafi's domestic base by striking at him in Chad appealed to Haig and Casey. The two officials directed their staffs to develop a coordinated policy to provide covert aid to the Chadian rebel Hissene Habré, whom the CIA described as the "quintessential desert warrior." Haig and Casey believed that a Libyan defeat in Chad would foment widespread disaffection within the officer corps of the Libyan armed forces, while heavy Libyan casualties would generate great unrest among Libyan rank and file. The two advocated a covert initiative that would, in effect, "bloody Qaddafi's nose" and "increase the flow of pine boxes back to Libya." Reagan approved a formal intelligence order or "finding" that authorized the CIA to conduct a covert operation in support of Habré's efforts to wrest control of the Chadian government from Goukouni Oueddei and remove Libyan influence from the country. The operation provided Habré with money, weapons, technical support, and political assistance.[48]

It was presumed that thwarting Qaddafi in Chad also would send a very strong signal to the Soviet Union. Since the 1970s the Soviets had established client states in Afghanistan, Ethiopia, and Angola virtually unopposed by U.S. administrations in the years following the Vietnam War. Haig emphasized that the Reagan administration's position regarding Soviet involvement in the Third World was decidedly different. "Our signal to the Soviets had to be a plain warning that their time of unrestricted adventuring in the Third World was over," he asserted, "and that America's capacity to tolerate the mischief of Moscow's proxies, Cuba and Libya, had been exceeded." The fact that Qaddafi did not act on behalf of the Soviet Union and therefore could not be considered a Soviet proxy was not important to Haig.[49] Libya and the Soviet Union enjoyed a close relationship by virtue of a few common interests, and that relationship caused some administration officials (such as the secretary of state himself as well as the hard-liners within his department) to regard Libya as a client of the Soviet Union.

Reagan signed another intelligence finding that directed the CIA to provide "nonlethal" aid and training to anti-Qaddafi groups. This aid operation was to proceed cautiously and deliberately first by recruiting reliable agents from the exile Libyan community and then by taking on the arduous task of developing viable opposition groups based outside the country. If the second step achieved a measurable degree of success the administration would then consider drafting a new finding that would support a plan to go forward with an anti-Qaddafi propaganda program and paramilitary operations.

In 1979 Dr. Muhammad Yusuf al-Muqaryaf, a senior Libyan bureaucrat and diplomat, defected to Egypt where he immediately denounced Qaddafi as a corrupt, brutal, and profligate dictator. In October 1981 Muqaryaf founded the National Front for the Salvation of Libya (NFSL), a group financed primarily by the CIA and Saudi Arabia. Based in Sudan, the NFSL set up a radio station that broadcasted news and opposition propaganda into Libya, and recruited other prominent exiles to join the anti-Qaddafi movement. Muqaryaf dedicated himself to abolishing the Qaddafi regime, through violence, if necessary. Casey did not expect the exiles to be powerful enough to overthrow Qaddafi, but he supported them as an inexpensive, low-risk means of making trouble for the Libyan dictator and as a new source of intelligence on developments inside Libya.[50]

In the summer of 1981 the covert operation in Chad got underway. After the CIA's deputy director for operations, Max Hugel, briefed the House Intelligence Committee on the operation, a number of committee members questioned the wording of the finding, which was vague enough that it could be interpreted as justification for directly challenging Qaddafi's hold on power. Concerned committee members sent a classified letter to Reagan in which they strongly protested the operation. The media soon caught wind of the letter and reported that several members of the Intelligence Committee were objecting to a CIA covert operation taking place in an unnamed African country. In a half-page article *Newsweek* described the operation as "a large-scale, multiphase and costly scheme to overthrow the Libyan regime of Col. Muammar Qaddafi." The article then reported that "the CIA's goal . . . was Qaddafi's 'ultimate' removal from power. To members of the House Intelligence Committee who reviewed the plan, that phrase seemed to imply Qaddafi's assassination."[51]

A scheme to assassinate Qaddafi, however, would be in direct violation of Executive Order 12333, signed by Reagan in 1981. According to the order, "No person employed by or acting on behalf of the United States government shall engage in, or conspire to engage in, assassination."[52]

Casey was furious about the leaks and subsequent news reports. The CIA's Directorate for Operations had carefully designed a covert support operation for Chad, a country in which the agency believed it had a reasonable chance of success and where U.S. allies France, Egypt, and Sudan were already involved. Reports of a plan to topple the Qaddafi regime undoubtedly would make the Libyan dictator more cautious and vigilant just as the CIA was trying to strike at him indirectly through Chad. In response to the *Newsweek* story the White House issued a statement that denied the contents of the article but acknowledged that some members of the House Intelligence Committee had written a letter to Reagan protesting an unspecified operation. *Newsweek* reporters then sought clarifying information about the operation from their source, who happened be a member of the committee. Soon afterward Congressman Clement J. Zablocki—Democrat of Wisconsin, chairman of the House Foreign Affairs Committee, and a member of the House Intelligence Committee—admitted to House staff personnel that he had been the source of the *Newsweek* story. Congressman Edward P. Boland, Democrat of Massachusetts and chairman of the House Intelligence Committee, rebuked Zablocki for the leak and informed him of his misunderstanding of the facts, but Boland did not pursue disciplinary action against his colleague.[53]

The next component of Reagan's Libya strategy to take shape was the calculated use of military power. One month into his presidency Reagan approved an assertive, comprehensive FON program that was designed to defend U.S. national interests against the unreasonable maritime claims of more than forty nations, including Qaddafi's Libya. Weinberger and the Joint Chiefs of Staff (JCS), particularly Admiral Hayward, urged Reagan to authorize a FON exercise for the Gulf of Sidra. Carter had blocked the most recent proposals for an exercise in the gulf, but Weinberger and Hayward did not want to follow the former president's policy of avoiding the disputed body of water. Conducting maneuvers in the gulf, they argued, would demonstrate U.S. determination to exercise its rights and would undermine Qaddafi's credibility since there was nothing he could do to prevent the Sixth Fleet from operating there. Reagan sided with the top officials at the Pentagon.

In the late spring of 1981 at a meeting of the National Security Planning Group (NSPG)—a gathering of the president's most senior advisers and chaired by the president himself—Reagan directed the Pentagon to plan a major Sixth Fleet exercise that would challenge Qaddafi's claim over the Gulf of Sidra. The exercise was tentatively planned for late summer. It would boldly yet peacefully assert U.S. rights in international waters and airspace and would demonstrate to America's friends and adversaries in the Middle East the United States' commitment to peace and stability in the region. The Pentagon spearheaded the planning of the exercise, but other departments and agencies were involved in the process owing to the sensitive nature of it. One day before the start of the exercise *Newsweek* reported that the Reagan administration "will test Qaddafi's reactions—and those of his allies in Moscow—by staging war games inside the gulf." According to the magazine the maneuvers would serve as the administration's "first direct challenge to the Libyan strongman."[54] (Details of the FON exercise and its surprising outcome are presented later in this chapter.)

Regarding the diplomatic components of the new Libya strategy, the administration pursued several initiatives. First it appealed to U.S. allies in Europe, Africa, and the Middle East to join the United States in condemning and isolating Libya. Several European governments advised the administration not to confront Qaddafi publicly because such an approach might strengthen him at home and enhance his stature throughout the Third World. On the other hand, President Sadat, who once described Qaddafi as "a lunatic," encouraged American efforts to pressure the Libyan leader. Second, the administration pledged diplomatic support and significant increases in military assistance to several of Libya's neighbors in North Africa, namely Egypt, Sudan, Tunisia, Algeria, and Morocco.[55] Meanwhile, strong evidence emerged that Qaddafi's liquidation campaign against Libyan exiles had reached the United States, which had a profound effect on diplomatic relations between the United States and Libya.

In October 1980 Faisal Zagallai, a graduate student at Colorado State University and one of the leaders of the Libyan exile dissident community, was grievously wounded when he was shot twice in the head by an assailant using a .22 caliber pistol. Incredibly, the Jamahiriyya Arab News Agency (JANA), the official information bureau of the Libyan government, announced that the attack had been carried out by one of Libya's revolutionary committees. The FBI traced the gun to a former U.S. Army Green Beret, Eugene Tafoya, who had been recruited by the Libyan government and was serving as a Libyan agent. When Tafoya was arrested on 22 April 1981 investigators found in his possession an address book containing the names of other Libyan exiles living in the United States. The publicity over Tafoya's arrest supported the Reagan administration's efforts to paint Qaddafi as an international outlaw and practitioner of state-sponsored terrorism. The arrest also led to the first public action taken by the administration against the Libyan government.[56]

On 6 May 1981 Haig ordered the closure of the Libyan people's bureau in Washington and gave the twenty-seven Libyan diplomats posted there five days to leave the United States.[57] The official State Department announcement cited "a wide range of Libyan provocations and misconduct, including support for international terrorism." The statement also noted that the United States was disturbed by "a general pattern of unacceptable conduct" by the Libyan government, which "is contrary to internationally accepted standards of diplomatic behavior." The State Department also warned U.S. citizens not to travel to Libya and advised all Americans living there to leave.[58] The closure of the people's bureau was Reagan's first signal to Qaddafi that more serious consequences were to follow if he did not curtail his involvement in international terrorism.[59]

One month later the Reagan administration took another step to isolate Qaddafi. On 2 June Chester Crocker, the assistant secretary of state for African affairs, announced that the United States would support all African states that opposed Libyan intervention in their countries. "The administration . . . is deeply concerned about Libyan interventionism in Africa and in particular the presence of Libyan troops in Chad," Crocker stated. The administration announced huge increases in military assistance to Qaddafi's neighbors in Africa and the Middle East: Egypt received $900 million in aid; Sudan, $100 million; Tunisia, $140 million; Morocco, $100 million; Somalia, $95 million; and Oman, $1 billion (for improvements to bases used by U.S. forces).[60]

Arguably the most important component of Reagan's Libya strategy was economic sanctions, since they could have the most immediate and profound impact on the Qaddafi regime. Nevertheless, concerns about the U.S. oil industry, about American citizens in Libya, and about the degree of allied cooperation greatly influenced the development of a package of economic sanctions against Libya. In early 1981 Libya was the third largest supplier of oil to the United States, with Libyan oil making up 10 percent of the total U.S. supply. As long as the United States purchased $7 billion of Libyan oil each year and upwards of two thousand American workers and their families provided Qaddafi with a ready pool of potential hostages, the administration was hampered in its ability to construct a tough, comprehensive strategy toward Libya. The United States continued to buy oil from Qaddafi because Libyan light crude was especially attractive on the American market. Its low sulfur content was well suited for producing gasoline with fewer pollutants. Most refineries along the East Coast of the United States specialized in processing Libyan light crude, which meant that an embargo on Libyan oil could cause an economic slowdown in that region of the country. Even if the United States did ban Libyan oil, the Libyan economy probably would not suffer because new customers in Europe would make up the difference.

Before it could implement a stringent economic policy toward Libya the Reagan administration had to make several tough decisions. It would have to cut off the importation of Libyan oil, shouldering the economic consequences of that action, and it would have to order all Americans out of Libya. At the same time the United States would seek the cooperation of its European allies. With their support the sanctions would have had a greater chance of success. The Europeans, however, were not ready to take drastic economic steps against Libya. They were more concerned with protecting their economic interests in Libya than with confronting Qaddafi over the issue of terrorism. A number of European countries, particularly Italy, France, and Germany, were dependent on Libyan oil, and several European companies benefited greatly from Libya's multibillion dollar development programs. The Europeans argued that until American rhetoric toward Qaddafi was matched by concrete actions, they would be unwilling to risk their economic relationship with Libya for what they considered a symbolic expression of disapproval of Libya's involvement in international terrorism. Furthermore, several European governments had their doubts about the effectiveness of economic sanctions, citing the failure of past British sanctions against Rhodesia and U.S.-led sanctions against the Soviet Union, Poland, Iran, and Nicaragua. Ultimately the decision to ban Libyan oil was not made for another year and only then when it was prompted by a series of extraordinary events: a dogfight between U.S. and Libyan aircraft over the Gulf of Sidra, the murder of Anwar as-Sadat by Muslim extremists, and reports of a Libyan plot to assassinate Reagan.

Fundamental policy decisions regarding the Libya strategy were made by political appointees and approved by Reagan. In the ensuing policy discussions several career diplomats, intelligence officers, and Pentagon officials objected to many of the steps advocated by the appointees. Briefly stated, the political appointees were more hard-line in their approach toward Libya and in their desire to take assertive, immediate, and, if necessary, unilateral actions to contain and embarrass Qaddafi and undermine his authority in the country. At a minimum they wanted to respond publicly to his support for terrorism and his efforts to destabilize friendly governments in the Middle East and Africa. On the other hand, the career bureaucrats believed that Qaddafi was not as big a threat as the administration was portraying him. They worried that confronting Qaddafi in public might turn him into an Arab hero standing up to the United States. The careerists also emphasized that the Europeans did not regard Qaddafi as an international outlaw and that a poorly crafted Libya policy might undermine America's fragile standing among moderate Arab leaders. They argued that the best way to handle Qaddafi was to ignore him, that is, not give him attention for his actions.

In the long run the careerists won most of the battles over the details of the Libya strategy. The individual components of the strategy were designed to produce a noticeable effect on Libya, but they were limited in scope. Each component was meant to heap considerable pressure on Qaddafi and induce a change in his behavior regarding terrorism, but none would directly assail his regime. Furthermore, many of the elements were to be carried out only after careful consultation with America's allies in Europe and the Middle East. On the other hand, although the political appointees compromised on specific details of the strategy, they nevertheless achieved their objective of altering U.S. policy toward Qaddafi. Henceforth the Reagan administration regarded Qaddafi as an enemy of the United States.[61]

Planning the Gulf of Sidra Operation

At the Pentagon the planning for the FON exercise in the Gulf of Sidra made steady progress. Ostensibly the purpose of the exercise was to demonstrate the right of the United States to navigate the international waters of the Gulf of Sidra and to train Sixth Fleet ships and aircrews in the employment of modern guided missiles. The real intent, however, was to make a powerful impression on Qaddafi with a tremendous demonstration of U.S. military power.

In light of Libya's track record of attacking U.S. aircraft in international airspace, Pentagon officials were gravely concerned about the risks associated with a major naval exercise inside the gulf. Coincidentally, the exercise was the first test of a new set of naval rules of engagement (ROE), formally titled the Worldwide Peacetime Rules of Engagement for Sea Borne Forces. The new ROE were the product of a thorough review of the existing ROE as ordered by Admiral Hayward in 1979.[62] Navy regulations already gave on-scene commanders the authority "to counter either the use of force or an immediate threat of the use of force" with military action.[63] The new ROE were appropriately nicknamed the "Reagan ROE" in military circles.[64] They described in uncomplicated language the circumstances under which a commander could take appropriate action without approval from higher authority to defend his ships, aircraft, and personnel against an opposing force committing a hostile act, demonstrating an imminent use of force, or exhibiting a continuing threat to use force.[65]

While the Pentagon was finalizing the exercise plan a multiagency national security working group was studying Qaddafi's likely reaction to a large-scale naval exercise in Libyan-claimed waters. The participants concluded that the chance of Libyan reaction was low for a number of reasons. First, Qaddafi understood that ordering a major attack on the battle force would be tantamount to sending his air force and navy on a suicide mission. Second, the Soviets would not come to Qaddafi's assistance in defending a territorial claim that they did not recognize.[66] Earlier in the year, during a conversation with Haig, the Soviet ambassador to the United States, Anatoly Dobrynin, made it clear that "Libya was an American problem."[67] Administration officials quickly determined that the Soviets did not think Qaddafi was worth the risk of fomenting a major confrontation with the United States. Finally, it was presumed that Libya would not harm Americans living in the country because of their crucial role in Libya's oil industry. In July the NSC reviewed the exercise plan and recommended its approval. The plan was forwarded to Reagan, who on 1 August gave the Pentagon the official go-ahead.[68]

The exercise plan contained several operational contingencies for dealing with escalating levels of Libyan aggression. Aside from action taken in self-defense, any military response under this program of graduated measures required Reagan's approval. Although the new ROE gave a great deal of discretion to the on-scene commander, a number of senior Pentagon officers accustomed to seeking permission first and shooting later still sought assurance from the White House that the new ROE were genuine.

At a cabinet meeting in early August Reagan received a thorough briefing on the details of the FON exercise, which carried the innocuous name Open Ocean Missile Exercise (OOMEX). Each year the Navy conducted several OOMEXs to maintain the efficiency of missile-firing ships and fighter squadrons. This particular missile exercise was to be performed in conjunction with the high-profile naval maneuvers in the Gulf of Sidra, and it incorporated the new ROE. According to the ROE the carrier-based fighters were to intercept all approaching aircraft and escort them until they were clear of the exercise area, opening fire only if fired upon first (a significant change from the ROE that had been in effect during the Carter administration). Under former rules American pilots were required to request permission from the task force commander before firing back. Furthermore, according to the old ROE a pilot had to hold fire if the enemy pilot disengaged and returned to his base.[69] At the meeting Reagan made it absolutely clear that his naval forces had the authority to take appropriate action to protect themselves. "Any time we send an American anywhere in the world where he or she can be shot at, they have the right to shoot back," he said. Enemy fighters would no longer get free shots at American aircraft. When asked by a cabinet officer how far a U.S. pilot could go in pursuit of Libyan planes that had fired on him, Reagan responded: "All the way into the hangar."[70] The individuals present at the briefing were satisfied that the new ROE were genuine and that Reagan would support any member of his armed forces who exercised self-defense against an adversary committing or threatening to commit a hostile act.

As a further precaution the JCS ordered Rear Adm. James E. Service—a veteran attack pilot who served concurrently as commander of Carrier Group Two, as commander of Battle Force Sixth Fleet (also known as Task Force 60), and as the officer in tactical command (OTC) of the upcoming exercise—to Washington for discussions on the operational details of the exercise and the circumstances under which his task force, particularly his aircrews, could engage a hostile military force. On 12 and 14 August the U.S. government issued a notice to airmen and mariners that announced that live missile firings would be conducted in a 3,200-square-mile hexagonal area of the Mediterranean on 18 and 19 August. The exercise area included a section of the disputed waters south of 32° 30'.[71]

Not surprisingly, the Libyan government protested the planned exercise, calling it a violation of Libya's territorial waters and airspace. In addition, one Libyan official accused the United States of coordinating the movement of the Sixth Fleet with Egyptian military forces that were conducting maneuvers near the Egyptian-Libyan frontier.[72] *Newsweek,* in the issue that arrived at newsstands on 17 August, substantiated this accusation when it reported that "Washington officials are . . . eager to see how Qaddafi will react to what they insist is a coincidence: Egyptian troops will conduct maneuvers along the Libyan border at the same time." Two days before OOMEX started Egypt canceled its plans for a military exercise near the Libyan border, fearing that if its maneuvers took place at the same time as the Sixth Fleet exercise Qaddafi might conclude that he was under a two-pronged attack and respond irrationally.[73]

The Open Ocean Missile Exercise

For the two-day surface and air exercise Rear Admiral Service commanded a large battle force consisting of the carriers *Nimitz* (CVN 68) and *Forrestal* (CV 59); Carrier Air Wings (CVW) 8 and 17 based on the *Nimitz* and the *Forrestal*, respectively; and thirteen escort and support ships.[74] The planned highlight of OOMEX was the destruction of target drones by Sparrow and Sidewinder air-to-air missiles fired from fighter aircraft and Standard surface-to-air missiles launched by the nuclear-powered guided missile cruisers *Texas* (CGN 39) and *Mississippi* (CGN 40). In addition to carrying out the missile exercise and the FON operation Admiral Service was fully prepared to intercept and escort all Libyan aircraft and naval vessels that approached the exercise area and, if necessary, to perform armed defense of the battle force.

With his carriers in position north of 32° 30' Service commenced OOMEX in the early hours of 18 August. Several F-14 Tomcats from the nuclear-powered aircraft carrier *Nimitz* and F-4J Phantom IIs from the *Forrestal* catapulted into the morning sky and established a barrier of seven combat air patrol (CAP) stations between Libya and the battle force. The two Tomcat squadrons based on the *Nimitz* were the "Black Aces" of Fighter Squadron (VF) 41 and the "Jolly Rogers" of VF-84. The "Bedevilers" of VF-74 and the "Fighting Silver Eagles" of Marine Fighter-Attack Squadron (VMFA) 115 flew Phantoms off the *Forrestal*. Pairs of F-14s filled four stations; pairs of F-4Js filled the other three. One Tomcat CAP station was located below 32° 30'. All of the U.S. aircraft operated in the Tripoli Flight Information Region (FIR), a Libyan-claimed air defense zone that extended out well into the central Mediterranean. The northern boundary of the zone was the 34th parallel. Within the FIR all aircraft were required to identify themselves to Libyan air traffic controllers.

At daybreak the guided missile destroyer *William V. Pratt* (DDG 44) and the destroyer *Caron* (DD 970) steamed south of 32° 30' and operated in the Gulf of Sidra for the next thirty-four hours.[75] For the duration of the exercise Qaddafi was in Aden conducting an official visit to South Yemen. According to U.S. intelligence Qaddafi had left Tripoli before the start of the exercise and had arrived in the capital of South Yemen earlier than planned. While in Aden he signed a treaty of cooperation with Ethiopia and South Yemen, effectively uniting three of the most radical states in the Middle East and Africa. A CIA analysis of the pact found that the tripartite alliance significantly increased the threat to U.S. interests in northeast Africa. According to the analysts a quick look at a map of the region showed U.S. allies Egypt and Sudan caught between Libya on the west and Ethiopia and South Yemen on the east. According to the terms of the treaty Qaddafi pledged hundreds of millions of dollars in economic and military assistance to his partners, and the three countries agreed to maintain a reserve military force of five thousand Libyan, five thousand Yemeni, and fifty thousand Ethiopian troops.

In Qaddafi's absence his lieutenants reacted swiftly to the American flight operations taking place in the Tripoli FIR and the northern section of the Gulf of Sidra.[76] On the first day of the exercise an assortment of aircraft from the Libyan Arab Air Force—consisting of French-built Mirage F-1s and Mirage F-5Ds, and Soviet-made MiG-23 Flogger Es and MiG-25 Foxbat As—took off from bases along the Libyan coast and flew as close as possible to the American battle force. The F-14 and F-4J crews performed thirty-five intercepts of seventy Libyan aircraft operating in pairs. Several of the intercepts evolved into "hassles," which is fighter pilot jargon for simulated dogfights. Most LAAF pilots turned back before entering the exercise zone, but on three occasions Libyan MiGs entered the restricted area and each time forced the fleet to suspend its missile-firing exercise. Navy fighters closely escorted each intruder until well clear of the exercise area.[77]

Most of the aviators in the battle force were too young to have flown combat missions in Vietnam, but the first day of OOMEX provided U.S. fighter crews with an excellent opportunity to practice combat maneuvering against a potential adversary flying Soviet- or French-built aircraft. The Americans noted that in general the Mirage pilots were more proficient at evasive maneuvering than the MiG pilots and were more difficult to intercept and hold in formation. Some Navy airmen speculated that the difference might have been due to the quality of the training provided by the French compared to that supplied by the Soviets.[78]

ABC News correspondent John K. Cooley was in Tripoli during the Sixth Fleet exercise. On the evening of 18 August he observed Libyan television announcers whip up the residents of Tripoli into a terrified frenzy with reports that the CIA was planning to overthrow or kill Qaddafi, that the American battle fleet was sailing toward Libya, that Egypt and Sudan were preparing to attack Libya with American support, and that the Libyan armed forces had been placed on high alert.[79] All of this, of course, was unknown to the aviators in the battle force who were preparing for another full day of flight operations over the Gulf of Sidra. The second day of OOMEX promised to be just as exciting as the first.

The Gulf of Sidra Incident

At 0545 local time on 19 August, the *Nimitz* and the *Forrestal* ordered their crews to flight quarters. By 0600 the ordnance men had armed the planes, and the aircrews had completed their mission briefings and were manning their aircraft. There was a gentle breeze that morning, and the forecast called for a deep blue sky that would provide clear visibility for several miles. The *Nimitz* and the *Forrestal* launched six F-14 Tomcats and four F-4J Phantoms, respectively. The ten fighters were to fill five CAP stations by first light. Tomcats from VF-41 were to occupy the three southern stations, while four Phantoms of VF-74 were to fill the remaining two. Both carriers launched antisubmarine aircraft to guard against the Libyan fleet of Soviet-built diesel submarines and attack aircraft for armed surveillance of Libyan surface vessels. This latter assignment was known as surface combat air patrol (SUCAP) and carried the code name "birddog." An unarmed E-2C Hawkeye from Carrier Airborne Early-Warning Squadron (VAW) 124 based on the *Nimitz* took station in the northern portion of the exercise area, out of the reach of Libyan fighters. Its mission was to provide long-range surveillance and fighter control for the battle force. Finally, the carriers launched KA-6D tankers to extend the on-station time of the CAP aircraft.

The Black Aces of VF-41 flew the most capable fighter plane in the world. The Tomcat's AN/AWG-9 radar could detect targets nearly two hundred miles away, and the aircraft's weapons control system could track twenty-four targets and simultaneously engage six with AIM-54C Phoenix missiles. During OOMEX the F-14s were armed with short-range AIM-9L Sidewinder heat-seeking missiles, medium-range AIM-7F Sparrow semi-active radar-guided missiles, and long-range Phoenix active radar-guided missiles. The Tomcats were also equipped with an M-61A1 Vulcan 20mm Gatling gun for close-in dog-fighting. The Bedevilers of VF-74 were armed with Sidewinders and Sparrows. The Navy version of the F-4 Phantom was not equipped with a gun system.[80]

A pair of Tomcats with radio call signs "Fast Eagle 102" and "Fast Eagle 107" was scheduled to fill the southernmost CAP station. Comdr. Henry M. "Hank" Kleeman, the commanding officer of VF-41, flew the lead F-14 fighter, Fast Eagle 102, and his wingman Lt. Lawrence M. "Music" Muczynski piloted Fast Eagle 107. Lt. David J. Venlet and Lt. (jg) James P. "Amos" Anderson served as the radar intercept officers (RIOs) in Fast Eagles 102 and 107, respectively. Muczynski later admitted that he would not have been disappointed had the sortie been completely uneventful. On the previous day, 18 August, he had seen plenty of action performing a pair of intercepts, one of which was against a powerful MiG-25. Once airborne Fast Eagles 102 and 107 topped off their fuel tanks then headed south to their CAP station at the southern end of the patrol area. While en route to their station they monitored on their radios a hassle that was taking place to the west between two Libyan MiG-25s and two VF-41 Tomcats. The Libyans eventually broke off and returned to base. Meanwhile, a pair of birddog A-7E Corsair II aircraft kept watch over a Soviet-built *Osa*-class missile patrol boat that had moved into the exercise area. Minutes later two Bedevilers swung south to intercept a pair of MiG-23 Flogger Es, which were heading north toward the battle force. The Tomcats arrived on station at sunrise and commenced a racetrack patrol pattern, cruising at twenty thousand feet at three hundred knots. The aircraft timed their patterns so that one plane was always pointed toward the Libyan coast while the other flew its northern leg.[81]

At approximately 0715, while the two Phantoms from VF-74 were escorting the two MiGs, Kleeman began what he thought was his last turn toward the coast before breaking off to refuel from an airborne tanker and returning to the carrier. Suddenly Venlet detected an air contact on his radarscope due south at eighty miles. It was proceeding north from the Libyan air base at Ghurdabiyah on the south shore of the Gulf of Sidra. The E-2C detected the contact at the same time and tracked its northward progress. Venlet immediately noticed the contact climb to twenty thousand feet and increase its speed to 550 knots. It was heading right for Fast Eagle 102. Venlet reported the contact to the E-2C and to the battle force antiair warfare commander (AAWC) stationed on the *Nimitz*. The AAWC, a senior officer in the battle force, had the authority to initiate defensive measures to protect the force from a hostile air threat. Venlet received no reply, however, because the radio circuit was busy with reports from the F-4Js escorting the MiG-23s.[82]

Muczynski and Anderson in Fast Eagle 107 also held the presumed-to-be-Libyan contact on their radarscope. Muczynski abandoned the racetrack pattern and swung his Tomcat into a combat formation known as a "loose deuce." This maneuver placed him four thousand feet above Kleeman and two miles off and slightly ahead of his skipper's right wing. The loose deuce, an aggressive and flexible formation, allows each fighter to protect the other and enables either plane—depending on who spots the enemy first—to initiate an attack. The attacker becomes the "engaged" fighter, while the other plane—the "free" fighter—climbs to a higher altitude to take advantage of the situation set up by the engaged fighter. More than likely the free fighter takes the first shot. The crews of Fast Eagles 102 and 107 had spent countless hours practicing this maneuver and they believed it was a great example of a good offense being the best defense. Kleeman banked twenty degrees to the right, starting a gradual turn that put him on the tail of the "bogey" (unidentified air contact), but the aircraft altered course and continued to close in on him. The VF-41 skipper altered course further to the right, but the Libyan plane, guided by ground control intercept (GCI) radar, again changed course to maintain an intercept on Fast Eagle 102. Unable to loop in from behind, Kleeman and Muczynski increased speed to 550 knots and proceeded directly toward the Libyan plane with Fast Eagle 102 flying at an altitude of eighteen thousand feet. They prepared to execute a demanding but effective combat maneuver known as an "eyeball-shooter intercept." Kleeman, acting as the "eyeball," steered directly for the contact while Muczynski, the "shooter," jockeyed into a position from which he could aim a Sidewinder at the tailpipe of the Libyan aircraft.[83] Still anticipating a routine intercept, Muczynski told Anderson to get his camera ready. They had taken pictures of Libyan pilots on the first day of the exercise and Muczynski believed that "there was no reason to expect anything different from the day before."[84]

With a relative closing rate of eleven hundred knots (eighteen miles per minute), it was only a matter of seconds before the American aviators saw the Libyan aircraft. Kleeman spotted the contact when it was approximately eight miles away. What had been a single blip on the AN/AWG-9 radar repeater was actually a pair of Libyan planes flying less than five hundred feet apart in a tight formation known as a "welded wing" (in which the lead pilot performs the aerial combat while the wingman protects the leader). At a range of two to three miles the skipper identified the aircraft as Soviet-built Su-22 Fitter Js (single-seat, single-engine ground attack planes).[85]

The Su-22 was no match for the F-14 in combat maneuvering ability and firepower. The Fitter was considerably slower than the Tomcat and unable to turn as tightly. It was armed with two internal 30mm cannons and a pair of AA-2 Atoll heat-seeking, air-to-air missiles. Unlike the all-aspect homing capability of the Sidewinder, the Atoll could not be employed with any probability of success unless it was aimed directly at an opposing jet's exhaust pipe. Ignoring the disproportionate odds in his favor, Kleeman carefully initiated an offset intercept of his unsophisticated foes.[86]

As Kleeman closed in on the pair of Fitters, Muczynski executed a hard left turn that placed him behind the Libyans. The rigorous maneuver pounded Muczynski's and Anderson's bodies with a force seven times that of gravity. At approximately 0718 Kleeman initiated a 150-degree turn to the left that would put him in an escorting position alongside the lead Fitter.[87] At the instant the lead Libyan was one thousand feet in front of and five hundred feet below Kleeman, the Libyan radioed to his wingman: "I'm preparing to fire." A fraction of a second later he called out: "I've fired!"[88] Kleeman immediately noticed the area under the Fitter's left wing erupt in smoke and fire. Shockingly, the Libyan pilot fired an Atoll missile at the tail of Kleeman's F-14. Simultaneously Kleeman and Muczynski shouted that the Libyan had launched a missile, and the two pilots banked hard to the left to avoid the heat-seeking missile, which passed safely under the tail of Fast Eagle 102. It flew unguided until it ran out of fuel. Kleeman managed to send an urgent report to the *Nimitz*, notifying the carrier that a pair of Libyan Fitters had attacked the Black Aces. In accord with the Reagan ROE, Kleeman and Muczynski took immediate action to defend themselves. Without hesitation they performed a crossover maneuver.[89] Kleeman told Muczynski, "You go for the guy that shot at us. I'm going for the wingman." Muczynski replied, "Roger that."[90] Since the Libyans had fired once already, Kleeman figured they might try it again. Then he thought, "The only acceptable course of action was to shoot at them."[91]

The moment the lead Fitter pilot carried out his desperate attack, the Libyan pilots broke their tight formation and headed in different directions. The leader executed a climbing left-hand turn then turned right toward the north. The wingman turned east in the direction of the morning sun. Satisfied that Muczynski was pursuing the lead Fitter, Kleeman settled in one-half mile behind the Libyan wingman but held off firing a Sidewinder lest the missile home in on the blazing solar disk instead of on the Fitter's tailpipe.[92] Kleeman knew he was not ready to fire. "I realized that that was not a good position to shoot," he recalled. "I waited about ten seconds until he cleared the sun, [and then] fired my missile. . . . There was no chance that I wasn't going to pull the trigger. It did go through my mind that it was likely to cause a ruckus, but I had no choice."[93] The AIM-9L streaked across the bright Mediterranean sky and slammed into the aircraft's tailpipe section. Kleeman recalled that "the missile . . . struck him in his tailpipe area causing him to lose control of the airplane, and he ejected within about five seconds." Kleeman observed the pilot descend in his parachute.[94]

Meanwhile, Muczynski streaked to a firing position one thousand yards behind the lead Fitter. He had to throttle back and apply his speed brakes to keep from flying past him. Muczynski hesitated for an instant before firing, debating in his own mind whether or not it was necessary to take out an adversary who was headed away from the action and no longer a threat to either Kleeman or himself. In his headset speaker he heard his skipper shout: "Shoot! Shoot! Shoot!"[95] The Libyan made a couple of futile attempts to shake off Fast Eagle 107, but Muczynski fired a Sidewinder just as the Fitter initiated a hard bank to the right. The missile struck the Libyan aircraft in the tailpipe and the massive explosion a fraction of a second later severed the tail section and engine from the rest of the fuselage. Muczynski maneuvered immediately to avoid the cloud of debris produced by the disintegrating Fitter.[96] "If you fly through this stuff, and it goes through your engine, you're finished," he recalled. "I said, 'My God, I've just shot myself down!' I just took the stick and buried it in my lap. I pulled straight up over the top, doing a seven-G pull-up."[97] Muczynski saw the pilot eject but never saw a parachute, which may have deployed automatically at a lower altitude.

Approximately three minutes after first detecting the Fitters the engagement was over. The air battle occurred approximately sixty miles off the coast of Libya and lasted barely a minute.[98] At approximately 0719 Fast Eagle 102 and Fast Eagle 107 joined up and headed back to the *Nimitz,* watching each other's "six" to ensure that no Libyan MiGs crept up behind them. While en route Kleeman reported the result of the engagement to the carrier: two Fitters shot down, both pilots ejected, one parachute observed. Muczynski remembered the understated reply from the carrier. "The admiral wants to talk to you, when you get back," responded the voice on the radio.[99]

Muczynski activated the autopilot in his Tomcat and let it fly the plane back to the vicinity of the carrier, all the while attempting to settle himself down. "We were so pumped up . . . I literally was shaking uncontrollably," he said.[100] Muczynski landed on his first try, trapping the number three wire. Kleeman was also excited. Rated the best pilot in the squadron at carrier landings, Kleeman took two "practice bolters" before landing on his third approach. After landing safely the four aviators were given an exhilarating heroes' welcome by a jubilant crowd of officers and sailors who instantly swarmed onto the flight deck.

The Libyans supposedly recovered their two hapless pilots, and later that day two fliers were presented alive and well on Libyan television. Meanwhile, the LAAF continued to probe the defensive perimeter of the battle force. A total of forty-five intercepts, including the two kills, were performed during the two-day exercise. Admiral Service concluded OOMEX on the afternoon of 19 August and withdrew the two-carrier battle force from the exercise area.

On 24 August, while anchored in Naples, Italy, the *Nimitz* provided the venue for a press conference attended by more than one hundred reporters representing news agencies from around the world.[101] Kleeman and the other Black Aces described the short air battle in great detail and answered several questions about the incident. They left little doubt that their actions were justified. Admiral Service and Vice Adm. William H. Rowden, commander of the U.S. Sixth Fleet, praised and supported the actions of the Black Aces. "The aircrews correctly reacted in self-defense," remarked Rowden, a surface warfare officer who had embarked in the *Forrestal* for the exercise. "They did not require or ask [for] any specific authorization from Admiral Service or anyone else. . . . Our pilots went out and they performed a duty, and they performed it perfectly. They performed as they had been trained and disciplined to do." Service added: "We had the superior airplane, superior pilots, and our weapons systems are . . . better."[102]

Several of Kleeman and Muczynski's fellow aviators were certain that the Libyan lead pilot must have fired by mistake, because his chances for success were overwhelmingly against him. Muczynski, however, thought the attack was deliberate. His opinion was validated when the crew of an electronic surveillance plane informed him that they monitored voice traffic between the Fitters and their ground controller. They overheard the lead pilot report that he fired a missile at one of the American fighters; he mentioned nothing about making a mistake.[103]

The Libyans may have selected low-performance Fitters for the attack to enhance the element of surprise. Their plan may have been to lull the American pilots into dropping their guard, fire a quick shot, and then run like hell for home. If they were counting on the Americans not to respond quickly with force they were dead wrong. Under the Reagan ROE there were no more free shots at Americans.

"You Fight Like You Train"

In the brilliant sunlit skies over the Gulf of Sidra, American fighter crews successfully acquitted themselves in their first aerial combat since the Vietnam War. The seeds for the unexpected victory had been planted during the latter years of the Vietnam War, when the U.S. Navy made a concerted effort to improve the combat performance of its fighter crews. During the Korean War, Navy and Air Force fighter pilots had enjoyed a kill ratio of thirteen to one against Communist pilots. During the first half of America's involvement in

Vietnam the kill ratio against enemy fighters fell to one loss for every two victories. By 1969 the ratio was approximately one for one. Particularly discouraging was the combat record of the high performance, four million dollar F-4 Phantom II. In combat against the one million dollar MiG-21 Fishbed, the Phantom won fewer engagements than its less sophisticated foe. Beginning in early 1968 a team of experienced naval aviators and technical experts studied the performance of Navy fighters in Vietnam. Capt. Frank Ault, former skipper of the USS *Coral Sea* (CVA-43) who had served a combat tour in the Tonkin Gulf off North Vietnam, led the team. After nine months of analysis the Ault Report found no single reason for the Navy's mediocre air combat record, but instead it identified several problems that seriously degraded combat performance. Among those problems were faulty missile performance, an emphasis on long-range intercept tactics, and insufficient training in basic fighter tactics. U.S. fighter crews flew extremely powerful aircraft but their overreliance on radar and air-to-air missiles diminished their basic dogfighting skills. They could not outmaneuver the MiG pilots and, arguably worse, they did not understand the physics of a successful air-to-air missile engagement. Learning to use missiles effectively was especially important to the Navy since their version of the F-4 was armed only with missiles. The Ault Report contained 242 recommendations for improving the Navy's fighter weapon systems, the most important of which was basic training in air combat maneuvering (ACM).

To its credit the Navy took assertive action to revamp fighter combat training during the Vietnam War, while the Air Force did not. In late 1968 the Navy began pulling together the staff and curriculum for what became the Navy Fighter Weapon School, better known as "Top Gun." Based at Miramar Naval Air Station near San Diego, the school graduated its first class of "Fighter Ph.D.s" in March 1969. After Top Gun graduates and fleet crews trained by Top Gun alumni began arriving in Vietnam in 1972, the Navy kill ratio soared to slightly over twelve-and-a-half enemy planes shot down for each Navy loss. With its overwhelming air victory in Vietnam the Navy fighter community learned an important lesson: the skill of the crew is just as important as the technology built into the aircraft. The crew deserved a capable fighter system and they had to be thoroughly trained in the latest dogfighting techniques.

The Top Gun motto—"You fight like you train"—was evident over the Gulf of Sidra on the morning of 19 August 1981. The Black Aces epitomized the aggressive tactics taught at Top Gun, particularly the use of the "loose deuce" formation. Kleeman and Muczynski immediately took command of the action and relentlessly prosecuted the engagement until their foes were destroyed. From the moment they catapulted off the deck of the *Nimitz* they regarded their sortie over the Gulf of Sidra as a potential combat mission. Top Gun had trained them well; they were prepared to defend themselves.[104]

Later that year Muczynski and Anderson participated in a seminar on fighter tactics at the annual Tailhook Reunion in Las Vegas. Needless to say, their discussion about the recent air battle was the highlight of the convention of carrier-based Navy and Marine Corps aviators. The two airmen were modest about their unexpected notoriety, stating that any aircrew in the wing could have engaged the Fitters and would have achieved the same outcome. They endorsed rigorous training in air combat maneuvering for fleet fighter crews and emphasized that continuous training had been instrumental in their recent success.[105]

American Reaction to the Gulf of Sidra Incident

The aerial victory over the Gulf of Sidra generated an avalanche of media attention and produced an outburst of national pride. Newspapers throughout the country carried photographs of the four aviators, and Americans from all walks of life cheered the outcome of the sixty-second dogfight. Countless fast food restaurants and car washes decorated their outdoor signs with messages that read "USA-2, Libya-0" or "Navy-2, Libya-0." After years of frustration the United States had scored a resounding victory over an international rogue.[106]

Despite the public euphoria, the reaction of the Reagan administration to the shoot down was positive but restrained. The State Department issued the following statement: "The U.S. Government is protesting, through diplomatic channels, this unprovoked attack which occurred in international airspace approximately sixty nautical miles from the nearest land." At a Pentagon press briefing Caspar Weinberger regretted "that the Libyans took this action and brought about these consequences." He commended the skill and professionalism of the aircrews and emphasized that they followed the ROE governing this type of situation and were not required to seek higher approval for their actions.[107] Meanwhile, Deputy Secretary of Defense Frank C. Carlucci sought to bring immediate closure to the incident. As he put it, "We filed our protests; our ships are moving out of the area; the exercise is over; and we consider the incident closed."[108]

Following up its earlier statement the State Department sent a formal note of protest to the Libyan government. It stated that Libyan aircraft had carried out an "unprovoked attack against American naval aircraft operating in international airspace." The Belgian government, which handled U.S. interests in Libya in the absence of diplomatic relations between Washington and Tripoli, informed the United States that the Libyan government refused to accept the note.[109]

On 20 August Reagan took time from his vacation at Rancho del Cielo, his ranch near Santa Barbara, to visit the aircraft carrier USS *Constellation* (CV-64) while it was stationed off the coast of California.[110] Although the visit had been arranged long before the Gulf of Sidra incident, the timing was remarkable. Using the carrier's public address system from the navigation bridge Reagan praised the crew of the *Constellation,* although his words could have applied to every American man and woman in uniform: "This ship represents a powerful force in an uncertain world, and we all sleep a little better at night knowing that you're on duty. Everything we as Americans hold dear is safer because of what all of you are doing."

During an impromptu press conference on the navigation bridge Reagan commented on the significance of the incident of the previous day. "Libya . . . created an artificial line, claiming waters that are actually international waters," he said. "We decided it was time to recognize what are the international waters and behave accordingly. . . . We responded as we will respond . . . when any of our forces are attacked. They're going to defend themselves." Reagan then left the navigation bridge and went down to the flight deck to observe a demonstration of naval striking power. Sitting in an armchair under a bright sunny sky, he watched F-14s scream by at near supersonic speed and felt the concussions of live bombs dropped into the dark blue water by A-6E Intruders.

After lunch Reagan addressed the *Constellation*'s crew assembled in the hangar deck. He again praised them and sent a stern message to the enemies of freedom: "You all make me very proud to be able to say I'm the commander in chief of all of you. The demonstration of firepower and efficiency by the air wing was . . . impressive to the enemies of freedom in the world. And we had an example of that just night before last on the carrier *Nimitz.* . . . You are ensuring peace just by doing what you're doing, because any potential enemy has to see the price of aggression is . . . more than he might want to pay, and that's the greatest service that can be performed."[111] The crew burst out in cheers several times during his brief remarks.

Perhaps the most significant development following the air battle was the absence of second-guessing of the actions of the fighter crews by administration officials. If there were any doubts that the aircrews had acted properly,

Reagan put those doubts to rest. He fully supported their split-second decision and reiterated his complete confidence in the talent and judgment of his armed forces. His "hands-off" approach to military operations attained its first success.

In his autobiography, *An American Life*, Reagan reflected on the message that the United States delivered to Qaddafi courtesy of the Sixth Fleet: "We weren't going to let him claim squatters' rights over a huge area of the Mediterranean in defiance of international law. I also wanted to send a message to others in the world that there was a new management team in the White House, and that the United States wasn't going to hesitate any longer to act when its legitimate interests were at stake."[112]

While Reagan Slept

Immediately after the shootdown a flash message was sent from the *Nimitz* to the headquarters of U.S. Naval Forces in Europe located in London, then forwarded to the headquarters of the European Command in Stuttgart, West Germany, and finally sent to the National Military Command Center at the Pentagon. It took less than six minutes for the message to travel from the *Nimitz* up the chain of command to the Pentagon command center. Lt. Gen. Philip J. Gast, USAF, director of operations for the Joint Chiefs of Staff, who was on duty in the command center, immediately notified Weinberger and the chairman of the Joint Chiefs of Staff, Gen. David Jones, USAF. Weinberger called National Security Adviser Richard V. Allen, who a few minutes later notified Counselor to the President Edwin Meese III. Both Allen and Meese were with Reagan at the Century Plaza Hotel in Los Angeles. Weinberger's call to Allen came in around 2300 Pacific Daylight Time. By that time Reagan had gone to bed. Meese decided to wait for a complete report on the incident from Weinberger before waking Reagan. Five hours later Meese and Allen had enough information. Shortly before 0430 the two aides woke Reagan and informed him of the incident. Reagan asked about the condition of the American aviators, he stated that he regretted the Libyan action, and he expressed his approval of the fleet's response. Satisfied that the situation was in good hands he went back to sleep.[113]

In the wake of the sixty-second air battle with Libya some journalists tried to stir up controversy when they learned that Reagan's staff had waited nearly five and a half hours before waking him and informing him of the dogfight. Reagan reacted to the "scandal" with his characteristic good humor: "There was no decision to be made or they would have . . . awakened me. . . . If our planes were shot down, yes, they'd wake me up right away; if the other fellow's [planes] were shot down, why wake me up?"[114] Besides, he quipped, "4:30 in the morning, California time, is as early as I want to be awakened."[115]

Libyan and International Reaction

The Libyans reacted to the incident with disinformation and venomous rhetoric. The Jamahiriyya Arab News Agency reported that the LAAF had combated eight F-14s and shot down one. A few thousand demonstrators took to the streets of Tripoli and Benghazi to shout anti-American slogans, but they seemed to be chanting from rote and lacked conviction.[116] At a rally in Aden Qaddafi charged that the United States threatened peace by "persisting in its provocations and terror."[117] A few days later in Addis Ababa, the capital of Ethiopia, Qaddafi accused the United States of "wanton provocation, an act of international terrorism, brigandage and brinksmanship."[118] He called on the Arab world to "declare a state of mobilization to face imperialist-Zionist and reactionary challenges," and he boasted that his country was "ready to defend the Gulf of Sidra even if it means a third world war."[119] "We are ready to die for the Gulf of Sidra," Qaddafi told a crowd celebrating the twelfth anniversary of the Libyan revolution. "We will make the Gulf of Sidra into a new Red Sea with our blood."[120]

The PLO and a number of radical Arab states such as Syria, South Yemen, and Algeria denounced the United States and expressed support for Libya. PLO Chairman Yasir Arafat, whom Qaddafi condemned for being too moderate in the struggle against Israel, called the incident "the beginning of a new phase in the conspiracy against Libya and the Arab nation."[121] In an illusory showing of Arab unity, several moderate Arab governments such as Saudi Arabia and Tunisia and the controlled media in their countries charged the United States with aggression against a fellow Arab nation.[122] The secretary general of the League of Arab States, Chadli Klibi of Tunisia, called the air battle "a violation of the peace and security" of the entire Arab world and stated that the incident "can only increase tension in the Middle East."[123] Privately many moderate Arab leaders praised the American action. After Reagan briefed Sadat on the upcoming exercise during the latter's visit to Washington in early August, the Egyptian leader exclaimed, "Magnificent!"[124] Sadat was undoubtedly delighted by the results of the air battle over the Gulf of Sidra.

Moscow offered perfunctory condemnation of the incident,[125] declaring that the Sixth Fleet's "piratical action had caused a storm of indignation around the world."[126] The planners in Washington had been right in their prediction: the Soviets did not come to the assistance of Qaddafi. The incident demonstrated the paradox of Moscow's relationship with Libya. The Soviets were willing to demonstrate a degree of support for an Arab leader who shared many of their interests, especially in the Middle East, and who purchased huge quantities of their weapons, but they could not champion many of Qaddafi's extreme policies and declarations. The Soviets took no further action on behalf of Qaddafi because they did not support his claim to the Gulf of Sidra.

Among America's allies only Israel lent unabashed support to the United States. Israeli Prime Minister Menachem Begin called the U.S. action "an act of self-defense—just like our raids on the Iraqi nuclear plant and on the PLO headquarters in Beirut."[127] In Western Europe the reaction to the incident was mixed. Governments and the press generally supported the United States for acting in self-defense in international waters but expressed some concern that the United States may have provoked the incident. One unlikely source welcomed the American show of force. In an editorial the left-leaning French newspaper *Le Monde* stated: "Restoring the power of the United States . . . is above all a question of showing that the country will not hesitate to act whenever it is challenged. The hesitations and the scruples of a Jimmy Carter thus are relegated to the antique shop." The Spanish newspaper *Dario 16*, however, best expressed the conflicting feelings held by many Europeans: "While Carter's excessive weakness was a threat to Western stability, the whole world now feels insecure after Reagan's show of force."[128]

The prospect of Libyan retribution against American citizens and interests in Libya was relieved one day after the incident when senior officials from the Libyan ministries of oil and heavy industry met with executives of the American oil companies operating in Libya. The Libyans assured the Americans that Libya would not retaliate against the United States by nationalizing the American oil companies, by placing an embargo on the sale of oil to the United States, or by harming the Americans living and working in Libya.[129] Furthermore, a Libyan diplomat in Paris stated that Libya had no intention of mistreating the Americans living and working in Libya because Libyans "differentiate between governments and peoples," and because the Americans have "a role to play in the Libyan economy."[130] In the aftermath of the incident the American expatriate community maintained an atmosphere of guarded calm, and oil field operations continued without interruption. Meanwhile Reagan, who was deeply concerned about the safety of the Americans living in Libya, sent a message to Qaddafi through diplomatic back channels. He warned Qaddafi "that any acts of terrorism directed against Americans would be considered acts of war, and we would respond accordingly."[131]

Qaddafi Plots Revenge

By most measures the air battle in the Gulf of Sidra was a minor military victory, but in a number of ways it was an enormous psychological and diplomatic triumph for Ronald Reagan. First, Qaddafi had been outmatched militarily. The U.S. Navy demonstrated that it was a powerful and effective force, one that Qaddafi was helpless to stop. Second, Qaddafi was intimidated. Western business executives and European diplomats reported that the Libyan government was obsessed with the threat of attack by the United States. Third, the incident demonstrated to Moscow and its clients that the United States was willing to use force to protect its vital interests around the globe. Finally, the battle reassured moderate governments in the Middle East and Africa that radical regimes were vulnerable and assumed an enormous risk if they challenged the United States. In his memoir *Fighting for Peace: Seven Critical Years in the Pentagon,* Caspar Weinberger commented on the political consequences of the recent action: "We had demonstrated not only a greatly increased American resolve, but also a greatly increased American capability for dealing with the enemy quickly and decisively. That alone did more to reassure our allies than any budget amounts we committed to spend, or any amount of rhetoric, no matter how well delivered."[132]

On 22 August Qaddafi was in Addis Ababa, the capital of Ethiopia, conferring with the country's Marxist ruler, Lt. Col. Mengistu Haile Mariam. Present at the meeting was a senior Ethiopian official allegedly on the bankroll of the CIA. The agency rated him as a "generally reliable" to "excellent" source of information. At the meeting Qaddafi declared that he was going to have Reagan assassinated. The informant forwarded this information to his local CIA handlers and added that Mengistu believed Qaddafi was serious. The report was forwarded to Washington with the recommendation that Qaddafi's statement be taken seriously.

Shortly afterward the National Security Agency (NSA) intercepted a telephone call from Addis Ababa to Tripoli in which Qaddafi repeated his vow to avenge the Gulf of Sidra debacle by assassinating Reagan. The CIA mentioned both reports in Reagan's daily intelligence brief. Although most administration officials lost interest in the reports after one week, William Casey remained keenly interested in the matter and directed the intelligence community to keep him informed of any new information concerning Qaddafi's threat to kill Reagan.[133]

The Assassination of Sadat and the Bright Star Exercise

On 6 October President Anwar as-Sadat of Egypt was brutally murdered by Muslim extremists as he viewed a military parade celebrating the eighth anniversary of Egypt's crossing of the Suez Canal during the October 1973 Arab-Israeli War. In a speech delivered only hours after the assassination Qaddafi applauded the killing and remarked that "the sound of the bullets that resounded firmly and courageously in the face of as-Sadat this morning was in fact saying this is the punishment of those who betray the Arab nation."[134]

Although no evidence that linked Libya to the crime could be uncovered, the United States took immediate action to assure regional allies and increase pressure on Qaddafi.[135] First, on 8 October Reagan signed National Security Decision Directive (NSDD) 14. The secret directive, titled "Security Considerations in Egypt and Sudan," directed the secretaries of state and defense to "undertake an immediate examination of steps to be taken to strengthen the position of Egypt and Sudan." The directive mandated increased military cooperation with both countries, and it envisioned that the enhanced cooperation would take the form of large increases in military aid, more visible demonstrations of military support, and promises to safeguard Egypt and Sudan. Additionally, it authorized the expansion of Bright Star '81, the large multinational exercise scheduled to take place in November in several locations throughout North Africa and the Middle East. The Reagan administration hoped that Bright Star would demonstrate a potent U.S. military commitment to the Middle East and North Africa and counter the influence of the radical tripartite alliance of Libya, Ethiopia, and South Yemen; that it would deter attacks on the new government in Egypt and other friendly governments in the region; and that it would assure regional allies that the United States would come rapidly to their aid during a crisis.[136]

Second, in mid-October Reagan dispatched two U.S. Air Force E-3A Airborne Warning and Control System (AWACS) aircraft to Egypt. The planes arrived on 15 October and immediately began monitoring the airspace around

Egypt. By deploying the two sophisticated planes the United States sought to project both a visible presence and a settling influence in the region following Sadat's assassination. The deployment demonstrated support for the new Egyptian president, Husni Mubarak, and served as a warning to Qaddafi not to exploit the tenuous situation in Egypt.

Bright Star '81 commenced on 9 November and continued for two weeks. During the exercise the United States demonstrated its ability to project power and operate military forces thousands of miles from their bases in the United States. A flight of B-52 Stratofortress bombers struck targets in Egypt's Western Desert after a nonstop flight from their bases in North Dakota. In Egypt approximately four thousand U.S. troops took part in joint-maneuvers with the Egyptian army. In Sudan U.S. Special Forces instructed Sudanese forces in counterinsurgency tactics. In Somalia medical and engineering units conducted training exercises for their Somali hosts. In Oman a thousand Marines carried out an amphibious landing near that country's border with South Yemen. By the time the exercise concluded on 24 November, the United States had demonstrated its commitment to regional allies, had blocked Libyan exploitation of the Sadat assassination, and had minimized the influence of the Libya–Ethiopia–South Yemen pact.[137]

Sadat's shocking death and its aftermath dominated the administration's Middle East policy during most of October and November. The matter of Qaddafi's threat to assassinate Reagan still remained, however, and by late fall the threat developed into a brief crisis.

3

The Wave of Terror

The Libyan Hit Squads

In the final months of 1981 the White House became increasingly concerned when the CIA received a number of intelligence reports that lent plausibility to Muammar al-Qaddafi's alleged threat to assassinate President Reagan.

In late August a CIA source in Europe reported that an important Palestinian official had met with a member of the Libyan general staff and agreed to participate in a coordinated attack on Reagan. In early September another CIA informant, who enjoyed excellent access to senior officers in the Libyan military, reported that Libya was planning to attack American interests in the Mediterranean area and was plotting to kidnap or assassinate Max Rabb, the U.S. ambassador to Italy. In September a European intelligence service reported that Italian authorities had arrested and deported several Libyans allegedly involved in the plot against Ambassador Rabb. A few days later the same intelligence service reported that a Palestinian faction had agreed to assist Libya in attacking Reagan and other prominent U.S. government officials. In mid-September the CIA reported that Libya was preparing to launch a suicide attack against the aircraft carrier *Nimitz*, which was still on deployment with the Sixth Fleet in the Mediterranean.

In early October a European intelligence service reported that, during a visit to Syria in August, Qaddafi had met with representatives of four terrorist organizations and solicited their help in striking American interests in Europe. In mid-October a CIA informant with good access to senior officials in the Libyan intelligence service reported that Libyan agents were traveling to Europe to assault the American embassies in Rome and Paris. A few days later the same informant reported that the U.S. embassies in Athens, Beirut, London, Madrid, and Tunis were possible targets. By the end of the month another well-placed informant corroborated the first report, stating that a five-man Libyan hit team had arrived in Italy. On 21 October Rabb was flown back to Washington for his own protection. In late October Italian intelligence informed the CIA that a Libyan hit team had traveled through Rome and was en route to an unknown destination.

By early November U.S. intelligence had "credible evidence" that Qaddafi had targeted the American embassy compounds in London, Paris, Rome, and Vienna.[1] On 12 November an unidentified assailant fired six shots at the American chargé d'affaires in Paris, Christian A. Chapman, as he left his home for the U.S. embassy. Fortunately Chapman was not harmed. The CIA believed that Libya was responsible for the attack.[2] Four days later a man proclaiming to be a terrorist walked into a U.S. embassy in Africa and claimed that he had been present at a terrorist training camp in Libya when Qaddafi approved the plan to send hit teams to the United States to assassinate Reagan. The informant described in detail how the terrorists practiced the ambush of a motorcade using rocket-propelled grenades. His story enjoyed considerable credibility because the plan was remarkably similar to a Libyan plot to assassinate Herman Eilts, the American ambassador in Cairo, in 1977. That earlier plot was foiled when a senior Libyan official approached the CIA with crucial information, and President Carter sent a personal note to Qaddafi informing him that he knew about the operation. This latest informant also stated that the assassins planned to go after Vice President Bush, Secretary of State Haig, and Secretary of Defense Weinberger if Reagan proved to be too well guarded. The CIA, FBI, and Secret Service questioned the informant. He took a polygraph test and passed.[3]

On 4 December the *New York Times* ran a story reporting that a five-man Libyan-trained assassination team had entered the United States the previous weekend. The *Times* reporter, who attributed the story to high-ranking federal law enforcement officials, reported that the plans to assassinate Reagan included shooting down Air Force One with a surface-to-air missile, destroying his limousine with a rocket, and firing at him with small arms. The FBI circulated composite sketches of the suspects as described by a key informant, and federal, state, and local law enforcement officers conducted a massive nationwide manhunt.[4]

Armed with several intelligence reports, many senior administration officials, particularly CIA Director Casey, were convinced that Qaddafi's threat to carry out a spectacular attack in the United States was serious and had to be thwarted. Reagan's personal security detail was immediately strengthened and security measures at the White House were significantly enhanced. Reagan's three closest White House aides, Counselor Edwin Meese, Chief of Staff James A. Baker, and Deputy Chief of Staff Michael K. Deaver, were given Secret Service protection. Security for Haig and Weinberger was also increased. The assassination attempt on Reagan in March, the shooting of Pope John Paul II in May, and the murder of Anwar as-Sadat in October were still fresh in the minds of Reagan's advisers. Whether the hit teams were real or not, they had a profound impact on the administration's Libya policy by accelerating many decisions that would normally have taken the bureaucracy months to achieve.[5]

Between November 1981 and March 1982 the administration responded to the apparent Libyan threat with a comprehensive set of military, diplomatic, and economic measures that were designed to increase Qaddafi's international isolation, embarrass his regime, and exploit his many political weaknesses.[6] According to Frank Fukuyama, an official serving on the State Department's Policy Planning Staff, the strategy could create "the conditions for an internal military coup."[7]

In late November Reagan signed NSDD 16, which established an interagency task force to implement the newest measures regarding Libya. The administration decided to ban the importation of Libyan oil and place restrictions on exports to Libya but delayed the announcement of these sanctions until most American workers were out of Libya and America's European allies had joined the U.S.-led effort against Qaddafi. A glut in the world oil market and the high price of Libyan crude made it easier for the administration to ban Libyan oil. At one point during the year the price of Libyan oil reached $41 per barrel before settling at $37.50 per barrel. Imports of Libyan oil dropped from 650,000 barrels per day in April 1981 to roughly 200,000 barrels per day in November (which meant that the amount the United States spent on Libyan oil each day dropped from $26 million to around $7.6 million). The administration believed that a ban would produce a negligible impact on the U.S. economy and would actually enjoy the support of American oil companies operating in Libya. They were losing money on the high-priced crude they extracted in

Libya, and the ban would help them persuade the Libyan government to reduce the price of its oil. Furthermore, if the United States banned Libyan oil, Qaddafi would lose his single largest customer. The United States purchased about 25 percent of Libya's oil exports.[8]

On the last day of November at a meeting of the NSPG, Reagan ordered his top aides to prepare plans for a "military response against Libya in the event of a . . . Libyan attempt to assassinate American officials or attack U.S. facilities."[9] One week later Haig, Casey, and Deputy Secretary of Defense Frank Carlucci (acting for Weinberger) presented a joint memorandum to Reagan that recommended that he "should immediately direct the Joint Chiefs of Staff to ready assets to carry out military action against Libya in self-defense, following a further Libyan provocation."[10] The memorandum outlined a series of five graduated responses to Libyan aggression: an air raid on terrorist training camps in Libya, an attack on Libyan airfields, a raid on Libyan naval bases, a strike on concentrations of stockpiled Libyan military equipment, and a commando raid on Libyan naval vessels in port.[11]

As a warning to Qaddafi administration officials leaked elements of the memorandum to the press. *Newsweek* reported that Reagan was prepared to use a number of military options in response to the next occurrence of Libyan-sponsored terrorism. The magazine, however, inaccurately reported that the options included a B-52 raid on terrorist training camps, an air strike on Libyan oil fields, and a naval blockade to halt the flow of trade to and from Libya. *Newsweek* quoted a senior official as saying, "If one of Qaddafi's terrorists fires a grenade into the Rose Garden, we aren't going to answer him simply by telling people to stop buying his oil."[12]

On Sunday, 6 December, Qaddafi participated in a live interview on the television program *This Week with David Brinkley*. Speaking from Tripoli, Qaddafi denied that he sent hit squads to the United States and demanded that Reagan produce the evidence against him. Senator Daniel P. Moynihan, Democrat of New York and vice chairman of the Senate Intelligence Committee, also appeared on the program. He stated that the United States had "concrete evidence" that Libya had targeted officials of the United States government.[13] "I wouldn't believe a word [Qaddafi] says," Reagan responded the next day. "We have the evidence and he knows it."[14] A few days later Reagan sent a top-secret personal letter to Qaddafi via the Belgians, which read: "I have detailed and verified information about several Libyan-sponsored plans and attempts to assassinate U.S. government officials and attack U.S. facilities both in the U.S. and abroad. . . . Any acts of violence directed by Libya or its agents against officials of the U.S., at home or abroad, will be regarded by the U.S. government as an armed attack upon the U.S. and will be met by every means necessary to defend this nation in accordance with Article 51 of the United Nations Charter."[15]

On 10 December Deputy Secretary of State William P. Clark called on, but did not order, the fifteen hundred to two thousand U.S. citizens residing in Libya to leave as soon as possible, and announced that all U.S. passports for travel to Libya were invalid. Citing a worsening "security climate for American citizens in Libya," Clark stated that these actions were being taken because of "Libya's well-known efforts over the course of many years to undermine U.S. interests and those of our friends as well as Libya's support for international terrorism." Once the Americans were out of Libya the threat of hostage taking would be eliminated, making it easier to mount a military operation.[16]

Later that day the State Department contacted the executives of all U.S. oil companies with employees in Libya to assess their reaction to the announcement. In general the executives reacted calmly to the president's decision; a few were angry. One executive stated that the withdrawal of his American employees would bankrupt his company. On the other hand, Armand Hammer, the chairman of Occidental Petroleum, stated that he supported the president and would make plans "for an orderly departure for those wishing to leave."[17] The United States was moving swiftly toward a total embargo of Libyan oil.

When Clark announced the recall of American citizens, Haig was in Brussels attending a meeting of NATO foreign ministers. Haig was confident that once the allies reviewed the intelligence on Libyan terrorism they would support American-led diplomatic and economic sanctions against the Qaddafi regime. Unfortunately, as Haig was about to launch his campaign for international sanctions against Libya, a major crisis in Poland dominated the attention of NATO foreign ministers and the task of garnering allied support for sanctions fell to lower-ranking administration officials. In general the Americans found the Europeans interested in the evidence against Qaddafi but not interested in joining the United States in confronting him.[18] At a news conference following the NATO meeting Haig accused the allies of using a moral double standard that enabled them to conduct "business as usual" with Qaddafi. For their part the Europeans pointed out the hypocrisy in Haig's comments: he was accusing them of following a double standard yet U.S. exports to Libya had nearly doubled during the previous year, and the United States continued to import huge amounts of Libyan oil.[19]

On 18 December the CIA's Directorate of Intelligence issued a report on the validity of the alleged Libyan plot to assassinate senior U.S. officials which stated that the first report of the Libyan threat—the meeting between Qaddafi and Mengistu in late August—came from a well-placed and highly reliable intelligence source. Follow-on reports, however, were attributed to sources with indirect access and of questionable credibility. "It is possible that some of the reporting may have been generated because informants are aware we are seeking this information," the CIA reported.[20] Furthermore, some of the reports may have been the product of a disinformation campaign conducted by an interested third party—most likely Israel—who would benefit from the maintenance of high-level tensions between the United States and Libya.[21] Later an analysis by the State Department's Bureau of Intelligence and Research (INR) also discounted subsequent reports of the Libyan assassination plot. The INR memorandum pointed out that "reporting breeds reporting where the U.S. is perceived to have an interest."[22]

Although the intelligence community cast doubt on the veracity of the reports of Libyan assassination squads, Reagan still believed they existed. In a televised interview with CBS News anchorman Dan Rather, Reagan stated that the reports were true: "We had too much information from too many sources, and we had our facts straight. . . . Our information was valid."[23]

There could be little doubt that the administration extracted maximum benefit from the "Libyan hit squads" episode. Reports of a terror campaign directed against the highest officials of the U.S. government were exaggerated and, in the words of one FBI official, "blown way out of proportion." While the administration may have appeared a little foolish by the time the crisis subsided, the episode achieved its goal of branding Qaddafi an assassin in the arena of public opinion. Moreover, the assassination threat gave the administration added justification for imposing diplomatic and economic sanctions against Libya. "It wasn't artificial," said a senior official, "just lucky timing."[24]

Immediately after the administration requested American citizens to leave Libya it began to de-emphasize the Libyan threat and the military consequences Qaddafi faced were he to launch a terrorist attack against officials of the U.S. government. On Christmas day an analyst with access to the latest intelligence told reporters that Qaddafi had "suspended" the operations of the assassination squads, and in mid-January 1982 a senior official stated that Qaddafi had "postponed" or "canceled" the plot to murder Reagan.

For several weeks the media and the public were growing suspicious that the administration had purposely leaked the story of the hit squads to the press and then exaggerated the situation simply to discredit Qaddafi and prepare the way for broad sanctions against Libya. In May a senior official admitted to a reporter that the administration had in fact deliberately exploited the reports of Libyan hit squads.[25] The press had been an unwitting, albeit willing, accomplice in the Reagan administration's propaganda campaign against Qaddafi. (The affair was not the last time that the administration manipulated the press in its efforts to increase pressure on Qaddafi.)

The Oil Embargo

At a meeting of the NSPG held on 25 February Reagan approved a ban on imported Libyan oil and a restriction on all exports to Libya. Administration officials informed the media that the sanctions would be implemented as soon as discussions were held with members of Congress, representatives of American oil companies, and allied governments. The administration emphasized that the new measures did not come as the result of any new development in U.S.-Libyan relations but were an important component in a "long-term program of opposing Qaddafi." The following day the General Accounting Office released a study that stated that the ban on the importation of Libyan oil might cause a brief revenue loss for Libya as it sought new customers but in the long run would have little effect on either the Libyan or the U.S. economy.[26]

On 9 March Reagan signed NSDD 27, which implemented measures designed "to reduce the threat posed by Libyan policies and actions." The directive, titled "Economic Decisions for Libya," placed an embargo on the importation of Libyan crude oil, required a valid license on all exports of U.S. goods and technology to Libya (except for food, medicine, and medical supplies), banned the export of any goods or technology with a military application, and prohibited the export of oil and gas equipment and technology that was not readily available from suppliers outside the United States. NSDD 27 also included a statement ordering an increase in both overt and covert assistance to North African governments opposed to the Qaddafi regime.[27]

On 10 March the administration announced that the economic measures against Libya had gone into effect. State Department spokesman Dean Fischer told reporters that the United States was "taking these measures in response to a continuing pattern of Libyan activity which violates accepted international norms of behavior. Libya's large financial resources, vast supplies of Soviet weapons, and active efforts to promote instability and terrorism make it a serious threat to a large number of nations and individuals, particularly in the Middle East and Africa." The U.S. government, Fischer added, has "no evidence

of a significant, lasting change in Libyan behavior; Libyan efforts to destabilize U.S. regional friends have continued. Accordingly, the Administration has
decided that further measures are appropriate at this time to underline our
seriousness of purpose and reassure those threatened by Libya."[28]

The Reagan administration had finally imposed major economic sanctions
against Libya but, by the time they were announced, the impact of those sanctions was greatly reduced and the measures became mostly symbolic. Libyan
oil was so expensive that the market had begun looking elsewhere for light,
sweet crude. U.S. oil companies had reduced the amount of Libyan oil they
were lifting and the U.S. market, which had imported more than 500,000 barrels
of Libyan oil per day earlier in the year, was getting by very well on less than
150,000 barrels per day. The percentage of Libyan oil making up total U.S. oil
imports had sunk to less than 3 percent.[29]

Although the economic measures announced on 10 March were forecast
to have a negligible impact on Libya, the administration's desire to construct
a consistent policy toward Libya influenced the decision to take this action.
Reagan realized that as long as the United States imported hundreds of thousands of barrels of Libyan oil each day he would be unable to condemn
Qaddafi's use of terror and subversion with any measure of credibility.[30]

Operation Early Call

By the summer of 1982 the CIA's covert operation in Chad was enjoying its first
string of successes. With Libyan forces encamped in northernmost Chad and
ignoring the presence of peacekeeping troops provided by the OAU, Hissene
Habré's guerrillas drove President Goukouni Oueddei's forces out of several
strategic towns in northern and eastern Chad. On 7 June 1982 about two thousand of Habré's men wrested control of N'Djamena from Oueddei's troops,
and Habré declared the establishment of Chad's Third Republic. Oueddei fled
to Tripoli and the remainder of his forces took refuge in the Tibesti Mountains
in northern Chad. Qaddafi's influence in Chad was shattered, and the Libyan
dictator now faced a hostile government that was supported by France, the
United States, Egypt, and Sudan on his southern border.[31] Embittered by this
stunning turn of events Qaddafi swore off—at least for the time being—any
further involvement in Chadian affairs.

Galvanized by Israel's crushing victory over the PLO in Lebanon in the
summer of 1982 and by his recent setback in Chad, Qaddafi's rhetoric at the

beginning of 1983 was bellicose and uncompromising. In early February he convened a meeting in Tripoli of dissidents from all over the Arab world called the "Pan-Arab Meeting of the Opposition and Popular Movements in the Arab Homeland." In his speech during the opening session of the conference Qaddafi attempted to inspire the participants to return to their countries and carry out acts of defiance, rebellion, and armed protest against Zionism, the United States, Arab governments friendly to the United States, and American-led peace initiatives. He shared his personal feelings of pain and frustration over recent Arab defeats in Lebanon and Chad and warned that confrontation with the United States—a friend of Israel and enemy of the Arab people—was inevitable and should not be feared.[32] Shortly after his speech the GPC passed a resolution calling for the arming of all able-bodied Libyans and the creation of "suicide squads" to attack Israel and those Arab countries which "follow the imperialist camp headed by the United States, the leader of world terrorism."[33] In light of Qaddafi's strident rhetoric it was no surprise that the United States and Libya became embroiled in two short-term crises in February and August 1983 when the United States acted in concert with other countries to thwart Qaddafi's efforts to destabilize northeast Africa.

In February the United States, Egypt, and Sudan foiled a Libyan plot to overthrow President Jafar an-Numayri's pro-Western regime in Sudan (though it was more likely that the leaders of the three countries had conspired to destroy Qaddafi's air force and just missed an opportunity to inflict a devastating and humiliating defeat on the Libyan leader). The United States and its two African allies very nearly enticed Qaddafi into sending his air force over Khartoum in support of a phony anti-Numayri group that had requested his assistance. (The anti-Numayri group had been set up by Sudanese intelligence operatives.) Qaddafi snatched the bait and began staging bombers, fighters, and transport planes at airfields in southeast Libya, near the Sudanese border. Reagan secretly dispatched four AWACS aircraft to Egypt. The planes would vector Egyptian fighters to intercept and shoot down Libyan aircraft that ventured into Sudanese airspace. American carrier-based fighters would patrol Egyptian airspace while the Egyptian fighters battled the Libyan planes. If Qaddafi failed to attack Khartoum, U.S. officials planned to explain that the quick deployment of the AWACS aircraft to Egypt had deterred Libyan subversion in Sudan. The scheme collapsed when the American press reported the deployment of the AWACS and the movement of the *Nimitz* aircraft carrier battle group (CVBG) to waters near Libya.

The plan to destroy Qaddafi's air force, given the code name "Early Call," was known to a very small number of administration officials. The plan predicted that the most likely window for a Libyan air strike on Khartoum was during Muslim noon prayers on Friday, 18 February. On Monday of that week four AWACS aircraft and four KC-10A Extender aerial tankers arrived in Cairo to rehearse the ambush operation with the Egyptian air force. The cover story, which was affirmed by both American and Egyptian authorities, was that the AWACS aircraft had been sent to Egypt for a joint training exercise.

Meanwhile, the Pentagon ordered the *Nimitz* CVBG to leave its station off Lebanon, take position off the coast of Libya, and make preparations to defend Egyptian airfields from attack by the Libyan air force. The *Nimitz* and her escorts took station eighty-five miles off the Libyan coast, and the air wing carried out flight operations in the Tripoli FIR and over the Gulf of Sidra. On Tuesday, 15 February, the only contact between U.S. and Libyan forces occurred when F-14s from the *Nimitz* intercepted two Libyan MiG-23 Floggers that had approached within sixty miles of the carrier but had not exhibited any menacing action.[34]

It would have been difficult to keep a lid on information about Early Call considering the deployment of eight large U.S. Air Force planes to Egypt, the arrival of approximately six hundred American support personnel, and the operation of the *Nimitz* battle group in waters near Libya. Not surprisingly, the operation began to unravel as soon as it got under way. The AWACS planes and tankers were supposed to land at the Cairo West Airport (which is located away from populated areas), but a dust storm forced three AWACS aircraft to land at Cairo's main commercial airport where they sat in plain view. Then on Wednesday, 16 February, the plan completely collapsed when John McWethy, ABC television's Pentagon correspondent, obtained information from a source within the administration about the AWACS deployment and the movement of the *Nimitz*. The network carried the story on its national news program that evening. "ABC News has learned that the United States has secretly deployed four early warning AWACS planes to Egypt on short notice and has rushed the aircraft carrier *Nimitz* and three escort ships from the coast of Lebanon to Libya," McWethy reported. With uncanny detail McWethy outlined the operational plan: "Intelligence sources say the movement is a direct result of an apparent military buildup by Libya spotted in the southeastern corner of that country, a buildup which Pentagon sources fear could foreshadow a move to overthrow the pro-American government of Sudan. . . . ABC News has been told if Libya does move militarily, Egyptian fighters, being guided by American AWACS planes, will make the intercept." Thus alerted to the ambush plan Qaddafi ordered his air force to relax its alert status. A well-conceived plan to devastate the Libyan air force and humiliate Qaddafi had been thwarted by a leak to the press.[35]

Speaking before the General People's Congress Qaddafi warned the United States to keep its naval forces away from the Gulf of Sidra. "Entering Sidra means an invasion of Libya," he declared. "The Libyan people want to live as free people and won't accept foreign occupation. The Gulf of Sidra will turn into a red gulf of blood if anyone tries to sail through it by force."[36]

At a press conference held the same evening that McWethy broke the story of the AWACS deployment and the movement of the *Nimitz*, Reagan denied any knowledge of naval maneuvers involving the *Nimitz* and emphasized that the aircraft had been sent to Egypt for a joint training exercise amid reports of increased tensions between Libya and its neighbors. Responding to a reporter's question about the movement of the *Nimitz*, the AWACS deployment, and the possibility of a Libyan attack on Sudan, Reagan answered: "I don't believe there's been any naval movement of any kind. And we're well aware of Libya's attempts to destabilize its neighbors and other countries . . . in that part of the world. But the AWACS, this is not an unusual happening. We have conducted joint exercises and training exercises with the Egyptian air force. . . . We'll do more in the future. And these planes have been there for quite some time . . . for this kind of exercise and that's what they're going to conduct."[37] Reagan's comment about the movement of the *Nimitz* CVBG from the coast of Lebanon to waters closer to Libya seemed to imply that its maneuvers were unrelated to the crisis between Libya and its neighbors. Furthermore, Reagan's claim that the AWACS deployment was "not an unusual happening" contradicted a message from the Joint Chiefs of Staff on 15 February that reminded key participants in Operation Early Call "of the unique sensitivity of these operations."[38] The Egyptians, in particular, wanted the AWACS aircraft sent to Egypt without publicity because they did not want to be seen as dependent on the American military for their security.[39]

When a reporter asked Reagan if he would use force against Qaddafi, Reagan replied: "I don't think there's any occasion for that; it's never been contemplated." The remark contradicted the Pentagon's position on the AWACS deployment, which had been outlined in a position paper used by Secretary of Defense Weinberger and the chairman of the JCS, U.S. Army Gen. John Vessey, at the NSPG meeting in which Early Call had been discussed and approved. The position paper emphasized that the objective in dispatching the AWACS aircraft to Egypt was to deter the Libyan threat and, if deterrence failed, to defeat Libyan forces through U.S. military action.

To say the least, Reagan's explanation for the movement of the *Nimitz* battle group was misleading and his statement about the AWACS deployment was implausible. Many viewers of the news conference simply believed that Reagan, the man who shunned details, had not gotten his facts straight.[40] More likely Reagan was being cautious about what he said concerning U.S. military action taken in response to the Libyan threat against Sudan. In the words of one administration official, Reagan was "trying to speak softly and carry a big stick."[41]

The following day a senior White House official, speaking on the condition that he not be identified, tried to clarify Reagan's news conference comments. (The official was presumably William Clark, Haig's former deputy at the State Department who succeeded Richard Allen as national security adviser in early 1982.)[42] The official emphasized that the AWACS training exercise required Reagan's approval but the movement of the *Nimitz* battle group, since it was limited to "normal ops within its Mediterranean assignment area," did not. Hence Reagan was technically correct when he had said there had been no naval movement related to the crisis.[43] The official denied press reports that Reagan had ordered the *Nimitz* to waters off Libya to deter a Libyan attack on Sudan, and insisted that the naval maneuvers and the AWACS deployment were unrelated events. He did, however, characterize the battle group's presence near Libya and the stationing of four AWACS aircraft in Egypt as a pleasant coincidence. He pointed out that the AWACS exercises had been planned and subsequently put on the back burner, but when the situation involving Libya flared up the United States and Egypt decided to carry out the exercises to reduce tensions in the area. He also stated that the United States viewed the exercises as an opportunity "to demonstrate resolve to our friends" in the region.

Despite the senior official's efforts, the administration's credibility problems continued. Pentagon sources informed the media that the *Nimitz* battle group had been stationed near Libya for the purpose of discouraging a Libyan attack on Sudan.[44] Meanwhile, a State Department official confessed somewhat humorously that it was difficult to believe that the movement of the *Nimitz* battle group and the deployment of the AWACS aircraft were unrelated, but "enough people have told me that, so I am beginning to believe it."[45]

On Saturday, 19 February, Reagan ordered the AWACS aircraft, the tankers, and the support personnel to leave Egypt by the middle of the following week and directed the *Nimitz* and her escorts to return to their station off the coast of Lebanon. Although the administration's efforts to explain its actions during the crisis of mid-February were in a shambles, Reagan's team could still claim that it had deterred a Libyan plot against the pro-Western government in Khartoum.[46] Four days after the AWACS deployment was made public the new secretary of state, George P. Shultz, appeared on *This Week with David Brinkley* and asserted that "the president of the United States acted quickly and decisively and effectively, and at least for the moment, Qaddafi is back in his box where he belongs."[47] Like the 1981 Gulf of Sidra FON exercise, the Early Call scheme was typical of the Reagan administration's strategy toward Libya: it was composed equally of deterrence and provocation.[48]

Operation Arid Farmer

Having cut his losses in Chad in the summer of 1982, Qaddafi waited patiently for an opportunity to reenter the contest. His next chance came as a result of the Arab world's reaction to the Israeli invasion of Lebanon and the introduction of Western military forces into the war-ravaged country. The crushing Israeli offensive and the subsequent deployment of U.S., French, Italian, and British peacekeeping troops diminished Arab enthusiasm for cooperation with the West, and the small opening created by events in Lebanon influenced Qaddafi's decision to commit his forces in support of deposed Chadian president Goukouni Oueddei. Qaddafi and his Chadian ally achieved some swift victories over President Habré, but the quick reaction of the United States, France, Egypt, Sudan, and Zaire preserved Habré's government and blocked Qaddafi's attempt to control his southern neighbor.[49]

In June 1983 Oueddei launched a military offensive against Habré's government. Within a month Oueddei's rebel army, reinforced by Libyan paramilitary forces, seized several towns in northern and eastern Chad, including the important crossroads town of Faya Largeau in north-central Chad. Habré began a counteroffensive in early July, and by the end of the month his troops had recaptured Faya Largeau and a number of other towns. In early August Qaddafi ordered his regular armed forces into combat, an action that dramatically escalated the conflict and prompted intervention by the United States and France. After a week of heavy bombing by the LAAF, Oueddei's rebel forces, which were reinforced by Libyan armor and artillery, moved into Faya Largeau.

Profoundly concerned that a victory by the Libyan-backed rebels in the Chadian civil war would have grave consequences for the security of Egypt and Sudan, the Reagan administration took decisive action against Qaddafi. In

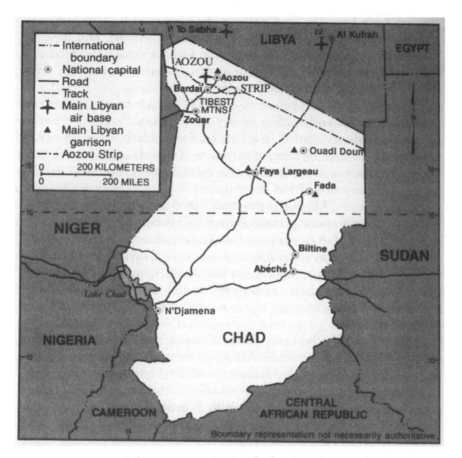

Libyan intervention in Chad, 1980–1987
Libya: A Country Study, ed. Helen C. Metz, 1989

early August it announced that the United States had a vital interest in preventing a Libyan victory in Chad and that America's closest allies in the area
could count on U.S. support against Libya. It approved twenty-five million dollars in emergency military aid for Chad and sent three U.S. Army instructors and
thirty Redeye shoulder-fired antiaircraft missiles to N'Djamena. It also ordered
the deployment of two AWACS radar planes, eight F-15 Eagle fighters, one
tanker aircraft, and approximately six hundred support personnel to bases in
Sudan. The operation carried the code name "Arid Farmer." For the duration
of the crisis the Sudan-based F-15s provided cover for the AWACS aircraft, which
monitored the flights of Libyan bombers that were attacking targets in Chad.

Reagan increased the pressure on Qaddafi by dispatching two additional AWACS aircraft to Egypt (where they arrived ahead of schedule for a planned exercise with the Egyptian air force), and by stationing the *Dwight D. Eisenhower* (CVN 69) CVBG just north of the Gulf of Sidra. The "Ike" was joined briefly by the *Coral Sea* (CV 43) CVBG. On 1 August JANA declared that the Libyan air force would crush the American naval force operating near the Libyan coast. The next morning two F-14 Tomcats from the Ike intercepted a pair of MiG-23 Floggers that were heading toward the battle group. The action took place over the Gulf of Sidra, approximately ninety miles from the carrier. The F-14s quickly achieved a favorable position behind the MiGs, but the Libyans suddenly broke away from the American planes and hastily retreated to the coast. The F-14s broke off the engagement and returned to their CAP station. On 14 August the Ike left its station off Libya to participate in Bright Star '83 in conjunction with units of the Egyptian armed forces and the U.S. Air Force.[50]

Beginning in the second week of August François Mitterand's government took vigorous steps to frustrate Qaddafi's designs on Chad. The French action served other purposes as well: it satisfied the Reagan administration, which was pressing hard for the involvement of France—a Western ally—in the crisis, and it boosted France's strategic position among its former colonies in central Africa.

Between 9 and 21 August the French airlifted approximately three thousand paratroopers to Chad. The troops immediately set up a defense line along the sixteenth parallel about two hundred miles north of N'Djamena. This act effectively ceded the northern half of the country to Libya and the Chadian rebels. Approximately three thousand rebels and an equal number of Libyan troops occupied the territory north of the line, while the French paratroopers plus about four thousand troops loyal to Habré and approximately two thousand Zairian troops held the southern half of the country.[51] President Mobutu Sese Seko of Zaire, the only African leader to offer direct military support to the Chadian government, visited N'Djamena in late August and proclaimed that "Chad does not stand alone" in opposition to Libyan aggression.[52] On 21 August the French dispatched four Jaguar ground attack planes, four Mirage F-1 fighters, and a KC-135 tanker aircraft to the airport at N'Djamena, which was well protected by a French air defense network. According to the French government the planes were sent to Chad to defend the paratroopers against attack from Libyan or rebel forces.[53]

With French paratroopers and tactical aircraft on the ground in Chad and with a military stalemate solidly in place, Reagan was confident that Qaddafi's designs on ousting Habré had been thwarted. Reagan recalled the military instructors from Chad and the aircraft and support personnel from Sudan by the end of August.

Libya, Terrorism, and the West

In December 1983 President Numayri of Sudan visited Washington and met secretly with the leader of the NFSL, Dr. Muqaryaf. A senior Sudanese official present at the meeting, a CIA informant, provided the agency with a complete account of the discussion between Numayri and Muqaryaf (and it is believed he may have provided the information with the knowledge of Numayri). The Sudanese president informed Muqaryaf that he was welcome to use Sudan as a base for his operations, including paramilitary activities, against the Qaddafi regime. Numayri pledged increased support for the NFSL in the form of training, arms, ammunition, and false passports. He also promised the full cooperation of Sudan's intelligence agency, the Sudanese Security Organization. In response to Numayri's largesse Muqaryaf informed him that as soon as his operatives had completed their next cycle of training, he intended to mount an operation in Libya that would establish the NFSL as a viable guerrilla organization. William Casey was buoyed by the prospect of an anti-Qaddafi guerrilla organization operating inside Libya. If Muqaryaf's NFSL could achieve some measure of success, Casey would have an easier time convincing Reagan to approve an intelligence finding that supported providing lethal aid to Libyan dissidents. By the end of 1983 Qaddafi was well ensconced in power and was ruthlessly pursuing opponents of his regime, whether they lived inside Libya or not.[54]

Reagan's policy of overt military, diplomatic, and economic pressures and nonlethal covert aid for anti-Qaddafi exiles appeared to have had a positive effect on Qaddafi's behavior because, according to the State Department, no terrorist incidents in 1982 and 1983 could be traced to Libyan sponsorship. In 1984 and 1985, however, Libya was linked to several acts of terrorism, subversion, and deadly mischief. The State Department identified some thirty terrorist incidents involving Libya during those two years.[55] The following is a description of several of those incidents.

In February 1984 Libyan revolutionary committees announced that all Libyan exiles must return home or face "the death penalty."[56] In May JANA announced that the "masses have decided to form suicide commandos to chase traitors and stray dogs wherever they are and liquidate them physically."[57] Over the course of the year Libyan agents attacked several dissidents in Britain, Greece, and Italy, killing six of them. In 1985 four dissidents living on Cyprus, in Italy, and in West Germany were murdered.[58]

In March an LAAF TU-22 bomber attacked the town of Omdurman, Sudan, near Khartoum in an unsuccessful attempt to knock out Sudan's main radio station, which was being used by anti-Qaddafi dissidents. In response to the raid, which killed five people, Reagan ordered two AWACS radar planes to Egypt to monitor the airspace in northeast Africa. The deployment was named "Operation Eagle Look." The planes were withdrawn the following month.

That same month four bombs exploded in London and Manchester, England, near the homes of Libyan exiles or in businesses frequented by them. Nine Libyans were rounded up as suspects, and five Libyan diplomats were expelled.

In April a person inside the Libyan people's bureau in London sprayed machine-gun fire at a group of about seventy Libyan anti-Qaddafi protesters gathered in front of the building. A British policewoman was killed and eleven demonstrators were wounded. London promptly expelled all individuals who had been inside the embassy, and severed diplomatic relations with Tripoli.

In May the FBI arrested two Libyan men near Philadelphia who were attempting to purchase handguns with silencers (the favorite weapon of Libyan assassination squads).

In November Egyptian security officials tricked the Libyan government into believing that one of its hit squads had killed a prominent Libyan exile, former Prime Minister Abd al-Hamid Bakkush, who was residing in Cairo. After JANA announced that Libyan agents had succeeded in their mission, the Egyptians presented to the media the very much alive and well former Libyan official and photographs of the faked incident, then announced that four would-be assassins had been arrested. Seeking some measure of revenge Qaddafi plotted to murder President Mubarak during a visit to Greece but the plot failed. Incredibly, one year later, in November 1985, the Egyptian government announced the arrest of another four Libyan would-be assassins, accusing them of plotting to murder Bakkush and other Libyan exiles gathered in Alexandria.[59]

In February 1985 the Chadian government announced at the United Nations that Libyan agents had attempted to assassinate Habré in September 1984. The government displayed a Libyan-made attaché case bomb which was set to go off at a cabinet meeting chaired by Habré.

In May the State Department reported that Egyptian security agents had foiled a plot to blow up the U.S. Embassy in Cairo with a truck bomb by militant Palestinians who were being supported by Libya.

In early July 1985 the U.S. government expelled an administrative attaché with the Libyan mission to the United Nations. Two months earlier the FBI had linked him to a plot to murder Libyan exiles in the United States.

In September a Libyan diplomat mailed several letter bombs to Tunisian journalists who had been critical of Tripoli's decision to expel over thirty thousand Tunisian workers from Libya. Several bombs exploded, wounding two postal workers and prompting the Tunisian government to break diplomatic relations with Libya. During that same month Zairian officials frustrated a Libyan-sponsored plot to assassinate Mobutu. According to government reports, Libya had been funding, training, and arming Zairian dissidents and sending them back to Zaire to perform acts of subversion and terrorism.[60]

Terrorism was not the only factor that adversely affected Qaddafi's relationship with his neighbors and the West. In 1983 and 1984 a number of his foreign policy initiatives directly challenged the security and interests of the United States and its European allies. During the brutal Iran-Iraq War, which began in 1980, Qaddafi allied his country with the revolutionary regime in Tehran primarily because of his antipathy for the secular ideology of Iraq's ruling *Baath* Party. Baghdad, on the other hand, was supported by every other Arab country except Syria, and was tacitly backed by the United States. Qaddafi supplied Iran with Soviet-made T-55 tanks, Scud surface-to-surface missiles, antitank weapons, antiaircraft artillery (AAA), and ammunition.

In the spring of 1983 the CIA received a timely report from a human intelligence source that several Libyan transport planes, scheduled to stop in Brazil on their way to communist Nicaragua, were carrying Soviet and Soviet bloc weapons, not medical supplies as the Libyans claimed. The planes were detained and, when searched, seventy tons of arms and explosives were found, providing the Reagan administration with a propaganda victory over both Libya and the Sandinista regime in Nicaragua.[61]

In the summer of 1984 persuasive circumstantial evidence linked the Libyan roll-on roll-off ship *Ghat* to the mining of the shipping lanes of the Gulf of Suez, an act of state-sponsored terrorism that menaced international commerce and caused indiscriminate damage to at least eighteen merchant vessels. Qaddafi may have been motivated to mine the Gulf of Suez as a way to embarrass President Mubarak, to harm the Egyptian economy by drastically reducing revenues from the Suez Canal, or to support Iran by intimidating Arab countries located on the Red Sea littoral that supported Iraq.[62]

In September 1984 Libya and France signed an agreement calling for the simultaneous and complete withdrawal of their troops from Chad. In November both countries announced that their forces had departed the country. In reality Qaddafi deceived the French into believing his troops had redeployed when in fact they had bivouacked in concealed positions in the northern part of the country.

By the mid-1980s Qaddafi had provided hundreds of millions of dollars in economic assistance to the Sandinista regime in Nicaragua. Furthermore, Qaddafi dispatched several dozen military advisers to Nicaragua, he financed the construction of a military airfield near the capital of Managua, and he attempted (unsuccessfully) to provide combat planes to the Nicaraguan air force. The Libyan military hardware that did reach Nicaragua included anti-aircraft artillery, SA-7 surface-to-air missiles, and small arms.

After Jafar an-Numayri was ousted in a coup in April 1985, Qaddafi exploited the renewal of diplomatic ties with Sudan to subvert the new government's attempt to establish a parliamentary democracy. Most important, he provided weapons, funds, training, and advice to the Sudanese Revolutionary Committee, a small insurgent group dedicated to the establishment of a Libyan-style government in Sudan.

Finally, to the extreme discomfort of the United States and its allies, Qaddafi allowed the Soviets greater access to Libyan military bases, anchorages, and airfields. Most notably, Soviet patrol aircraft frequently operated out of Tripoli Military Airfield and monitored Sixth Fleet maneuvers; Soviet ships were anchored off Tobruk where they performed repairs and loaded stores; and the Libyans constructed a Soviet-designed airfield at al-Jufrah in the Libyan Desert.[63]

Except for a few tactical victories, by the middle of 1984 the Reagan administration had accomplished very little in its campaign to isolate Qaddafi. The administration's record was particularly unsuccessful when weighed against its rhetoric. More than a thousand Americans still lived in Libya, even though the State Department had strongly urged them to leave and had invalidated their passports for travel to that country. Furthermore, with the Sixth Fleet's principal assets concentrated off Lebanon in support of the U.S. Marine Corps deployment in Beirut since the fall of 1982, the Navy was unable to keep up the pressure on Qaddafi with frequent FON exercises in the Gulf of Sidra. Between September 1982, when the Marines landed in Beirut, and February 1984, when they were withdrawn, Sixth Fleet ships operated near Libya only twice—the *Nimitz* CVBG in February 1983 and both the *Dwight D. Eisenhower* and the *Coral Sea* CVBGs in August 1983. Nearly a year later the Sixth Fleet finally returned to the vicinity of Libya when the *Saratoga* (CV 60) CVBG conducted a FON operation in waters near the Gulf of Sidra. On the night of 25–26 July 1984, F-14 Tomcats twice penetrated the Gulf of Sidra, reasserting the U.S. right to conduct flight operations over international waters while avoiding a confrontation by taking advantage of the LAAF's poor night flying capabilities. Finally, the CIA's effort to destabilize the Qaddafi regime by providing non-lethal aid to Libyan dissidents had accomplished very little. Meanwhile, the NFSL, for which Casey had high hopes, suffered a disastrous defeat. On 8 May 1984 NFSL operatives launched a major coup attempt against Qaddafi. The anti-Qaddafi forces had trained in Sudan and infiltrated Libya from Tunisia. The rebellion, the largest ever mounted since the revolution, involved a commando assault on Qaddafi's headquarters compound in Tripoli and resulted in a pitched battle in the downtown area that lasted about five hours. For the first time anti-Qaddafi groups both in the country and in exile had joined forces and coordinated their actions. The coup attempt collapsed when three conspirators were captured at the Tunisian border. Under torture they revealed the Tripoli hideouts of about fifteen rebels. With this valuable information Qaddafi's forces gained the upper hand before the remaining plotters could get into position. The NFSL paid a heavy price for its courageous attempt to overthrow Qaddafi. The military wing of the movement, the Salvation Corps, was annihilated, and its commander, Ahmad Ahwas, a former Libyan military officer and diplomat, was killed. In the wake of the failed coup Qaddafi's security forces made thousands of arrests and hanged hundreds of suspects. The regime purged the military of disloyal officers, executing seventy-five of them.[64]

Crafting an Effective Libya Policy: The Broad and the Bold Approaches

In William Casey's view the coup attempt demonstrated that Qaddafi was vulnerable and represented an opportunity to further weaken his base of power. "It proves for the first time [that] Libyans are willing to die to get rid of that bastard," the CIA director remarked.

Hoping to take advantage of this dramatic development, Casey approached George Shultz, a highly respected and influential member of the Reagan cabinet who had succeeded Haig as secretary of state in July 1982, and encouraged him to take the lead in developing a more assertive policy toward Libya. Shultz concurred and directed Deputy Secretary of State Kenneth W. Dam to conduct a thorough review of U.S. policy toward Libya. On 18 May the INR presented Dam with a paper, titled *Countering Libyan Terrorism*, which listed ten options for dealing with Qaddafi. The options ranged from one extreme—doing nothing —to the other—taking one of several positive steps (attacking carefully selected targets in Libya in response to Libyan acts of terrorism, carrying out covert activities "to preempt, disrupt and frustrate Libya's plans," or seeking a change in the regime). In the meantime the State Department had asked the CIA's Directorate of Intelligence to prepare an analysis of the threat posed by Qaddafi to U.S. interests worldwide.[65]

As it turned out, the CIA's national intelligence officer for the Near East and South Asia, Graham Fuller, was already supervising an interagency assessment of Qaddafi's vulnerabilities. Representatives from the CIA, INR, NSA, and DIA all agreed that the U.S. oil embargo and other trade restrictions had had little effect on the Libyan economy, whereas a complete withdrawal of all American and British oil workers might cause a short-term drop in Libya's oil production by upwards of 50 percent. The officials also agreed that the United States should approach Egypt and Algeria—the strongest military powers in North Africa—to bring armed pressure on Libya, and should support covert activities directed at Qaddafi. Many of Egypt's disagreements with Qaddafi were well known; Algeria opposed the Libyan dictator because of his intervention in Chad, his meddling in the internal affairs of countries of the Sahel region of Africa, and his support for Algerian dissidents. The officials acknowledged, however, that Egypt and Algeria would be reluctant to cooperate with the United States in activities directed at the overthrow of Qaddafi because of their concern that the United States would not give its full support and attention to the undertaking and would be unable to keep the operations secret.

The representatives from the CIA, the DIA, and the NSA were confident that there was significant opposition to Qaddafi within the Libyan military and that "successful internal operations, on a relatively spectacular level and with some frequency, combined with other external pressures and setbacks, could serve to spark action against Qaddafi by some disaffected elements in the military."[66] The representative from the INR challenged their conclusion, however, by questioning the quality of current intelligence on Libya and emphasizing that Qaddafi continued to be a popular figure among the Libyan populace with his grip on power still tight despite his unpredictable behavior and unconventional policies.[67]

The CIA, DIA, and NSA representatives brushed aside the arguments of their State Department colleague and advocated a program of forceful action on behalf of the exiled dissident community. "Exile groups, if supported to a substantive degree, could soon begin an intermittent campaign of sabotage and violence which could prompt further challenges to Qaddafi's authority," they wrote. "If exile activity were [to be] coupled with other factors—increased propaganda, visibly deteriorating relations with foreign countries and broad economic pressure—disaffected elements within the military could be spurred to assassination attempts or to cooperate with the exiles against Qaddafi."

The assessment, which—it could be argued—flew in the face of the presidential executive order prohibiting assassination, was a provocative document. It concluded "that no course of action short of stimulating Qaddafi's fall will bring any significant and enduring change in Libyan policies." It pointed out that Qaddafi's vulnerabilities could only be successfully exploited through a comprehensive program of political, economic, and paramilitary actions carried out in concert with key countries such as Egypt and the Western Europeans. Isolated and halfhearted measures would have no effect on Qaddafi.[68]

Graham Fuller issued the top-secret interagency intelligence assessment on 18 June over the formal objection of the State Department representative. Its call for major covert action and its tacit encouragement of the Libyan military to remove Qaddafi from power or assassinate him caused a sensation among the small number of administration officials privy to the document.

In early July the CIA issued the top-secret threat analysis on Libya that the State Department had earlier requested. It reported that Qaddafi was a continuous threat to American interests around the world but that it would be very difficult for him to launch a successful terror campaign in the United States. The analysis pointed out, however, that Sudan was particularly vulnerable to Libyan-sponsored subversion.[69]

Meanwhile, top officials at the CIA threw cold water on the interagency assessment of Libyan vulnerabilities, particularly its recommendation to take major covert action. Deputy Director John McMahon, who had served as deputy director for operations in the Carter administration, considered the exiles incapable of mounting a successful insurgent campaign against Qaddafi, as demonstrated by the results of the 8 May coup attempt. He argued that "they were still too weak, too scattered, and too divided to put any pressure on Qaddafi."[70] Surprisingly, Casey agreed with McMahon, pointing out that neither the allies nor a significant number of senior administration officials would support a major covert initiative against Libya at the present since Qaddafi had done nothing to warrant such a move. If the United States went forward with the covert option it would find itself acting alone, and the covert action would certainly fail. "With the Nicaragua operation in trouble in Congress, Casey was in no mood for another fight," wrote Bob Woodward in his book *Veil: The Secret Wars of the CIA 1981–1987*, which chronicled CIA operations during the Reagan presidency. "The 1984 presidential election was several months off.

There was no way Casey wanted to step off a cliff, though he was sure that an operation against Qaddafi would be popular with his two most important constituencies—the public and Ronald Reagan."[71]

With the CIA reluctant to support deliberate action against Qaddafi, Donald Fortier, the NSC's director of political-military affairs, spearheaded another drive to construct an effective strategy toward Libya. In late December 1984 the NSC's Policy Review Group (PRG), the body that coordinates covert operations, proposed that the CIA draft a presidential finding which authorized the agency to provide lethal aid to anti-Qaddafi opposition groups. The proposal would be discussed at an upcoming meeting of the NSPG.

To grease the skids for the PRG proposal Fortier asked Vincent Cannistraro, an NSC staff member and veteran CIA officer who had served in Libya, to prepare a background memorandum that listed all options for dealing with Qaddafi. Cannistraro completed the report in mid-January 1985. "A consensus within the intelligence community has developed concerning Qaddafi's increasing adventurism and his ability and determination to undermine U.S. interests around the world," read the report. "A number of new terrorist incidents sponsored by Qaddafi can be forecast[,] as well as new efforts to subvert allies and governments friendly to the West." Cannistraro recounted the recent increase in incidents of Libyan roguery and argued that Qaddafi was a threat, not merely an irritant, to U.S. strategic interests. "In the absence of any real penalties resulting from his impudent involvement in other nations," he concluded, "the constraints on Qaddafi's adventurism are diminishing. . . . Continued American vacillation on Libyan policy conceivably may result in a Libya even more hostile and more dangerous to U.S. interests."[72]

In echoing Fuller's assessment, Fortier and Cannistraro believed that Qaddafi was vulnerable, pointing out that his huge arms purchases and massive public works projects were depleting Libya's foreign currency reserves at such a rate that they could be exhausted in two years. From June 1981 to January 1985 Libya's cash reserves had declined from $14 billion to $3.1 billion. To head off the depletion of cash reserves Qaddafi could impose spending cuts for social welfare programs and public works projects, but such a course of action could foment discontent among the general population. Fortier and Cannistraro pointed out, however, that the administration was hamstrung in its ability to capitalize on Qaddafi's vulnerability because of its own reluctance to provide lethal aid to Libyan opposition groups.

Fortier and Cannistraro warned, however, that increasing the pressure on Qaddafi carried some risks. Active support for anti-Qaddafi exiles could "result in the removal of the last restraints against Libyan-sponsored terrorism directed at American citizens and officials." Furthermore, provocative naval demonstrations in the Gulf of Sidra could prompt Qaddafi to sign a treaty of friendship and cooperation with the Soviet Union.[73] Fortier and Cannistraro recommended a two-pronged approach for dealing with Qaddafi: a "broad" approach and a "bold" approach. The broad approach contained three elements. First, the administration would increase the pressure on the remaining American citizens and companies to get out of Libya. Second, it would inform Mubarak that it was pursuing an assertive policy with regard to Libya, and would invite the Egyptian military to participate in contingency planning and would pledge U.S. support in the event of hostilities between Egypt and Libya. Finally, it would conduct FON exercises off Libya, "coupling these exercises with provocative ship movements into the Gulf of Sidra."

The bold approach would involve "a number of visible and covert actions designed to bring significant pressure to bear upon Qaddafi and possibly to cause his removal from power." To implement the bold approach the administration would, first, encourage Egypt and Algeria "to seek a casus belli for military action against Tripoli and plan with these countries U.S. military support to their possible joint action" and, second, it would supply arms, ammunition, and intelligence information to Libyan opposition groups that were conducting a sabotage campaign against critical economic, military, and government installations in Libya. Fortier and Cannistraro theorized that "actions carried out by the Libyan armed opposition, if successful in augmenting significant pressure on Qaddafi and diminishing the stability of his regime, may lead to action by moderate Libyan army officers who are discontented with Qaddafi's policies." They cautioned, however, that the bold approach also could produce undesired consequences: it could alienate America's European allies who wanted to maintain important commercial relations with Libya, and it could force Qaddafi and the Soviets into a closer relationship.[74]

Although progress was being made behind the scenes, the development of an effective Libya policy was not achieved until the United States had suffered several spectacular and violent attacks at the hands of terrorist groups based in the Middle East.

NSDD 30, NSDD 138, and the Shultz-Weinberger Debate

Of the many contentious issues that shaped U.S.-Libyan relations in the mid-1980s, it was Tripoli's sponsorship, support, and high-profile encouragement of international terrorism that made a military showdown with the United States inevitable. During the first five years of the Reagan administration terrorists had killed and wounded approximately 660 American civilians and military personnel. By the end of 1985, after nearly three years of what seemed to be an unrelenting terrorist assault on American citizens and interests, the patience of the American people had worn out. They were angry and frustrated that very few perpetrators had been caught and brought to justice, they were disheartened by a sense of helplessness and vulnerability, and they were anxious for Ronald Reagan to make good on his promise of "swift and effective retribution" against the elusive enemy and its benefactors. The violence committed by Middle Eastern terrorist organizations against Americans from 1983 to 1985 roused national feelings of shock, outrage, and—to a large degree—impotence. Reagan stood at a crucial moment in his presidency. Secretary of the Navy John F. Lehman Jr. recognized the magnitude of the crisis facing the president. In his autobiography, *Command of the Seas,* Lehman wrote: "It now appeared that despite our great power—and our rhetoric—terrorism would succeed against Reagan as it had against his predecessor."[75]

In late September 1982 Reagan ordered U.S. Marines to Lebanon to serve as peacekeepers in the multinational force (MNF). The mission of the MNF was to promote the establishment of a viable central government. Lebanon had been embroiled in civil war since 1975, and in the summer of 1982 the country suffered a huge Israeli invasion designed to crush the Lebanon-based Palestinian guerrillas loyal to Yasir Arafat. On 18 April 1983 a car filled with explosives detonated next to the U.S. embassy in Beirut, killing sixty-three persons, including seventeen Americans. On 23 October 1983 a truck loaded with six tons of TNT crashed into the compound of the U.S. Marines peacekeeping force at the Beirut airport, and the ensuing explosion completely destroyed the headquarters-barracks building. The attack killed 241 American servicemen. A radical Shia Muslim organization with close ties to Iran, Islamic *Jihad* (Islamic Holy War), claimed responsibility for both bombings.

Despite the enormous losses suffered in the barracks attack, however, Reagan never ordered a retaliatory air strike although the Sixth Fleet had been poised to carry out one. A number of factors could explain his decision. First, his attention was consumed by the U.S. invasion of Grenada, which took place two days after the bombing. Second, U.S. intelligence could not determine the exact location of the perpetrators responsible for the bombing. Finally, many of his key advisers effectively pointed out the dangers of a retaliatory strike. They warned that U.S. bomber crews could be lost and innocent civilians could be killed, and they argued that unless the raid hit those directly responsible for the barracks bombing, military action could put the Marines in greater danger of further terrorist attacks. Reagan's failure to respond certainly did not improve security for the Marines in Beirut. Pinned down at their airport base by Muslim snipers and artillery fire, they could no longer perform their mission and, by early 1984, Reagan had had enough. In February he ordered the Marines to redeploy from the airport to amphibious ships offshore.

Meanwhile, on 12 December 1983 a truck bomb destroyed an entire wing of the U.S. embassy in Kuwait City, killing four persons. The Kuwaiti government charged another militant Shia organization, *ad-Dawa* (the Call) with carrying out the attack on the U.S. embassy and other targets in Kuwait City. On 20 September 1984 a van packed with explosives exploded at the main entrance to the U.S. embassy annex in east Beirut. The bomb killed sixteen persons, including two servicemen. Islamic Jihad claimed responsibility for the act. In December a Kuwaiti airliner en route to Pakistan was hijacked to Tehran by radical Shias demanding the release of seventeen co-religionists who were in prison for the December 1983 bombings in Kuwait City. During the five-day standoff at the Tehran airport the hijackers tortured a number of American passengers and killed two.

Throughout 1984 the Reagan administration struggled to develop a viable and coherent strategy against terrorists and the countries that sponsored or supported them. Two year earlier, in April 1982, Reagan signed NSDD 30 for the "efficient and effective management of terrorist incidents." The secret directive, appropriately titled "Managing Terrorist Incidents," stated in its opening paragraph that the "successful management of terrorist incidents requires a rapid, effective response, immediate access to institutional expertise, and extensive prior planning." It established the special situation group (SSG) under the direction of the national security adviser to advise the president on appropriate policies to guide a response and actions to take during a terrorist incident. It designated lead agencies to coordinate U.S. government action during a terrorist incident. The lead agency for incidents occurring abroad was the State Department; for domestic incidents it was the FBI; and for air hijackings it was the Federal Aviation Administration. It set up the terrorist incident working group (TIWG) comprised of representatives from the State Department, Pentagon, CIA, FBI, Federal Emergency Management Agency, and NSC. The TIWG was charged with providing operational assistance to the SSG, ensuring interagency coordination, and offering recommendations to the SSG during a terrorist incident. According to the directive the appropriate lead agency would manage the incident under the supervision of both the SSG and the TIWG. It established an interdepartmental group on terrorism (IG/T), under the direction of the State Department, which was "responsible for the development of overall U.S. policy on terrorism, including . . . policy directives, organizational issues, legislative initiatives, and interagency training programs." Finally, it authorized "active measures" to deter or disrupt terrorist attacks on U.S. citizens and interests.

In 1983 the Reagan administration initiated active measures—in the form of CIA operations that were aimed at killing (not assassinating) the leaders of radical Islamic movements whom the administration believed were responsible for the bombing of U.S. facilities in Beirut. According to the CIA's general counsel, "assassination" referred to the murder of heads of state and was prohibited by executive order. On the other hand, "killing" referred to the elimination of terrorists and lower-ranking government officials and was considered "preemptive self-defense."[76] Although NSDD 30 codified procedures for handling terrorist incidents and sanctioned steps to preempt and retaliate against terrorist attacks, the directive generated a major debate within the administration over how and under what circumstances an active response would be used against a terrorist group that had attacked or was about to attack the United States.

Bitterly disappointed that the United States had not retaliated for the bombing of the Marine barracks in Beirut and still smarting from the withdrawal of the Marines from Lebanon, Shultz became the leading voice advocating the use of force, either overt or covert, to combat terrorism. He felt that the United States had been driven from Lebanon by terrorists and realized that the problem could not be solved diplomatically. As far as Shultz was concerned, retaliation or preemptive action was all that the terrorists and their state supporters would understand. Since covert activity and military force were likely instruments in the war against terrorism, Shultz sought the involvement of the CIA and the Pentagon in the development and implementation of a stronger antiterrorist strategy. Casey supported tougher action against terrorists, but CIA career officers generally favored more cautious measures. They fell in line with Shultz and Casey, however, after William Buckley, the CIA station chief in Beirut, was kidnapped in March 1984 by members of the Iranian-backed Shia organization *Hizballah* (Party of God). On the other hand, Weinberger was reluctant to use Pentagon resources to fight terrorism. He could not help but recall that the 16-inch guns of the battleship USS *New Jersey* had failed to halt shelling and sniper fire directed at the Marines in Beirut and were unable to check the advance of antigovernment forces.

Without attaining agreement on the use of force among his senior advisers, Reagan's antiterrorism strategy would be severely hamstrung. Therefore, to find common ground concerning active measures to fight terrorism, National

Security Adviser Robert C. McFarlane, who had succeeded William Clark in October 1983, proposed a thorough review of the then-current counterterrorism policy and options for dealing with the terrorist threat.[77] The effort culminated in the promulgation of NSDD 138, which Reagan signed on 3 April 1984. The secret directive endorsed, in principle, the use of "proactive" operations—that is, preemptive raids and retaliatory strikes—to fight terrorist organizations and states that support them. The word "proactive" replaced language in an earlier draft of NSDD 138 that spoke of operations designed to "neutralize" terrorists. To many officials the word "neutralize" sounded too close to "assassinate," which was illegal.[78] The directive also ordered twenty-six federal departments and agencies to develop plans for combating terrorism.[79]

On 16 April the *Los Angeles Times* broke the story that Reagan had signed a new policy directive that authorized the use of preemptive strikes and retaliatory raids against terrorists operating overseas. In an interview with the *Times*, Deputy Assistant Secretary of Defense Noel C. Koch, the official responsible for developing the Pentagon's antiterrorist programs, admitted that the new directive represented "a quantum leap in countering terrorism, from the reactive mode to recognition that pro-active steps are needed."[80] On 18 April 1984 the *Washington Post* reported that Reagan had approved a secret presidential directive that contained a "decision in principle" for "taking the offensive" against terrorists.[81]

In response to press reports about NSDD 138 the White House provided the media with an unclassified statement outlining several components of the administration's new antiterrorism strategy. The statement, read to the media by presidential spokesman Larry Speakes on 17 April, had been carefully drafted by members of the NSC. Although the statement did not specify the circumstances under which the United States would take preemptive or retaliatory action in response to acts of terrorism, it contained the following warning: "While we have cause for deep concern about the states that now practice or support terrorism, our policies are directed against all forms of international terrorism. The states that practice terrorism or actively support it cannot be allowed to do so without consequence." The statement described the following steps the United States would take to protect itself and its friends from the actions of terrorist states:

> As a first step in dealing with these states, every channel of communication that is available to us will be used to dissuade them from the practice or support of terrorism. We will increase our efforts with other governments to obtain and exchange the information needed about states and groups involved in terrorist activities in order to prevent attacks, warn our people, our friends

and allies, and reduce the risk. We will also do everything we can to see that acts of state-sponsored terrorism are publicized and condemned in every appropriate forum. When these efforts fail, however, it must be understood that when we are victimized by acts of terrorism we have the right to defend ourselves—and the right to help others do the same.

An unclassified extract of NSDD 138 released by the NSC emphasized that the right of self-defense extended to terrorist acts being planned or about to be carried out: "Whenever we have evidence that a state is mounting or intends to conduct an act of terrorism against us, we have a responsibility to take measures to protect our citizens, property, and interests."[82] Secret portions of NSDD 138 sanctioned the creation of CIA and FBI paramilitary teams and authorized the use of unconventional tactics against terrorist groups by the new CIA and FBI counterterrorist squads and special warfare units, such as the Navy SEALs and Green Berets. The directive authorized deception, sabotage, preemptive and retaliatory strikes, and murder—but not assassination—against terrorists. The directive also ordered an expanded intelligence collection program aimed at suspected terrorists and their sympathizers and put special emphasis on oper- ations directed against those states believed to be the most active supporters of international terrorism. In a speech delivered the day that Reagan signed NSDD 138 Shultz identified those terrorism-sponsoring states as Iran, Syria, Libya, and North Korea.[83]

While NSDD 138 codified the administration's antiterrorism strategy and created a mechanism for conducting the war against terrorism, it did not quell the debate among Reagan's closest advisers over which active measures should be used against terrorists and their supporters. On the contrary, after the White House revealed the existence of a new policy the debate between Shultz and Weinberger became more shrill and threatened to obstruct effective U.S. action as terrorist violence against the United States continued to mount.

Shultz spoke out vigorously on the issue of international terrorism, hoping that a public debate would sharpen the administration's thinking on the problem and strengthen its policy. He believed that if a government was aware that a rogue state or its surrogate was conducting or planning to carry out a terrorist attack, then that government had the right and the responsibility to confront that state or group with appropriate political or military consequences. He urged Western democracies to recognize the need for "active defense" against the terrorist threat. He feared that if it became evident that the practitioners of terrorism could achieve their political goals then they would become bolder and the threat would become greater.

At a meeting of the Trilateral Commission held on 3 April Shultz stated that the United States must "take on the challenge of terrorism boldly and be willing to use force under the right circumstances." He advocated a proactive strategy but expressed a number of concerns about the use of force by a democratic society. "Certainly we must take security precautions to protect our people and our facilities; certainly we must strengthen our intelligence capabilities to alert ourselves to the threats," he stated. "But it is increasingly doubtful that a purely passive strategy can even begin to cope with the problem. This raises a host of questions for a free society: in what circumstances—and how—should we respond? When—and how—should we take preventive or preemptive action against known terrorist groups? What evidence do we insist upon before taking such steps?"

Shultz rejected the idea, born of the legacy of Vietnam, that military force should be used only in exceptional cases and with strong public support in advance. He argued that certain situations exist in which a discrete application of force is justified or appropriate for limited objectives. He declared that the United States should not "turn automatically away from hard-to-win situations that call for prudent involvement."

Shultz professed that a country can effectively combat terrorism and still abide within the rule of law. On 24 June, in a speech before the Jonathan Institute (an Israeli foundation dedicated to educating the public on the nature of terrorism), Shultz stated that a democratic country can do both: "It is time to think long, hard, and seriously about more active means of defense—about defense through appropriate preventative or preemptive actions against terrorists before they strike." He acknowledged that practicing active defense was a "slippery slope" but emphasized that "terrorists had to see costs to themselves and active opposition."

On 25 October Shultz's campaign for a policy of active defense reached its height in a speech before the congregation of the Park Avenue Synagogue in New York City. Outraged that opponents of the use of force had prevented Reagan from ordering retaliation against the latest act of terrorism—the bombing of the U.S. embassy annex—and confident that his views were consistent with the president's he passionately called on the U.S. government to drop its reluctance to use appropriate measures against terrorists groups and their supporters. "Fighting terrorism will not be a clean or pleasant contest, but we have no choice," he stated. "We must reach a consensus in this country that our responses should go beyond passive defense to consider means of active prevention, preemption, and retaliation. Our goal must be to prevent and deter future terrorist acts. . . . The public must understand *before the fact* that occasions will come when their government must act before each and every fact is known—and the decisions cannot be tied to the opinion polls."[84]

Weinberger, on the other hand, accused Shultz of advocating an "'unfocused' response" to terrorist attacks directed at the United States or one of its allies. In particular he opposed "immediate retaliatory action" such as bombing cities of a state believed to be sponsoring or supporting acts of terrorism. He argued against a "simple 'revenge' approach" and believed that Reagan agreed with him by opposing "anything that could hurt or kill innocent people." Weinberger pushed for a "'focused' response" whenever the terrorists responsible could be positively identified. According to the secretary of defense a focused response would be appropriate to the incident and would serve to discourage states and groups from committing acts of terrorism in the future.[85]

After Shultz's speech at the Park Avenue Synagogue, Weinberger articulated his views on the use of force. Speaking before the National Press Club on 28 November he presented a six-point policy, later known as the "Weinberger Doctrine," that delineated the circumstances under which the United States would send its military forces into battle.

> First, the United States should not commit forces to combat . . . unless the particular engagement or occasion is deemed vital to our national interest or that of our allies.
>
> Second, if we decide it is necessary to put combat troops into a given situation, we should do so wholeheartedly and with the clear intention of winning.
>
> Third, if we do decide to commit forces to combat . . . we should have clearly defined political and military objectives. And we should know precisely how our forces can accomplish those clearly defined objectives. And we should have and send the forces needed to do just that.
>
> Fourth, the relationship between our objectives and the forces we have committed . . . must be continually reassessed and adjusted if necessary.
>
> Fifth, before the United States commits combat forces . . . there must be some reasonable assurance we will have the support of the American people and their elected representatives in Congress. . . .
>
> Finally, the commitment of U.S. forces to combat should be a last resort.

Borrowing a line from a reporter, Shultz referred disdainfully to Weinberger's policy as "the Capgun Doctrine." According to the secretary of state, "Cap's doctrine bore relevance to a major, conventional war between adversarial armed forces. In the face of terrorism . . . however, his was a counsel of inaction bordering on paralysis. . . . This was the Vietnam syndrome in spades, carried to an absurd level, and a complete abdication of the duties of leadership."[86]

Reagan, whose grasp of foreign affairs was not as strong as his understanding of domestic issues, was not confident enough to referee the disagreement between Shultz and Weinberger over the use of force. Reagan respected Shultz's advice and the strength of his arguments, but Shultz was a recent addition to the Reagan team, having been pressed into service when Haig suddenly resigned in June 1982. Weinberger, on the other hand, had worked for Reagan while the latter was governor of California.[87] Since Reagan was reluctant to act without the support of his secretary of defense, Weinberger's views on the use of force effectively blocked Reagan from retaliating whenever a terrorist act was committed.

The failure of the United States to respond to acts of terrorism overlay a profound disagreement over the application of American power that, according to Lehman, "constantly distorted decision-making during Reagan's first term and often paralyzed the administration. . . . When you combined Pentagon paralysis with State Department bellicosity, the results were stupefying. Loud talk and no reaction repeatedly followed the taking of American hostages [by Hizballah in Lebanon]. We remained unwilling to risk the use of our military power."[88]

While the American public and many administration officials thought that NSDD 138 would serve as a declaration of war against terrorist organizations, it did not live up to those expectations. "No part of it was ever implemented," declared the Pentagon's Noel Koch. "The president's signature on a document meant no more to the conflicted elements of his administration than his pro forma threats against terrorism meant to the terrorists."[89] Nevertheless, NSDD 138 marked a significant milestone in the evolution of the use of offensive tactics against terrorist groups and their supporters, and it functioned as Reagan's counterterrorism policy for nearly two years. Its longevity—in political terms—was evident when McFarlane broadly discussed its contents in a speech before the Defense Strategy Forum on 25 March 1985, fifty-one weeks after Reagan signed the directive. Aware of the document's classification, McFarlane strongly suggested that the administration had embraced a proactive strategy to defend U.S. citizens and interests when they are threatened by acts of state-sponsored terrorism. According to McFarlane the United States recognized that "the practice of international terrorism must be resisted by all legal means" and that it had "a responsibility to take protective measures whenever there is evidence that terrorism is about to be committed."[90]

In mid-1985 terrorism against U.S. citizens and interests attained a new and higher level of violence. For seventeen days in June America suffered through the traumatic ordeal of TWA Flight 847. On 14 June gunmen belonging to Hizballah commandeered the aircraft and its 153 passengers and crew during a flight from Athens to Rome. The hijackers, who demanded the release of more than seven hundred prisoners, mostly Shias held in Israel, diverted the plane to Beirut and Algiers twice before settling in Beirut. During an earlier stop in Beirut the gunmen murdered a U.S. Navy petty officer, Robert Stethem, and dumped his body on the tarmac. While three crewmembers stayed with the aircraft, the remaining thirty-seven hostages, all American men, were removed to sites in and around southern Beirut. Understanding the risks that a military solution would involve, Reagan told reporters on 18 June that he would "have to wait it out as long as those people are there and threatened and alive."[91] According to Reagan biographer Lou Cannon, "The hijacking had become a kidnapping that mocked Reagan's vow of taking swift and effective retribution against terrorism."[92] The president set aside all of his antiterrorist rhetoric and decided to win the freedom of the hostages through painstaking negotiations. Through the intercession of Syria president Hafiz al-Asad and moderate Lebanese Shia leader Nabih Birri a deal was finally reached: Hizballah freed the hostages on 30 June, and Israel released the Lebanese Shia prisoners.

"Senior national-security principals realized that the Administration had been fortunate compared to the 444 days of the Carter Iran hostage crisis," wrote Bob Woodward. "But they realized that TWA Flight 847 had further exposed the weaknesses of the administration's antiterrorist capability and the lack of an effective policy."[93] Before the year was over the United States suffered even greater and more spectacular terrorist violence, and the administration was thwarted twice in its efforts to seriously undermine Qaddafi.

Operations Flower, Tulip, and Rose

Fortier's policy initiative was given a powerful boost both by the hijacking of Flight 847 and by Reagan's rhetoric in its aftermath. Although Qaddafi was not tied to the hijacking, David Martin and John Walcott, authors of *Best Laid Plans: The Inside Story of America's War Against Terrorism*, noted that "the seventeen days of helplessness, the murder of another innocent American, and the ease with which the culprits slipped away, all fed an urge to lash out against terrorism."[94] Anxious to satisfy the American public's demand for action, Reagan's closest advisers realized that the hijacking demonstrated just how vulnerable the United States was to terrorism and agreed that a determined stand had to be taken against it once and for all. Reagan informed his advisers that the continuous television coverage of the hijacking had been unbearable for him, and he privately vowed that the United States would respond appropriately in the future.[95] In a speech before the American Bar Association on 8 July Reagan labeled Iran, Libya, North Korea, Cuba, and Nicaragua "a confederation of terrorist states." As a measure of gratitude for Asad's role in ending the TWA hijacking, Syria was deliberately omitted from the list. "The American people are not . . . going to tolerate intimidation, terror and outright acts of war against this nation and its people," Reagan told the audience.[96] "And we are especially not going to tolerate these attacks from outlaw states run by the strangest collection of misfits, Looney Tunes, and squalid criminals since the advent of the Third Reich."[97]

While Iran and Syria were just as heavily involved in terrorist activity as Libya, Qaddafi was by far its most galling and vulnerable supporter. By focusing on Libya the administration could fight Qaddafi and terrorism at the same time. Moreover, the CIA had more intelligence on Libya than on the other state sponsors of terrorism. While Iran and Syria were careful to cover their tracks, Qaddafi's terrorist operations often left clues that pointed to Libyan sponsorship. His terrorist network generated a huge volume of encrypted radio traffic that was easily deciphered by the NSA because he employed unsophisticated codes and cryptographic equipment.[98]

The CIA maintained a steady flow of finished intelligence on Libya, striving to keep information on and analysis of Qaddafi's activities foremost in the minds of key policymakers. For example, in March 1985 the CIA issued an SNIE titled *Libya's Qaddafi: The Challenge to the United States and Western Interests.* The secret report predicted that Qaddafi would continue to undermine U.S. interests around the world for the next year-and-a-half, providing "money, weapons, a base of operations, travel assistance, or training to some thirty insurgent, radical, or terrorist groups."[99] A color-coded world map in the SNIE identified the countries in which Qaddafi supported insurgent groups and terrorist organizations. Those countries included El Salvador, Guatemala, the Dominican Republic, Chile, Colombia, Spain, Turkey, Iraq, Lebanon, Oman, Bangladesh, Pakistan, the Philippines, Thailand, Burkina Faso, Chad, Mauritania, Morocco, Namibia, Niger, Somalia, Sudan, Tunisia, Uganda, and Zaire. The map also highlighted countries in which Qaddafi supported radical politicians or opposition groups, including Austria, Great Britain, Australia, Costa Rica, Honduras, Nicaragua, Antigua, Dominica, St. Lucia, Benin, Ghana, Kenya, and Nigeria.[100] The assessment predicted that the Libyan leader "would directly target U.S. personnel or installations, if he believed he could get away with the attack without U.S. retaliation [and] he believed the U.S. was engaging in a direct threat to his person or was actively attempting to overthrow his regime."[101]

Casey thought the SNIE painted an accurate picture of Qaddafi's propensity to stir up trouble, but the State Department mildly disputed the assessment's conclusions. The INR argued that Qaddafi's first priority was the destruction of his opposition and that practicing subversion came in second.[102]

Working in concert with the CIA, McFarlane kept Libya on the NSC agenda during the first few months of 1985. This emphasis culminated on 30 April with Reagan's approval of NSDD 168, titled "U.S. Policy towards North Africa." The secret directive recognized "the region's geo-strategic position opposite NATO's southern flank, the potential for increased Soviet regional influence, and the dangers of Libyan adventurism."[103] It called for efforts to isolate Libya and increases in military assistance to Algeria, Morocco, and Tunisia.[104] It also established an interagency group, supervised by the National Security Council, "to review U.S. strategy toward Libya, and to prepare policy options to contain Qaddafi's subversive activities." Among those options were the broad and bold approaches conceived by Fortier and Cannistraro. The directive ordered the Pentagon to "review [the] Stairstep Exercise program [the code name for military exercises off the coast of Libya] and forward options and recommendations."[105]

In the aftermath of the traumatic TWA hijacking the Reagan administration began planning for direct action against terrorist organizations in general and against Muammar al-Qaddafi in particular. At an NSPG meeting in mid-July McFarlane pointed out to Reagan and his senior advisers that U.S. economic and diplomatic sanctions had not reined in Qaddafi, and that a more forceful strategy was warranted. Surprisingly, Shultz, Weinberger, and Casey all agreed with McFarlane's assessment, and the remarkable consensus spurred a number of studies, discussions, meetings, and even targeting sessions aimed at Libya.

On 20 July Reagan signed NSDD 179, which directed Vice President Bush to head a government-wide task force to study the broad issue of combating terrorism. The task force was born out of the humiliation of TWA Flight 847 and reflected the reality that the administration still had not reached definitive agreement over when and how force would be used against terrorists. On page one the directive stated: "The United States Government has an obligation to protect its citizens and interests against terrorists who have so little regard for human life and the values we cherish. To the extent we can, we should undertake action in concert with other nations . . . to combat the menace of terrorism. We must, however, be prepared to act unilaterally when necessary. It is, therefore, imperative that we develop a sustained program for combating terrorism." The task force was to study and evaluate the effectiveness of existing counterterrorism policies and programs and make appropriate recommendations to the president by the end of the year. Among its duties the task force was to assess the effectiveness or appropriateness of earlier directives or executive orders, such as the existing organization for dealing with terrorist incidents as established by NSDD 30, the intelligence-gathering responsibilities mandated by NSDD 138, and the prohibition on assassination stipulated by Presidential Executive Order 12333. It would also assign "responsibilities and accountability for ensuring interagency cooperation and coordination before, during, and after a terrorist incident"; would review and evaluate "present laws and law enforcement programs dealing with terrorism"; and would evaluate "current . . . programs of international cooperation and coordination." Though not stated in the confidential directive, the task force's most important assignment was the development of a set of guidelines for the preemptive or retaliatory use of force against terrorists that would gain the support of other democratic countries.[106]

Meanwhile, senior NSC officials embraced the two-pronged Libya strategy that Fortier and Cannistraro had developed earlier in the year, and gave it the code name "Flower." The NSC restricted access to the top-secret plans to about two dozen officials. Flower contained two subcomponents: "Tulip" and "Rose." Tulip was the code name for the CIA covert operation designed to overthrow Qaddafi by supporting anti-Qaddafi exile groups and countries, such as Egypt, that wanted Qaddafi removed from power. Rose was the code name for a surprise attack on Libya to be carried out by an allied country, most likely Egypt, and supported by American air power. If Qaddafi was killed as a result of Flower, Reagan said he would take the blame for it. His statement removed concerns over an operation that might result in Qaddafi's death.[107] Bob Woodward explained the unique relationship between the two phases of Flower: "The covert pressure in Tulip and the military planning in Rose were designed to reinforce each other. But if they failed, together they might force a state of alert and crisis in Libya, so that anti-Qaddafi elements in the Libyan military could overthrow him."[108]

At the CIA, Deputy Director for Intelligence Robert Gates completed a quick study for Casey on the pros and cons of Rose. The top-secret paper, dated 15 July, assessed the military balance between Egypt and Libya, the support Egypt would require if it fought Libya, and likely reactions by the Libyans, Arabs, and Soviets to an Egyptian invasion of Libya.[109] It concluded with the statement that the daring operation presented an opportunity "to redraw the map of North Africa."[110] Casey was so impressed by the paper that he ordered a study of possible Libyan targets that U.S. forces could attack in support of an Egyptian military operation against Libya.[111]

Fortified by Gates's analysis the NSC immediately set out to coordinate plans for a joint U.S.-Egyptian attack on Libya, but opposition to the operation appeared from two important quarters: the Pentagon and the State Department.[112] Weinberger (who described the plan as "silly") and the Joint Chiefs of Staff were worried that the United States might be drawn into a ground war in the event the Egyptian offensive stalled in the Libyan Desert.[113] Furthermore, the JCS did not like the idea of American planes flying over Libyan territory while escorting Egyptian transports.[114] Shultz thought the plan was risky and ill conceived—he considered the scheme "crazy"—and did not think that Mubarak would ever agree to it. Yet he was so exercised over the proposed military offensive that he summoned Nicholas Veliotes, the U.S. ambassador to Egypt, back to Washington to lobby for revisions to the plan that would make it acceptable to both the United States and Egypt. Their efforts obviously paid off, because Rose was changed from an offensive operation to one consisting of reactive and defensive contingencies only.[115]

While McFarlane was preoccupied with preparations for the first summit meeting between Reagan and the new Soviet leader, Mikhail Gorbachev, scheduled for November, his deputy, Vice Adm. John M. Poindexter, took over the coordination of Flower. Poindexter was so committed to Rose that he, Donald Fortier, and a senior CIA officer visited Cairo over the Labor Day weekend to discuss the plan with Mubarak and senior officials in the Egyptian Ministry of Defense. Shultz was confident that Poindexter's talking points with the Egyptians were more in line with the State Department's position than with the original plan, which called for a joint military operation against Libya. Before Poindexter could begin his briefing, however, the Egyptian president pulled the rug out from under the whole enterprise. Doubting the ability of the United States to keep such a complex and extremely sensitive operation under wraps, Mubarak told his American guests that he was in no way ready to commit Egypt to an invasion of another Arab country with the assistance of the United States.[116] "Look, Admiral," he said abruptly. "When we decide to attack Libya it will be our decision and on our timetable."[117] Poindexter and his entourage enjoyed a better reception at the Defense Ministry, but Mubarak's attitude severely weakened the prospects for Rose.[118]

In October Tulip was activated when Reagan signed an intelligence finding that authorized the CIA to support efforts already underway in Egypt, Algeria, and Iraq to organize, train, and arm Libyan opposition groups. By the mid-1980s Baghdad had emerged as the leading backer of anti-Qaddafi guerrillas after Libya tilted in favor of Iran in its war with Iraq. The plan had two main goals: it would work to interrupt, preempt, and thwart Qaddafi's subversive and terrorist activities, and it would try to lure Qaddafi into some foreign adventure or terrorist deed that either would give dissidents in the Libyan military an opening to seize power or would present one of his neighbors in North Africa (namely Egypt or Algeria) a pretext to challenge Qaddafi militarily.

After the administration explained the covert plan to the Senate and House intelligence committees, each committee approved the plan by the narrowest of margins. Senate Intelligence Committee members Senator David Durenberger, Republican of Minnesota, and Senator Patrick Leahy, Democrat of Vermont, the chairman and vice chairman, respectively, raised strong objections to the plan. They were concerned that lethal support for anti-Qaddafi dissidents could result in Qaddafi's assassination. Casey responded that the purpose of Tulip was to assist those groups that wanted Qaddafi removed from power. They might try to kill Qaddafi but that was not the objective of the operation. The two senators were not satisfied with Casey's explanation. They wrote a top-secret letter to Reagan in which they argued that the plan was in essence an assassination plot and they threatened to cut off funding for the operation. The White House replied that there was no deliberate plan to assassinate Qaddafi and reiterated that the purpose of the operation was to support Qaddafi's opposition. In early November an unidentified source—most likely from within the administration, not someone on the intelligence committees—leaked news of the covert plan to the *Washington Post*, which ran a front-page story about it on 3 November 1985. Reagan was disappointed but Casey was furious. Tulip had been exposed by an individual opposed to the plan and had to be abandoned.[119]

If there was any consolation for Reagan and the proponents of Flower it was that only Tulip had been exposed. Egyptian participation in Rose continued after Veliotes personally assured the Egyptian minister of defense, Field Marshall Abdul Halim Abu Ghazala, that the military operation had not been compromised and that the individuals responsible for leaking the information about the covert operation would be prosecuted. Meanwhile, at the Pentagon planners continued to study the Rose operation, although not with much enthusiasm since, after all, Rose had been an idea generated by the NSC and not the Defense Department. Weinberger and the JCS did not like what their planners were telling them: U.S. logistical support of an Egyptian invasion of Libya could develop into a major ground operation—requiring as many as six divisions, or about ninety thousand troops—if the Egyptians ran into serious trouble. They did not believe Libya was worth a war.[120]

The Rome and Vienna Massacres

By the fall of 1985 the administration's policy toward Libya was still sputtering, trying to get on track. It might have remained in the starting blocks indefinitely had terrorist attacks against Americans and others not become so remarkably gruesome during the last three months of the year and had Qaddafi not teamed up with the notorious Palestinian terrorist Abu Nidal.

In early October 1985 four heavily armed men belonging to the Palestine Liberation Front (PLF), a faction hostile to Arafat, seized the Italian cruise ship *Achille Lauro* with its four hundred passengers and crew while it sailed between the Egyptian ports of Alexandria and Port Said. The gunmen demanded the release of fifty Palestinians jailed in Israel. Following two days of intense negotiations the hijackers surrendered to PLO officials in Egypt after they won a promise of safe passage out of Egypt. Soon afterward the U.S. government learned that the gunmen had shot an elderly, wheelchair-bound American man, Leon Klinghoffer, and thrown his body overboard. The United States urgently requested that Egypt hold and prosecute the assailants, but Egyptian authorities permitted the four men to leave the country on a commercial airliner. Thereupon, four F-14s from VF-74 and VF-103, based on the carrier *Saratoga*, intercepted the EgyptAir plane and forced it to land at the NATO air base in Sigonella, Sicily. The four hijackers were arrested by Italian authorities and charged with kidnapping and murder. Muhammad Abu Abbas, the leader of the PLF and the alleged mastermind of the hijacking, was also on the jetliner but he was allowed to leave Italy despite U.S. warrants issued for his arrest.[121] Nevertheless, at a White House news conference the day after the hijackers were apprehended a beaming Ronald Reagan savored a rare victory in the struggle against international terrorism. "I am proud to be the commander in chief of the soldiers, sailors, airmen, and Marines who deployed, supported, and played the crucial role in the delivery of these terrorists to Italian authorities," he told assembled reporters. "These young Americans sent a message to terrorists everywhere, a message, 'You can run, but you can't hide.'"[122] Unfortunately, the victory would be short-lived. Abu Nidal was plotting his own revenge for the *Achille Lauro* debacle. He was planning an airline hijacking to punish the Egyptians and an airport assault to strike back at the Italians. The airport attack in Italy and a duplicate operation in Austria also targeted the Israelis.[123]

Abu Nidal, whose real name was Sabri al-Banna, deserted the mainstream PLO in 1974 after Yasir Arafat denounced terrorist attacks outside Israel and the occupied territories. Abu Nidal was dedicated to destroying all efforts at mediation between Israel and moderate Arab states and was dependent on radical Arab states such as Iraq, Syria, and Libya for refuge, funding, and logistical support. As Abu Nidal's organization, Fatah—The Revolutionary Council (FRC) —became increasingly more violent in the mid-1980s, his supporters either abandoned him or attempted to restrict his operational freedom. For instance, Iraq expelled him and Syria imposed a tight reign on his activities. By mid-1985 Abu Nidal had found a kindred spirit in Muammar al-Qaddafi, who was also vehemently opposed to a negotiated settlement to the Arab-Israeli conflict. Abu Nidal took up part-time residence in Tripoli and conspired with Qaddafi to destabilize the government of Egypt.

On 23 November 1985 three members of the FRC seized EgyptAir Flight 648 while it was en route from Athens to Cairo. After a harrowing in-flight shootout with an Egyptian sky marshal, the gunmen forced the plane to land in Malta. Over the next few hours the hijackers shot two Israelis and three Americans and dumped their bodies onto the runway. Miraculously, two of the Americans and one Israeli survived. The following evening Egypt's Force 777 commandos blasted their way into the plane, and during the ensuing firefight several passengers were indiscriminately wounded and a horrifying conflagration broke out and swept through the cabin. A total of sixty people died of smoke inhalation or wounds they received in what turned out to be the deadliest airplane hijacking until 11 September 2001. Meanwhile, U.S. intelligence had collected evidence that Libya had played a major role in the bloody hijacking. The CIA learned that Qaddafi had paid five million dollars for the operation. Intercepted cable traffic between Tripoli and the Libyan people's bureau in Malta indicated that Libya had known about the hijacking in advance and had passed instructions to the terrorists on the ground in Malta.[124]

Two days after Christmas the Abu Nidal organization struck again with deadly precision. Shortly after nine o'clock in the morning, at the Leonardo da

Vinci airport in Rome four assailants armed with machine-guns and grenades attacked bystanders and employees at the El Al, TWA, and Pan Am airline ticket counters and a nearby snack bar. Strung out on amphetamines, the terrorists screamed and laughed like wild men. The bloody rampage left sixteen civilians dead and over seventy people wounded. Five Americans were killed, including an eleven-year-old girl. Italian security personnel killed three of the gunmen and captured the fourth. Almost simultaneously, at Vienna's Schwechat Airport three terrorists attacked travelers waiting at the departure gate for Israel's El Al Flight 364 to Tel Aviv. Four people were killed and more than forty were wounded in a violent barrage of machine-gun fire and grenade explosions. Police killed one assailant and captured the other two after a brief car chase.

Shortly after the attacks a radio station in Malaga, Spain, received a phone call from an individual who stated that the Rome and Vienna massacres were the work of the FRC. Moreover, the three surviving terrorists admitted being members of the FRC, and a note carried by one of them stated that the attacks were in reprisal for Israel's bombing of the PLO headquarters in Tunis two months earlier. That raid had killed more than seventy Palestinians and Tunisians.[125] Another note—this one found on the body of one of the dead Rome gunman—was more ominous. It read: "Zionists, as you have violated our land, our honor, our people, we in exchange will violate everything, even your children, to make you feel the sadness of our children. The tears we have shed will be exchanged for blood. The war started from this moment." The note was signed by "The Martyrs of Palestine."[126] Italian and Austrian investigators soon established a Libyan connection to the two assaults when they traced the Tunisian passports carried by the Rome and Vienna terrorists to a batch that Libyan authorities had confiscated from Tunisian guest workers who had been expelled from Libya earlier in the year.[127]

Reagan, who was enjoying the holidays at Rancho del Cielo, was shocked by the brutal massacres. Crisis meetings were immediately convened in his absence at the White House. The CIA suspected that both Libya and the Abu Nidal organization were responsible for the attacks, but the early evidence was either circumstantial or conflicting. For instance, the CIA had an intelligence report that Qaddafi had once deposited one million dollars in an Abu Nidal bank account in Bulgaria, but that had happened several years earlier. Furthermore, while the Italians and Austrians had uncovered a significant tie between Tripoli and the terrorists, the surviving Rome assailant told investigators that he had received training in the Biqa Valley in Lebanon by Syrian agents who then traveled with him from Syria to Rome. Officials at the Pentagon began studying Libyan targets for a retaliatory strike but at the same time raised an important concern. The Soviets had more than two thousand advisers in Libya and several hundred directly involved in air defense. Was the U.S. willing to risk killing Soviet citizens in order to strike at Qaddafi? That question would have to wait for Reagan's return to Washington.[128]

Qaddafi called the airport attacks "an act of revenge for the Israeli action against Tunisia." JANA described the massacres as "heroic actions," and Qaddafi publicly defended the reputation of Abu Nidal, comparing him to a famous American freedom fighter. "If Abu Nidal is a terrorist, then so is George Washington," he remarked.[129] Once again the galling Colonel Qaddafi was proving to be his own worst enemy. Within days of the Rome and Vienna attacks the Reagan administration accused Tripoli of aiding the perpetrators and providing a safe haven for Abu Nidal. Since the terrorists had targeted El Al in both operations, many U.S. officials fully expected the Israelis to strike back against Libya.

The Israeli government accused Libya of supporting Abu Nidal, and it appeared likely that Israelis would indeed retaliate.[130] "These beasts know no borders, and we will hit them wherever they are," declared Deputy Prime Minister David Levy.[131] As the hours wore on, however, the prospects for an Israeli attack declined. Although El Al facilities and passengers had been attacked at both airports, the majority of the killed and wounded were not Israelis. Officials in the Israeli government were reluctant to take on "the burden of being the spear-carrier for antiterrorism." In their view the weight of retaliation should not be theirs alone.[132]

Qaddafi denied any involvement in the Rome and Vienna atrocities. Instead, he launched a verbal counterattack, accusing the United States and Israel of preparing a joint attack on his country and warning of drastic consequences if that occurred. "Aggression on Libya means war," he announced. "Libya will not act in a limited fashion. Libya will declare war in the Middle East and in the Mediterranean zone."[133]

4

Operation Prairie Fire

Reagan Sets the Stage for Military Action

Before President Reagan returned to Washington, his new national security adviser, Vice Adm. John M. Poindexter, chaired a meeting of the NSC's Crisis Pre-Planning Group to develop a list of military options that Reagan could use against Libya. The participants generated a list of options that included air raids by either carrier-based Navy attack aircraft, F-111F fighter-bombers based in the United Kingdom, or B-52 Stratofortress bombers based in the continental United States as well as precision strikes by ship- or submarine-launched Tomahawk land attack cruise missiles. Each Tomahawk was armed with a 1,000-pound high explosive warhead and was equipped with a digital scene-matching area correlation (DSMAC) computer system that guided the missile with great accuracy over hundreds of miles of tree top–level flight to the target. An advantage of using Tomahawks was that no American aircrews would be exposed to Libyan air defenses.[1]

At the same time, Pentagon planners were preparing a contingency list of Libyan targets, ranging from antiaircraft sites to terrorist-related facilities to government buildings. The JCS favored terrorist targets directly connected with the Abu Nidal organization and ones that were located where U.S. forces could strike them without endangering innocent civilians. Unfortunately, the number of terrorist sites meeting these criteria was small since many of the targets were located in or very near civilian-populated areas.[2]

Reagan was convinced that the evidence linking Libya to the terrorist attacks at the Rome and Vienna airports was "irrefutable."[3] On 6 and 7 January he chaired two meetings of the NSPG to discuss strategies for confronting Muammar al-Qaddafi. Reagan's senior advisers gathered to debate not whether but how to deal with the Libyan leader. At the first meeting Reagan ordered CIA Director Casey to press ahead with covert operations supporting dissident Libyans who were working to destabilize the Qaddafi regime, and he directed the Pentagon to continue working with the Egyptians on Operation Rose. Reagan and his advisers began discussing a military response to Libya's involvement in the Rome and Vienna massacres, but the president postponed further deliberations and a decision until the next day.[4]

At the second NSPG meeting Secretary of State Shultz read an opinion from the State Department's legal counsel, which stated that according to Article 51 of the United Nations Charter terrorism constituted "armed aggression" and that military force could be used in self-defense.[5] Shultz urged Reagan to authorize an immediate retaliatory air strike on Libya to show Qaddafi that he "could not avoid responsibility for attacking American civilians and others by using Palestinian terrorists to do the job."[6] Shultz was opposed for several reasons by Secretary of Defense Weinberger, Chairman of the Joint Chiefs of Staff Adm. William J. Crowe, and the CIA's Casey. They argued that an attack might put Americans living abroad at greater risk of a terrorist attack and that the Americans living and working in Libya might be taken hostage. They emphasized that U.S. pilots conducting the strike might be shot down and taken prisoner and that innocent people might be killed if the strike did not carefully target the actual perpetrators. They also pointed out that diplomatic and economic options had not been exhausted and that the available evidence—Reagan's personal convictions notwithstanding—linking Qaddafi to the airport attacks was strong but not conclusive. The talk of Americans being taken hostage or of U.S. airmen being shot down had a sobering effect on the participants. As the discussion progressed Reagan realized that he would have to give political and economic sanctions enough time to influence Qaddafi's behavior. Only then could he hope for critical support at home and abroad for future military actions. He agreed with Weinberger and Crowe that any retaliation against a terrorist incident must be focused and proportionate, and not a simple act of revenge that could endanger innocent lives. Reagan also needed stronger evidence of Qaddafi's hand in the spate of recent terrorist attacks and information on the identity and whereabouts of specific perpetrators. The president's view, of course, was not shared by Shultz.[7]

Another factor influenced the debate over the use of military force. As noted earlier, Syria and Iran were just as active as Libya in the support and sponsorship of international terrorism and their actions often wrought deadlier results. Syria had trained and provided logistical support for the terrorists who attacked the Rome and Vienna airports, and Iran's surrogates in Lebanon had killed nearly three hundred Americans since 1983 (while they presently held six Americans hostages). Nevertheless, the administration did not consider Syria and Iran for retribution for a number of reasons. Syria possessed a formidable air defense network and was the Soviet Union's most important ally in the Middle East. An attack on Syria might result in the capture or loss of American airmen and produce a confrontation with the Soviet Union. On the other hand, the United States was secretly courting Iran to use its influence to free the American hostages held by militant Shias in Lebanon. Furthermore, increased military and economic pressure on Iran might drive the country into a closer relationship with the Soviets. Thus, by the end of 1985 America's war against terrorism focused on Muammar al-Qaddafi, whose regime represented the most obvious and immediate danger to American citizens abroad.[8] In early 1986 journalist George J. Church made the following observation: "Qaddafi has been the most open supplier of money, weapons, training and refuge to terrorist groups around the world. He has broadcast the most inflammatory public appeals for attacks on Americans. He has issued the most insolent taunts and threats of blood and death. And he happens to be the weakest militarily and the most isolated politically of the world's suspected terrorist leaders, despised even by many of his fellow Arab leaders and regarded nervously by his Soviet supporters."[9]

Shultz backed away from his earlier advocacy of immediate military retaliation and instead advocated a package of diplomatic and economic sanctions that would effectively curtail all trade between Libya and the United States. In the aftermath of the massacres in Rome and Vienna policymakers at the State Department dropped their usual resistance to strict economic sanctions and endorsed a proposal, drafted by Elaine Morton (the State Department's former North Africa officer and currently an NSC staff member), to break all economic ties with Libya. Shultz also proposed a major FON exercise in the Gulf of Sidra to exert military pressure on Qaddafi. He envisioned an operation that would be larger in scope than the maneuvers carried out by the *Nimitz, Eisenhower,* and *Coral Sea* CVBGs in 1983 and by the *Saratoga* CVBG in 1984. He hoped that the combination of sanctions— in concert with Western allies, he hoped—and a large naval demonstration off the Libyan coast would induce a change in Qaddafi's behavior and obviate the use of military force. Reagan approved Shultz's proposal and directed him to line up allied support for stricter economic and diplomatic measures. Allied backing was crucial if such measures, especially the economic sanctions, were to have any chance of success. If European companies filled the commercial void left by the departure of American businesses and technicians, Qaddafi would not feel the effects of the rupture of economic ties with the U.S.

Ironically, America's commercial relationship with Libya had expanded since the Reagan administration imposed diplomatic and economic sanctions in 1981 and 1982. Five American petroleum companies—Amerada Hess, Conoco, Marathon, Occidental, and W. R. Grace—still lifted seven hundred thousand barrels of crude oil per day, and several engineering and construction firms were awarded lucrative public works contracts, including a portion of Qaddafi's Great Man Made River project (designed to tap desert aquifers and carry water to coastal agricultural areas). American exports to Libya during the first ten months of 1985 reached $260 million, a nearly 60 percent increase over the same period of the year before, and approximately fifteen hundred Americans still worked and lived in Libya—each one a potential hostage.[10]

Overriding the concerns of his secretary of defense, Reagan directed the Pentagon to develop contingency plans for striking economic, military, and terrorist-related targets in Libya. Since taking office at the Pentagon in January 1981 Weinberger regarded Reagan's huge military buildup as a means to preserve the peace, not conduct war. He consistently argued that military force should only be used as the last resort in a crisis that affected national interests and only in adequate strength to achieve clear obtainable objectives. He communicated his convictions at the 7 January meeting of the NSPG.

Reagan listened to his military advisers and ruled out the use of B-52s and Tomahawk cruise missiles. They argued that repositioning the strategic bombers and cruise missile platforms for training or staging them for an attack would alert the Soviets, who would likely warn Qaddafi. Furthermore, using Tomahawks could result in the compromise of sensitive cruise missile technology if a missile were to be shot down over Libya. Therefore the Pentagon tasked the European Command (EUCOM)—the U.S. unified military command in Europe—to develop strike plans that used other theater assets.[11]

Later that day Reagan exercised his authority under the International Emergency Economic Powers Act of 1977 and signed Executive Order 12543, which stated that "the policies and actions of the Government of Libya constitute an unusual and extraordinary threat to the national security and foreign policy of the United States" and declared "a national emergency to deal with that threat." The executive order banned all travel and commercial transactions between the United States and Libya. Most of the sanctions took effect immediately. The prohibition against all economic activities was, in effect, an order for Americans still living in Libya to leave because U.S. citizens would no longer be able to engage in any financial transactions, including paying rent and buying food. On 1 February the ban on U.S. citizens taking flights out of Libya would go into effect. The earlier ban on travel to Libya, imposed in December 1981, failed to get all Americans out of the country because Qaddafi allowed them to enter and leave Libya without getting their passports stamped, thus making it impossible to enforce the ban. The five American oil companies working in Libya were given until 30 June 1986 to sell off their operations in order to prevent the Libyan government from earning windfall profits after their departure.[12]

At a press conference that evening Reagan blamed Abu Nidal and his terrorist organization for the attacks at the Rome and Vienna airports and charged Qaddafi with abetting and supporting the murderers and with "armed aggression against the United States . . . just as if he had used . . . [his] own armed forces." He outlined the economic measures against the Libya and urged all Americans living in Libya to leave immediately. "Civilized nations cannot continue to tolerate in the name of material and self-interest the murder of innocents," Reagan continued. "Qaddafi deserves to be treated as a pariah in the world community. We call on our friends in Western Europe and elsewhere to join with us in isolating him." Finally, he warned, "If these steps do not end Qaddafi's terrorism, I promise you that further steps will be taken."[13]

In his diary entry for 7 January Reagan reviewed his strategy for dealing with Qaddafi. "I finally came down on the side of an executive order bringing Americans and American businesses home from Libya and canceling relations —trade, etc. . . . with them," he wrote. "At the same time we beef up the Sixth Fleet in the Mediterranean Sea. If Mr. Qaddafi decides not to push another terrorist act, okay, we've been successful with our implied threat. If on the other hand he takes this for weakness and does loose another one, we will have targets in mind and instantly respond with a h—l of a punch."[14]

Although the administration expected the impact of the executive order on the Libyan economy to be minimal—annual trade between the United States and Libya totaled only $300 million—it served two very important purposes: it increased the pressure on the allies to take action against the Qaddafi regime and it served as a warning to Qaddafi that more drastic measures were a strong possibility.[15] Qaddafi responded to Reagan's announcement by calling the president a "stinking, rotten crusader." He also stated that Reagan's decision to sever economic ties was "tantamount politically to a declaration of war." He warned that any U.S. military action against Libya would result in attacks on Americans carried out by "suicide groups." "If they threaten us at home, we shall threaten them at home," he declared.[16]

On 8 January Reagan signed NSDD 205, which outlined the economic sanctions against Libya and committed the administration "to seek allied implementation of comparable economic sanctions and agreement not to replace U.S. business and personnel" in Libya and to "initiate a global diplomatic and public affairs campaign to isolate Libya."[17] Attached to the confidential directive, which was titled "Acting against Libyan Support of International Terrorism," was a top-secret annex that ordered additional intelligence operations and military deployments. The purpose of the latter, which included multicarrier operations in the Gulf of Sidra, was to "signal U.S. resolve, reduce the potential risk to American citizens in Libya, heighten the readiness of U.S. forces to conduct military action, and create uncertainty regarding U.S. intentions." The annex directed Weinberger to submit to the NSC by 9 January the draft plans for the FON operations.[18]

Shultz dispatched Deputy Secretary of State John C. Whitehead and Robert Oakley, the acting ambassador-at-large for counterterrorism, to Canada and Europe to urge the allies "to reduce their purchases of Libyan oil, to ban sales of military hardware to Qaddafi, to stop extending official credits to Libya, to condemn Libya by name for supporting terrorism, and to shut down Libya's people's bureaus, which continued to function as recruiting offices and command posts for terrorist activities."[19] The reaction of the members of the European Community (EC) to Reagan's call for action against Libya was lukewarm at best. On 27 January EC foreign ministers agreed to cut off arms sales to Libya, to end guaranteed credit for Libya and other states supporting terrorism, and to place restrictions on the entry and movement of Libyans in EC countries. The foreign ministers also pledged to do everything possible to prevent businesses in their countries from capitalizing on the departure of American firms from Libya. On the other hand, France, Greece, Italy, and Spain—countries with close ties to the Arab world—successfully thwarted efforts led by Great Britain to secure agreement on measures aimed at condemning Libya for its support of terrorism and cutting back purchases of Libyan oil. Greece even refused to join the other members in the arms embargo against Libya. The countries that opposed more stringent measures believed that economic sanctions did not work, and they were concerned that the Reagan administration had not presented enough concrete evidence of Libyan involvement in the airport attacks.[20] "It is hard enough to get the Common Market to agree on simple things such as butter and wine," complained an American diplomat based in Rome. "But to talk of something as monumental as Libya . . . and try to get some meaningful policy from that is all but impossible."[21] "The Europeans don't have the political will or the backbone to do what needs to be done to cope with terrorism," asserted terrorism analyst Yonah Alexander. "The short-term benefits are more important to them than their long-term interests."[22] Following his tour of the allied capitals Oakley expressed polite praise for the governments of Italy, Canada, and Great Britain for enacting additional diplomatic measures against Libya.[23] Upon his return to Washington a disappointed Whitehead pointed out to reporters that the president had "reserved the right to come back to the military option in case the nonmilitary, peaceful measures don't work."[24]

Although the United States was in effect dealing with Qaddafi alone, the preliminary elements of Reagan's strategy were firmly in place. The United States had laid a moral foundation for future military action. If diplomatic and economic sanctions and demonstrations of military force failed to curb Qaddafi's lawlessness, Reagan was prepared to raise the stakes. Further Libyan provocations would be met with a disproportionate response.[25] "In the future, no one will be able to suggest that the president hasn't been measured and considered in his actions," insisted a senior administration official. "And if stronger action is required, the burden will be on the terrorists who caused it rather than on the president."[26]

Initial Military Preparations

Immediately after the attacks on the Rome and Vienna airports the Reagan administration was confronted with the reality that most Americans believed that the time was long overdue to strike at nations that sponsored or supported international terrorism. According to a Harris Poll taken at the time, 72 percent of the public indicated that countries supporting terrorism should be threatened with military attack, and 79 percent supported the death penalty for terrorists. The growing outrage against terrorism certainly made it easier for the administration to go forward with its preparations for military action against

Qaddafi. "We're a half step behind the newspapers and the congressmen," one relieved administration official commented. "They're asking why we aren't acting, not why we are."[27]

Preparations for military operations against Libya had begun within hours of the Rome and Vienna airport attacks. Late on the evening of 27 December 1985 the Pentagon issued a top-secret warning order to key Navy and Air Force commands in EUCOM. The order, code named "Prime Pump," outlined a long-range strike mission and called for feasibility studies without identifying specific targets. In the early hours of 1 January 1986 Col. Sam Westbrook, commander of the U.S. Air Force's 48th Tactical Fighter Wing (48 TFW) based at Lakenheath, England, and Comdr. Byron Duff, commander of Carrier Air Wing 13, based on the USS *Coral Sea* in the Mediterranean, were ordered by their respective service commanders in Europe—the commander in chief of U.S. Air Forces Europe (USAFE) in Ramstein, West Germany, and the commander in chief, U.S. Naval Forces Europe (CINCUSNAVEUR), in London—to send small strike-planning teams to Ramstein where they would receive further instructions.

After arriving in Ramstein each team was directed to develop plans for raiding two targets in Libya: the Tripoli Military Airfield located south of the Libyan capital, and the Benina Airfield located near Libya's second largest city, Benghazi, four hundred miles to the east. In three days the Air Force and Navy officers were to present their strike plans to U.S. Army Gen. Bernard Rogers, commander in chief, European Command (CINCEUR). David Martin and John Walcott observed that "an air raid against Libya's two main airfields would serve as a mirror-image retaliation for the massacres at the Rome and Vienna airports just four days earlier."[28]

On Saturday morning, 4 January, at CINCEUR headquarters in Stuttgart, West Germany, an Air Force lieutenant colonel, the commander of one of Westbrook's F-111F squadrons, stood before Rogers and his deputy, U.S. Air Force Gen. Richard Lawson, to brief the Air Force strike plan. (To date this officer has not been identified by the Air Force out of concern for his safety and that of his family.) Against each Libyan air base the Air Force planned to send six F-111Fs on a low-level night run that would cross the Libyan coast, circle around behind the airfield, turn outbound and clobber the planes parked on the ramp using dozens of 500-pound bombs. Although the Libyan air defense network was one of the largest in the world, the lieutenant colonel had very low regard for its operational efficiency. He noted that many antiaircraft guns and missile batteries were not even manned at night. To defeat the Libyan defenses he planned to rely on the element of surprise instead of a large support package of airborne jammers and missile-firing SAM-suppression aircraft. In his opinion the presence of a huge attack and support force would tip off the Libyans.[29]

The Navy strike plan contained essentially the same assumptions and elements that were contained in the Air Force plan. In his briefing Commander Duff expressed his disdain for the operational capability of the Libyan air defenses and advocated the use of a small number of attack planes to exploit the element of surprise.[30] Meanwhile, just after the start of the year the Navy had increased its combat readiness in the Mediterranean by transferring on very short notice a detachment of EA-6B Prowlers (electronic countermeasures [ECM] aircraft) from Tactical Electronic Warfare Squadron (VAQ) 135, based at Whidbey Island, Washington, to the *Coral Sea*. The Navy also shipped seventy-five high-speed antiradiation missiles (HARMs), designed for use against enemy radar systems, to the Sixth Fleet.[31]

During the first week of the year an outbreak of "war fever" swept through the American and European media. On New Year's Eve the *NBC Nightly News* stated that the Pentagon was drafting a set of plans to strike terrorist camps in Libya. On New Year's Day the Associated Press reported that the Joint Chiefs of Staff sent Reagan a set of military recommendations for dealing with Middle Eastern terrorism.[32] On 3 January the *Washington Post* reported that "the military contingency planning has looked at the use of F/A-18 bombers on the carrier USS *Coral Sea* . . . F-111 fighter bombers in Britain and B-52 bombers based in the United States."[33] By 5 January television news crews from the American broadcast networks, CNN, the BBC, and British independent television were camped outside the main gate and along a road that ran beside the runway at RAF Lakenheath, the home of 48 TFW. Their presence marked the beginning of a barrage of news stories that detailed various options for a U.S. strike against Libya. With this much reporting, surprise was impossible to maintain and contingency planning became increasingly difficult and complicated. After a week of intense coverage the media concluded that the United States was not about to launch a military strike against Libya. The frenzy over imminent hostilities between the United States and Libya subsided—at least for the time being.[34]

In Washington the administration established an ad hoc targeting committee under the direction of Assistant Secretary of Defense Richard Armitage. Representatives from the NSC, JCS, State Department, and CIA served on the committee. Almost immediately the representatives from the JCS and NSC began sparring over what they considered appropriate Libyan targets. NSC staff members wanted to go right for Libya's jugular by striking key economic targets, particularly facilities serving the oil industry. On the other hand, JCS representatives wanted to limit the choice of targets to those directly related to Qaddafi's support for terrorism and subversion. NSC representatives also advocated the use of Tomahawk cruise missiles and secret F-117 "stealth" fighters to make a dramatic impression on Qaddafi. The Pentagon strenuously rejected the idea, arguing that an attack on Libya was not worth the risk of compromising the sensitive technologies contained in the Tomahawk missile and the stealth fighter. The JCS argued for a conventional air strike carried out by carrier-based attack planes or F-111F fighter-bombers based in England. (The selection of targets and the method of attacking them would not be finalized until the strike on Libya was only a few hours away.)

Over the next three months the Pentagon forwarded 36 probable targets to 48 TFW at Lakenheath and 152 targets to the carrier battle groups operating in the Mediterranean. For the officers directly involved the strike planning was a very strenuous and painstaking task. Since the planners had to know the exact layout and condition of each target, a special courier service was established to keep the Air Force and Navy strike planners supplied with the latest satellite intelligence photos. For each location the satellite photographs had to be studied carefully, Libyan air defenses had to be analyzed and their coverage plotted, the ingress and egress routes had to be selected, the size of the attacking force had to be determined, and the specific weapons load had to be calculated. To compound the demands of the project, all of the work had to be accomplished while maintaining the normal tempo of European theater peacetime operations. "The possibility of going decreased, but the workload didn't," commented Col. Robert E. Venkus, the deputy commander of 48 TFW. He recalled that the JCS frequently contacted 48 TFW in the late afternoon, demanded a strike plan for a new target, and insisted that the plan be completed by the following morning. Sometimes the small circle of Lakenheath planners—less than two dozen people—was unable to meet the assigned deadline. "We had to cry uncle a few times," Venkus remembered.

As Air Force and Navy strike planners went about their duties, they admitted that they could no longer count on the element of surprise due to the intense media scrutiny of the first few weeks of 1986. "It became obvious that strategic surprise was no longer an option," Westbrook recalled. "The chances of our getting down there undetected—the chances of catching the Libyans sitting on their front porches smoking their pipes—were very, very slim." Air Force and Navy staffs had to prepare a plan for each target that included the suppression of enemy air defenses (SEAD). Therefore, in addition to the bombers each attacking force would by necessity include support aircraft to deceive or destroy Libyan air defenses as well as fighters to protect the bombers from Libyan interceptors. While the Air Force could send EF-111 electronic jamming aircraft in company with the U.K.-based F-111Fs, it would have to rely on the Sixth Fleet carriers to provide fighter cover and additional SEAD aircraft. "That presented us at Lakenheath with significant problems," Westbrook said. "We didn't do much with the U.S. Navy. Our focus was on Central Europe." With interservice cooperation a necessity, Air Force and Navy liaison officers shuttled back and forth between 48 TFW and Sixth Fleet carriers, working to become familiar with the opposite service's tactical doctrine and operating procedures.[35]

NSDD 207: The National Program for Combatting Terrorism

In Washington work on Operation Rose went forward. In late January Reagan approved the visit of Lt. Gen. Dale Vesser, the chief planning officer for the JCS, to Cairo to coordinate U.S.-Egyptian planning, but a leak to the *Washington Post* forced Poindexter to postpone the mission for several weeks. In response to the newspaper's queries about the mission the national security adviser convinced the editors of the *Post* of its sensitivity. He argued that publication of an article about the mission would undermine the administration's strategy for dealing with Qaddafi and would prompt the Egyptians to cancel Vesser's visit, inflicting yet another setback for the bold scheme. For their part the editors agreed to bury the item about Vesser's trip inside a 24 January article on the movement of two aircraft carriers near the Libyan coast. The article stated that Reagan ordered "an envoy be sent to Egypt for further discussions about coordinating possible military options." The Egyptians failed to notice the passage about the unnamed envoy, and Operation Rose miraculously survived the leak. When Vesser arrived in Egypt he was authorized by Poindexter to discuss four options with the Egyptians. The first three options were defensive, all meant to come to Egypt's aid in case of a Libyan attack; the fourth was a deliberate Egyptian attack on Libya. Vesser reported to Poindexter that his discussions with the Egyptians had been "very productive."[36] Evidently the NSC was still considering the possibility of offensive action by Egypt against Libya, even though Shultz had effectively quashed this option four months earlier.

On 20 January Reagan approved NSDD 207 to implement the recommendations of Vice President Bush's Task Force on Combatting Terrorism. The top-secret directive, titled "The National Program for Combatting Terrorism," provided a comprehensive statement of U.S. policy on counterterrorism. The directive affirmed that the U.S. government considered "the practice of terrorism by any person or group a threat to . . . national security" and that it would "resist the use of terrorism by all legal means available." According to NSDD 207 the government was "prepared to act in concert with other nations or unilaterally when necessary to prevent or respond to terrorist acts." It declared that countries which practice or support terrorism "will not be allowed to do so without consequence"; it promised that it would make no concessions to terrorists; and it pledged that it would take action "against terrorists without surrendering basic freedoms or endangering democratic principles." The directive attempted to resolve the Shultz-Weinberger disagreement over the use of force in response to a terrorist incident. "Whenever we have evidence that a state is mounting or intends to conduct an act of terrorism against us, we have a responsibility to take measures to protect our citizens, property, and interests," it asserted. The directive also declared that all appropriate assets of the U.S. government must be mobilized in the struggle against terrorism. Moreover, to ensure that the government's response to a terrorist incident was completely integrated and fully supported, it strengthened the organization of both the Terrorist Incident Working Group and the Interdepartmental Group on Terrorism, which were established by NSDD 30 in 1982.[37] Finally, a secret annex provided for centralized operational authority in the event of a terrorist incident by creating the Operations Sub-Group (OSG), a small interagency group, which operated from the White House and had the power to direct the actions of other government agencies.[38]

On 6 March Bush released the *Public Report of the Vice President's Task Force on Combatting Terrorism,* the unclassified version of NSDD 207. "We should reiterate the willingness of our administration to retaliate and retaliate swiftly when we feel we can punish those who were directly responsible," Bush informed the press.[39] Listening to Bush it seemed as though the administration had finally resolved the issue of using military force to preempt or retaliate against a terrorist attack, but the report addressed the question of military action gingerly. It pointed out that "counterterrorism missions are high-risk/high-gain operations" and that American "principles of justice will not permit random retaliation against groups or countries." Nevertheless, it mentioned that "a successful deterrent strategy may require judicious employment of military force to resolve an incident."[40] Bush acknowledged that "there isn't any simple answer" to the matter of using force. "We haven't been able to solve that problem," he stated, "and I wish we could have."[41]

In the weeks following Reagan's announcement of economic sanctions, tension between Libya and the United States steadily increased. On 13 January two Libyan MiG-25 Foxbats intercepted a U.S. Navy EA-3B Skywarrior electronic warfare plane that was operating 150 miles north of Tripoli. The *Coral Sea* launched alert F/A-18 Hornets to rescue the EA-3B, but the effort would have been in vain if the Libyans had intended to shoot down the lumbering, defenseless aircraft. Later that month the Libyans finished construction of an SA-5 Gammon surface-to-air (SAM) battery (that consisted of twelve launchers) at Surt on the south shore of the Gulf of Sidra. The Soviet-made SA-5s, each of which was fifty-four feet long, weighed eleven tons, and had an estimated range of 150 miles, could challenge U.S. aircraft operating in the Gulf of Sidra and portions of the Tripoli FIR. Although too slow to hit fighters and other high-performance aircraft, the SA-5 could threaten larger aircraft such as AWACS planes, RC-135 electronic surveillance aircraft, and P-3 antisubmarine warfare planes. Finally, the Soviets transferred the flagship of their Mediterranean fleet, a large submarine tender outfitted with intelligence-gathering equipment, to the harbor at Tripoli where it could provide the Libyan government with information on the movement of the Sixth Fleet.[42]

When Abu Nidal's terrorists attacked the Rome and Vienna airports, the *Coral Sea* was the only carrier stationed in the Mediterranean, a situation that helped Weinberger argue successfully against an immediate retaliatory attack. With tensions rising between the United States and Libya he wanted the Sixth Fleet to have more than enough firepower to deal with Qaddafi's military. In early January Weinberger ordered a second carrier battle group into the Mediterranean and directed a third carrier battle group to deploy from the United States as soon as it was ready.[43] The *Saratoga* and her escorts, which spent Christmas in Singapore, departed the island base of Diego Garcia in the Indian Ocean and performed a high-speed transit to the Mediterranean via the Suez Canal. On 15 January the *Saratoga* CVBG, commanded by Rear Adm. David E. Jeremiah, rendezvoused with the *Coral Sea* CVBG, commanded by Rear Adm. Jerry C. Breast.[44] Jeremiah, a surface warfare officer, was commander of Cruiser Destroyer Group Eight, while Breast, an attack aviator and test pilot, was commander of Carrier Group Two.

The two battle groups comprised a large Task Force 60 under Jeremiah's command. He would conduct a series of operations named "Attain Document" but popularly known in the Sixth Fleet as "Operations in the Vicinity of

Libya" or OVL (pronounced "oval") for short. The Attain Document series would reaffirm the right of the United States to operate ships and aircraft freely in the international waters and airspace of the Tripoli FIR and the Gulf of Sidra and would serve as a powerful demonstration of American resolve in the struggle against international terrorism. Subsequent operations would be bolder and more complex and would culminate in a major FON operation carried out after the arrival of the third aircraft carrier, USS *America* (CV 66). In accordance with Weinberger's order, *America,* her air wing, and her escorts deployed from their homeports and bases on the East Coast on 10 March, ten days ahead of schedule.

The Attain Document series was carefully crafted to satisfy both the "hawks" and the "doves" within the Reagan administration. The former hoped to provoke a military confrontation with Libya by probing increasingly deeper into the Gulf of Sidra and eliciting an armed response from Qaddafi, thus giving the Sixth Fleet the pretext to clobber his armed forces. The latter, on the other hand, considered the maneuvers a FON exercise and insisted that the fleet was being sent into the disputed waters slowly and incrementally, thus giving Qaddafi plenty of time to contemplate each of his moves. The plans for Attain Document were developed by Vice Adm. Frank B. Kelso II, commander of the U.S. Sixth Fleet, who emphasized that the primary purpose of each phase of the operation was "to show we could operate in international waters and not be blackmailed by Qaddafi into thinking the Gulf of Sidra is his lake."[45]

The immediate objective of both Attain Document I and Attain Document II was to operate ships and aircraft in the Tripoli FIR. No surface or air operations were scheduled for the area south of 32° 30' north latitude. Jeremiah planned to establish between Libya and the task force a barrier of fourteen CAP stations, three of which would be filled around the clock. During the day pairs of fighters would fill the CAP stations; at night a single fighter would perform the duty. The fighter squadrons on the *Saratoga* flew F-14s; the Navy strike fighter and the Marine fighter-attack squadrons on the *Coral Sea* flew F/A-18s. The fighters were armed with Sidewinder heat-seeking air-to-air missiles, Sparrow semi-active homing air-to-air missiles, and 20mm guns. As the Attain Document series unfolded, a few F-14s were equipped with long-range active homing Phoenix air-to-air missiles. These Tomcat crews craved the opportunity to fire a Phoenix at extreme range against some hapless Libyan fighter. In addition to fighters the air wings operated E-2Cs for long-range airborne surveillance and fighter control; EA-6Bs for electronic countermeasures (ECM); and A-6E Intruders, A-7E Corsair IIs, and F/A-18s for SUCAP against

Libyan surface vessels. Depending on the model, the SUCAP aircraft were armed with a variety of antisurface ordnance including Harpoon antiship cruise missiles, Rockeye cluster bombs, and HARMs. The SUCAP Hornets were also armed with air-to-air weapons, permitting them to back up the CAP aircraft. KA-6D tankers refueled the fighters during mid-cycle to maximize their on-station time and to provide them with an adequate amount of fuel if they were forced into combat. SUCAP planes flew a normal cycle without refueling. Each carrier planned to conduct approximately thirteen hours of flight operations each day and maintain an alert status when not operating aircraft.[46] Lt. Comdr. Robert E. Stumpf, an F/A-18 pilot serving in VFA-132 based on the *Coral Sea*, described first-hand the rigors of maintaining CAP twenty-four hours per day:

> A barrier CAP . . . demanded on-station relief of CAP, no small task when stations were often more than 150 nautical miles from the ship. The *Coral Sea* launched her fighters first on a normal cycle. They would buster ("buster" is the command given to carrier pilots to proceed at best possible speed) to station to relieve the off-going CAP, who would buster back to make the last part of the carrier's recovery cycle. This 300-plus-mile transition often took forty minutes or more during which the ship steamed into the wind, which delayed the respot for the next launch and thus decreased time allotted for aircraft refueling and maintenance. This created an extremely demanding environment on the flight deck—both for men and machines.[47]

On 24 January, a few days after the Pentagon announced that the Sixth Fleet planned to conduct air and naval maneuvers in the Tripoli FIR, Qaddafi placed his armed forces on "total alert" and informed the journalists who were visiting him in his tent inside Tripoli's Bab al-Aziziyah Barracks compound that the U.S. exercises prove "that America is practicing state-organized terrorism against a small, stable and peaceful country like Libya and is threatening the peace in the Mediterranean."[48] The next day Qaddafi boarded the missile patrol boat *Waheed* in the port of Misratah, 125 miles east of Tripoli. He proclaimed that he was sailing to Benghazi on the eastern shore of the Gulf of Sidra to demonstrate that the entire body of water belonged to Libya. Sporting a tailored jump suit, sunglasses, and an admiral's hat, the Libyan leader held a shipboard news conference for about two-dozen reporters who were brought to Misratah by the Libyan government just for the occasion.[49] "Libya cannot be patient forever to live under America's international terrorism," Qaddafi exhorted. "I am going out to the parallel 32.5, which is the line of death, where we will stand and fight with our backs against the wall. . . . The

Gulf of Sidra is part and parcel of Libyan territory. . . . We call on the international community to prevent the United States [from] carrying out military maneuvers inside Libya's economic zone."[50] After the press conference the *Waheed,* with Qaddafi embarked, left port accompanied by another patrol boat and headed for Benghazi, nearly three hundred miles to the east. The small flotilla soon returned to port because of rough seas.[51]

The ROE for Operations Attain Document I and Attain Document II were identical to those used in 1981, but Kelso went a step further and granted to Jeremiah (the on-scene commander) the authority to designate Libyan forces as hostile if they exhibited the imminent use of force or a continuing threat to use force and to order an armed response to defend the battle force.[52] If tactical circumstances warranted a vigorous reaction, the commanders, airmen, and surface operators of Task Force 60 could exercise self-defense without consulting higher authority, as they had done in 1981.

Prior to the start of Attain Document I in late January, Kelso, the former skipper of two nuclear-powered attack submarines, visited the battle force and met with the airmen of CVW-17 on the *Saratoga* and those of CVW-13 on the *Coral Sea.* He discussed the objective of the operation and the ROE and cautioned them to exercise sound judgment and to act with restraint if they encountered LAAF aircraft. Libyan pilots had a long history of acting unpredictably and what might appear to be a routine intercept could turn deadly. "Do the job professionally, and be ready to defend yourself and your ship—but only within the guidelines of the rules of engagement," Kelso advised. "Admiral Kelso's visit built an atmosphere of intense anticipation in the ready room," Stumpf recalled. "Pilots continued to study tactics, equipment recognition features, and capabilities of the Libyan Arab Air Force and Navy." Kelso's aviators had a very healthy respect for Qaddafi's armed forces, since the Libyans possessed a huge arsenal of modern Soviet and French weaponry and were assisted by hundreds of foreign technical advisers. Of utmost concern to both air wings was the large inventory of sophisticated fighters in the LAAF and Libya's extensive air defense network.[53]

Operation Attain Document I

After a month of rising tensions and several days of demanding workups, Jeremiah commenced Operation Attain Document I on 26 January. That morning two Libyan MiG-25 Foxbats, armed with AA-6 Acrid air-to-air missiles, entered the Tripoli FIR and headed toward a CAP station filled by a pair of F/A-18s from the *Coral Sea*. Under the control of an E-2C and mindful of the all-aspect firing capability of the AA-6, the Hornets executed a stern intercept and took up firing positions on the rear hemispheres of the MiGs. The Libyans showed little reaction to the intercept and only slightly maneuvered during the encounter. After being tailed by the Americans for about ten minutes the Fox-bats broke off and returned to their base.[54]

Over the next four days Task Force 60 fighter crews carried out eight intercepts on a variety of LAAF aircraft: MiG-25 Foxbats, MiG-23 Floggers, Su-22 Fitters, Mirage-Vs, and Mirage F-1s. The Libyan planes were usually armed with at least two radar-guided or heat-seeking air-to-air missiles, but the LAAF pilots never engaged in all-out air combat maneuvering, and none achieved a firing position on a U.S. fighter. Breast commented that "our initial impressions were that the LAAF had poor flight discipline, poor look-around doctrine, maneuvered sluggishly, and were not aggressive."[55] Nevertheless, the American fighter crews were constantly aware that the Libyans were very unpredictable and realized that a hostile reaction from the Libyan military was always a possibility. Although most of the aviators spent the four-day exercise without gaining even so much as a radar contact, they never relaxed their vigilance and took full advantage of every flying hour. "U.S. pilots flew CAP missions as though their lives depended on it," Stumpf remarked. "They practiced non-tactical aspects of maintaining the barrier—such as relieving on station, data link coordination with the E-2C radar control aircraft, and tanking—until they became routine."[56]

Jeremiah concluded Attain Document I on 30 January, and Task Force 60 withdrew north of the Tripoli FIR. The ships and aircraft of Battle Force Sixth Fleet would return to waters near Libya in less than two weeks for the next phase of Attain Document.

Operation Attain Document II

While the level of Libyan air activity during Attain Document I had been low, the tempo during Attain Document II, which began on 12 February, afforded nearly every carrier-based fighter pilot the opportunity to intercept a Libyan aircraft. Duff commented that the Libyans "came out with anything and everything."[57] During Attain Document II the Libyans exhibited more aggressive maneuvering, more advanced intercept tactics, and more effective ground control vectoring, but none of their aircraft ever achieved an offensive firing position against an American fighter. In the official report, "Lessons Learned from

Operations in the Vicinity of Libya," Navy officials attempted to explain the change in Libyan demeanor: "This aggressive Libyan response may have been due to emphasis from Soviet advisers to demonstrate existing capabilities. Also, the Libyans may have perceived a hostile intent during [Attain Document] I, but felt more confident after [U.S. Navy] forces withdrew without challenging their claim to the Gulf of Sidra."[58]

The powerful radar of the E-2C detected Libyan aircraft as soon as they were airborne. The Hawkeye's air controllers then vectored F-14s and F/A-18s toward the Libyan planes. With this advantage the U.S. fighters were able to achieve firing positions on the rear hemisphere of their opponents on practically every intercept.

During the four-day operation American aviators performed 140 intercepts. "When the opposing sections closed to within ten miles," Stumpf noted, "the U.S. pilots could often maneuver at will to arrive at a firing position behind the MiGs." GCI radar operators provided LAAF pilots with accurate vectors to the American CAP stations, but the Libyans were totally outmatched once the intercept phase began.[59] "It was incredible how poor they were at what they were trying to do," commented Comdr. Robert Brodsky, commander of CVW-17 based on the *Saratoga*. "These guys were grapes."

A typical F-14 intercept took place as follows: A section of Tomcats would patrol at twenty thousand feet, and from that altitude they could detect LAAF aircraft on radar out to one hundred miles. The F-14s would descend to ten thousand feet and slip unnoticed into an offensive position several miles behind the Libyan fighters. While the Americans watched their opponents on television from a distance of fifteen miles, the unsuspecting Libyans continued to search the skies with their naked eyes.[60]

Some Libyan pilots attempted to lure Navy fighter crews south of 32° 30' by flying a leisurely pattern that gradually moved southward, but the disciplined Navy and Marine Corps fighter pilots always broke off and returned to station before crossing "the line of death." Conversely, the Americans almost always tried to draw the Libyan fighters northward in order to conserve fuel and gain the advantage of being closer to the layered defense of the battle group. Only once during Attain Document II did Libyan aircraft approach one of the carriers. A flight of several MiG-25s passed over the *Coral Sea* but, with F/A-18s closely escorting them, the Libyans wisely elected not to make any threatening moves.[61]

LAAF aviators exhibited an assortment of behaviors during Attain Document II. Some pilots waved at American fighter crews during close-up photo opportunities, while others, according to Stumpf, "appeared to slide down in the cockpit, as though they could keep from being shot by not exposing their upper torso through the canopy." He noted that a few LAAF aviators "made vain attempts to shake the Hornets or Tomcats off their tails. Hard oblique weaves, supersonic accelerations, and decelerations to very slow airspeeds were typical maneuvers, tried mostly by the Flogger pilots."[62] On several occasions Libyan pilots used Soviet tactics in an attempt to lure American fighters into a firing position for their wingmen, but these tactics never succeeded.[63] One Tomcat pilot serving in VF-103, based on the *Saratoga,* noted that the "Libyan aircraft seemed to just 'go home' rather than attempt to disengage via high speed 'bug out' maneuvers."[64]

Libyan fighter pilots rarely flew after dark. If they did they usually operated within sight of their lighted air bases. Soviet-made IL-76 Candid transports were the only LAAF aircraft that operated over water at night. The Libyans kept one Candid airborne throughout Attain Document II, flying an east-west pattern in the northern portion of the Tripoli FIR. A-7Es or F/A-18s escorted the IL-76, while it reconnoitered the American fleet.

During Attain Document II Tomcat and Hornet crews practiced a number of advanced tactical maneuvers. Newly arriving CAP aircraft often relieved on-station fighters, while the latter performed an intercept or escorted a Libyan fighter. Alert CAP was frequently pressed into service during periods of heavy air activity to shore up the CAP defensive barrier. "Taking a vector off the catapult," Stumpf recalled, "alert pilots often found themselves intercepting inbound MiGs quite soon after launch, while still completing combat checks and coordinating with the E-2C. In this multiple target arena, correlation between E-2C contacts and on-board radar contacts was essential to ensure that the object of the intercept was truly an adversary and not another U.S. Navy fighter."[65]

Having conducted flight operations above 32° 30' north latitude unchallenged for four days, Jeremiah ended Attain Document II as planned. On 15 February the ships of Task Force 60 departed the Tripoli FIR and proceeded to Mediterranean liberty ports or other assignments.

During the first two phases of Attain Document, American pilots and surface operators acquired a wealth of practical experience and intelligence officers gathered valuable information on LAAF operations and capabilities. "The greatest satisfaction for the U.S. Navy fighter pilots, other than completely dominating the Libyans, was the exposure to genuine Soviet hardware—equipment they had scrutinized for years," Stumpf remarked.[66] Qaddafi had been challenged forcefully but not provocatively. Unfortunately, the demonstrations of naval force had not elicited a change in Qaddafi's behavior regarding terrorism.

Attain Document III, which was scheduled for late March, would significantly increase the pressure on the Libyan strongman. A third carrier battle group was en route, and the Sixth Fleet was preparing for major surface and air operations south of 32° 30'.

Preparing for Operation Attain Document III

The objective of Attain Document III, scheduled for 23–29 March, was to conduct a large-scale FON exercise south of 32° 30' that would discredit Qaddafi's claim over international waters and airspace and demonstrate America's resolve in the struggle against international terrorism. White House and Pentagon officials understood that an excellent chance existed that the bold operation might precipitate a military confrontation with Libya, thus giving Reagan an opportunity to take military action against Qaddafi. As the planning for Attain Document III progressed, Kelso became extremely concerned for the safety of Task Force 60. He believed strongly that once his ships and aircraft crossed the "the line of death" the Libyans would counter with military force. Consequently, he submitted a request to the National Command Authority—the president and the secretary of defense—via CINCEUR and the JCS, for a set of supplemental ROE that would give him the authority to conduct preemptive defense of the battle force following the first Libyan hostile act.

Crowe believed that an armed confrontation between the United States and Libya was highly likely and directed his staff to develop a new set of rules, which eventually became known as the Peacetime Rules of Engagement for U.S. Forces (PROE). The new ROE authorized on-scene commanders to respond to hostile threats more forcefully and with less provocation. "Requiring our units to wait until they were actually fired on put American lives at risk," Crowe wrote in his memoirs, *The Line of Fire*. "I wanted them to be able to defend themselves as soon as a threat was apparent."[67] W. Hays Parks elaborated on the purpose of the PROE: "The intent remains to permit the commander responsible maximum flexibility to respond to threats with appropriate options, to limit the scope and intensity of any armed confrontation, and to discourage escalation, while terminating hostilities quickly and decisively and on terms favorable to the United States. The PROE further provides that any responses must be proportionate to the threat."

Kelso's request was endorsed by his seniors in the chain of command and forwarded to Reagan, who signed an NSDD authorizing Kelso to use the draft

PROE during the upcoming exercise. Although Weinberger sanctioned use of the new rules, he did not approve their permanent adoption until 26 June 1986.[68]

It is worth pointing out the major difference between the ROE of 1981 and the PROE of 1986. In the past, Brodsky explained, "you could retaliate only against the particular party which committed the hostile act. For the March exercise, the rules changed. If one [Libyan] fires, then anybody else who has hostile intent is to be fired upon. Hostile intent is defined as being in a position to fire."[69] Therefore, if any unit of the Libyan armed forces committed a hostile act toward the battle force, Kelso planned to issue the code word "table top." If announced, the code word would declare all Libyan ships, planes, or missile sites in position to strike an element of the Sixth Fleet as hostile and open to attack.[70] As Kelso asserted, "We went at it with the idea that if one American was shot at, we weren't going to wait around for number two to be shot at."[71]

In mid-March plans for Attain Document III were finalized under the direction of National Security Adviser Poindexter. Admiral Poindexter, a nuclear-trained surface warfare officer who had served on the NSC staff since 1981, effectively guided the national security bureaucracy through all phases of this latest confrontation with Libya, from the earliest contingency planning to the drafting of the execute order for Attain Document III. He made sure the White House remained in the forefront of operational planning, thus ensuring that Reagan's goal of responding with military force against Libyan aggression was translated into action.

On 14 March at an NSPG meeting devoted to Libya, Reagan approved the outline of Operation Attain Document III and signed the NSDD authorizing the use of the new Peacetime Rules of Engagement. NOTAMs covering the period 23 March–1 April were issued on 21 March.[72] Attain Document III contained a contingency operation, code named "Prairie Fire," which delineated a set of graduated responses to varying levels of Libyan aggression. At previous NSPG meetings Shultz had argued for swift attacks on several Libyan targets ranging from terrorist facilities to industrial sites. Weinberger, on the other hand, had insisted that the fleet exercise restraint during the operation and, if attacked, respond proportionately. Poindexter effectively managed the disagreement between the two secretaries by ensuring that each man had an opportunity to express his views on the use of force in private meetings with Reagan. Poindexter would sit in on the meetings, guaranteeing that he knew exactly what Shultz or Weinberger had told the president.[73] As the planning for Attain Document III progressed, Poindexter bridged the views of Shultz and Weinberger using the familiar military concept of "proportional response."[74]

Under the first stage of Prairie Fire, in response to a Libyan hostile act Kelso "would put Task Force 60 on a full wartime footing, free all weapons for task force defense, and permit proportionate preemptive and retaliatory surface and air strikes against Libyan ships, planes, and shore facilities."[75] Second, if Libyan action caused American casualties Reagan would authorize a strike against military and terrorist-related targets. Finally, in response to an all-out Libyan attack Reagan would order a strike on important industrial sites, including oil pipelines and pumping stations. The third stage would disrupt the Libyan economy and deliver a devastating blow to the Qaddafi regime. Under the guidelines of Prairie Fire, Kelso had the authority to respond to each Libyan military act in kind, but retaliation beyond self-defense would require White House approval. For the duration of Attain Document III, F-111Fs stationed at Lakenheath would be on alert, just in case.[76]

The naval maneuvers set for Attain Document III were anything but ordinary, since it was highly probable that they would elicit a bellicose response from Qaddafi. Kelso planned to operate ships below 32° 30' and fly aircraft right up to the twelve-mile limit. By keeping the pressure on Qaddafi, Reagan hoped the Libyan dictator would commit a hostile act. "Of course we're aching for a go at Qaddafi," a Pentagon official admitted.[77] A number of officials, including Secretary of the Navy Lehman and Kelso, expected Qaddafi to order his air force to attack the Sixth Fleet. It was presumed that the subsequent turkey shoot would deal a fatal blow to Qaddafi's stature as a leader and his prestige in the Arab world.[78]

Poindexter and Donald Fortier, now deputy national security adviser, believed that if the Sixth Fleet walloped the Libyan military, Qaddafi's officers would conclude that the humiliating defeat had been brought about by Qaddafi's irrational foreign policy and his support for terrorism and they might be prompted to topple his regime. Casey, on the other hand, had reservations about the value of military operations aimed at Qaddafi, believing that any military action would strengthen the Libyan leader's domestic authority, build sympathy with his fellow Arabs, and buttress his assertion that the United States was the world's leading imperialist state. Furthermore, since the Libyan exiles were not measuring up to Casey's expectations, he was ready to approach Reagan with a new intelligence finding that would permit the CIA to act directly against Qaddafi, not in concert with or through dissident exiles. Casey, however, kept his concerns to himself when he observed the White House staff's obsession with the preparations for Attain Document III.[79]

In early March Weinberger and Crowe met in Wurzburg, West Germany, with their two top generals in Europe, Rogers and Lawson. The purpose of the meeting was to review the plans for Attain Document III and, more important, to discuss the PROE that Kelso planned to employ in the Gulf of Sidra. Weinberger and Crowe were adamant that every official in the chain of command as well as the commanders on the scene understand that the ROE had undergone a substantial change and that the rules meant exactly what they said. "You just don't put [the PROE] in a message and say that takes care of it," Crowe reflected. "It's hard to persuade guys [who] for fifteen years now have been told 'Don't get us in a war,' that you're serious that if the guy challenges us, we're going to shoot him. . . . You have to persuade people the mood has changed, that the situation is now different."[80]

Kelso did not attend the meeting in Wurzburg, so he traveled to London to discuss with Weinberger Attain Document III and the PROE. The secretary made it clear to Kelso that he had the authority to attack any Libyan aircraft, vessel, or shore site that threatened the Sixth Fleet once the Libyans fired the first shot. On the other hand, if hostilities were to break out Weinberger did not want the situation to escalate. He directed Kelso to keep his fleet's response appropriate and proportional to each Libyan attack or provocation, and he urged the admiral to minimize the destruction of Libyan forces by using "smart" weapons as much as possible.[81] "I want you to know," Weinberger told Kelso, "that I will back and support you to the full in action *you* feel you have to take."[82] Lehman and Crowe also traveled to Europe to meet with Kelso and discuss the upcoming operation and the new ROE.[83]

On 19 March, the *America* CVBG, commanded by Rear Adm. Henry H. Mauz Jr., a surface warfare officer and commander of Cruiser Destroyer Group Twelve, passed through the straits of Gibraltar and joined Task Force 60.[84] The three-CVBG task force now comprised twenty-six combatant vessels, 250 aircraft, and twenty-seven thousand officers, sailors, and Marines.

Kelso visited each carrier and reviewed the goals of the operation and the revised ROE with air wing personnel and each warfare-area commander.[85] Underscoring the likelihood of Libyan hostilities, he emphasized the following points: "There can be no doubt that the risk to our forces has . . . increased. When in range of Libyan forces every unit must be at high state of alert and prepared to defend itself. . . . Every unit commanding officer [and] pilot . . . [must] clearly understand he has the right to defend himself and . . . will be prepared to do so."[86]

Jeremiah compiled a set of code words that covered several contingencies and would enable the entire battle force to switch simultaneously to different categories of ROE as the situation dictated. "We knew exactly what to do," stated the task force commander.[87]

By 22 March the three CVBGs of Task Force 60—designated Battle Force Zulu for the operation—were on station in the Tripoli FIR and ready to commence Operation Attain Document III. Jeremiah placed the *America, Coral Sea,* and *Saratoga* in an east-west line approximately 150 miles north of the "line of death." A flotilla of escorts, including the Aegis cruiser *Yorktown* (CG 48), three other guided missile cruisers, three guided missile destroyers, one destroyer, three guided missile frigates, and nine frigates screened the three carriers. Jeremiah assigned each of the carriers and escorts an operating sector as defined by a grid superimposed over the central Mediterranean. The tactical disposition was known as the 4W—pronounced "four whiskey"—grid. A surface action group (SAG), comprised of the Aegis cruiser *Ticonderoga* (CG 47), guided missile destroyer *Scott* (DDG 995), and destroyer *Caron* (DD 970), was poised to operate south of 32° 30'. The SAG was commanded by Capt. Robert L. Goodwin Jr., commodore of Destroyer Squadron Twenty, who embarked in the *Caron.* The two Aegis cruisers with their sophisticated AN/SPY-1 multipurpose phased array radars significantly enhanced the command and control and the air and surface surveillance capabilities of the battle force. The SPY-1 radars continuously searched the skies in all directions to a distance of over 200 miles.

Each carrier was prepared to conduct flight operations for roughly sixteen hours per day. The *America* was to cover the period from noon to 0345, local time; the *Saratoga* from 2015 to noon. The *Coral Sea,* which flew F/A-18 Hornets in both fighter and strike roles, was to operate its air wing from 0345 to 2015, providing dual-CVW coverage when Libyan air and naval activity was expected to be heaviest. With two air wings the battle force could keep continuously airborne twelve CAP aircraft, eight SUCAP planes, four S-3A ASW aircraft, two E-2Cs, two EA-6Bs, and two SH-3s.[88]

Breast noted the unique versatility of the Hornets based on his flagship. "We had found that spotting 22 F/A-18s on [*Coral Sea's*] flight deck meant that we could count on 22 being available continuously," he stated. "The quick deck launch capability of the Hornet and the ability to hang a recoverable strike/fighter armament load meant that those 22 F/A-18s could be catapulted as STRIKE/CAP to fill either attack (SUCAP) or fighter (CAP) roles."[89]

Fighter aircraft would fill fourteen CAP stations in the Tripoli FIR and two in the northern portion of the Gulf of Sidra. SUCAP would be in position to respond immediately to any Libyan surface threat. A dedicated E-2C would coordinate the surface picture during daylight hours, and SH-60B Seahawk Light Airborne Multipurpose System (LAMPS) MK III helicopters, based on the guided missile frigates *Halyburton* (FFG 40) and *Dewert* (FFG 45), would fly an east-west pattern north of 32° 30' and provide continuous radar coverage of the Gulf of Sidra.[90]

For the operation Kelso elected to go to sea in his flagship *Coronado* (AGF 11). Jeremiah would exercise tactical command from the *Saratoga*. Breast and Mauz embarked in the *Coral Sea* and the *Yorktown*, respectively. In a brief message to the battle force Jeremiah exhorted all personnel to "be prepared for sustained combat operations. . . . Take all steps necessary within individual unit capacity to ensure max readiness including damage control measures. . . . The fat lady is practicing her scales; it's time to get out the song books and get on with it."[91]

Jeremiah commenced Operation Attain Document III at 0100 local time on 23 March. Throughout most of the first day the air wings operated north of 32° 30'. At 2015 aircraft from the *Saratoga* and the *America* crossed the "line of death," and Tomcats occupied the two CAP stations in the gulf. The Square Pair fire-control radar of the SA-5 Gammon missile battery at Surt locked on to Navy aircraft that came within range. All radar and electronic warfare operators in the battle force were intently watching their scopes for the first indication of a missile launch from the battery. It was reported that the Libyan missile operators worked under the supervision of Soviet technicians.[92]

At 1200 on 24 March, the SAG crossed the line of death under the protective umbrella of CAP and SUCAP. At 1352 the Square Pair radar locked on to a pair of *America*-based VF-102 Tomcats patrolling at CAP station one, the station closest to Surt. The CAP station was about sixty miles off the coast and about eighty miles from the missile site. Suddenly the Libyans fired two Gammons at the "Fighting Diamondbacks." The F-14s, which were warned of the activation of the Square Pair radar by the Hawkeyes, avoided the lumbering missiles by diving to the surface. While EA-6B Prowlers jammed the fire control radar, the SA-5s continued their long-range, high-altitude flight before crashing harmlessly into the sea. Immediately after launch the *Ticonderoga* and the *Yorktown* detected the missiles with their SPY-1 radars, they tracked their trajectories, and they recorded the flight data for later analysis.[93]

American intelligence analysts believed the SA-5 battery at Surt operated under Qaddafi's direct authority. Therefore, firing the Gammons was a very deliberate action on Libya's part. "The decision to engage us was a national command decision as opposed to a pilot who might accidentally have reacted," Jeremiah noted. "The SA-5 site fired for the whole nation of Libya," Brodsky remarked.[94] Stumpf recalled that the mood of the fleet's aviators changed dramatically following the SAM launches. "Any previous jocularity was replaced by firm resolve to respond violently to the Libyan action," he stated. "During this period of hostilities, they knew that any Libyan target encountered would be fair game. Having recently seen so many targets centered in their gun sight, a trigger squeeze was all that separated a fighter pilot from a MiG-killer."[95]

A few hours later two MiG-25s approached the exercise area but were quickly intercepted by a pair of F-14s from VF-74 based on the *Saratoga*. The MiGs soon disengaged and returned to their base. This was the only reported intercept of LAAF aircraft during Attain Document III. The MiG pilots were extremely lucky that Kelso had not yet declared all Libyan forces hostile. Qaddafi's air force, which probably realized that any act perceived as hostile would prove fatal, restricted its sorties to the vicinity of their airfields for the remainder of the operation.[96] Breast speculated that the LAAF refrained from over water flights "to avoid the implication that they were either forced down or shot down."[97]

By firing SA-5s at the F-14s the Libyans ostensibly committed a deliberate hostile act, but Kelso refrained from activating the first phase of Operation Prairie Fire until he was absolutely sure that the launching of the SA-5s had been deliberate, not an accident. When he received confirmation that the Square Pair radar had indeed locked on to the Tomcats, he knew the missile firing was no accident. Accordingly, at 1538 he sent a flash precedence message to the fleet, executing table top and authorizing the fleet "to engage Libyan units closing the force in international waters and airspace."[98] Although Kelso had the authority to attack the Surt missile battery, he elected to wait until nightfall before ordering a retaliatory strike.[99] His carefully calculated response, however, did not satisfy the hawks at the NSC who were monitoring the action in the White House Situation Room and did not understand why the Sixth Fleet had not attacked the SA-5 site. After all, Qaddafi had committed the very miscalculation for which they had long waited. At EUCOM headquarters in Stuttgart Lawson received several anxious phone calls from Washington, demanding to know why Kelso had not attacked the missile battery or demanding to know when Kelso was going to do something. "Everybody is raising Cain with me, because the pilots didn't shoot at the SAMs," Lawson recounted. "The pressure to fire was clearly there," Kelso acknowledged, "but I didn't want to do it until we could do it safely."

Kelso and Jeremiah carefully planned their next move. They did not like the idea of a daylight strike on Surt. The SAM site was located on the southern coast of the Gulf of Sidra, and Libyan aircraft approaching from the east and west could flank an attacking force. Furthermore, if the Libyans were expecting an immediate retaliatory raid they would be primed and ready for action. The admirals decided to take their time and do it right. They were not going to be pressured into repeating the same mistakes of the ill-fated daylight raid on Syrian antiaircraft batteries in Lebanon on 4 December 1983. That poorly executed mission resulted in the needless death of one aviator and the capture of another, as well as the loss of two carrier-based aircraft and damage to a third. "It was getting dark," Kelso recalled. "I liked the game plan at night. We operate very well at night. They don't."[100]

At 1600 Kelso received an intriguing message, sent via commercial teletype, from the commander in chief of the Libyan Arab Air Force which read: "Unless the aggressive acts are stopped against [the] Jamahiriyya we are bound to destroy the CV carriers/Stop/In doing that [we] will have the political and military support of the world states/Stop/Maintain in peace you will leave in peace/Stop/Best regards."[101] Shortly after receiving the curious telegram Kelso gave Jeremiah the go-ahead to destroy the radars at Surt. At 1830 the battle force commander ordered a pair of A-7Es to attack the site using HARMs. At 1844, as the planes approached the target, the Libyans fired one, possibly two, SA-5s at the lead Corsair. With the element of surprise lost, Jeremiah canceled the attack and ordered all aircraft to proceed immediately north of 32° 30'. About ten minutes later the battery launched an SA-2 Guideline—the famed "flying telephone pole" of the Vietnam War. At 1914 another SA-5 rocketed out of Surt. The SAMs were foiled by the deft maneuvering of American pilots and effective ECM. JANA, on the other hand, reported to the home front that Libyan missiles had shot down three U.S. planes.[102] Before Jeremiah could order another attack on the radar site he had to neutralize a more menacing threat.

Shortly after 2000 the *Ticonderoga* and an E-2C detected the *Waheed*, a French-built *La Combattante II-G*–class fast missile attack craft. The missile boat was tracking east-southeast at twenty-four knots from the port of Misratah and heading right for the SAG. The 161-foot, 311-ton *Waheed* was a potent threat to the ships of Task Force 60 because she carried four Italian-made Ottomat antiship cruise missiles. The Ottomat had an effective range of nearly forty miles and was armed with a 460-pound warhead.[103] Like many other officers watching the situation unfold on radar, Breast recognized immediately that the first priority for the battle force was the destruction of the Libyan missile boat. "My focus was, let's get those bastards before it gets dark," Breast declared. After all, the missile patrol boat might get lucky and sink one of the ships of the battle force.[104]

A few minutes later two sections of SUCAP steered toward the Libyan missile boat, which was now within striking range of the ships of the SAG. Two A-6Es of Attack Squadron (VA) 34, the "Blue Blasters" based on the *America,* were armed with AGM-84A Harpoon antisurface cruise missiles. The other A-6Es, a pair of VA-85 "Black Falcons," based on the *Saratoga,* carried Mark 20 Rockeye cluster bombs, each containing 247 small but destructive armor-piercing bomblets.[105] The pilot of one of the Harpoon-armed A-6Es radioed the *Saratoga* to verify that he did in fact have permission to fire. The flagship responded instantly: "The admiral says, 'Smoke 'em.'"[106]

Once they were cleared to fire, the four Intruders set up an attack. At 2017 each Blue Blaster fired a single Harpoon from a range of sixteen miles—well outside the *Waheed*'s SAM envelope. The missiles skimmed the surface of the Gulf of Sidra at about 650 miles per hour and zeroed in on the Libyan patrol boat. The 13-foot, 1,160-pound active-homing cruise missiles plowed into the superstructure of the *Waheed,* and the 500-pound warheads exploded a fraction of a second later, reducing the Libyan vessel to a shattered, burning hulk. The Black Falcons finished it off with a devastating Rockeye attack. The *Waheed* sank immediately along with most of her crew, becoming the first victim of a Harpoon missile fired in anger. The next day the Spanish oil tanker SS *Castillo de Ricote* rescued sixteen survivors.[107]

Shortly before 2100 the operators at Surt reactivated the Square Pair radar. This time, however, a quartet of A-7Es—two VA-81 "Sunliners" and two VA-83 "Rampagers" based on the *Saratoga*—was ready to put it out of service. A pair of Sunliners, led by Brodsky, approached Surt at high altitude and in clear view of the Square Pair radar. They served as decoys while the two Rampagers, each armed with AGM-88 HARMs and flying at five hundred feet, approached within effective range of the missile battery. The Libyans took the bait and locked their radars on to the high-flying A-7Es. Brodsky and his wingman maintained their course and altitude. "It was a beautiful night," Brodsky recalled. "I was about fifty miles away from the SA-5, and I was sure I could have seen a launch."[108] Before the Libyans could launch a salvo of Gammons, however, the wave-skimming Corsairs each fired one 14-foot, 800-pound HARM missile, which followed the Square Pair radar beam at twice the speed of sound back to Surt more than thirty miles away. One AGM-88 hit the Square Pair antenna, but the second missile narrowly missed. The explosion and warhead fragments transformed the Square Pair antenna into a pile of jagged debris. The warhead cut power lines, damaged control consoles, and caused death and injury to the operators and technicians on duty.[109] "HARM worked exactly as advertised," remarked Comdr. Richard J. Nibe, the skipper of VA-83.[110] In spite of heavy damage to one of its main radars, the SA-5 battery was back in operation in about four hours.[111]

Meanwhile, a second surface engagement was unfolding in the eastern half of the Gulf of Sidra. Surface and airborne radars detected a 197-foot, 780-ton Soviet-made *Nanuchka II* missile corvette heading west from the naval base at Benghazi. The *Nanuchka* was armed with four Soviet-built SS-N-2C Styx antiship cruise missiles. The Styx was twenty-one feet long, weighed two and half tons, carried a potent 1,100-pound warhead, and had a range of approximately twenty-five miles. At 2235 a pair of A-6Es from VA-85 attacked the Libyan corvette with Rockeye cluster bombs, damaging the ship's combat systems equipment and topside electronics suite. The Black Falcons were unable to execute the coup de grâce with Harpoons because a merchant ship was in the vicinity of the engagement. The Libyan patrol boat very astutely warded off further attacks by taking refuge near the merchantman. The bruised corvette hobbled back to Benghazi, reaching port before first light.[112]

The next two surface engagements were arguably the most unusual events of Operation Prairie Fire. Off and on for over two hours the F-14s in CAP station five in the western half of the Libyan FIR reported muzzle flashes (possibly from AAA or small arms) and the activation of fire control radar in their vicinity. The F-14s, which were from *America*-based VF-33, believed that they were being taken under fire. At 2350 the guided-missile cruiser *Richmond K. Turner* (CG 20) launched one RGM-84A Harpoon at an unidentified surface contact to the southwest at a range of fifty miles. (This position was in the general area of CAP station five.) *Turner* claimed that it hit a *La Combattante*–class vessel, but an E-2C that tracked the flight of the missile reported holding no radar video that corresponded to a surface contact. Furthermore, a search of the area by SUCAP found neither a target nor any debris. The contact may have been flotsam from the *La Combattante* destroyed earlier that evening. Perhaps some armed and angry survivors were exacting their last measure of defiance against the overwhelming American naval force.

Around 2300 the Aegis cruiser *Yorktown,* operating in the task force defensive screen north of 32° 30', acquired a small surface contact on its SPY-1 radar at a range of about forty miles. At approximately twenty-five miles the contact was picked up by the ship's AN/SPS-49 air search radar. The target was tracking toward the battle force at slow speed. SUCAP was dispatched to investigate but could not locate the vessel. A few minutes after midnight the contact suddenly increased speed to over forty knots and appeared to activate its fire control radar. To the officers and men in the *Yorktown*'s Combat Information Center, it seemed as though the vessel was making a high-speed run toward the center of the battle force. The contact was already within striking range of the *Coral Sea* as it moved southward, refueling alongside the replenishment ship *Detroit* (AOE 4). With a disastrous situation unfolding ahead of them, the two vessels conducted an accelerated breakaway and went to general quarters. The cruiser also went to battle stations and prepared to engage the target. When the unidentified vessel closed to approximately eleven miles, the *Yorktown* fired a pair of Harpoons. The missiles streaked toward the contact and within a minute sonar operators reported two loud surface explosions—apparent hits. Aircraft investigated the site shortly afterward and found no traces of wreckage. The *Yorktown* reported that it sank a *Wadi* (renamed *Assad*)–class missile corvette, but intelligence analysts soon accounted for all surviving Libyan naval vessels. The *Yorktown*'s skipper, Capt. Carl A. Anderson, concluded that his ship had successfully engaged and destroyed an unidentified high-speed surface craft, and circumstantial evidence supported that conclusion.[113] Crowe, on the other hand, called the *Yorktown*'s target "a radar shadow." Breast referred to it as "a flock of sea birds."[114] A few days after the incident the Pentagon reported that the *Yorktown* had attacked a target with "undetermined results."[115] Post-combat analysis of the *Yorktown*'s SPY-1 radar data recorded during Attain Document III revealed that the mysterious target vessel was actually an air contact that the Aegis combat system had incorrectly designated as a surface target. The true identity of the air contact remains a mystery.[116]

While the *Richmond K. Turner* and the *Yorktown* were dealing with their ghostly surface contacts, the Libyans reactivated the Square Pair radar at Surt. At 0047 on 25 March, a pair of *Saratoga*-based A-7Es launched one HARM each at the radar antenna and knocked it out of action again. The radar site was soon repaired, but the Libyans wisely decided to leave the radar turned off until after the departure of the Sixth Fleet.[117] For the remainder of the night the Libyans refrained from making threatening moves against the American fleet. Shortly after 0600, however, an E-2C detected a Libyan naval vessel proceeding northwest at more than twenty-five knots from Benghazi. Initially identified as a *La Combattante II-G*–class missile boat, the vessel was later identified as the *Nanuchka II*–class corvette *Ean Mara*. It is highly likely that it was the same patrol boat that had escaped destruction the previous evening.[118]

A few minutes later an A-6E from VA-55 swooped down and dumped two Rockeyes on the Libyan vessel, partially disabling it. Believing they were up against a *La Combattante,* the A-6E crew was unaware that they had been inside the envelope of the *Nanuchka's* SA-N-4 surface-to-air missile system. Almost immediately after the Rockeye attack an Intruder from VA-85 arrived in the vicinity and prepared a Harpoon attack against the stunned Libyan corvette. From a range of nine miles the A-6E fired an AGM-84 that achieved devastating results.[119] "The shot went real smooth," said the pilot, who could watch the Harpoon attack unfold on his FLIR scope because of the unlimited visibility in the Gulf of Sidra that morning. "The targeting and launch went just the way it was supposed to. . . . It went in pretty quick, and I doubt if the Libyans saw it coming."[120] The missile struck the ship on its starboard beam, ripped open the hull, and ignited a blistering oil fire, the smoke from which could be seen for twenty miles. The *Saratoga*-based A-6E then delivered the coup de grâce, dropping two Rockeyes on the stricken vessel. Survivors scrambled onto life rafts as the inferno engulfed the ship. Task Force 60 aircraft later watched the Libyan rescue efforts but made no attempt to interfere. The ROE had been amended to permit the Libyans to conduct a recovery operation. Unbeknownst to the men of the battle force, the destruction of the *Ean Mara* would be the last combat action of Operation Prairie Fire.[121] "We never heard another peep," Duff recalled.[122] The Libyans assumed a strict defensive posture, keeping their naval vessels within territorial waters and restricting LAAF fighters to sorties over land.

For the next two-and-a-half days the ships and aircraft of Task Force 60 operated unopposed in the international waters and airspace of the Gulf of Sidra and Tripoli FIR, effectively destroying Qaddafi's illegal claim over the disputed waters. The three carrier air wings kept up the brutal around-the-clock flight schedule. Tomcats and Hornets manned CAP stations below the "line of death," and several fighters conducted "blue darter" operations, flying directly toward the Libyan coast and keeping Libyan radar operators at several SAM sites on the edge of their seats. Stumpf noticed that the radar "emissions were of short duration, an obvious and successful attempt to keep the radars from once again being struck by HARMs." Meanwhile, the *Ticonderoga, Scott,* and *Caron* steamed unchallenged in the Gulf of Sidra.[123]

Satisfied that the battle force had successfully challenged Qaddafi's illegal claim to the Gulf of Sidra and had done so in dramatic fashion, Weinberger ordered Kelso to terminate Attain Document III on the afternoon of 27 March, more than two full days ahead of schedule. Shultz was extremely disappointed by Weinberger's action. He believed that the United States had passed up a great opportunity to deliver a devastating blow to the Qaddafi regime.[124] Similarly, Lehman wrote in his memoirs of his "consternation and astonishment" over Weinberger's decision. "While Kelso had executed the operation flawlessly, its fullest effect was frustrated by premature termination," Lehman wrote. "Qaddafi seized upon the withdrawal to proclaim victory, which he probably believed."[125]

Although the operation ended early, the United States sent an unequivocal message to Qaddafi. In resounding fashion the U.S. Navy reaffirmed its legal right to operate freely in the international waters and airspace of the Gulf of Sidra. It defied the Libyan leader's illegal territorial claims and easily repulsed his attempts to back up his claims with force. In a message to the officers, sailors, and Marines of the Sixth Fleet, Reagan praised their professionalism and bravery in defense of freedom of the seas: "During the past five days, the Sixth Fleet has once again served as the spear and shield of American policy in a troubled and volatile region. . . . You have sent a message to the whole world that the United States has the will and, through you, the ability to defend the free world's interests. Your determination and tireless response to Libyan threats make this world a safer place."[126]

The Sixth Fleet's accomplishments during Attain Document III were impressive: it had destroyed two Libyan naval vessels, it had put Qaddafi's most sophisticated missile battery out of action, and it had effectively grounded the LAAF. According to intelligence estimates seventy-two Libyans were killed in the fighting while six Soviet technicians at the Surt SA-5 site were wounded. The Libyan Arab Air Defense Command (LAADC) fired at least five and as many as twelve SAMs at Sixth Fleet aircraft without scoring as much as a near miss. The carrier air wings flew 1,546 sorties, 375 of which traveled south of 32° 30'. The SAG operated for seventy-five continuous hours in the Gulf of Sidra, penetrating forty-two miles below the "line of death." Several new U.S. weapons systems—Aegis, the F/A-18 Hornet, Harpoon, HARM, and LAMPS MK III—performed well in a combat environment.[127] Weinberger called the Sixth Fleet's performance "a remarkable professional achievement."[128]

The ships of the *Saratoga* battle group departed the Mediterranean and returned to their home ports along the East Coast. The *Coral Sea* and the *America* battle groups headed for well-deserved liberty in friendly ports around the Mediterranean.

An analysis of the Sixth Fleet's combat performance in the Gulf of Sidra identified three factors that contributed significantly to the lopsided American victory. First, Task Force 60 enjoyed superior organization and the highest level of operational readiness. The *Saratoga* and *Coral Sea* battle groups were on forward deployment for several months, while the *America* battle group participated in a number of grueling Second Fleet exercises in the months immediately preceding its arrival in the Mediterranean Sea. The three battle groups readily formed a gigantic battle force, implemented an integrated command structure, and immediately began multicarrier workups for Attain Document III. Second, the sophisticated weaponry and electronic systems of Task Force 60 functioned as they were designed, a tribute to advanced American technology and the talented operators in the battle force. With superior equipment and the ability to use it effectively, the task force struck Qaddafi's military establishment at extreme range but with devastating accuracy in both daylight and darkness. Finally, the American naval force in the Mediterranean operated under effective local command. Kelso and his subordinate commanders responded swiftly and decisively to threats posed by Libyan forces without consulting higher authorities.

For their part the Libyans were totally unprepared for combat in the Gulf of Sidra. They appeared thoroughly disorganized and without purpose, and their actions seemed completely uncoordinated and utterly confused. Qaddafi's armed forces were incapable of carrying out a well-planned and determined naval attack against the American armada. Nevertheless, the Libyan leadership ordered a few patrol boats to perform an impossible mission, and several Libyan sailors paid the ultimate price. "The Libyans thought they could penetrate the battle group, shoot their missiles, and run like hell," said Comdr. Bob Day, the skipper of VA-85, "but we didn't give them a chance."[129]

"Qaddafi had sent his forces into a battle they couldn't win," observed David Martin and John Walcott. "He seemed to relish the role of the Arab David against the American Goliath, but he could only play it for so long. If he kept it up, his armed forces would be either destroyed or turn against him."[130]

Reactions to Operation Prairie Fire

The American public and members of Congress from both sides of the aisle were supportive of Reagan's handling of the brief shooting conflict with Libya. According to a *Newsweek* poll, 75 percent of those surveyed indicated that the U.S. military action was justified. Sixty-three percent said the action was worth it, even if it resulted in more terrorist attacks on Americans.[131] "The administration's handling of this matter is on the right course," said House Speaker Thomas P. O'Neill, Democrat of Massachusetts. "Its actions in protecting America's armed force in international waters is [sic] justified." Senate Minority Leader Robert C. Byrd, Democrat of West Virginia stated that "if we're going to get fired on in international waters, we will fire back."[132] "The U.S. Navy task force was fully justified in retaliating with a limited surgical strike in response to the wholly unwarranted Libyan attacks," Senator Dan Quayle, Republican of Indiana, commented.[133]

A few Members of Congress, most notably House Foreign Affairs Committee Chairman Dante B. Fascell, Democrat of Florida, complained that Reagan failed to satisfy the requirements of the War Powers Act by not consulting with Congress before deploying U.S. forces to an area "where imminent involvement in hostilities was a distinct possibility." Under the provisions of the War Powers Act of 1973 the president can send troops into combat or situations where "imminent hostilities are likely" for no more than sixty days without the concurrence of Congress.[134] Administration officials responded that prior consultation was not necessary because the fleet maneuvers took place in international waters and had been publicly announced in advance. Nevertheless, the White House forwarded a report on the operation to Congress.[135] "It wasn't an unusual thing we set out to do," Reagan stated, reminding his critics that the United States had a long-standing freedom of navigation exercise program. The president also was quick to point out that Qaddafi had opened "hostilities, and we closed them."[136]

During the confrontation in the Gulf of Sidra large street demonstrations took place in Tripoli and Benghazi and many frenzied young men shrieked that they would carry out suicide attacks against the United States. Meanwhile, Libyan government representatives announced that Libyan air defenses had shot down several American warplanes. They also warned the Sixth Fleet that if it continued its aggression it would suffer "a sea of blood and fire."[137] Government-controlled radio made no mention of Libyan casualties and declared that the Libyan people had "scored a glittering victory over the imperialist invaders of the gulf of death." The country "had risen to the level of being a match for a superpower . . . which they fought and triumphed over."[138] In a statement delivered 25 March before a large crowd of supporters shouting anti-American slogans, Qaddafi declared that the opportunity for a peaceful resolution to the conflict had passed: "It is not a time for speaking. It is time for confrontation—for war. . . . The Gulf of Sidra is ours. . . . If they want to expand the struggle, we will carry it all over the world."[139] At a rally three days later Qaddafi exhorted the crowd,

> This confrontation must make us more determined to achieve our right to live. We have baptized our right to the Gulf of Sidra with blood. We have reaffirmed that the 32nd parallel is the line of death. Actually we are prepared to die at this line. We have done so and this happened. It suffices that

the American Sixth Fleet was compelled to withdraw, dragging behind it its tail of disappointment, shame, and fatigue without achieving its aims. . . . Even if they return to challenge us we will challenge them. . . . The struggle will continue until victory and until imperialism falls, and until the banners of freedom are raised everywhere in the world.[140]

Moderate Arab states, the PLO, and Iran expressed general solidarity with Libya in its conflict with the United States. The Council of Foreign Ministers of the League of Arab States condemned the "American aggression against Libya" and called on all Arabs to help Libya "repulse this aggression."[141] On the other hand, the harshest condemnation of the United States came from Syria, Algeria, and radical Palestinian factions, such as the Syrian-backed Palestine National Salvation Front, which proclaimed that it would "take necessary measures to deter the U.S. by attacking every single American target or interest in the Middle East."[142]

The Soviet Union condemned the United States for precipitating a military confrontation in the Mediterranean and for creating a situation that would "poison the atmosphere" of improved relations between the United States and the Soviet Union that had resulted from the summit meeting between Reagan and Soviet leader Gorbachev in Geneva in November 1985.[143] Israel applauded the Sixth Fleet's action, calling it a legitimate exercise in self-defense and a demonstration of American resolve. The majority of America's European allies expressed guarded support. A few of the Europeans, however, notably Italy, Spain, and Greece, were concerned that the conflict might endanger the peace and stability of the Mediterranean region.[144]

The Smoking Gun: The Bombing of La Belle Discothèque

Coming as it did after the diplomatic and economic sanctions announced in January and the Sixth Fleet's operations in January and February, Operation Prairie Fire was Reagan's last message to Qaddafi to alter his behavior regarding terrorism or suffer more severe consequences. In less than a day of combat Reagan's navy had crushed or neutralized Qaddafi's armed forces in the entire Gulf of Sidra basin. The Libyan leader failed to back up his anti-American rhetoric with conventional military force. His regime had been thoroughly humiliated. To retaliate against the United States he once more resorted to terrorism. On the second day of the operation the director of the Libyan intelligence service sent a cable to Libyan agents in the people's bureaus in Belgrade, East Berlin, Geneva, Madrid, Paris, and Rome,[145] and ordered them to carry out terrorist attacks against American military and civilian targets that would "cause maximum and indiscriminate casualties." The cable was intercepted and decoded by the National Security Agency.[146] With the issuance of this order Qaddafi "crossed the Rubicon" in his conflict with Reagan. The United States and Libya were irreversibly headed for a deadly showdown.

On 26 March the State Department announced that it had sent warnings to U.S. diplomatic posts and military installations abroad. It advised Americans to be aware of the increased likelihood of terrorist activity and to take added precautions. The department also issued travel advisories for Americans planning to travel overseas. On 27 March the administration also took an extraordinary step to save American lives when a U.S. diplomat met secretly with representatives of the Soviet and East German governments. The American official apprised them of the threat that the people's bureau in East Berlin posed to American citizens and property in West Berlin and called on them to use their influence to forestall any terrorist attacks planned by Libyan agents in East Berlin. The Soviet and East German diplomats promised no action. Instead they demanded that the U.S. government produce evidence of its allegations against Libya.[147]

It was not long before Qaddafi's call for violence against the United States netted deadly results. An obscure Syrian-backed terrorist group, the Arab Revolutionary Cells, planted a bomb on TWA Flight 840, which exploded during the plane's descent into Athens on 2 April. The blast killed four American citizens.[148] The terrorists declared that the bombing was carried out in retaliation for America's military actions in the Gulf of Sidra. Qaddafi publicly congratulated the terrorists, but no evidence tying him to the monstrous act could be found. The bomb was believed to be the handiwork of the infamous Palestinian bomb maker Abu Ibrahim. The device, which consisted of one pound of plastic explosive, was hidden under a seat cushion and was set off by a change in cabin pressure. The prime suspect was a Lebanese woman who, on the earlier Cairo-to-Rome leg of the flight, had occupied the seat where the bomb was planted. The woman was identified by Italian authorities as May Elias Mansur, a known terrorist who belonged to the Revolutionary Brigades, a radical pro-Syrian terrorist group with no known ties to Qaddafi or Abu Nidal.[149]

Less than three days later, in the early hours of Saturday, 5 April, Libyan agents set off a bomb in a restroom of La Belle discothèque in West Berlin, a popular hangout for African-American GIs. The blast killed Sgt. Kenneth Ford and a Turkish woman instantly, and mortally wounded Sgt. James Goins; 229 people, including seventy-eight Americans, were injured.[150] Before the discothèque bombing the Libyan people's bureau in East Berlin had informed Qaddafi that "a joyous event"—a terrorist operation—would be carried out soon and he would be pleased with the results. The cable was intercepted and decoded by the General Communications Headquarters (GCHQ), the NSA's British counterpart. The intercept was immediately passed to U.S. intelligence. After the attack the people's bureau reported to Qaddafi that the operation had succeeded and even mentioned the time of the attack. The GCHQ intercepted this cable as well.

U.S. intelligence sent an urgent warning to the operations center of the U.S. Army brigade stationed in West Berlin, stating that a terrorist attack against American military personnel was highly probable. The brigade commander, Brig. Gen. Thomas Griffin, gave his military police the nearly impossible task of searching West Berlin's nightclubs and discothèques for suspicious persons, objects, or activities. One team of MPs was a quarter of a mile from the discothèque when the bomb exploded.[151] "We were about fifteen minutes too late," General Rogers lamented. But even if the MPs had gotten to the club in time, it would have been very difficult to locate the bomb.[152]

With transcripts of the Tripoli–East Berlin cables in his possession, Reagan at last had direct proof or "a smoking gun" linking Qaddafi to a specific terrorist attack. The cables of late March and early April were arguably ambiguous, but taken together they contained the key elements of a state-sponsored terrorist operation: motive, execution order, time, place, and after-action report. Neither Qaddafi nor the Libyan intelligence service actually directed the attack on La Belle discothèque; target selection and timing had been left up to Qaddafi's operatives in East Berlin.[153]

Some administration officials were so impressed with the quality of the evidence against Libya that they made inappropriate public comments about it. The U.S. ambassador to West Germany, Richard R. Burt, commented that "there is very clear evidence that there is Libyan involvement" in the disco bombing. Meanwhile, Rogers revealed in a speech in Atlanta on 9 April that "indisputable evidence" supported allegations of Libyan responsibility for the attack.[154]

IN THE AFTERMATH of the reunification of Germany in the early 1990s, countless records of the former East German security service—the Stasi— were scrutinized by Western intelligence services. Investigators located several files that confirmed that Libyan agents operating out of the people's bureau in East Berlin carried out the attack on La Belle discothèque under orders from Tripoli and that officials in the East German government knew of the plot in advance. According to German investigators and U.S. intelligence, the mastermind behind the attack was Said Rashid, a senior Libyan intelligence operative who since the early 1980s had directed several terrorist operations aimed specifically at Americans. German prosecutors ultimately brought charges against five suspects with the help of evidence found in the Stasi archives, using the testimony of former East German agents, and relying on confessions from some of the suspects themselves. Two Palestinian men, Yasir Shraydi and Ali Chanaa, and a German woman, Verena Chanaa, were charged with three counts of murder and several counts of attempted homicide. A former Libyan diplomat, Misbah Abu al-Qasim at-Tayr, and a second German woman, Verena's sister Andrea Haeusler, were charged as accomplices. According to German prosecutors Shraydi had planned and directed the attack on the discothèque, Ali Chanaa had manufactured the bomb, and Chanaa's wife Verena had planted it in the nightclub. In November 1997 the trial of the five bombing suspects opened in Berlin.[155]

On 13 November 2001 a Berlin judge found Verena Chanaa guilty of murder and Shraydi guilty of multiple counts of attempted murder. He sentenced each assailant to fourteen years in prison. The judge also convicted Ali Chanaa of attempted homicide and at-Tayr of acting as an accomplice. He sentenced these men to twelve years in prison each. Haeusler was acquitted because the prosecutors could not prove that she knew Verena Chanaa was carrying a bomb in her handbag.[156] Moreover, they were unable to prove that Qaddafi had personally ordered the attack on the discothèque, largely because of "the limited willingness" of the U.S. and German governments to provide them with intelligence related to the case. Despite this failure the judge found that the bombing had been planned by both the Libyan intelligence service and the Libyan people's bureau in the former East Berlin. In his verdict he noted that "Libya bears at the very least a considerable part of the responsibility for the attack."[157]

President Ronald Reagan and Secretary of Defense Caspar Weinberger one week after taking office. Over the next five years, Reagan found it easier to promise military action against terrorists than carry it out.

U.S. Army

USS *Nimitz,* Carrier Air Wing 8, and escorts in the Mediterranean Sea. In 1981 President Reagan ordered the U.S. Sixth Fleet to challenge Qaddafi's claim over the Gulf of Sidra.

U.S. Navy

Colonel Muammar al-Qaddafi. By the late 1970s, many Western leaders considered Qaddafi one of the world's most notorious practitioners of international terrorism.

Corbis: Wally McNamee

Morgan I. Wilbur painting of F-14 Tomcat launch of heat-seeking Sidewinder
missile, Gulf of Sidra, 19 August 1981
NHC: Morgan I. Wilbur

Comdr. Hank Kleeman (*right*), skipper of
VF-41, and Lt. David Venlet simulate for
reporters the air battle over the Gulf of
Sidra that occurred on 19 August 1981.
U.S. Navy

USS *Saratoga* with CVW 17 and the warships and auxiliaries of her battle group steam through the Mediterranean in November 1985.

U.S. Navy

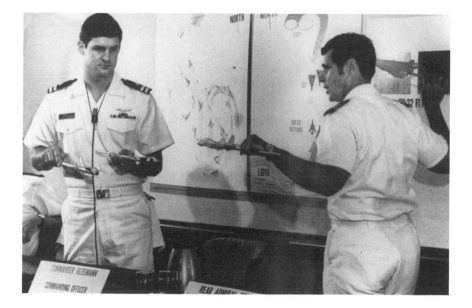

USS *Coral Sea* with Carrier Air Wing 13. In 1986 the "Ageless Warrior" participated in all three phases of Operation Attain Document and Operation El Dorado Canyon.

U.S. Navy

U.S. Navy F/A-18 Hornet escorts Libyan MiG-23 Flogger during Operation Attain Document II, February 1986.

U.S. Navy

U.S. Marine Corps F/A-18 Hornet escorts Libyan MiG-25 Foxbat during Operation Attain Document II, February 1986.

U.S. Marine Corps

Left to right: Donald Regan, Caspar Weinberger, President Reagan, and John Poindexter confer in spring of 1986.

Ronald Reagan Library

USS *America* with Carrier Air Wing 1. The escalating crisis between the United States and Libya caused the *America* and her escorts to deploy to the Mediterranean ten days ahead of schedule.

U.S. Navy

Rear Adm. David E. Jeremiah (*left*) looks on as Rear Adm. Jerry C. Breast welcomes Vice Adm. Frank B. Kelso II (*right*) aboard the *Coral Sea*.

U.S. Navy

The guided missile cruiser USS *Ticonderoga* formed the core of a three-ship surface action group that operated south of Qaddafi's "line of death" during Operation Attain Document III.

U.S. Navy

An A-6E lands safely aboard the *Coral Sea*. In the spring of 1986, three Sixth Fleet A6-E squadrons distinguished themselves in combat against Libya.

U.S. Navy

Morgan I. Wilbur painting, "Moment of Impact, Operation Prairie Fire," depicts destruction of Libyan missile boat *Waheed*, 24 March 1986.

NHC: Morgan I. Wilbur

A Soviet-built SA-2 surface-to-air missile and launcher. The SA-2 and other Soviet- and French-built SAMs, AAA, and advanced radars made the Libyan air defense network one of the world's most deadly.

U.S. Air Force

An A-7E Corsair II fires a high-speed antiradiation missile (HARM). Task Force 60 A-7Es used HARMs to silence Qaddafi's most sophisticated air defense system: the SA-5 SAM battery at Surt.

U.S. Navy

Libyan missile corvette *Ean Mara* burns out of control, 25 March 1986. The destruction of the *Ean Mara* was the last combat action of Operation Prairie Fire.

U.S. Navy

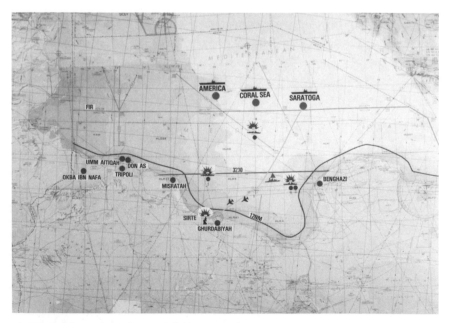

Gulf of Sidra combat action of 24–25 March 1986.

U.S. Department of Defense

President Reagan and his senior advisers discuss military action against Libya, April 1986 in the aftermath of the Libyan-sponsored bombing of La Belle discothèque in West Berlin.

Ronald Reagan Library

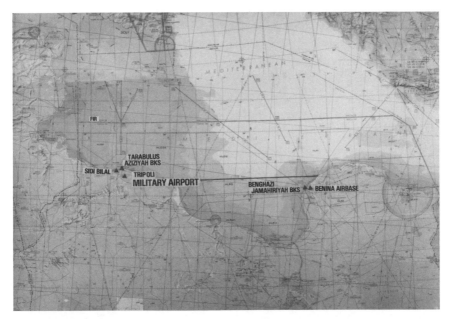

Chart showing five Libyan targets attacked by Air Force and Navy bombers during Operation El Dorado Canyon, 14–15 April 1986.

U.S. Department of Defense

A U.S. Air Force F-111F fighter bomber of the 48th Tactical Fighter Wing, based at Lakenheath in Great Britain.

U.S. Air Force

President Reagan and his senior advisers brief congressional leaders on Operation El Dorado Canyon, three hours before Air Force and Navy bombers struck targets in Tripoli and Benghazi.

Ronald Reagan Library

A U.S. Air Force KC-10A Extender tanker with boom extended as it prepares to refuel aircraft.

U.S. Air Force

Map of the nearly 6,000-mile route taken by F-111Fs to and from Libya after the French and Spanish governments refused overflight of their countries.

U.S. Department of Defense

An F-111F drops Snakeye Mark 82 high-drag bombs during a training exercise.

U.S. Air Force

The crew of the USS *America* prepares to launch an F-14 Tomcat, an A-7E Corsair II, and an EA-6B Prowler for Operation El Dorado Canyon.

U.S. Navy

Soviet-built IL-76 Candid transport planes at Tripoli Military Airfield, captured by FLIR camera aboard F-111F.

U.S. Air Force

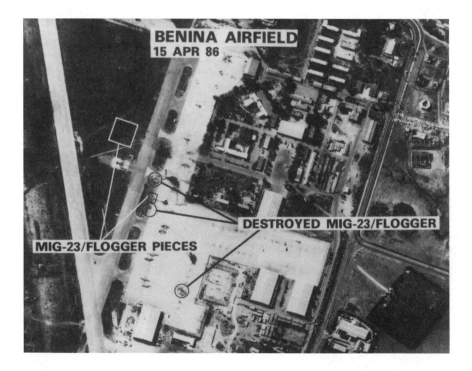

Air Force Chief of Staff Gen. Charles Gabriel briefs President Reagan and advisers on U.S. Air Force raid on Tripoli.

Ronald Reagan Library

Reconnaissance photograph of damage inflicted on Libyan MiG-23 Floggers at Benina Airfield by six A-6Es.

U.S. Department of Defense

5

Planning to Strike Qaddafi

Selecting the Right Targets

Very early on Saturday morning, 5 April, National Security Adviser John Poindexter woke President Reagan and informed him that a bomb had exploded in a discothèque in West Berlin, killing one U.S. serviceman and injuring several Americans. Later that morning transcripts of the cable traffic between Tripoli and the East Berlin people's bureau reached the White House Situation Room and were immediately forwarded to Reagan, who was taking a short vacation at Rancho del Cielo. That same day Adm. William Crowe phoned Gen. Richard Lawson at EUCOM and requested a list of Libyan targets that could be attacked in short order. Two days later, at a meeting with his principal advisers at the White House, Reagan reviewed the evidence of Libyan involvement in the bombing and received an intelligence briefing on Muammar al-Qaddafi's plans for a wave of terrorist attacks on American citizens and interests overseas. Reagan was convinced of Qaddafi's complicity in the West Berlin attack, and on Wednesday, 9 April, he approved "in principle" a military operation against Libya and authorized the NSC to finalize the necessary plans.

Reagan and his senior advisers believed that attacking Qaddafi would achieve important military and political objectives. Militarily it would be a legitimate act of self-defense that could save innocent lives by interrupting Qaddafi's ability to orchestrate acts of terrorism. Politically it would send a clear message to those who support or sponsor terrorism that they could not do so without paying a very heavy price. An armed response also would soothe public outrage by avenging a terrorist attack that had been aimed directly at American citizens.[1] "There comes a time in these events and affairs," remarked Crowe, "when you've got to retaliate just because people are doing things to you they don't have a right to do, and you've got to stand up."[2] Secretary of State Shultz very accurately and concisely captured the sentiment of those present at the meeting on 9 April: "We have taken enough punishment and beating. We have to act."[3]

Reagan made his wishes clear: if any military operation went forward it had to destroy critical elements of Qaddafi's terrorist infrastructure while minimizing both American losses and Libyan civilian casualties. By destroying major components of Qaddafi's terrorist command, training, and support facilities Reagan was determined to thwart a significant number of terrorist attacks aimed at Americans in Europe, the Middle East, Africa, and Latin America. According to the intelligence reports, which Reagan reviewed on 7 April, Qaddafi was planning about three dozen operations against American diplomatic missions, military installations, and commercial interests overseas. A report from the CIA, which detailed nine Libyan operations either ordered by Qaddafi or already underway, caused grave concern and created a powerful sense of urgency for the administration. In early April Qaddafi's agents failed in their attempts to attack the U.S. visa office in Paris and the American embassy in Beirut and to kidnap the American ambassador in Rwanda. Reports existed that Qaddafi was attempting to buy the American hostages held by Hizballah in Lebanon. Reagan and his advisers believed that using force could not make the current situation any worse and might improve it by deterring or disrupting planned terrorist operations.[4]

Contingency planning for military operations against Libya had been under way since Task Force 60 and 48 TFW received warning orders from the Pentagon immediately after the Rome and Vienna airport massacres. Following Reagan's meeting with his advisers on 7 April, preparations for the operation proceeded at a furious pace. Reagan and his team were determined to execute the operation before Qaddafi could carry out any more of his planned assaults.[5] General Rogers designated Admiral Kelso as the officer in tactical command of the operation and ordered him "to coordinate detailed joint planning and deconfliction efforts, to integrate other command assets, and to conduct the actual operations."[6] The operation carried the code name El Dorado Canyon.

On 8 April Kelso ordered the *Coral Sea* and her escorts to remain in the

Mediterranean. The *Coral Sea* was in Malaga, Spain, where her officers and men were enjoying what they thought was their last port visit in the Mediterranean before starting the homeward transit across the Atlantic. Two days later the "Ageless Warrior" got under way and sailed eastward to join the *America* in the Tyrrhenian Sea. While en route she topped off her supply of ammunition and conducted air wing training, while her strike planners resumed their eighteen-hour workdays. Meanwhile, the *America* left the port of Livorno, Italy, and on 12 April she rendezvoused with the *Coral Sea*. The two carriers conducted a practice strike, an antiair warfare exercise, and a joint-C3 exercise with units of 48 TFW. As expected, journalists noted with keen interest the movements of the two battle groups in the central Mediterranean. Several reporters chartered daily press flights out of Rome and Naples to report on the movements of the Sixth Fleet.[7] Admiral Breast quipped that the pilots of the press planes "were considerably more intrepid and aggressive than the LAAF."[8]

EUCOM's contingency plans grouped Libyan targets into three categories: economic, military, and terrorist-related. Striking economic infrastructure targets such as oil fields, pumping facilities, and loading jetties would have the greatest impact on the Qaddafi regime, but a number of administration officials argued that this option was neither proportionate nor directly related to Qaddafi's sponsorship and support of international terrorism. Moreover, attacking Libyan industrial sites might inflict casualties within the foreign worker community—Italians, Britons, Germans, and some Americans—and ruin domestic and international support for military action.[9]

Libyan military facilities appeared to be more legitimate as targets, but several officials pointed out that they were not directly connected to terrorist activity either. Furthermore, despite the Libyan military's record of carrying out hostile acts against American forces, Reagan and his national security advisers did not want to alienate the one segment of Libyan society that was most deeply frustrated by Qaddafi's terrorist policies and had the best chance of toppling his regime: the officers and soldiers of the regular army. Several Libyan army officers were highly suspicious of Qaddafi and his plan to replace the regular army with paramilitary forces drawn from the very loyal Popular Resistance Forces. Moreover, a significant number of Libyan soldiers were demoralized by Qaddafi's open distrust of the military, his costly foreign adventures (namely, the debacle in Uganda and the quagmire in Chad), and his preposterous claims of victory over Hissene Habré's army and the Sixth Fleet. Judging from the considerable number of mutinies, refusals to fight, and coup attempts that had occurred in recent years, outside observers might have concluded that the Libyan armed forces were close to launching a full-scale revolt against the Leader. Consequently, to maintain the wedge between Qaddafi and his regular armed forces, U.S. planners considered attacking only those military targets such as fighter bases and SAM batteries that could impede the passage of U.S. strike aircraft to and from terrorist-related targets.[10]

Qaddafi commanded a number of personal military contingents, each of which provided a target for U.S. retaliation more appropriate than the units of the regular Libyan armed forces. To keep weapons and ammunition out of the hands of potentially mutinous troops and to protect the regime against disloyal elements of the Libyan army, Qaddafi placed units of the Popular Resistance Forces in charge of supply bases and arsenals. Qaddafi also controlled three brigades of the paramilitary Islamic Legion, whose members were recruited (some by force) from all over Africa to carry out his policy of subversion. For his personal security Qaddafi relied on the following outfits: a deterrent battalion whose members were drawn exclusively from members of his own tribe, al-Qaddafa; a coterie of radical Jamahiriyya Guards; and an East German security battalion.[11]

During the previous three months Task Force 60 and 48 TFW planners had drafted dozens of strike plans for terrorist-related targets as well as plans for economic and military targets. Several of Reagan's senior advisers argued that terrorist facilities should be the focus of a retaliatory military operation. On Monday, 7 April, Lawson forwarded to Crowe a list of Libyan targets that included important industrial facilities, airfields, naval bases, a terrorist training camp, terrorist command and control facilities, Qaddafi's desert camp, an intelligence command center, and Qaddafi's headquarters-residence complex in Tripoli. On Tuesday Crowe presented the list to Reagan, who planned to discuss the target list with his advisers at the NSPG meeting scheduled for the next day. Their goal was to produce a short list of targets.

On Wednesday, 9 April, Reagan met with Shultz, CIA Director Casey, Crowe, Poindexter, White House Chief of Staff Donald Regan, and Deputy Secretary of Defense William H. Taft IV (who was filling in for Secretary of Defense Weinberger while Weinberger was on an official trip to Asia and the South Pacific). At the meeting Reagan studied maps of Libya spread out on the floor of the Oval Office, reviewed each target, and listened carefully to the opinions of his advisers. Shultz, Casey, Regan, and Poindexter argued for a devastating attack in response to the latest act of Libyan-sponsored terrorism, but the secretary of state had misgivings about attacking Qaddafi's Tripoli complex.[12] "We wouldn't get him," he declared, and "it would be seen as an attempt by us to kill him that failed." To Shultz's surprise Taft supported the use of military force but stressed that it should only be used against targets with a direct connection to terrorist activities.[13] On the other hand, Crowe argued that the United States should hit Qaddafi "where it would hurt and where it would do us the most good." Crowe wanted to attack important military installations, such as airfields, SAM batteries, and armor bases, and he asserted that there was no point in bombing terrorist facilities unless they were populated with terrorists. "I wanted to destroy his capacity to do us harm in the event we had to come back, or if we found ourselves engaged more deeply than we expected," he stated. He firmly believed that the most devastating impact on Qaddafi could be achieved by clobbering his military installations, because the greatest amount of force could be brought to bear with the smallest risk to Libyan civilians.[14]

After listening to his advisers and evaluating the advantages and disadvantages of each target, Reagan approved for further consideration the following targets: the Tripoli Military Airfield, the Tripoli Naval Base, the Benghazi Naval Base, the Benina Airfield near Benghazi, the terrorist training facility at Murat Sidi Bilal on the coast near Tripoli, the Libyan intelligence service headquarters in Tripoli, Qaddafi's desert camp, his bunker-residence at the Bab al-Aziziyah Barracks in Tripoli, and the Benghazi barracks of his Jamahiriyya Guards. The list included military and terrorist-related targets as well as a number of sites closely connected to the Qaddafi regime. Reagan was confident that the targets were appropriate for a military operation aimed at upsetting Qaddafi's terrorist infrastructure since they could be attacked with precision weapons and hitting them would not present extraordinary risks to either U.S. forces or Libyan civilians.[15]

The White House winnowed the list even further and directed EUCOM to finalize strike plans for the following terrorist-related targets: the Bab al-Aziziyah Barracks, which served as Qaddafi's residential compound, as the headquarters and command center for terrorist operations, and as a billeting area for his personal security forces; the Murat Sidi Bilal Training Camp, which served as a school that specialized in training naval commandos and terrorist frogmen in amphibious assaults, ship hijackings, port seizures, and underwater demolitions; the Tripoli Military Airfield, which served as the base for about nine IL-76 Candid transport planes that were used to support terrorist activity abroad and military operations in Chad; and the Benghazi Military and Jamahiriyya Guard Barracks, which served as the alternate terrorist command center, as a billeting area for Qaddafi's personal guards, as guest quarters for representatives of various terrorist organizations, and as a storage and assembly facility for MiG aircraft.

One military target, the Benina Airfield near Benghazi, was added to the list to prevent Libyan fighters from intercepting Navy strike aircraft bound for or returning from the Benghazi barracks. About a dozen MiG-23 Floggers were based at the Benina Airfield, and intelligence reports indicated that guest pilots from countries such as North Korea, Syria, Pakistan, from the PLO, and even from the Soviet Union flew MiGs from the base.[16]

A number of important political and tactical factors were carefully considered in developing the final target list. First, allowing only minimum risk to the American attacking force (which more than likely would consist of high performance attack aircraft) was a high priority. For instance, as Kelso emphatically informed Breast (the chief strike planner for Task Force 60), "I don't want any of our aviators walking down the street with a noose around his neck." To minimize the risk only targets near the coast were selected. The longer a plane spent over Libya, the greater were its chances of being shot down.

Second, Libyan collateral damage had to be kept to a minimum. The Reagan administration wanted to disrupt Qaddafi's ability to conduct terrorist operations, not punish the Libyan people. In constructing the target list planners sought targets with distinctive physical features that made them recognizable by using radar, infrared equipment, or the naked eye. Three of the five targets were located away from crowded neighborhoods and were easy to identify with radar.[17] One possible target, the intelligence service headquarters, did not make the final list because it was located in a densely populated area that included several diplomatic residences.

Third, the attack had to make a devastating impact on Qaddafi. For that reason two targets, the Bab al-Aziziyah Barracks in Tripoli and the Jamahiriyya Guard Barracks in Benghazi, were included on the final list. They were important political, as well as terrorist-related, targets.[18] A senior administration official referred to them as the "nerve center" of Libyan terrorism,[19] that is, targets whose destruction would dramatically undermine Qaddafi's will to commit future acts of terrorism aimed at the United States. As important as the two targets were, successfully disabling them presented serious problems for both bomber crews and Libyan civilians on the ground. Both targets were located in heavily populated and well-defended areas. They would be very difficult to locate amid the urban clutter while flying a high-speed, low-level profile at night. A near miss could have devastating consequences for many unsuspecting Libyans, and getting to and from the targets would be very hazardous for the attacking forces.[20] Breast did not like the target in Benghazi: "Jamahiriyya was not a good target, not a good radar target. It was a bunch of flat barracks." Because of these concerns Breast's planners never worked up a strike plan for the Jamahiriyya Barracks.[21] Similarly, Col. Sam Westbrook said that Bab al-Aziziyah "was very difficult in terms of trying to find it and in terms of collateral damage since it was right in the middle of a populated area and in the middle of all their defenses." Westbrook's planners held enough reservations about Aziziyah to cause them to never develop a detailed plan to attack it. It was too tough and dangerous a target. Breast remarked that he "would not have chosen to go against those targets at night."

Reagan selected the two urban targets because of their obvious connection to the Qaddafi regime and Libyan terrorism. "I wanted Qaddafi's compound," Lawson said, conveying the sentiment of many senior officials in Washington and Europe. Although Crowe acknowledged the difficulties in striking the two targets, he observed that "there was strong sentiment for psychological purposes that we should do something in his personal compound and get his communications center and headquarters." Bab al-Aziziyah (the splendid gate) was the nexus of Qaddafi's political power structure. The two hundred–acre compound was enclosed by a fifteen-foot wall, it was guarded by Soviet-made tanks, and the area was honeycombed with underground bunkers. In addition to barracks for his personal security services, the compound contained communications facilities, military staff headquarters, the house where his wife and seven children lived, and the Bedouin-style tent where he received visitors.[22]

Although Qaddafi's headquarters-residence complex was the most prominent target in the package, the Libyan leader was never deliberately targeted for assassination. One member of the NSC staff who assisted with the planning of El Dorado Canyon recalled the views of Reagan and his senior advisers concerning this very controversial issue: "Killing him was never part of our plan. On the other hand, we certainly made no attempt to protect him from our bombs. By law, we couldn't specifically target him. But if Qaddafi happened to be in the vicinity of the Aziziyah Barracks in downtown Tripoli when the bombs started to fall, nobody would have shed any tears."[23] Moreover, the White House press secretary's office was prepared to call Qaddafi's death "a fortuitous by-product of our act of self-defense."[24]

Constructing the Strike Force

El Dorado Canyon planners studied the composition and size of the strike force as they developed the target list. At the outset Kelso considered a range of attack options but immediately ruled out the use of battleships, Tomahawk cruise missiles, and special operations forces. The battleships were rejected for a number of reasons. First, although all Libyan targets except the Benina Air-field were within range of the 16-inch guns of the Navy's *Iowa*-class battleships, none of the dreadnoughts were deployed to the Mediterranean in the spring of 1986. Second, a single battleship would be unable to attack targets in both Tripoli and Benghazi on the same evening. Third, the battleship's main batter-ies lacked the precision required to hit targets in crowded urban areas. Finally, the battleship and her supporting task group would be operating close in to the Libyan coast where they would be susceptible to attack. If the battleship or any of her supporting ships suffered any damage, Qaddafi would score an enor-mous propaganda victory. Tomahawks were eliminated for the same reason they had been rejected in January: few missiles had been programmed for and were available for conventional missions in Libya. Special operations forces were not a practical option either, since their use required ample preparation time and a covert means of insertion and extraction, they involved compli-cated tactics on the ground, and they presented a high probability of American casualties.[25] After weighing a number of critical factors such as weapon accu-racy, weight of payload, proximity of targets to civilian population centers, time over target, and survivability of attacking forces, the planners decided that tac-tical strike aircraft would be best able to provide the safest and most effective means of carrying out the attack. In the words of W. Hays Parks, "Tactical air offered the ability to place the greatest weight of ordnance on the targets in the least amount of time while minimizing collateral damage and providing the greatest opportunity for the survival of the entire force."[26]

Mindful of the tragic consequences of the 4 December 1983 daylight raid on Syrian antiaircraft batteries in Lebanon, planners decided to strike at night. At night the Libyan air defense system would be at its lowest state of readiness —for example, shoulder-fired optically sighted SAMs would be severely ham-pered—and the LAAF, owing to its operational history, would least likely chal-lenge any attacking aircraft. A night strike would significantly reduce the chance that an American flier would be taken prisoner, and the civilian popu-lation on the ground would be at lower risk, since fewer people would be on the streets. Furthermore, since Qaddafi had confiscated all small arms from his military for fear of a coup and had turned the armory keys over to loyal revo-lutionary committees and components of the Popular Resistance Forces, strik-ing aircraft could fly a low-altitude approach and skirt below Libyan radars. The United States had in its inventory only two strike aircraft capable of perform-ing precision, low-level night or all-weather missions: the Navy's A-6E Intruder and the Air Force's F-111F. (Fighter crews had unofficially christened the F-111 the "Aardvark" because of its long snout and sprawled posture when parked.)[27]

The *Coral Sea* and the *America* each carried ten of the most updated version of the A-6E, which had joined the fleet in 1980 and was equipped with the powerful AN/APQ-148 search radar and the sophisticated AN/AAS-33 Target Recognition and Attack Multisensor (TRAM) system. With the radar and TRAM's forward-looking infrared (FLIR) sensor, the bombardier-navigator (B/N) sitting to the right of the pilot acquired and tracked targets at night and in adverse weather conditions. The TRAM's laser designation system illuminated a target for laser-guided bombs (LGBs) or provided highly accurate range information for the automatic release of unguided bombs. (LGBs are basically unguided or "dumb" bombs converted to "smart" bombs with the addition of laser guidance kits.) For a strike mission the Intruder typically carried Mk-84 2,000-pound, Mk-83 1,000-pound, or Mk-82 500-pound general-purpose bombs, in addition to CBU-59 antipersonnel-antimateriel (APAM) cluster ordnance. The A-6E enjoyed a high target kill rate at altitudes as low as two hundred feet and at speeds around 450 knots. It was a highly capable combat aircraft that could deliver a considerable ordnance package, but Kelso did not have enough planes at his disposal to hit all five targets simultaneously.

If forced to conduct the operation with an all-Navy strike force, Kelso could deploy his bombers in one of three ways: he could spread his assets very thin and hit all five targets at the same time, he could order two consecutive raids to inflict substantial damage on all five targets, or he could drop one target and hit only four targets at once (using one carrier's planes to hit a pair of targets in Tripoli and the other carrier's planes to strike two targets in the Benghazi area). None of these options appeared satisfactory; Kelso needed Navy and Air Force attack planes in order to conduct a simultaneous devastating attack on all five Libyan targets.[28]

Contrary to the opinion of some critics of Operation El Dorado Canyon, the British-based F-111Fs were not included in the strike force merely to give the Air Force a piece of the action or to dramatize an ally's support for the operation. "Given that we would be permitted only one strike, the Sixth Fleet was too limited in the weight of ordnance it could deliver," Crowe explained. "The element of surprise combined with the F-111s' superb fire control ideally suited them for a low-level one-pass night attack against heavy flak. In my mind, these advantages were decisive."[29]

Forty-eight TFW, based about eighty miles northeast of London at RAF Lakenheath in Suffolk, England, was the only tactical fighter wing in the European theater equipped with the most advanced version of the Aardvark—the F-111F—which had joined the service in 1973. Westbrook took command of 48

TFW—nicknamed the "Statute of Liberty Wing"—in 1984. He was a Vietnam combat veteran and experienced F-111 pilot.[30]

The F-111F was the Air Force's principal night or adverse weather interdiction aircraft, capable of low-altitude, high-speed strikes deep within enemy territory. Equipped with an advanced electronics suite and powerful TF-30P-100 Pratt and Whitney afterburning turbofan engines that generated nearly 50 percent more thrust than similar engines installed in other F-111s, the Aardvarks at Lakenheath were a significant improvement over the original F-111 or "tactical fighter experimental" (TFX) of the 1960s. The TFX program was championed by then–Secretary of Defense Robert S. McNamara in an attempt to save money by developing a common Navy–Air Force fighter design. Although the Navy soon abandoned the project, the Air Force had flown the F-111 in Vietnam with varying degrees of success. Rushed into combat in March 1968, the first batch of F-111s experienced numerous crashes that killed some of the most talented aircrews in the service. Three of the initial eight aircraft that flew in combat were lost in the first two weeks of duty. At one point half of the F-111s based in Thailand were lost in less than a month. Over the next two years fifteen planes were lost to mechanical failure, not enemy action. With this horrendous record the planes were withdrawn from the war. Since the plane's mission required it to fly solo at night, many of the crash sites were never found and the causes went unexplained. Of the wrecks that were located, a thorough investigation established the cause of each crash. Investigators determined that in several instances the F-111's terrain-following radar (TFR), an integral feature of the aircraft, could not cope with the heavy rains of Southeast Asia. Once this problem was corrected the aircraft returned to combat in 1972 and performed its difficult and dangerous missions reasonably well for the remainder of the war.[31]

The F-111F's TFR tracked the topography in front of the aircraft and automatically flew the 45-ton plane 200 to 1,000 feet over the ground at speeds greater than five hundred knots. With TFR the Aardvark could fly below enemy radars and exploit the terrain to mask its path of attack. Col. Robert Venkus, a veteran of 169 combat missions in Vietnam flying the F-105 Thunderchief, described flying the F-111F with TFR as "the first unnatural act I ever performed that I did not enjoy."[32]

The F-111Fs were equipped with the AN/AVQ-26 Pave Tack, a night or all-weather, electro-optical target acquisition, laser designation, and ordnance delivery system, contained in a pod mounted on a rotating cradle in the weapons bay of the F-111F. With Pave Tack the F-111F crew could identify a target in the dark and under conditions of reduced visibility such as fog, drizzle, or light smoke. The pod deployed downward during the ingress phase of a strike run. The sophisticated electronics package, which was operated by the plane's Weapon Systems Operator (WSO), consisted of a search radar, a low-light television, a FLIR imaging system, and a laser designator. The FLIR camera permitted target acquisition, identification, and tracking, and the laser designator, whose aiming reticle was slaved to the infrared sight, allowed precise targeting of laser-guided ordnance. The Pave Tack system enabled the Aardvark to deliver GBU-10 Paveway II Mk-84 2,000-pound LGBs with devastating accuracy. The LGB followed a ballistic trajectory until it detected laser energy reflected from the target, then it homed in on the target, adjusting the final seconds of its flight with maneuverable control fins.[33]

The F-111F delivered its LGBs using a maneuver called the "Pave Tack Toss." In a typical toss the aircraft closed in on the target at high speed and low altitude. Depending on the unique ballistics of the bombs carried, the pilot could initiate a sudden pull-up at a predetermined distance from the target. The nose would climb to a specific pitch angle (usually fifteen to thirty degrees) until the bombs were automatically released. After the bombs were released the pilot would turn hard away and force the nose hard down, descending to the safety of a low altitude. This convulsing maneuver had to be performed deliberately since the plane would be diving toward the ground at a frightening rate. After the F-111F became steady at the lower altitude, the pilot could resume TFR and make a rapid escape from the target area.

The WSO had a very difficult task during and after the Pave Tack Toss. As the nose started up the WSO switched the display on the scope from radar to FLIR and searched for the target. Once the WSO acquired the target he placed the reticle directly on it and activated the laser. As the plane violently turned, pitched over, and dove, the WSO had to keep his face buried in his scope, struggling to keep the laser on the aim point until the bombs hit. The Pave Tack Toss —from the moment of pull-up to the instant of bomb impact—took less than forty-five seconds. "During that short interval, there are a thousand ways to screw it up," Venkus commented.[34]

The F-111F could also carry a load of BSU-49 Snakeye Mk-82 high-drag bombs, which were 500-pound general purpose bombs equipped with balloon-parachute ("ballute") stabilizers. The high-drag Snakeyes enabled the F-111F to perform low-level, high-speed bombing runs with little risk to aircraft and crew. Although Pave Tack did not guide the Mk-82s, the laser designation system determined the exact range to the target and facilitated accurate delivery. The Aardvark typically carried a load of four Paveway IIs or a dozen 500-pound bombs on a strike mission.[35]

The F-111Fs of 48 TFW were a powerful EUCOM asset that the United States could use to deliver a considerable blow against Qaddafi, but their use—more specifically, the use of the British bases—in a non-NATO mission required the consent of the British government, as stipulated in a 1951 agreement signed by U.S. president Harry S. Truman and British prime minister Clement Attlee. Earlier in 1986 Prime Minister Margaret Thatcher had made it clear that she would not condone the use of military force to retaliate against terrorism. Its use was acceptable only in self-defense and only against terrorist targets. After reviewing the target list for the first time on 8 April, Reagan sent a secure message to Mrs. Thatcher asking for the cooperation of her government in the event he ordered an attack on Libya. On 9 April she sent a message to Reagan requesting additional information on the purpose and objective of such a mission. The members of her cabinet were nearly unanimous in their opposition to giving the United States permission to use the airfields. They were profoundly concerned that terrorists would target British citizens, embassies, and commercial interests overseas. Mrs. Thatcher overruled them, arguing that she would support Reagan so long as he justified the operation on the grounds of self-defense.[36]

In a nationally televised news conference on the evening of 9 April Reagan refused to comment on press reports that he had decided to attack Libya in retaliation for the bombing of the West Berlin discothèque. "This is . . . not a question that I feel that I could answer," he stated. "Except that you all know that you've heard me on the record for several years now—that if and when we could specifically identify someone responsible for one of these acts, we would respond. And so . . . we're trying to . . . find out who's responsible for . . . that dastardly attack in West Berlin." He also refused to comment on reports that the United States had intercepted communications between Qaddafi and the Libyan people's bureau in East Berlin. He did, however, stoke the war of words between Libya and the United States when a reporter asked him to speculate on the reason why Americans are so often the targets of terrorism. "We know that this mad dog of the Middle East has a goal of a world revolution," he declared. "Where we figure in that I do not know. . . . But there's no question but that he has singled us out more and more for attack and we're aware of that." Near the end of the press conference Reagan was asked if a state of undeclared war existed between the United States and Libya. "Not on his side, he's declared it," he responded. "We're going to defend ourselves . . . and we're certainly going to take action in the face of specific terrorist threats."[37]

After the press conference a news blackout descended over the administration. At his press briefing the following morning White House Press Secretary Larry Speakes announced that he would not answer questions pertaining to

Qaddafi or Libya. Despite the embargo on official information, the national media was buzzing with speculation that an attack on Libya was in the works.[38]

"A Gross Tactical Error Was Being Made"

Reacting to media reports that a U.S. air strike was highly likely, Qaddafi threatened to take Americans and other Westerners hostage and move them to probable target sites. It was obvious that all military and civilian officials involved in planning El Dorado Canyon did not have a moment to lose. In their race to finalize the strike plans before Qaddafi could carry out his anti-American terrorist campaign or before he could take hostages, Kelso's Navy and Air Force planners (working primarily at the CVBG staff, air wing, and squadron levels) made the many crucial decisions regarding force composition and weapons selection. According to the final version of the execute order, which was released only two days before the raid, Kelso planned to employ two strike groups in a simultaneous attack against all five targets. The Air Force would hit the three targets in Tripoli while the Navy would strike the two targets in the Benghazi area. This division of responsibility would simplify operational planning and prevent conflicts in the command and control aspects of the raid. Air Force and Navy planners completed their work within five days of Reagan's tentative go-ahead of 9 April.[39]

Forty-eight TFW planners realized that the wing's participation in the raid depended on the approval of Mrs. Thatcher's government, and they were fully aware that her concurrence in the mission was far from certain. Furthermore, if Mrs. Thatcher did grant approval, they hoped that either the French or Spanish governments would permit the bombers and their support aircraft to fly over their countries to and from Libya. If the French and Spanish refused overflight the mission would require a huge flotilla of tanker aircraft and the Air Force aircraft would be forced to fly 2,800 miles one way around the Iberian Peninsula, through the Straits of Gibraltar, and across the western half of the Mediterranean to Libya. Furthermore, the longer flight to Libya would dictate four mid-flight refuelings instead of three. Despite the uncertainties surrounding the cooperation of the British, French, and Spanish governments, Air Force officers proceeded with strike preparations.

In a mission as complex as El Dorado Canyon, in which timing was crucial, a streamlined method for refueling the bombers had to be included in the plan. Following a standard refueling plan opened the way for too great a chance of reaching Libya late. In a standard plan bombers would rendezvous with tankers at designated points along the way. For example, tankers flying out of the Azores would meet up with and refuel bombers flying from the United States to Europe. However, flying at night in radio silence and with a huge formation of aircraft, the rendezvous method was too complex for an operation that had to run on time. Therefore, the Air Force decided to scrap the rendezvous option and have the tankers fly in company with the F-111Fs from takeoff to landing.[40]

During the first three months of 1986 the JCS expanded the list of potential Libyan targets for 48 TFW planners from a handful to three dozen. Over the same period the JCS sent a list of 152 prospective targets to the carrier air wing staffs in the Sixth Fleet.[41] As they worked out detailed plans for each target, Westbrook's staff believed that if an attack was ordered they would be tasked to perform a surgical strike mission, hitting one target with about a half-dozen F-111Fs. This contingency was dubbed "the twenty-hour option"— a plan to hit a specific target involving an approximately twenty-hour round-trip mission for Lakenheath-based F-111Fs. Planning for this option included the following assumptions: mission tasking would stem from a national contingency dealing with Libya, the target would be selected from a short list of very important targets, overflight would not be granted, tanker support would be required, and the attack would be carried out at night. The Air Force's twenty-hour option could be ordered in conjunction with a Navy strike or independently, and it could take place with or without significant external support from the Navy or other Air Force units. Since a surgical strike required just a handful of aircraft, only a small portion of the wing's aircrews underwent the intense, specialized training for the mission. In an early training exercise a half-dozen F-111Fs departed Lakenheath, flew nonstop to Turkey, dropped 2,000-pound practice bombs on a range near Konya in the southwest part of the country, then landed at the NATO airbase at Incirlik, Turkey, a couple of hundred miles further east. The elapsed time from takeoff to time over target (TOT) was more than five hours.[42]

On 21 March, 48 TFW staged a small-scale rehearsal using some of the crews designated to participate in an actual strike. Westbrook and Maj. Gen. David C. Forgan—the deputy chief of staff for operations at USAFE, who in January was named the head of Air Force contingency planning by Gen. Charles L. Donnelly, the commander in chief of USAFE—embarked in a KC-10A Extender tanker, which served as the command ship for the mission. The strike force for the exercise consisted of a pair of Lakenheath-based F-111Fs and an Upper Heyford–based EF-111A Raven electronic warfare plane. After topping off their fuel from the KC-10A, the F-111Fs and EF-111A flew across France and simulated bombing a Sixth Fleet ship positioned in the central Mediterranean. After "hitting" the target the strike force and Sixth Fleet units practiced communications and rehearsed flight procedures that were designed to prevent a "blue-on-blue" engagement during an actual raid. The Aardvarks and Raven later rendezvoused with the KC-10A, refueled, and returned to their bases in England. During the exercise liaison officers were present in both the 48 TFW and Task Force 60 command centers. A naval officer flew with Forgan and Westbrook in the KC-10A, while an Air Force officer joined the staff of the carrier battle group. The exercise lasted six hours, and its success demonstrated that the two services could work effectively with each other. (It is interesting to note that the March rehearsal was originally conceived by the Third Air Force (3 AF), the major USAFE component based in the United Kingdom, and took place before the scope of contingency planning was significantly expanded prior to the start of Attain Document III.) In mid-March USAFE directed 48 TFW to develop strike plans for several new targets.[43]

In the aftermath of the bombing of La Belle discothèque, any thought of a small surgical strike was tossed in the trash bin. Reagan administration officials and senior commanders in Europe wanted to inflict "maximum visible damage" to the seat of Qaddafi's power, a demand that would have deadly consequences for 48 TFW.

On Thursday, 10 April, the Pentagon's execute order for Operation El Dorado Canyon arrived at 48 TFW. Westbrook and his planners studied the order and interpreted the strike as an all-Navy operation because the order indicated that "it is doubtful . . . diplomatic clearance from the United Kingdom will be forthcoming." A short time later, Mrs. Thatcher gave her assent to Reagan's request to use U.S. Air Force assets based in Great Britain, and the Pentagon immediately modified the execute order. The revised order directed 48 TFW to plan for a raid against one target using six F-111Fs.[44] On Saturday morning Col. Tom Yax, 48 TFW's director of operations, traveled to USAFE headquarters in Ramstein, Germany, where he picked up a second revision to the execute order. The newest order listed the three Tripoli targets—Bab al-Aziziyah Barracks, Tripoli Military Airfield, and Murat Sidi Bilal—but did not specify how many targets were to be attacked. It stated that the number of targets would depend on the status of overflight. If overflight was granted, eighteen F-111Fs would attack all three targets. If it was refused, six planes would attack only one target.[45] Doubting that the F-111Fs and their supporting aircraft would be allowed to take a shortcut and figuring on six planes against one target, Yax flew back to Lakenheath.

Immediately upon his return to Lakenheath, Yax was phoned by Forgan and was informed that eighteen planes would be used in the raid. Soon after that Maj. Gen. Thomas G. McInerney, 3 AF commander, and Westbrook flew to Ramstein to meet with Donnelly. They sought to confirm the size of the strike and clarify some of the wording in the execute order. They wanted to know how the F-111F crews could achieve the seemingly incompatible goals of inflicting "maximum visible damage" and assuring "minimum collateral damage." Did one goal have priority over the other? Donnelly made it clear that no one expected that the air strike would be carried out without causing some collateral damage. Therefore, inflicting "maximum visible damage" on targets connected to Qaddafi's terrorist network took priority over minimizing collateral damage. Donnelly also expressed his concern that some American planes might be lost in the raid. Surprised by Donnelly's statement, McInerney commented that no target in Libya was worth the loss of one airman. Donnelly responded by saying that the Air Force has the duty to destroy the targets it is assigned, even if doing so places its crews in harm's way. Donnelly told McInerney and Westbrook to plan on using eighteen F-111Fs and to arm the planes with weapons necessary to inflict considerable damage.[46]

Within days of the mission USAFE was instructing 48 TFW to prepare for a large raid against the Tripoli targets. Venkus commented on the formidable task now facing Westbrook and his staff:

> For over three months, we had been planning for a small, surgical raid by no more than six jets. Now, however, with very little time left to adjust, the size of the mission had been tripled. . . . It was incredible to all of us that major changes to the targets . . . and especially to the raid's size were all being made within forty-eight hours of the planned takeoff time. The impact on all aspects of the final planning was amazing. The biggest contributor was the sheer number of aircrews brought into the planning process at the last minute. . . . Those new crews found a hornets' nest of activity at Lakenheath as everyone worked feverishly to make the mission work.[47]

The immediate problem facing 48 TFW was the selection of crews to man the additional bombers. Up to that point no more than a dozen crews had been preparing for a surgical raid. Now at least twice that number would be needed to launch as primary and backup crews. Westbrook assigned the task of crew selection to his three squadron commanders—all experienced lieutenant colonels who had flown with and observed their pilots and WSOs on a daily basis. Since the scope of the mission had been expanded, they would have to select younger and less-experienced crews.[48]

The other critical problem facing 48 TFW was the distribution of the eighteen bombers among the three targets in Tripoli. According to the final strike plan nine Aardvarks, each armed with four 2,000-pound Paveway IIs, would attack Aziziyah. Three F-111Fs, also armed with Paveway IIs, would bomb the Murat Sidi Bilal training facility. Laser-guided weapons were required for these targets because of their proximity to civilian neighborhoods. The remaining six bombers would tear up the Tripoli Military Airfield with 500-pound Snakeye high-drag bombs. The F-111Fs would be formed into attack elements of three aircraft each, and each element would have its own radio call sign. The planes attacking Aziziyah would be identified as "Remit," "Elton," and "Karma." "Jewel" would strike Murat Sidi Bilal, and "Puffy" and "Lujac" would target the Tripoli Military Airfield.[49]

The planners at Lakenheath vehemently disagreed with the decision to allocate the Tripoli strike force in this manner. When the wing was informed on Saturday morning that eighteen planes would attack the Tripoli targets, Westbrook and his staff assumed that six planes would be used for each of the three targets. Later in the day Lt. Col. Bob Pastusek, chief of 48 TFW's offensive operations branch and one of the key figures in the wing's planning efforts, was asked by the USAFE staff how the wing would allocate the bombers if the decision were left up to them. Pastusek took the question to the pilot of Remit-31, one of the wing's squadron commanders and an experienced Vietnam combat pilot who would lead the attack on Tripoli. (This was the same officer who had briefed General Rogers back in January.) The pilot studied each of the targets and the surrounding defenses and recommended that three F-111Fs be used against Murat Sidi Bilal, a maximum of six against Aziziyah, and nine against the Tripoli airfield. He stated that Murat Sidi Bilal contained only a few valuable targets and therefore could be hit convincingly with three bombers. He suggested that nine Aardvarks attack the Tripoli airfield because it was away from the city, was lightly defended, and presented several highly visible targets: Qaddafi's fleet of Candid transports. Nine bombers could achieve devastating results there with little risk to crews and civilians. The officer recommended that no more than six planes should be sent against Aziziyah. According to Venkus, the pilot based his recommendation on the following factors:

> Aziziyah was a relatively small target complex in the center of an urban area. For that reason, precision weapons—laser guided, 2,000-pound GBU-10 bombs—would be utilized. For these weapons to guide correctly, the target must remain visible to both the bomb and the attacking aircraft. Sending six jets raised the possibility that aim points would be obscured by smoke and debris from preceding attackers even if the winds were exactly as forecast.

The proximity to urban Tripoli also increased the odds that unintended collateral damage could occur. A mistake made in attacking Sidi Bilal or Tripoli airport would be bad, but not as bloody as what might occur in downtown Tripoli. Sending more jets against Aziziyah would increase the chances that this might happen.

Finally, Aziziyah was the most heavily defended target. . . . Attacking this target with a large number of aircraft increased the odds that one or more of them would be damaged or shot down. . . . Six jets across Aziziyah was a maximum; even that number might produce casualties.[50]

According to the strike plan under development, Remit-31 would be the first plane across Aziziyah, carrying a full load of 2,000-pound LGBs and heading in the direction of the predicted surface wind. The pilot would be aiming for a two-story rectangular building, Qaddafi's headquarters-residence, at the extreme southeastern edge of the compound. If the winds were as predicted, dust and smoke from this pilot's bombs would not obscure the aim points of the planes in trail behind him. The plan also called for at least thirty seconds of spacing between jets as a margin of safety for a night attack. Assuming nine planes were used to attack Aziziyah, the pilot in that ninth plane, Karma-53, would not deliver his ordnance until four minutes after the pilot of Remit-31 had dropped his.[51]

Early Saturday evening, 12 April, Pastusek took the pilot's recommendations to Westbrook, who heartily agreed with his squadron commander's proposal. Pastusek then relayed the wing's recommendation directly to Forgan, who expressed his concurrence without reservation. Pastusek hoped that there would be no further changes. A few hours later Forgan phoned 48 TFW and informed an officer on duty of a momentous change: 48 TFW would hit Aziziyah with nine F-111Fs, not six; the Tripoli Airfield with six, not nine; and Murat Sidi Bilal with three. At about 0100 U.K. time on Sunday morning, 13 April, Pastusek was notified of the change and immediately phoned USAFE headquarters. Despite the unusual hour he was able to reach Forgan. He strenuously communicated the wing's disagreement with the change and indicated that the 48 TFW believed it was a "high-risk, low-payoff" gamble. Forgan indicated that either the commander in chief of USAFE, General Donnelly, or a higher authority at EUCOM had made the decision and firmly stated that 48 TFW now had its orders. "A gross tactical error was being made," Venkus recalled, "and it was being done against the best judgment of the people who were planning and flying the mission."[52]

In the opinion of the wing's officers, sending a stream of nine jets over Aziziyah was a poor tactical decision for the reasons noted earlier. Most important, it raised the odds of American casualties because attacking planes would spend at least four minutes over a target that was being protected by alerted defenders. The situation would be particularly harrowing for the last three bombers in the raid—the Karma element.[53] "All of our planning in the months preceding the raid had been based on the premise that, next to the success of the mission defined by bombs on target, preventing the loss of an airplane was the paramount consideration," Venkus commented. "This goal had been stressed in several of the directive messages from above the wing. For that reason, we had never recommended assigning more than six jets to a target so that the total time over target would not exceed two-and-a-half minutes."[54]

It is appropriate to mention here a peculiar incident that occurred at the mission briefing on Sunday. The pilot who would lead the Karma element across Aziziyah was pulled aside by General McInerney and given a remarkable piece of advice. The general advised him to abort his section's attack if Libyan defenses appeared too formidable. Apparently McInerney was confident that the pilot of Karma-51, a Vietnam combat veteran, would be able to use his own judgment to make the right call. The pilot was astonished by McInerney's suggestion. "Here they were asking me to fly six thousand miles with the possibility of aborting my flight because of threat reaction," he stated. The pilot recalled that he had never been given that option in seventy-six combat missions over Vietnam.[55]

Forgan also had profound reservations about using nine planes to attack Aziziyah. He was concerned that smoke and dust would interfere with the WSO's ability to see the target and illuminate it with the laser beam. If dust and smoke from earlier explosions hid the target, then the 2,000-pound bombs would fall unguided. "We finally concluded that although it was not the optimum, it was do-able," Forgan said.[56] David Martin and John Walcott reported —and Venkus supported—the conclusion that it was Donnelly who made the decision to increase the number of planes targeting Aziziyah.[57] In *Best Laid Plans,* Martin and Walcott describe how the USAFE commander arrived at his controversial decision:

> For each structure in the compound, Donnelly's staff calculated a "probability of damage." With one plane, the chances of knocking a building out were less than 50 percent. Laser-guided bombs were more accurate than "iron bombs," but they still had a probable error of seventy feet. That's how much they might miss by if everything went right. . . . Add to the forces of nature the possibility of a bent fin or a shaky hand and the bomb could miss

the target completely. There was also the "probability of arrival" to consider—the chances that the plane would reach its target without being shot down. So, said Donnelly, "you keep adding aircraft until you arrive at a desirable PD [probability of damage]."[58]

Venkus later disputed Donnelly's rationale. He argued that "PD against any particular aim point only increases if the number of aircraft attacking that aim point goes up." In the case of Qaddafi's compound in Tripoli, five of the seven aim points would be attacked by one aircraft each. Therefore, no cumulative increase in PD would be achieved.

The officers of 48 TFW planned to brief McInerney on the strike plan on Sunday afternoon. If the plan was going to be changed and the tactical error corrected, the best place to start that process was at the briefing for McInerney. Perhaps he would seize on the error and convince Donnelly to reallocate the F-111Fs. In addition to McInerney, those attending the briefing were Westbrook, Venkus, Yax, Col. Ed Dunivant (48 TFW's deputy commander for operations), Col. Steve Ridgeway (3 AF's deputy commander for operations), and the squadron commanders of 48 TFW. The pilot of Remit-31, the squadron commander who would lead the attack, was the principal briefer.[59]

The briefing went smoothly until the pilot presented the plan to attack Aziziyah. McInerney immediately detected the error. He stated that nine jets were too many for a target located in downtown Tripoli and that the wing should expect considerable criticism if an aircraft was lost using this plan. A number of 48 TFW officers made it clear to him that the wing had recommended a different allocation of bombers but had been overruled by USAFE or another higher authority. Aware of the plan's Achilles' heel, McInerney asked if there was anything he could do to ensure the mission's success. Westbrook did not respond but, after some hesitation, Venkus spoke up. Unaware of Donnelly's comment to McInerney and Westbrook of the day before, that planes might be lost in the operation, he asked McInerney if he could work to get the bomber allocation changed. "A return to the numbers per target that the wing had recommended on Saturday night would be one option," Venkus recalled. "If there was not enough time for that, a reduction in the size of the attack from eighteen to fifteen aircraft would also work—simply scrub the last three F-111Fs slated for Aziziyah and their affiliated support forces."[60]

McInerney listened carefully to Venkus but he had resigned himself to a large raid on Bab al-Aziziyah. Westbrook also accepted this reality. They had heard Donnelly's views the day before and understood that either he or even higher authority had made the decision. Inflicting "maximum visible damage" to Qaddafi's means of conducting or supporting terrorist operations was the paramount goal. Other considerations, such as minimizing the risk to American forces and reducing the potential for civilian casualties, were secondary. Therefore, despite his offer to help, McInerney decided he would make no effort to change the plan.[61]

At the conclusion of the briefing McInerney conferred with Westbrook and recommended that the last two groups of F-111Fs slated for Aziziyah should monitor the situation unfolding ahead of them. If the defenses appeared formidable they should be ready to abort their attacks rather than risk being shot down. McInerney's advice was passed on to the pilot of Remit-31 and the six pilots of the Elton and Karma elements, one of whom was the pilot of Karma-51. "The only option they were given was an untenable one," commented Venkus. "It is utterly against both the training and the instinct of fighter crewmen to abort a mission because they might be hurt."[62]

Meanwhile, Navy planners finalized their plans for the two Benghazi targets. Planning for them was not nearly so complicated or controversial. Against the barracks and the airfield Kelso would send fifteen carrier-based A-6Es. Seven VA-34 Blue Blasters from the *America* would strike the Benghazi Military and Jamahiriyya Guard Barracks with Snakeyes, while eight VA-55 Warhorses off the *Coral Sea* would hit the Benina Airfield with a combination of Snakeyes and CBU-59 cluster bombs. The attack plans for the two A-6E squadrons were nearly identical. The planes in each squadron would rendezvous, descend to an altitude below the radar horizon, perform a series of timing turns to achieve a forty-second separation between aircraft, and execute a single-plane ingress to and egress from the targets at an altitude of five hundred feet.[63]

Taking Care of Every Last Detail

In the days running up to the strike Kelso demanded that his Navy and Air Force planners adhere to the strict guidelines handed down by President Reagan when he gave the preliminary go-ahead for the operation. To maximize surprise, overwhelm Libyan air defenses, and minimize the risk to U.S. forces and Libyan civilians, the targets would be struck simultaneously while targets not positively identified would not be attacked. All combat systems had to be fully operational for any aircraft to drop its bombs, and the attack planes would be authorized only one pass over the target area. There would be no re-attack of any target.[64]

A huge armada of Navy, Marine Corps, and Air Force aircraft would fly in support of the attack force. Two SAM suppression groups would neutralize the air defenses around Tripoli and Benghazi. Four EF-111A Ravens, nicknamed "Spark Varks" by their crews, would accompany the F-111Fs to the vicinity of Tripoli. Marking their combat debut, the EF-111As would operate as standoff, high-power jammers. (Their crews would have to endure the same level of fatigue as the F-111F crews.) The EF-111As, which were identified by the call sign "Harpo," were from 42d Electronic Combat Squadron of 20 TFW based at RAF Upper Heyford near Oxford, about sixty miles northwest of London. One Marine Corps EA-6B Prowler based on the *America* would join the Ravens. Rounding out the Tripoli SAM busters would be six A-7E Corsair IIs, also based on the *America*. The Benghazi SAM suppression group would consist of eight F/A-18 Hornets based on the *Coral Sea,* two *America*-based A-7Es, and three EA-6Bs off both the *Coral Sea* and the *America.* Both the EF-111As and EA-6Bs were equipped with the AN/ALQ-99 advanced tactical ECM system. The A-7Es were armed with either AGM-88A HARM or AGM-45 Shrike antiradiation missiles; the F/A-18s carried HARMs. Although the Shrike was of Vietnam vintage, it was particularly suitable for attacking Qaddafi's SA-2 SAM system. Two EA-3B Skywarriors, one from each carrier, would provide additional electronic warfare support. The Navy would provide MiG CAP—a defense against Libyan fighters —for both strike groups. Four *America*-based F-14s would protect the F-111Fs, while four Hornets off the *Coral Sea* would cover the Navy strike on Benghazi. Four F/A-18s would shield the battle force, and two Hornets would safeguard search and rescue (SAR) operations. Each carrier would operate two E-2C Hawkeyes for long-range surveillance, strike coordination, fighter control, and SAR coordination. A fleet of seven KA-6D and two KA-7 tankers would provide aerial refueling services for the carrier-based aircraft. Operation El Dorado Canyon would bring together more than a hundred attack and support aircraft from England and carriers in the Mediterranean in total darkness for an air raid that would last about twelve minutes.[65]

During the weekend of 12-13 April, while the crisis over the number of F-111Fs allocated to strike Bab al-Aziziya took center stage, Westbrook, his squadron commanders, and several other members of his staff furiously hammered out the seemingly countless details of the mission: the order of attack, timetable, aim points, and ordnance load. The squadron commanders of 48 TFW huddled with Pastusek to review the desired mean points of impact (DMPIs—pronounced "dimpies") for each target. The DMPIs marked the exact locations where the bombs would be aimed. Each plane would strike one aim point. For Aziziyah, Pastusek marked nine aim points on an intelligence photograph of the compound. With nine planes attacking the compound the selection of DMPIs had to be calculated carefully. Furthermore, the predicted surface winds had to be taken into account to determine the order in which the aim points would be hit. If the sequence was chosen incorrectly or if the winds at the time of the strike were not as forecast, the F-111Fs flying over the target later would have their aim points obscured by smoke and debris from earlier bomb impacts.[66] Two planes—Remit-31 and Karma-53, the first and the last of the group—would each strike Qaddafi's headquarters-residence building with a full load of 2,000-pound LGBs. The crews of those two aircraft would aim their bombs at the air conditioning unit on the roof of the building. Two other planes would bomb a large administration building in the middle of the compound. Each of the remaining five planes would hit a single building—a barracks or a storage shed—within the compound.

Assigning two planes to attack Qaddafi's headquarters-residence building certainly increased the chances of killing or wounding Qaddafi, but that was not the mission's objective. "The purpose was not to kill Qaddafi," Donnelly asserted. "It was to make a point to Qaddafi." Yax recalled that the wing was not "concerned about structuring a strike to actually catch him." The strike planners at Lakenheath had no way of knowing where Qaddafi would be at the time of the attack but, as Forgan put it, "If we caught Qaddafi in bed that would be a bonus, but that was not the goal."[67] At the final intelligence briefing before the start of the mission, the F-111F crews were informed that Qaddafi's whereabouts were unknown.[68]

The Pentagon wisely assumed that the F-111Fs would be forced to fly around the Iberian Peninsula to Libya. Therefore, with the weekend about to begin it ordered several KC-10A Extender tankers based in the United States to deploy to Great Britain. On Sunday afternoon KC-10As from Barksdale Air Force Base in Louisiana, March AFB in California, and Seymour Johnson AFB in North Carolina began arriving in England to augment the KC-135R Strato-tankers of the European Tanker Force. Twelve KC-10As and nine KC-135Rs were staged out of RAF Mildenhall in Suffolk, about eighty miles northeast of London, while five KC-10As and four KC-135Rs were based at RAF Fairford in Gloucester, about seventy miles west of London. Each KC-10A was capable of transferring about 200,000 pounds of fuel; each KC-135R transferred about 120,000 pounds.[69]

Many tanker crews were not informed of their deployment to Great Britain until Saturday afternoon, April 12. With barely enough time to get their planes preflighted, their flight plans filed, and their personal gear rounded up, they took off for England. The fliers knew nothing about the operation they would be supporting. A few hours after their arrival they received their first operational briefing. After the briefing several tanker crewmen huddled with 48 TFW's squadron commanders and the tanker commander from RAF Mildenhall, an experienced tanker officer, and worked out the refueling plan. What emerged was a simple plan known as "mother tanker," which facilitated silent refueling operations. According to the plan the KC-135Rs would refuel the KC-10As, which in turn would refuel a four-plane cell of F-111Fs and EF-111As. The bombers would stay with their tanker until they reached the drop-off point for the attack run. The tanker crews would perform four silent refuelings of the strike force while en route to the target area. With the refueling plan completed the tanker crews refueled their planes, reviewed the operational details of the mission, and grabbed some shuteye.[70]

One of the KC-10As was configured as the airborne command post for Forgan and Westbrook. After much deliberation Westbrook decided to fly in the command KC-10A rather than lead the strike force in one of the F-111Fs. Venkus later provided unique insight into Westbrook's decision:

> Sam Westbrook made the very logical decision that the raid's success was too important to risk. One of the wing's squadron commanders, who had been . . . receiving extra training for over three months, would be more likely to achieve that success. . . . It is fair to say that some number of those who would have made the emotional decision to be out front would have also made inadvertent errors that could have jeopardized the mission. Col. Sam W. Westbrook III held his ego in check and made the right call; the chances for the success of Operation El Dorado Canyon were significantly enhanced as a result.[71]

The thirty F-111F crews selected by 48 TFW's squadron commanders were briefed on the operation at 1500 U.K. time on Sunday, 13 April. Thirty crews were briefed to ensure ample backups. According to the plan twenty-four F-111Fs would take off from Lakenheath. Eighteen planes would be designated primary aircraft for the mission while the remaining six planes would serve as spares. The pilots and WSOs in all twenty-four F-111Fs would thoroughly evaluate the systems in their aircraft and, if the crew in one of the primary aircraft identified an equipment malfunction, that plane would be replaced by a fully operational spare. After the last briefing on Sunday night most of the crews stayed around until well after midnight to study their mission folders, which contained the details of the mission. Several men found time to update their wills or seek the counsel of one of the base's chaplains. Each crew member was ordered to get a good night's sleep, and directed to report back to the base by 1400, Monday. Although the pilots and WSOs were offered quarters at the base, most of them slept in their own beds that night, all the while trying not to betray to their families their apprehension and excitement about the operation about to unfold. Flight surgeons offered the airmen a newly developed sleeping tablet that was designed to induce immediate deep sleep but after eight hours would allow them to waken refreshed with the drug completely out of their bloodstream. Several fliers needed the sleeping pill to settle their nerves and bring on sleep. A number of men could not manage a satisfactory night's sleep even with the pill.[72]

Over the weekend 48 TFW tried to keep up a normal routine at RAF Lakenheath. Luckily a long-scheduled NATO exercise, code named "Salty Nation," was set to commence on Monday morning. Preparing for and conducting the exercise provided excellent cover when the media started asking questions about unusual developments taking place at the air bases in England. For example, public affairs officers could explain the presence of a large fleet of tanker planes by saying that the planes had flown in from the United States to support Exercise Salty Nation. At noon on Sunday the maintenance and ordnance crews arrived at Lakenheath, presumably to prepare the aircraft scheduled to participate in the exercise. Instead the crews were ordered to load live ordnance on the planes. "The crews knew this was unusual," Westbrook stated. "We told them what was going on, that this was a real go."[73]

Meanwhile, Battle Force Zulu, under the command of Admiral Mauz, was in the central Mediterranean completing its preparations for the air strike.[74] The air wings had conducted flight operations to sharpen aircrew efficiency, and battle force strike planners had selected attack routes and aim points, determined munitions load, and drafted the air defense suppression plan.[75] "The planning and briefing stages of the strike were extremely thorough," Commander Stumpf observed. "Although complex, the plan allowed each pilot and naval flight officer to concentrate on a single task, such as strike, CAP, or air defense suppression, rather than having one aircraft perform several missions." By virtue of extensive contingency planning and considerable experience operating near Libya, Mauz's force was soon ready and awaiting further orders.[76]

Easily overlooked yet vital to the successful preparation for the mission were the liaison officers who facilitated the joint efforts of the Navy and Air Force staffs. Officers in both services quickly realized that their technical vocabulary and tactical jargon were different and that extensive coordination was necessary to avoid interference between Air Force and Navy attack planes and support aircraft. As the contingency planning gathered momentum early in the year, Navy and Air Force liaison officers began traveling back and forth between the carrier battle groups in the Mediterranean and Lakenheath. They helped bridge differences in terminology and operational philosophy and helped finalize many details of the mission. One of 48 TFW's most experienced colonels spent considerable time on the *America* with Task Force 60 planners. During the final hectic days before the raid he coordinated air defense suppression and fighter cover with Task Force 60 planners and ensured that the mission time-table worked out by 48 TFW's planners conformed to the schedule promulgated by Kelso. Furthermore, his presence in the fleet allayed the fears of many Air Force crews that their planes might be shot down by Navy air defense systems. Similarly, by virtue of having one of their own at Lakenheath, Task Force 60 planners were confident that their strike plans were compatible with those of the Air Force.[77] According to W. Hays Parks, "Joint planning and command-to-command interface took place . . . in a highly professional atmosphere free of the acrimony and interservice rivalry frequently attributed to such military operations." During the raid a naval aviator flew on the KC-10A command plane and the colonel from 48 TFW was present with the Task Force 60 staff.[78]

Eleventh Hour Diplomacy

On Wednesday, 9 April, Admiral Crowe and Lt. Gen. Richard Burpee, the director of operations for the JCS, drove from the Pentagon to Fort Meyer to deliver the execute order to General Rogers, who was in the United States on official business. The original order had been signed by Deputy Secretary of Defense Taft, who was still acting in Weinberger's stead. On Thursday Rogers carried the order to his headquarters in Mons, Belgium. There he stopped long enough to change from his commander's aircraft, which was routinely watched by the Soviets, to a less-conspicuous executive jet. He then flew to Stuttgart, the headquarters of the European Command, and delivered copies of the order to Lawson, Donnelly, and Kelso. Kelso took off for the carrier *America* with his copy of the execute order. Donnelly took his copy and departed for his headquarters in Ramstein.[79] Westbrook received a copy of the order later that day.

Although President Reagan would retain the authority to cancel the operation, he insisted that Kelso control the timing and details of the attack. Kelso was free to execute Operation El Dorado Canyon as soon as he was satisfied that his forces were ready. He could abort the attack right up to the last moment, if weather conditions or operational factors warranted it.[80]

In addition to the intense military planning, important efforts were being made on the diplomatic front. On Friday, 11 April, Reagan dispatched retired Army Lt. Gen. Vernon A. Walters, who was serving as U.S. ambassador to the United Nations, to Europe to persuade allied leaders to join the United States in imposing a package of strict diplomatic and economic sanctions on Libya that would obviate U.S. military action. During high-level consultations in London, Madrid, Bonn, Paris, and Rome, Walters presented evidence of Libyan involvement in recent terrorist attacks, addressed the possibility of American military action if the allies failed to close ranks with the United States, and sought their support in the event the United States was forced to exercise that option. Realizing that failure to achieve a united front with the United States could hasten military action, the twelve EC foreign ministers agreed to meet in The Hague on Monday, 14 April, to discuss the adoption of additional sanctions against Qaddafi.[81]

Reagan was not optimistic that any of the new measures as proposed by the allies would be strong enough to influence Qaddafi's behavior. Moreover, he believed that all efforts to deal with Qaddafi thus far had been unsuccessful. Of immediate concern to Reagan was Qaddafi's threat to move foreign nationals to key military installations in order to "protect" those sites from American bombers.[82]

In London, Walters and Charles Price, U.S. ambassador to the United Kingdom, persuaded Prime Minister Thatcher to permit the F-111Fs to fly from their British bases. She was satisfied that the targets were terrorist-related, that the planned use of force was proportionate, and that the United States was acting in self-defense according to Article 51 of the UN Charter. It probably helped Reagan's cause that the United States supported Great Britain during the 1982 Falklands War with Argentina; that Qaddafi supported the Irish Republican Army, which in 1984 had attempted to assassinate Mrs. Thatcher with a bomb planted in a hotel where she was staying; and that in 1984 a Libyan gunman had killed a British policewoman who was trying to control a crowd of anti-Qaddafi demonstrators outside the people's bureau in London.[83] She later explained to the House of Commons how she arrived at the decision to support the United States: "In view of Libya's promotion of terrorism, the failure of peaceful means to deter it, and the evidence that further attacks were threatened, I replied to the president that we would support action directed against specific Libyan targets demonstrably involved in the conduct and support of terrorist activities."[84]

In the words of Secretary of the Navy Lehman, Mrs. Thatcher "came through like gang-busters."[85]

To help make up her mind Mrs. Thatcher had carefully examined British and American intelligence on the Libyan role in the discothèque bombing. Fortunately, she had her own transcripts of message traffic between Tripoli and East Berlin, which had been intercepted by the GCHQ. The prime minister urged Reagan to make public the evidence of Libyan involvement in the bombing of La Belle discothèque, even over the concerns of the intelligence community.[86] It is reasonable to conclude that Reagan would still have ordered the strike on Libya even without the support of at least one ally, especially in light of the evidence linking Qaddafi to the West Berlin bombing and the fact that Qaddafi was planning to launch several terrorist operations against American citizens and interests. Since the United States did not act unilaterally, the political benefits of the air raid were greatly increased.

Walters did not meet with similar success in Paris and Madrid. President François Mitterand of France and Prime Minister Felipe Gonzales of Spain refused his request for overflight in the event the United States elected to strike Libya with the F-111Fs based in Great Britain.[87] As if the refusal was not enough, Mitterand brashly offered gratuitous advice to the United States on how to conduct the raid: "Don't inflict a mere pinprick."[88] Following the raid the French Foreign Ministry made a vain attempt to justify the government's decision: "Informed of the intentions of the government of the United States, France refused to allow its air space to be used by American planes. It . . . deplores the intolerable escalation of terrorism which has led to an action of reprisal which in itself renews the chain of violence."[89]

The Reagan administration had first approached the French government about overflight in January. General Burpee, Navy captain James Stark of the NSC staff, and an officer from EUCOM traveled to Paris and asked senior French officials what their government would do if the United States decided to take military action against Libya from bases in Great Britain. The French gave an equivocal answer. They did not refuse overflight initially but emphasized that the United States should give them plenty of time to consider the request. The U.S. defense attaché in Paris presented the formal request to the French government on Saturday, which probably was not enough time for the Mitterand government. That evening the men at Lakenheath received the official notification that they long expected: the F-111F strike force would not be flying over France.[90] In his autobiography Reagan revealed his views on the French refusal to permit overflight. "The refusal upset me, because I believed all civilized nations were in the same boat when it came to resisting terrorism," he wrote. "At least in the case of France, however, economic considerations prevailed: while it publicly condemned terrorism, France conducted a lot of business with Libya and was typically trying to play both sides."[91]

When Rogers learned of the decisions of the French and Spanish governments he phoned Crowe, who expressed his concern that the extreme length of the flight would put the mission in jeopardy. When Crowe and Rogers learned that the pilots at 48 TFW were absolutely confident that they could carry out the mission, the two officers recommended that the operation should go forward. On Sunday afternoon Weinberger, who had returned earlier that day from his overseas tour, met with Taft and the joint chiefs at the Pentagon to review the plans for El Dorado Canyon. Weinberger was satisfied that the targets were linked to Libyan terrorism, that U.S. forces were adequate for the mission, and that reasonable precautions were being taken to minimize risks to both the attacking force and to Libyan civilians. The secretary of defense reported to Reagan that the plans were thorough and complete. Later that day Reagan gave final approval for Operation El Dorado Canyon.[92] Whether his actions were regarded as "self-defense" or "swift and effective retribution," after five years of tough talk Ronald Reagan was finally going to strike with punishing resolve against international terrorism.

Unaware that Reagan had ordered a retaliatory strike on Libya, the EC foreign ministers approved several diplomatic measures which they hoped would prevent an American attack. The sanctions, which British foreign secretary Geoffrey Howe described as a "credible response" to Libyan terrorism,[93] reduced the size of Libyan diplomatic and consular missions, restricted the movements of Libyan diplomats, and imposed stricter requirements for Libyans seeking visas.[94] For the first time the EC openly condemned Libya by name for its support and sponsorship of international terrorism. Nevertheless, the package of diplomatic sanctions fell far short of what the United States wanted: closure of the people's bureaus and the imposition of strict economic measures. Although the Europeans disliked Qaddafi's regime and abhorred his involvement with terrorism, they neither approved economic sanctions nor condoned American military action against Libya. They believed that the use of force would prompt terrorist reprisals against American targets in Western Europe and result in the loss of innocent European and American lives. Walters privately dismissed the action by the EC foreign ministers.[95] He noted that "it wasn't until they felt an American operation was imminent that they began to get together in great haste . . . and drew up that document."[96] Although the EC communiqué was a step in the right direction, Reagan was convinced that it would not stop Libyan terrorist operations currently underway. Recognizing the need to act urgently and decisively, Reagan refused to cancel or postpone Operation El Dorado Canyon.[97]

"Retribution Will Be Swift and Sure"

On the morning of 14 April, Kelso, who had embarked in *America* for the operation, convened a meeting onboard the carrier of all commanders and commanding officers in the battle force. He reviewed the execute order and led a discussion of the operational details of the mission. After the meeting the skippers "heloed" back to their ships, embarked staffs and squadrons, and informed their officers and men of the impending attack.

In the days leading up to the attack the *Coral Sea* and the *America* deliberately made as much "noise" as possible to focus the world's attention on the Sixth Fleet and, in the words of Admiral Breast, "to let everybody know where we were." Then, as the two battle groups prepared to commence high-speed runs to their launch points off Libya, their respective commanders terminated flight operations and imposed a strict emission control plan or "radio silence" on their ships. The plan, known as EMCON Alpha, required sailors throughout the force to secure all communications equipment, radars, and navigation aids—any source of an electronic signal that could compromise the position of either battle group.[98]

While Qaddafi and the world media tracked the movements of the U.S. Sixth Fleet, General McInerney skillfully completed the staging of his strike, support, and tanker forces in Great Britain. On 14 April he informed Kelso that the Air Force was ready to conduct Operation El Dorado Canyon. Kelso then sent orders to Mauz and McInerney, setting the TOT for 0200 Libya time, Tuesday, 15 April (1900 Washington time on Monday, 14 April).[99]

About six hours before the strike Mauz sent the following message to the commanders and commanding officers in Battle Force Zulu: "TF 60 and USAF F-111s are about to conduct strikes at a series of military targets in Libya in reprisal for clear and certain Libyan responsibility in recent attacks of terrorism. These strikes will represent a[n] historical milestone in dealing with state-sponsored terrorism. Those who sponsor such acts will perhaps for the first time, understand that retribution will be swift and sure as they contemplate their future activity."[100]

6

Operation El Dorado Canyon

Departing for Tripoli

Colonel Westbrook launched and recovered planes at RAF Lakenheath for Exercise Salty Nation until 1500 U.K. time on Monday, 14 April. After that time all planes taking off from the British base would be bound for Tripoli.

The F-111F mission crews started gathering at 48 TFW in the early afternoon, and those slated to bring up the rear in the nine-plane raid on Bab al-Aziziyah immediately checked to see if the plan had changed. None of them displayed any emotion when they realized that the plan had not been revised. The airmen then assembled in the crew room of the 494th Tactical Fighter Squadron (TFS) for the final briefing on the critical details of the mission: weather, latest intelligence on Libyan defenses, radio communications, refueling procedures, altitudes, speeds, turn points, radar offset points, aim points, escape and evasion plans, and hundreds of other vital pieces of information.

After the formal briefing Westbrook took the floor and addressed his pilots and WSOs. He reminded them that of the twenty-four F-111Fs that would take off from Lakenheath only the eighteen best planes would proceed to Libya. If a plane developed an equipment problem it would return to base, even if it was being flown by one of the squadron commanders or the hottest pilot in the wing. Westbrook reiterated that the ROE were extremely clear and would not be relaxed. The risks to both U.S. aircrews and Libyan civilians had to be kept to a minimum, and therefore a bomber's electronic systems had to be in full operating order or it would not deliver its ordnance.[1]

Westbrook concluded his presentation by telling his men that another person present wanted to speak to them. He was referring to the chief of staff of the Air Force, Gen. Charles Gabriel. Both events—Exercise Salty Nation and Gabriel's visit to Lakenheath—had been scheduled well before 48 TFW began its Libya contingency planning. Gabriel had spent the day with Westbrook touring the base, observing the exercise, and gathering first-hand information on Operational El Dorado Canyon. The chief of staff strode from the back of the room to the front, catching many of the men by surprise. He told the F-111F crews that they were not being ordered to do anything they had not been trained to do.[2] "If everybody followed the plan and no one tried to be a hero, the mission would succeed," he said. "We don't need any heroes. . . . They're a liability."[3]

After the briefing the pilots and the WSOs attended to some very basic needs. They ate a high-protein lunch and packed a substantial "in-flight meal" of sandwiches, fruit, cookies, juice, and a bottle of water and then visited the latrine before climbing into their aircraft. During the long mission, if a flier had to relieve himself he could urinate into a plastic "piddle pack," which contained absorbent material and could be tightly sealed.[4]

At about 1600 Westbrook and General Forgan, the mission commander who had arrived from Ramstein earlier in the day, drove to Mildenhall where they boarded the KC-10A tanker that would serve as their airborne command post. Aboard the plane technicians were busy checking out the radio equipment that would enable the two officers to stay in contact with the other planes on the mission and with the command centers at Lakenheath, Ramstein, Stuttgart, and in the carrier America. Admirals Kelso and Mauz would operate from the tactical flag command center in the America.[5]

The launch plan for Operation El Dorado Canyon was very complex. Its objective was to put nearly sixty bombers, electronic warfare planes, and tankers into the air from four different bases and do so without tipping off everyone in Great Britain that a large-scale military operation was underway. After the tankers began taking off the F-111Fs and EF-111As would commence launching in a "comm out," or complete radio silence status. They would join their designated tankers, which would carry out all necessary communications with air controllers on the ground. The Aardvarks and Ravens would fly in close formation with their tankers, and keep their IFF—identification friend or foe—

transponders turned off. The Air Force hoped that the strike force would appear to unsuspecting radar operators along the route simply as an unarmed flight of Air Force tankers.[6]

The giant tankers were the first aircraft to depart for Libya. A fleet of twenty-nine KC-10A Extenders and KC-135R Stratotankers began taking off from their bases at RAF Mildenhall and RAF Fairford at 1713 U.K. time (1213 Washington time). The tankers attracted some attention, but with Exercise Salty Nation in progress the British press did not link the departing tankers with the crisis involving the United States and Libya.[7]

At 1735, exactly four minutes after the command KC-10A took off from RAF Mildenhall, the first wave of eight F-111Fs began launching from their base at RAF Lakenheath. The Puffy element was the first to get airborne, since its target, the Tripoli Military Airfield, was the farthest away. Other F-111Fs followed at twenty-second intervals. If everything worked according to plan, in exactly six-and-a-half hours the crew of the lead Puffy aircraft would streak over the tarmac of the Tripoli airfield and drop twelve 500-pound bombs on a row of Il-76 Candid transport planes. At 1805 the second wave of sixteen F-111Fs started taking off and, at 1831, the first of five EF-111As launched from RAF Upper Heyford.[8] One of the Ravens was a mission spare.

The Aardvarks, Ravens, and tankers passed north of London, rendezvoused over southern England, and formed into their flight cells. The task force then proceeded southwestward toward the Atlantic. For ninety minutes the twenty-four F-111F crews checked and rechecked their aircraft systems and reported the results to their squadron commanders to ensure that the eighteen best planes continued the mission to Tripoli. The other six planes with their bitterly disappointed crews would return to Lakenheath. The departure of the unneeded aircraft would reduce the number of F-111Fs and EF-111As per tanker from four to three—one on each of the tanker's wings and one under the tanker's belly.[9]

Near Land's End the six F-111Fs (Remit-34, Elton-42, Karma-54, Jewell-64, Puffy-14, and Lujac-21), and one EF-111A (Harpo-75) were ordered to return to their bases. The strike force had seven fewer planes but it was nevertheless a sizeable armada, consisting of eighteen bombers, four electronic warfare planes, and twenty-nine tankers. Fliers called a force this size a "gorilla package." Following the departure of the spare planes the force turned south across the Bay of Biscay. Flying over three hundred knots at an altitude of twenty-six thousand feet, the planes commenced their first in-flight refueling operation.[10]

The dangerous operation was choreographed in advance to eliminate the need for radio communications. As the lead plane in each cell approached the

KC-10A's fueling boom, the other aircraft waited their turn in close formation. At night in radio silence the boom operator, who was lying face down inside the tanker, coached the pilot of the lead plane into position by flashing small signal lights located on the underbelly of the tanker. Once the plane was in position the boom operator guided the fuel probe into the receptacle located behind the cockpit of the fighter. After topping off his fuel tanks the pilot disengaged and slipped to the side, making way for the next customer.[11] In the words of one 48 TFW pilot, in-flight refueling conducted at night with no radio communications was simple. It's "just like day refueling," he said, "except you can't see a fucking thing!"[12] Subsequent refuelings en route to Libya would take place off the coasts of Portugal, Algeria, and Tunisia.[13]

During the long flight to Tripoli each pilot and WSO continuously evaluated his plane's combat systems and electronics suite. They performed a comprehensive "fence check," which automatically inspected the inertial navigation system, the terrain-following radar, the attack radar, the self-defense electronic warfare equipment, the Pave Tack FLIR and laser designator, and the switches on the weapons release panel. The crewmen held their breath each time they performed one of the checks. If a problem was detected they would have to abort the mission, considering the stringent rules of engagement. "The hope in every cockpit was that no last-second, hair-on-fire major malfunction would occur," noted Colonel Venkus.[14] If a problem cropped up it could mean a fourteen-hour, butt-numbing ride for nothing.

The arduous flight put extraordinary demands on the skill and endurance of every cockpit crew. "That's a long way to fly formation," the pilot of Remit-31 said. "My arm got tired. My neck got tired. . . . From time to time I would turn on the autopilot just to give myself a rest, but it couldn't hold formation for very long."[15]

Earlier in the day, at approximately 1030 local time, the *America* and the *Coral Sea* battle groups had commenced high-speed transits from the Tyrrhenian Sea to their scheduled operating areas north of the Tripoli FIR. The *Coral Sea* and her escorts sprinted through the Straits of Messina, while the *America* battle group swept around the west coast of Sicily and passed south of Malta. Battle Force Zulu was operating under EMCON Alpha, the complete shutdown of all radios and radars. Mauz hoped that the combination of speed and strict radio silence combined with the onset of darkness would foil the Soviet surveillance vessels that were prowling the central Mediterranean in search of the American fleet. Both battle groups successfully eluded an intelligence-gathering trawler, a *Sovremennyy*-class destroyer, and a modified *Kashin*-class DDG that were operating near Sicily and a pair of Soviet IL-38 May patrol aircraft that were flying out of their temporary base in Libya.

While the carriers steamed to their launch areas—the *America* to the west and the *Coral Sea* to the east, in a line approximately 180 miles off the coast of Libya—flight deck crews spotted, fueled, and armed the "go birds," and maintenance crews and electronics technicians performed preflight checks on each aircraft. For the attack planes "go" criteria meant a fully operational bombing and navigation system, mode IV IFF system, chaff dispenser, and radar homing and warning (RHAW) system. The chaff and RHAW systems were used for defense against enemy SAMs. Ordnancemen stenciled bombs with personal messages on behalf of friends or loved ones back home or slogans such as "To Muammar: For all you do, this bomb's for you" or "I'd fly 10,000 miles to smoke a camel." Meanwhile, the nuclear attack submarines *Dallas* (SSN 700) and *Dace* (SSN 607) established an invisible barrier to block Libya's fleet of six Soviet-built *Foxtrot*-class diesel-electric submarines from reaching the battle force.[16]

Consulting Congress, Notifying the Soviets, and Coping with the Media

At 1600 Washington time, President Reagan and his senior national security advisers met with House and Senate leaders to brief them on Operation El Dorado Canyon.[17] "At the conclusion of this meeting, I could call off the operation," Reagan emphasized. "I am not presenting you with a fait accompli. We will decide in this meeting whether to proceed." After Reagan and his advisers spoke and after each congressional leader had an opportunity to ask questions and express his concerns about the operation, the president asked if any of the senators or representatives believed that the operation should be canceled. None did. Reagan thanked them for their support and cautioned them about the sensitivity of the information contained in the briefing. After the meeting the lawmakers avoided making comments to reporters that might jeopardize the operational security of the mission.[18]

The Reagan administration waited until the mission was well underway to notify the Soviet government. The Soviet chargé d'affaires in Washington was called to the State Department where Secretary of State Shultz apprised him of the evidence of Libyan involvement in the West Berlin terrorist bombing, informed him of the operation, and assured him that the impending raid was in no way directed against his country.

Inevitably, several journalists examined the circumstantial evidence—Task

Force 60 was at sea, Ambassador Walters had completed a tour of allied capitals, and Reagan had just conducted a high-level meeting with congressional leaders—and concluded that an attack was imminent. The flood of news reports coming out of Washington had a very unsettling effect on the aviators of Task Force 60.[19] Commander Stumpf described their reactions thus: "These broadcasts listed target areas and proposed target times, which coincided almost exactly with the actual missions. Many believed chances for success without significant losses had been seriously jeopardized, since a major tactical feature of the strikes was the element of surprise. There was talk of postponing everything until whoever was compromising this vital information could be throttled. Aircrews whose missions would involve flying within enemy SAM envelopes were particularly alarmed by this breach of security."[20] Fortunately, the press was discussing U.S. military options and probable Libyan targets in very general terms. Crowe was confident that the element of surprise had been preserved. He remarked that "while there was a great deal of talk in the newspapers about the raid and so forth, we went to some effort, and I think we were successful in concealing the time of the raids and the actual targets." Also reassuring was the fact that the press was focusing its attention on Kelso's Sixth Fleet, not on the gorilla package plodding southward over the Atlantic.[21]

Closing in on Libya

Shortly after midnight Tripoli time, on 15 April (1700 Washington time on 14 April), the carriers went to flight quarters. The *America* and the *Coral Sea* began catapulting their planes into the dark, moonless night at 0045 and 0050, respectively. The *America* launched six A-6Es and eight SAM-suppression A-7Es. A seventh A-6E developed a problem with its TRAM system and aborted on the flight deck. The *Coral Sea* launched eight Intruders and a half-dozen anti-SAM F/A-18s, but two A-6Es aborted due to malfunctions with their RHAW and TRAM systems. The carriers also launched other crucial support aircraft: four EA-6Bs and two EA-3Bs for the suppression of the Libyan air defense network; F-14s and F/A-18s for protection of the Tripoli and Benghazi strike groups, defense of the battle force, and support of SAR operations; E-2Cs—a pair for each target sector—for strike coordination, long-range surveillance, CAP control, and SAR coordination; KA-6D and KA-7 tankers for in-flight refueling; and SH-3 helicopters for "lifeguard" duty during launch and recovery cycles and potential SAR missions. In all more than seventy aircraft were launched from the two carriers. Although *America*-based aircraft flew primarily in support of the

Air Force attack on Tripoli, three EA-6Bs and two A-7Es from CVW-1 supported the Navy strike on targets in the Benghazi area.

Flight deck personnel, air controllers, and aircrews carried out the launch in radio silence and with radars in standby or "non-radiate" status. Both launch cycles were completed by 0124. All aircraft planned to operate "zip-lip" until they reached the radar horizon of the Libyan air defense network.[22]

Meanwhile, as the Air Force planes arrived over the western Mediterranean, the pilot of Remit-31 realized that the strike force had fallen more than ten minutes behind schedule and, during a routine radio check, called out the word "time" to draw attention to the fact that the mission was running late. The situation had to be corrected immediately or the entire operation would be placed in extreme jeopardy. In a strike mission employing two separate forces timing is critical, because all surprise vanishes as soon as the first piece of ordnance explodes. If the Navy attacked the Benghazi targets on time but the Air Force planes were late, the Libyan defenders would be fully alerted by the time the F-111Fs arrived over Tripoli. Furthermore, if the bombers were late getting to Tripoli the effects of the Navy SAM suppression efforts would be nullified.

The Tripoli strike force could have fallen behind schedule for a number of possible reasons. It took the EF-111As more time than planned to join the formation. The KC-135Rs experienced difficulties refueling the KC-10As, which caused the formation to slow down. The formation encountered headwinds stronger than forecasted. Perhaps the best explanation was that tanker crews routinely use air speed when planning their missions, while fighter crews rely on ground speed. The latter more accurately tracks a plane's progress along a planned route, because it takes into account prevailing winds. Air speed equals ground speed only when no wind is present. Furthermore, during the final planning efforts no one from 48 TFW made it absolutely clear to the tankers that the bomber drop-off points in the central Mediterranean had to be reached on time. With drop-off points less than two hours away, urgent action needed to be taken to get the formation back on schedule. Agreeing with a recommendation from one of Westbrook's staff officers, Forgan ordered the task force to increase speed and shave some distance off the planned route by cutting the next turn. These actions eventually made up the lost ten minutes, but the increased speed made the next refueling extremely difficult, since F-111F controls become very sensitive—or "goosey," in fighter pilot jargon—at higher speeds. Venkus described the mood in the cockpits of the F-111Fs during this nerve-wracking phase of the transit to Libya: "As the delicate refueling maneuvers continued at airspeeds approaching four hundred knots, some F-111 crews silently cursed the tanker crews whom they mistakenly blamed for the entire problem. But they also breathed a sigh of relief as it became clear that they would make, though barely, their planned drop-off times. Because of the error, they would be operating at airspeeds much higher than normal for up to two hours. Flying night formation and refueling at these speeds was anything but fun."[23]

Off the coast of Tunisia the F-111Fs and EF-111As took their fourth and final pre-attack drinks from the tankers, still flying at twenty-six thousand feet. It was necessary to top off to ensure that the bombers had enough fuel to find their tankers in the dark or, if they were damaged during the raid, to fly clear of enemy territory. As each plane finished it dropped away from its tanker and started a gradual descent to its attack altitude of a few hundred feet.[24]

Meanwhile, back at Lakenheath at less than an hour before TOT, General Gabriel, Lt. Gen. John Shaud (an officer on Gabriel's staff), and General McInerney entered the wing's command post to monitor the attack. Until about 1500 U.K. time the command post had operated in a normal exercise mode. At two hours before takeoff British personnel were asked to leave and status boards containing operational information about the mission were uncovered. The Statue of Liberty Wing was now operating on a combat footing.[25]

Puffy-11, the plane slated to be the first to cross into Libyan territory, left its tanker at 0114, Tripoli time. With five F-111Fs trailing behind it Puffy-11 rushed toward the Tripoli Military Airfield, more than 350 miles away.[26] The other F-111Fs formed into their attack groups after topping off their tanks: nine planes for Aziziyah and three for Murat Sidi Bilal. As the bombers neared Tripoli some Air Force crews detected the silhouettes of SAM-busting A-7Es from the *America* moving into their firing positions. When he reached fifty miles from the beach the pilot of Puffy-11 turned off his navigation lights, armed his 500-pound bombs, and performed a final test of his plane's systems. Once over land he would depend on the TFR to carry him safely over the desert landscape that was speeding below. At 0152 Puffy-11 crossed the beach. The plane was southeast of Tripoli, sneaking up on the airfield through the back door. Just moments before that the WSO in Puffy-11 had updated the plane's inertial navigation system (INS) by locking on to an offset aim point (OAP), a natural or manmade geographical feature discernible on his radar. Updating the INS before the plane entered Libyan territory was crucial, because the F-111F's navigational system has an error rate of a quarter mile every hour.[27]

Meanwhile, equipment failure and pilot error had reduced the Aziziyah strike force to seven planes before the force reached the Tripoli target area. In Elton-44 the pilot completed the fourth refueling but did not break off until his tanker had turned toward its holding station located near Sicily. The pilot should have directed the tanker southward to facilitate his reaching the drop-off point on time. He realized that he could not reach the target on time without depleting his safety margin of excess fuel. He had no choice but to abort the mission, thus depriving the Aziziyah raiding force of one fully operational jet. Just before reaching Tripoli Elton-41 suffered a major equipment malfunction and it, too, had to abort. Additionally, one of the EF-111As, Harpo-72, experienced an equipment failure and was unable to carry out its mission.[28]

Hitting Qaddafi

On the evening of 14 April the attention of the Qaddafi regime was still focused on the carriers of Task Force 60, not the F-111Fs approaching from the west, but that was about to change. As the F-111Fs and their support aircraft traveled the long way in getting to Libya, they were detected by early-warning radars in several countries. While the radar operators in France, Spain, and Portugal kept silent, their counterparts in Italy alerted Malta, a country sympathetic to Qaddafi. About thirty minutes before the strike the Maltese warned Tripoli of a formation of U.S. Air Force planes flying over the central Mediterranean. Nevertheless, this new information apparently had little impact on the level of readiness of Libyan air defenses. "The steady sequence of building pressure from 3 to 14 April did not produce increased Libyan vigilance but fatigue," observed military historian Daniel Bolger, the author of *Americans at War, 1975–1986: An Era of Violent Peace*. "Tripoli evidently ignored the flurry of late afternoon and early evening conjectures as the American forces assembled."[29]

At 0150 Tripoli time, while the F-111Fs and A-6Es hugged the deck and bore down on their targets in Tripoli and Benghazi, the jammers and SAM busters went to work against what Secretary of the Navy Lehman described as "one of the most sophisticated and thickest" air defense systems in the world.[30] EF-111As and EA-6Bs began smothering Libyan air search radars with powerful electronic noise, and a couple of minutes later the pilots of the A-7Es and F/A-18s, who knew the locations and operating frequencies of most of the Libyan SAM radar sets, began unleashing a devastating barrage of HARM and Shrike missiles. The missiles knocked out radars serving SA-2 Guideline, SA-3 Goa, SA-6 Gainful, SA-8 Gecko, and French-built *Crotale* SAM batteries, and opened paths for the attacking aircraft. Sixteen HARMs and eight Shrikes were fired at Tripoli air defenses; twenty HARMs and four Shrikes were launched at radar sites in Benghazi.[31] The exploding warheads devastated active radar sites, shredding delicate antennas and raining hot, jagged fragments on support equipment and control facilities.

The operators of the SA-5 battery at Surt did not activate their radar until the strike aircraft had completed their attack runs and were outbound over the Mediterranean. Most likely the operators elected to stay out of the action, having learned their lesson the hard way on the night of 24–25 March.[32]

Meanwhile, the mission commander of an *America*-based E-2C described the exhilaration he felt the moment he switched his AN/APS-125 radar from standby to radiate: "The excitement really started . . . when we actually started picking up the people on our systems, when we started seeing these guys coming in from the western Mediterranean. . . . One of the most incredible things I've ever seen is that large number of Air Force aircraft come in. Their timing was incredible—right on the money, within seconds of when they were supposed to be there."[33]

Comdr. Jay Johnson, commander of *America*-based CVW-1, observed firsthand the state of Libyan readiness from the cockpit of his F-14 at his MiG CAP station twenty-five miles from Tripoli: "I came in at a low altitude and popped up on the clock and said, 'Holy Cow, this is a city that's asleep!' . . . They didn't have a clue."[34] Streetlights were shining in both Tripoli and Benghazi, and in the capital floodlights bathed the largest buildings and the minarets of the central mosque. Stumpf discovered that the Libyans had not extinguished the runway lights of the Benina Airfield, "which provided a visual beacon for the bombing runs."[35] The shining street and runway lights could have led one to conclude that the Libyans did not think an attack was imminent, but the element of surprise did not last long.

As the bombers approached their targets the Libyans threw up a dense volume of SA-2s, SA-3s, SA-6s, SA-8s, Crotales, and radar-guided ZSU-23/4 AAA. To the low flying F-111Fs and A-6Es the most deadly threats in Qaddafi's arsenal were the Crotales and AAA, both of which were far more capable against low-altitude targets than any of the Soviet-built SAMs. Luckily, most of the SAMs were not guided, thanks to the effectiveness of the U.S. jammers and ARM-firing aircraft. Errant missiles and wild AAAs streaked through the black skies over Tripoli and Benghazi, having little effect except to paint a terrifyingly surreal nocturne for the Air Force and Navy bomber crews as they bore down on their targets.[36] "Once we proceeded inbound to the target, there were a couple of SAMs launched," an A-6E pilot heading for Benina observed. "We were lit up, so they were looking for us, and they were shooting at us, but as far as I could tell . . . [the missiles] weren't guiding."[37]

As seven F-111Fs pressed their attack on Bab al-Aziziyah at an altitude of a couple hundred feet and 600 miles per hour, adrenaline was pumping and tension was palpable in each cockpit. Several concerns occupied the thoughts of the pilot of the lead plane, Remit-31. He worried about the performance of the terrain-following radar, so he constantly monitored its performance to make sure it did not fly his plane into the ground. He worried that he was not going fast enough and would arrive late over the target, so he kept his hand on the throttle to adjust air speed. He worried that the wind over the target might have shifted, thus obscuring aim points for the bombers following him. He worried that his WSO would not be able to locate the radar offset point—an operation crucial to the success of the mission.[38] And he worried about the Navy SAM-busters taking up their positions on time. "I had no idea whether the Navy had launched," he said. "The first time I ever saw or heard another airplane was forty seconds prior to my bomb release, when I looked up and saw a Navy A-7 firing a Shrike at a radar emitter. And boy that gave me a warm, fuzzy, good feeling inside."[39]

A few moments later the instruments on the pilot's console in Remit-31 indicated that the plane was 71,000 feet from Qaddafi's headquarters-residence building. As the plane roared over Tripoli harbor the pilot noticed several boats firing off flares. At just that moment a beeping sound went off in his headset, which indicated that he was being tracked by Libyan fire control radar. To evade the radar he descended to an even lower altitude which, although a good tactic, made it more difficult for his WSO to acquire his radar offset point—a set of piers in the harbor—on his radarscope. The WSO had loaded into the F-111F's computer the precise bearing and range of the aim point from the piers. If the WSO could lock his radar on to the offset point the computer would steer the plane automatically to the target. Therefore, for their attack to have any chance of success, it was essential that he find the piers. The plane's current speed and altitude made the task extremely difficult. He urged his pilot to pull up, but an instant later he located the offset aim point. "Yeah, we're looking good," he told his partner. He was confident that they were heading for Aziziyah.[40]

While Remit-31 was closing in on Aziziyah a number of network TV correspondents in Tripoli spoke over open telephone lines with their anchors back in the United States. It was exactly 0200 in the Libyan capital and 1900 on the East Coast. NBC correspondent Steve Delaney reported hearing the roar of a jet outside the window of his hotel room. Seconds later, millions of viewers of NBC Nightly News heard explosions and the crackle of gunfire.[41] "Tom, Tripoli is under attack!" Delaney told Tom Brokaw, the anchorman in New York.[42]

At the command center in the Pentagon Admiral Crowe and Secretary of Defense Weinberger waited for reports from CINCEUR headquarters in Germany and from the Sixth Fleet in the Mediterranean. In the meantime they listened to the CNN correspondent in Tripoli describe the city as calm and quiet but very tense. Suddenly the reporter shouted, "I'm hearing bombs and gunfire! . . . I can see rockets! I think there's an attack going on!" Crowe and Weinberger broke out in wide smiles. The strike was right on time.[43]

As Remit-31 hurtled toward Aziziyah, the pilot asked his WSO for the range to the target. At first the WSO could not respond, because he had not yet located the target building using the FLIR camera mounted beneath the aircraft. "Range!" demanded the pilot. An instant later the WSO replied: "Target direct." On his FLIR screen he could see Qaddafi's headquarters-residence building with the air-conditioning unit centered on the roof. As the range to the building ticked down to twenty-three thousand feet, the WSO warned his pilot, "Ready." When the range hit twenty-three thousand feet the WSO shouted, "Pull!" The pilot immediately initiated a Pave Tack Toss, pulling the nose of his plane up sharply and sending the four-ton payload straight to the heart of Qaddafi's terror network. After the bombs were released the pilot wrenched his plane into a 4G left-hand turn.[44] As he was the first plane over Aziziyah he had the luxury of making his attack before the Libyan defenders were fully alerted. Nevertheless, as he performed the evasive maneuver he watched as a stream of ZSU-23 tracers tried in vain to catch the bomber's tail. To evade the AAA the pilot turned even tighter.[45]

While the pilot performed the toss and escape maneuvers the WSO kept his head buried in his FLIR screen, struggling to keep the laser beam fixed on the target. He was able to hold the beam on the target until a second before impact. At that instant the plane's sharp turn caused the laser to slip from the target. "You pulled too hard!" the WSO shouted. For the last second of their flight the bombs were in an unguided free fall. That single second made all the difference between a direct hit and an extremely near miss. At the stroke of 0200, four 2,000-pound bombs impacted a few yards from the building that served as Qaddafi's headquarters and living quarters.

After the bombs hit the pilot immediately sought the safety of a lower altitude. "I'm going down," he told his WSO, pushing the plane down to three hundred feet. "We hit 'em big time!" the WSO reported, his FLIR screen filling with billowing smoke and dust. Remit-31 was back over the Mediterranean in less than a minute. He reported "feet wet"—meaning he was flying safely away from the Libyan coast—to the Navy E-2C and the Air Force command KC-10A, then followed his statement with the code word "tranquil tiger," which indicated a successful attack.[46]

Realizing he was a few seconds behind schedule, the pilot of Remit-32 frequently used his afterburner to make up the time. He had almost reached the point twenty-three thousand feet from the aim point and was about to perform the Pave Tack Toss but was forced to abort when, at the last instant, his WSO realized he was targeting the wrong aim point—a problem caused by an equipment failure that had gone undetected. The pilot retained the four 2,000-pound bombs, took manual control of the aircraft, and performed a high-speed, low-level escape from downtown Tripoli. Remit-32 barely eluded the determined efforts of Libyan gunners, whose notice was attracted by his excessive use of afterburner. After reaching the Mediterranean he reported "feet wet" and "frosty freezer," which meant that his attack had been aborted. He later jettisoned his bomb load at sea.[47]

More than a minute after Remit-31 dropped its bombs, Remit-33 carried out its attack on Aziziyah. After the four 2,000-pound bombs were released, the WSO could not hold the target on his FLIR scope. The surface winds had shifted from their predicted direction and the smoke and debris thrown up by the bombs from Remit-31 obscured the target. Consequently, the bombs fell to earth unguided. Nevertheless, they still impacted a couple of hundred feet from the target: a large administration building within the Bab al-Aziziyah compound. Remit-33 also escaped just ahead of a heavy SAM and AAA barrage.[48]

Although the 2,000-pound bombs dropped by Remit-31 and Remit-33 did not achieve direct hits, they did cause considerable damage to Qaddafi's compound. The Paveways had collapsed walls and caved in the roofs of several buildings within Aziziyah. *New York Times* reporter Edward Schumacher toured the facility two days after the raid and counted eight large bomb craters extending in a line from the front of Qaddafi's house to an administration building located atop the colonel's reinforced bunker. He noticed that the line of bombs passed within fifty yards of Qaddafi's ceremonial tent, knocking out a number of supports within and collapsing part of its cover. Schumacher reported that two bombs had hit within thirty yards of Qaddafi's residence, devastating the building. The 2,000-pound bombs shattered windows, blew out doors, collapsed ceilings, and demolished the contents of several rooms. *Washington Post* correspondent Christopher Dickey also toured the compound. He guessed that one of the 2,000-pound bombs had exploded within sixteen yards of the front entrance of the residence, producing a crater four feet deep and fifteen feet in diameter.[49]

Elton-43, the fourth plane in line to attack Aziziyah, developed a bleed air casualty to one of its engines when it was just short of the target. The problem disrupted the crew's concentration at the critical moment of their attack run and forced them to abort.

Immediately after releasing their bombs, the pilot and the WSO in Karma-51—the fifth plane over Aziziyah—realized that the attack had not gone well. The WSO had been unable to update his plane's inertial navigation system after the strike force took the shortcut to get back on schedule. After dropping away from the tanker he fixed his plane's position using a small island in the central Mediterranean as a reference point, but unbeknownst to him the location of the island, according to the plane's computer software, was off by several hundred feet. This inaccuracy, along with the pressures of high-speed, low-altitude flight, made it extremely difficult for the WSO to locate his offset aim point. Consequently, as the plane raced toward the Libyan coast he had inadvertently selected the wrong aim point. The computer placed the target in another location-one-and-a-half miles away—and it dutifully guided the plane to that position. As a result, Karma-51 dropped its bombs late and long. The pilot noticed that the bombs took a few more seconds to release than they should have, and the WSO searched his FLIR screen for the aim point in the Aziziyah compound but could not find it. In fact, nothing on the screen resembled Bab al-Aziziyah. Since he was unable to find the target, the WSO could not use the laser designator. Therefore, he had no choice but let the bombs fall ballistically. The four 2,000-pound LGBs smashed into a civilian neighborhood near the compound. The bombs demolished a number of houses and apartment buildings and damaged—ironically—the French Embassy. Unfortunately, several innocent Libyans were killed and injured in the regrettable attack. The Austrian, Finnish, Iranian, and Swiss Embassies also reported sustaining minor damage. During the attack the crew of Karma-51 had been in great danger. After their return to Lakenheath an analysis of their mission tape revealed that a Libyan SAM had locked on to their plane.[50]

Several F-111Fs used their afterburners to get through the volleys of SAMs and AAA as quickly as possible. The airmen who had flown combat missions in Vietnam acknowledged that the Libyan AAA was not as dense as they had experienced over Hanoi, but the Tripoli SAMs were more formidable. Fortunately, due to the effectiveness of the jammers and ARM-firing aircraft, most Libyan air defense crews were forced to launch their weapons optically. Although the afterburners provided a tremendous burst of energy, the long sheets of flame spewing from the exhaust pipes provided a brilliant target for Libyan gunners. As the raid progressed the density of SAMs and AAA steadily increased, but none of the weapons hit the first five planes over Aziziyah. Each crew breathed a huge sigh of relief as their plane reached the coast. The sixth plane in the stream over Aziziyah, Karma-52, was not so fortunate. It was hit by either a SAM or AAA prior to reaching the target. Making a beeline for the coast, the plane caught fire and went out of control. The pilot, Capt. Fernando Ribas-Dominicci, and the WSO, Capt. Paul Lorence, ejected seconds before their F-111F exploded and the huge fireball slammed into the sea. Unfortunately, their ejection capsule hit the water before the chutes could fully deploy. The fliers were knocked unconscious and subsequently drowned. Karma-52 would not be declared missing until all surviving F-111Fs had marshaled with their tankers for the first post-strike refueling. Libya soon recovered the body of Captain Ribas-Dominicci but did not return it to the United States until 1989. An autopsy determined the cause of death to be drowning, not massive physical trauma. Although there is not enough information to determine exactly what caused the loss of Karma-52, the autopsy finding and the eyewitness accounts of several aviators who saw the explosion and the descent of the fireball to the sea support the conclusion that Karma-52 was shot down by a SAM or AAA. The fact that Ribas-Dominicci's body did not contain evidence of fractures or internal injuries challenges the theory that Ribas-Dominicci simply flew his plane into the water due to pilot error.[51]

Karma-53, the last plane in line to attack Aziziyah and the one slated to drop a second set of 2,000-pound bombs on Qaddafi's headquarters-residence building, experienced a last-second combat systems malfunction and was forced to abort in the vicinity of the target.[52]

As Karma-53 passed over Aziziyah the Jewell attack group commenced its strike on the terrorist training facility at Murat Sidi Bilal. The Libyan defenses were lighter there, because the target was located a few miles west of downtown, but the winds at the target, like those at Aziziyah, were significantly different from what had been forecasted.[53] The first two planes to attack Murat Sidi Bilal—Jewell-61 and Jewell-62—delivered their 2,000-pound bombs using the Pave Tack Toss, churning up a tremendous amount of smoke, dust, and debris. Meanwhile, the third plane—Jewell-63—closed in on its target: the building that contained the swimming pool used to train commando frogmen. At a point exactly twenty-three thousand feet from the aim point, the pilot executed a Pave Tack Toss and released his four 2,000-pound bombs. As the bombs arced toward the laser energy reflecting from the building, the WSO coaxed his bombs on to the target: "This one's for you, Colonel!"[54] Then, an instant later he yelled out in disgust: "Ah, clouds, clouds, clouds!"[55] The dust and smoke from the other bombs had interrupted the laser guidance system and had caused the bombs to fall ballistically. The bombs slammed into the base mess hall, missing the building containing the swimming pool by about a dozen yards. Post-mission damage analysis determined that none of the bombers of the Jewell group scored a direct hit. They did, however, severely damage the mess hall, a classroom building, and an administration-support building and destroyed several small training vessels.[56]

After crossing the beach the six planes in the Puffy and Lujac attack groups flew a long overland route to the Tripoli Military Airfield, a trip that required full use of their terrain-following radars. As the TFRs guided the F-111Fs over the irregular Libyan terrain, the crews constantly monitored the performance of their "Auto-TF" systems. Each pilot kept his hand behind the stick and was ready to raise the nose of the aircraft in an instant, if it looked as though the TFR was about to fly the plane into the desert floor or at an unexpected outcropping. During the transit to the target the strike force was reduced to five aircraft when Puffy-12 developed a problem with its TFR and had to abort.

Flying with TFR over unfamiliar territory was very stressful, but the crews received one important break. As they approached the airfield they realized that they had caught the Libyans completely off guard and would not have to contend with a determined and effective defense. The crews were tempted to catch more than a fleeting glance at the huge fireworks display that was taking place in Tripoli to the north—streaking SAMs, AAA tracers, and exploding 2,000-pound bombs—but they had plenty of work to do studying their own consoles. The pilots kept an eye on the TFR, and the WSOs searched their FLIR screens for the parking ramp with the Il-76 transports.[57]

At 0206 the airmen of Puffy-11 commenced their attack on the airfield. As the plane roared in at less than five hundred feet, the pilot observed the terminal lights ablaze and asked the WSO if he had the parking ramp on his scope. The WSO, his face pressed into the rubber hood covering his scope, responded affirmatively and aimed his laser beam on the middle plane of five transports parked on the flight line. Although the laser-designator system would not guide the 500-pound bombs, it provided crucial data to the pilot. It recommended the correct heading to steer and informed him when to drop his ordnance. Just a few seconds before bomb release the pilot came to the right to center his plane on the target.[58] When the WSO saw the middle Il-76 filling up his FLIR scope, he exclaimed: "Oh baby!" "I'm on the pickle button," the pilot stated an instant later, as he depressed the bomb-release button. "Here come the bombs." A string of a dozen 500-pound bombs—each slowed by the ballute drag device—quickly fell behind Puffy-11 and immediately hit the transports parked on the tarmac.[59]

The bombing run performed by Puffy-11 was immortalized by a few feet of videotape shot by the camera mounted in the belly of the F-111F. The exceptionally clear video, which was shown repeatedly on news broadcasts all over the world, displayed hard maneuvering (as the crew struggled to line up on the target), a line of bombs stretching downward toward one of the parked Il-76s, an explosion, and a huge cloud of dust and debris. After delivering his ordnance the pilot of Puffy-11 increased the throttle, turned west to avoid the SAMs and AAA coming out of Tripoli, then streaked north toward the safety of the Mediterranean and the orbiting tankers.

The Snakeyes dropped by Puffy-11 scored several hits and touched off a number of fires and explosions. Two transports were destroyed and three others suffered considerable damage. As it turned out, Puffy-11 performed the only completely successful attack on the Tripoli airfield. Minor equipment malfunctions and mistakes had hindered the performance of the other four crews, all of which had failed to score a direct hit on the transports. Instead they caused minimal damage to a number of helicopters parked near the transports and to an operations building.[60]

On the other side of the Gulf of Sidra six *Coral Sea*–based VA-55 Warhorses bore down on the Benina Airfield. "A-6 crews . . . saw the incoming HARMs' orange cones of destruction, smothering SAM sites in their paths," Stumpf recalled. "SAMs that were launched created a sensational effect in the night sky, but none guided effectively."[61] At exactly 0200 local time the Warhorses—one armed with Snakeye high-drag bombs, and five carrying CBU-59 APAMs—devastated the Benina Airfield. The Snakeyes cratered the runway and torched the alert MiG-23s, while the APAM submunitions blanketed the parking apron and battered several aircraft.[62] "The last of the six A-6s across the airfield noted several airplanes on the ramp below burning furiously," Stumpf said, and "as the Intruders raced for the ocean and safety, they could see the giant bomb explosions of the *America*'s A-6s on target near the city."[63]

The attack on Benina demolished three, possibly four, MiG-23 Floggers; two Mi-8 Hip helicopters; one F-27 Friendship propeller-driven transport; and one small fixed-wing aircraft. Damaged planes included one Mi-8, two Boeing 727 transports, one propeller-driven transport, two fixed-wing aircraft, and an undetermined number of MiG-23s, which were probably moved out of sight before the United States could perform a post-strike battle damage assessment (BDA). The Benina hangars received moderate damage, while four other buildings and several vehicles and pieces of ground equipment were destroyed.[64] After the raid the airmen of VA-55 proudly called themselves "the East Coast's largest distributor of MiG parts."[65]

An F/A-18 pilot flying support off Benghazi was profoundly relieved when he detected the lights of the city. "If the lights were out, we were in trouble," he recalled. "It was all lit up like Norfolk or Jacksonville or any other major city."[66] At the exact moment the Warhorses hit Benina, six VA-34 Blue Blasters off the *America* struck the Benghazi Military and Jamahiriyya Guard Barracks. They had great difficulty identifying the barracks on radar, since the target was located in a crowded downtown area. Encountering a barrage of SAMs, each Blaster released a "stick" of sixteen 500-pound Snakeye high-drag bombs, which hit the barracks and an adjacent warehouse that served as a MiG-23 assembly facility. Four aircraft shipping crates were destroyed while a fifth was damaged. Unfortunately, two bombs fell a few hundred yards wide of the target and struck a civilian neighborhood, damaging two houses.[67]

From an unparalleled vantage point off the coast the last U.S. aircraft to leave the target area—a pair of F/A-18s assigned to support SAR operations— saw the Benghazi "skyline ablaze with secondary fires from the downtown areas, backdropped by a softer glow from fires burning at the airfield which was several miles inland."[68] In Tripoli and Benghazi the Libyans kept up a vigorous fusillade in a desperate attempt to knock down what they thought were more attacking aircraft. Several nights would pass before the sporadic firings at phantom bombers would cease, a clear indication of the frayed state of Libyan nerves.[69]

"Today, We Have Done What We Had to Do"

At approximately 1913 Washington time, Weinberger and Crowe received their first post-strike report. CINCEUR tersely stated, "Raid commander reports all aircraft feet wet." Everyone in the command center was overjoyed. It appeared that the raid had been carried out without any American losses, but the elation was quickly doused when a very discomforting message reached the Pentagon: "First report possibly not correct. We cannot account for one aircraft. Polling our group again." A follow-up report confirmed that one of the F-111Fs was indeed missing.[70]

At 1920 Reagan's press secretary, Larry Speakes, officially announced the air strike to the White House press corps and a national audience watching on television. On his way to the press briefing room Speakes had stopped by Admiral Poindexter's office to obtain last minute details. Poindexter was joined by Shultz, and Speakes noticed that both men exuded "a mood of quiet satisfaction." They were not jubilant—one American plane was missing—but they were obviously relieved that the United States had finally clobbered the world's most notorious advocate and practitioner of international terrorism.[71]

At 2100 President Reagan appeared on television from the Oval Office and informed the American public that units of the Air Force and Navy had conducted air strikes "against the headquarters, terrorist facilities, and military assets that support Muammar Qaddafi's subversive activities," and that according to preliminary reports the operation was a success. "Today, we have done what we had to do," Reagan said somberly. "If necessary, we shall do it again." He expressed hope that this military action "will not only diminish Colonel Qaddafi's capacity to export terror, it will provide him with incentives and reasons to alter his criminal behavior." Reagan emphasized that the United States had not attacked Libya in haste. "We tried quiet diplomacy, public condemnation, economic sanctions, and demonstrations of military force," he stated. "None succeeded. Despite our repeated warnings, Qaddafi continued his reckless policy of intimidation, his relentless pursuit of terror. He counted on America to be passive. He counted wrong."[72]

In a speech before a group of business leaders the next day Reagan told his audience that "the United States won but a single engagement in the long battle against terrorism. We will not end that struggle until the free and decent people of this planet unite to eradicate the scourge of terror from the modern world." He also sent a blunt warning to Qaddafi: "We would prefer not to have to repeat the events of last night. What is required is for Libya to end its pursuit of terror for political goals. The choice is theirs. . . . Colonel Qaddafi ought not to underestimate either the capacity or legitimate anger of a free people."[73]

On Wednesday, 16 April, Reagan forwarded to Congress a report on Operation El Dorado Canyon in accordance with the terms of the War Powers Act. In his letter Reagan stated that the air strikes on Libya "were conducted in the exercise of our right of self-defense under Article 51 of the United Nations Charter. This necessary and appropriate action was a preemptive strike, directed at the Libyan terrorist infrastructure and designed to deter acts of terrorism, such as the Libyan-ordered bombing of a discothèque in West Berlin on April 5."[74]

Getting Back to "Home Plate"

After the Air Force and Navy bomber crews dropped their bombs, their immediate attention was focused on reaching the safety of their post-strike marshaling areas as quickly as possible. Besides running the gauntlet of alerted Libyan SAM and AAA batteries, they were concerned about pursuit from Libyan fighter planes, some of which might be flown by Syrians or other foreign pilots serving with the LAAF. Nearing the coast the Air Force pilots and WSOs became gravely worried about transiting through the air defenses of Task Force 60 and avoiding a blue-on-blue incident. Fortunately, the battle force had constructed a very simple and effective "delousing" plan for distinguishing returning strike aircraft coming off the beach from Libyan MiGs trailing behind. By following a pre-briefed flight path, which stipulated specific altitude and airspeed parameters, the F-111Fs and A-6Es identified themselves as friendly aircraft to Battle Force Zulu's antiair warfare commander. The procedures ensured that any LAAF fighters attempting to pursue the friendly planes would be intercepted and shot down by F-14s or F/A-18s performing MiG CAP duty.[75]

By 0213 Tripoli time all Navy and Air Force strike aircraft, except Karma-52, had reported feet wet to the E-2Cs and, in the case of the Air Force bombers, to the command KC-10A.[76] The skipper of the *Coral Sea,* Capt. Robert H. Ferguson, remembered his crew's reaction when he informed them over the ship's 1MC (general announcing circuit) that all Navy and Marine Corps aircraft were heading back to their carriers. "You could feel the ship vibrate with enthusiasm and confidence that they had done a good job," he recalled.[77]

While the Hawkeyes and fighters guarded against an LAAF counterattack, the carriers recovered their strike and support aircraft. All Navy and Marine planes were safely on deck by 0253.[78] The actions of a *Coral Sea* ordnance handler epitomized the concern all personnel in the battle force felt for the men who had just carried out a very difficult mission. "I stayed up all night and counted them as they came back," the young sailor remembered. "It's like family out here, you might say. You just don't like to lose any of your shipmates."[79]

"The only disappointed pilots were those dedicated to the fighter missions in defense of the force," commented Admiral Breast. "They had expected some opposition but the Libyan Arab Air Force had chosen not to fly that evening."[80] Lehman predicted that if the LAAF had gone into action "it would have been a real turkey shoot."[81] A few Libyan fighters took off but wisely decided not to pursue the retreating U.S. aircraft. There were reports that LAAF GCI radars had been rendered useless by the jamming, and that the commander of the Benina Airfield had deliberately disobeyed a direct order to attack the departing Navy bombers and fighters.

For the next three days Task Force 60 maintained a defensive posture north of the Tripoli FIR. It was ready to repulse a Libyan attack and carry out White House–directed contingencies.[82] As the F-111Fs passed through the defenses of Task Force 60, their crews could not relax because they had to confront two monumental realities. First, several airmen witnessed what looked like an F-111F going down in a gigantic fireball. Did a missile or AAA hit one of the planes? If so, which crew was lost? The definitive answer would not be known until the F-111Fs had joined their tankers and the roll call of surviving crews had been completed. Second, many of the F-111Fs were getting low—desperately low, in a few cases—on fuel and had to find and rendezvous with their tankers as quickly as possible. The post-strike rendezvous procedures had been given very little attention at the mission briefings back at Lakenheath. "There was little said beyond 'get a vector, head north, find your tanker, join on him, and get gas,'" recalled one pilot. According to the plan, the E-2C that served as the command and control platform in the Tripoli sector would give each F-111F a vector, or recommended heading, to its assigned tanker. In general the vectors proved to be very inaccurate, forcing several crews to rely on their tactical air navigation (TACAN) equipment, which provided them with the heading to a particular tanker broadcasting a unique code.[83]

The pilot of Karma-51 captured the tension present in many F-111F cockpits with the comment that the anxious search for the tankers was "almost more nerve-wracking than the actual attack." Most of the F-111Fs were below their projected fuel states because more afterburner had been used during the mission than anticipated. To make the search even more difficult, the tankers orbiting near Sicily were flying in the middle of several layers of high cirrus clouds. Discovering the inaccuracy of their vectors and realizing their tankers were hidden in the clouds, the pilots and WSOs nervously scoured the skies with air search radars and their eyeballs. No airman could breathe a sigh of relief until every bomber safely rejoined a tanker. Eventually, all surviving F-111Fs were back on a tanker, although not necessarily their assigned tanker.[84]

A couple of incidents demonstrated just how low the fuel state was in some of the planes. In the first instance the pilot of Remit-31 came to the aid of another pilot, who was having difficulty locating his tanker, by doing "a little torching."[85] The first pilot dumped some fuel and ignited it with his afterburner, creating a huge explosion that both lit up the sky and pointed the direction to the tanker. For a few nervous moments many airmen thought that there might have been a midair collision. In the second case Puffy-11 successfully rendezvoused with its assigned tanker and was taking on fuel when another F-111F suddenly appeared alongside it, flying extremely close to Puffy-11. The second plane was so desperate for fuel that it seemed to be trying to shove Puffy-11 away from the tanker. After a few moments the pilot of Puffy-11 dropped off the tanker, giving way to the other plane.[86]

As the F-111Fs joined up with the tankers the officers in the command

KC-10A performed the difficult task of determining whether or not a plane was missing and, if so, which plane it was. The pilot of Karma-51 notified the command plane that he never heard Karma-52 report feet wet. "I don't think Karma-52 made it," he said. Several radio calls to Karma-52 over the military distress circuit went unanswered, yet every man held out a slim hope that Karma-52 had only been damaged, that the damage had prevented the plane from communicating, or that the plane would show up soon either in formation or at one of the emergency divert bases in the Mediterranean area. As the minutes ticked by it became increasingly unlikely that Karma-52 would appear.[87]

Venkus described what it was like for the pilots and WSOs as the process of identifying the missing plane dragged on. "In some F-111F cockpits, this somber delay was especially confusing and difficult," he noted. "Some crews did not have complete lineup cards, so they were unsure which of their friends matched up with particular call signs. As it became clear that one aircraft had been lost, these crewmen listened closely to the repeated roll calls, trying to recognize voices in order to determine who was missing. Eventually they realized which crew had not returned, and their thoughts turned to their friends' present plight."[88]

Meanwhile, one of the ships in Task Force 60 reported that it had received a very short series of beeps, possibly the signal from the downed F-111F's emergency radio beacon, then immediately lost the signal. A Navy patrol plane flew over the area where the fireball had been seen, hoping to catch the signal from the F-111F's emergency beacon. It heard nothing.[89] For more than an hour the Air Force planes loitered in the skies near Sicily, hoping that Karma-52 would join up. By 0314 Forgan and Westbrook were certain that Captain Ribas-Dominicci and Captain Lorence were missing, and Forgan reluctantly ordered the huge strike force back to England. Meanwhile, back at Lakenheath Venkus organized two teams to perform the solemn duty of officially notifying the families of Ribas-Dominicci and Lorence that their loved ones were missing.[90]

Kelso ordered a search and rescue operation for the missing fliers. The SAR effort, which included a P-3 Orion maritime patrol aircraft and a submarine, found no traces of either of the men or their plane, and the search was terminated at 1700 local time, 15 April.[91]

The Air Force mission was still long from over, and huge challenges still had to be overcome. The pilots had to perform seven hours of grueling, night formation flying and one more in-flight refueling. With the strike and the rendezvous behind them and with their adrenaline worn off, the airmen had to struggle to keep up their concentration and fight off the tendency to relax. A single instant of inattention could result in a midair collision. If an airman became tired he could take a couple of "go pills" or amphetamines that had been provided by the wing flight surgeons.

The early phase of the flight back to England proved to be very interesting for Elton-43. The bleed air problem that had forced the crew to abort their attack on Aziziyah had not been resolved. The "Wheelwell Hot" alarm light indicated that a pipe near the main landing gear was leaking very hot engine air. The emergency demanded quick action to prevent an in-flight fire and possible loss of the aircraft. With the problem showing no signs of improving, Forgan ordered Elton-43 to divert to the U.S. naval air station at Rota, Spain. The plane landed safely at Rota at 0524 local time. The engine was eventually repaired and Elton-43 finally returned to RAF Lakenheath at 2201 U.K. time on 15 April. Since the Spanish government was very concerned about negative political ramifications stemming from any association with the air strike, the emergency recovery of Elton-43 at Rota was not officially announced to the public for a number of weeks.[92]

One at a time sixteen F-111Fs descended through the thinly overcast early morning skies over England and made their final approach to the runway at Lakenheath. At an altitude of one thousand feet their landing lights became visible to the hundreds of ground personnel waiting anxiously on the flight line. Many of those standing on the tarmac—jet engine mechanics, electronics technicians, ordnance handlers, refueling crews, and other wing personnel—had contributed directly to the success of the mission. Three generals—Gabriel, Shaud, and McInerney—also waited to greet the F-111F crews. As the planes landed and taxied to their hardened shelters they were greeted in a scene reminiscent of the B-17s returning from their bombing missions over Germany in World War II. Several individuals in the crowd waved signs, welcoming the fliers home and praising their heroic mission. A few of the pilots and WSOs, their legs very wobbly, needed a little assistance getting out of their cockpits.[93]

Just seconds after climbing down from his F-111F and getting his weary legs back on solid ground, the pilot of Karma-51 was greeted by the generals, who shook his hand and congratulated him on his outstanding effort. Gabriel then asked the Vietnam veteran to compare the defenses over Hanoi to those encountered in Tripoli. The pilot graded Tripoli's defenses as follows: "On a scale of one-to-ten, . . . the missiles were a *fifteen!*" He would probably have gotten little argument from the other men who had just flown the mission.[94]

At 0810 U.K. time on 15 April, the last F-111F touched down at RAF Lakenheath. The longest fighter mission in U.S. history, lasting fourteen hours and thirty-five minutes, was over.[95]

Honoring Captain Fernando Ribas-Dominicci
and Captain Paul Lorence

According to Air Force regulations, in his capacity as unit commander West-brook had both the duty and authority to declare Captain Ribas-Dominicci and Captain Lorence killed in action, provided there was a preponderance of evidence to support such a determination. After two days Westbrook concluded that the men were dead. He justified his decision on a couple of factors. First, the Navy's SAR efforts found no evidence that either man had survived. Second, the men did not appear on Libyan television. No one doubted that Qaddafi would have displayed his prisoners for propaganda purposes. After making this weighty decision Westbrook compassionately informed the wives and families of Ribas-Dominicci and Lorence that their husbands and fathers would not be coming home. On Thursday, 17 April, the Air Force formally declared the two fliers killed in action.[96] President Reagan telephoned the wives of the two lost airmen and in an attempt to temper their grief called the officers "heroes of our heart."[97]

On Monday, 21 April, a memorial service for Ribas-Dominicci and Lorence was conducted in a hangar at RAF Lakenheath. A huge crowd came to honor the brave men who had lost their lives in Operation El Dorado Canyon. Ambassador Price delivered a moving speech in which he lauded their courage, discipline, and devotion to duty. The emotional ceremony concluded with a formation of Air Force jets performing the missing man flyby—the traditional military salute to lost comrades.[98]

Libyan Reaction to the Raid

The Libyan government claimed that its air defense forces shot down three American aircraft and went so far as to say that it had recovered an F-111F from the sea and was turning it over to the Soviet Union. In a desperate attempt to retaliate against the United States, Qaddafi ordered his army to launch two Soviet-built SS-1 Scud B ballistic missiles at the U.S. Coast Guard long-range navigation station on the Italian island of Lampedusa, located approximately 170 miles north of Tripoli. The missiles detonated harmlessly two miles off-shore, sending two large columns of water into the air and shaking the homes of the island's six thousand residents.[99]

The Libyan government announced that the U.S. raids on Tripoli and Benghazi killed thirty-seven Libyans and injured ninety-three, but their figures do not specify how many of those individuals were civilians killed or wounded by stray American bombs, how many were military personnel operating Libyan air defense equipment, how many were people present at the five targets, or how many were persons killed or injured by SAM components falling back to earth. Qaddafi was reportedly in his underground command bunker at the time of the bombing while his wife and children were asleep on the ground floor of their residence within the compound. Qaddafi survived the attack on Aziziyah rattled but unharmed, but other members of his family were not so fortunate. According to JANA the attack killed Qaddafi's fifteen-month-old adopted daughter and seriously injured his two youngest sons, aged three and four. The news about Qaddafi's daughter surprised many Western analysts and journalists, because no announcement had ever been made that he had adopted a child. His wife supposedly had adopted a baby girl about ten months earlier.[100] There was no denying that the U.S. air strike killed innocent men, women, and children, but a huge moral distinction can be made between killing Libyan civilians by accident and deliberately murdering Americans through acts of terrorism.[101]

"Red Flag," "Strike U," and Results

The successful execution of Operation El Dorado Canyon can be traced to several initiatives taken by the Air Force and Navy to improve their strike warfare proficiency in the decade following the Vietnam War. Among the steps taken by the Air Force were the procurement of sophisticated weapons, the development of innovative delivery tactics, and the establishment in 1975 of the "Red Flag" training program,[102] which emphasized "train as you fight" realism.[103] Red Flag, the massive strike exercise conducted at Nellis AFB in Nevada, was designed to give bomber and fighter crews a training experience that was as close as possible to actual combat. During a typical exercise crews flew several sorties against a series of heavily defended targets. They practiced tactics designed to defeat enemy air defenses, elude enemy fighters, and put bombs squarely on target.[104] The air warfare skills honed at Red Flag were heroically demonstrated in the night sky over Tripoli.

The Navy's badly executed raid on Syrian antiaircraft batteries in Lebanon on 4 December 1983 spurred the service to revamp its strike warfare methodology. The raid failed to use tactics that would have taken advantage of new weapon systems and technologies developed after the early 1970s.[105] Secretary Lehman, an A-6 B/N in the naval reserve, immediately identified the deficiency:

"The Navy air wings produced what had been trained into them, and what had been trained into them was a twenty-year-old Vietnam daytime 'Alpha' strike, and it was totally inappropriate."[106] In a typical Alpha strike attack planes crossed the beach at twenty-thousand feet, gradually descended to ten thousand feet, dove to three thousand feet, released their bombs, pulled out, and ran for the coast. Those tactics did not fool Syrian gunners in the Biqa Valley.[107]

The outcome of the Lebanon mission prompted Lehman to establish a naval warfare center devoted to the development of strike warfare doctrine and tactics—an attack aviation version of "Top Gun." In May 1984 the Naval Strike Warfare Center opened at Lemoore Naval Air Station in California. One year later "Strike U"—as it is known throughout the Navy—moved to Fallon NAS in Nevada, where aircrews could enjoy wide open spaces and year-round, near-perfect weather while they carried out their training programs. Prior to departing on its overseas deployment a carrier air wing would spend three weeks at Fallon studying the latest doctrine, practicing all facets of a strike mission, and participating in a realistic, full-blown war game that provided an opportunity for the wing to practice the tactics and skills that Strike U had validated.[108] With a training syllabus that emphasized night attacks, terrain-following flight profiles, and standoff weapons, Strike U had an immediate and positive effect on the Navy's attack community. "When the navy flew over Libya in the spring of 1986, they knew their business," wrote Daniel Bolger. Since the "Sixth Fleet planned the mission, the new Fallon mentality . . . permeated the operation."[109]

In addition to renewed Air Force and Navy proficiency in strike warfare, a number of important factors contributed to the operational success of Operation El Dorado Canyon, America's strike against international terrorism. First, Admiral Kelso had been entrusted with control over nearly all of the operational aspects of the mission by his superiors in Washington and Europe. Kelso, his principle subordinate commanders—Admiral Mauz and Colonel Westbrook —and their staffs, planned the strike, marshaled their resources, and executed the mission when their forces were ready.[110] A senior Pentagon official who testified before Congress on the lessons of El Dorado Canyon emphasized that one of the most significant elements accounting for the success of the operation was that command and control of the mission was entrusted to the on-scene commander, Kelso. "The Sixth Fleet commander was given the time frame to attack, and he had the responsibility of putting it all together," stated the official. "He also had the flexibility and authority to cancel the strike right up until the last moment if it looked like weather or operational factors could be a problem."[111]

Second, the precision with which the strike was conducted caught Qaddafi's armed forces completely off guard. In a magnificent feat of planning and execution, separate Air Force and Navy attack groups operating from bases nearly three thousand miles apart struck their targets at exactly the same instant. In less than twelve minutes all targets were hit and all planes, except one F-111F, reached the safety of the Mediterranean. The 0200 TOT stunned the Libyans who, despite the warnings they had received for several days, were totally unprepared to defend against the raid.[112] "Runway lights were on and continued to burn during the attack," noted W. Hays Parks. "Although antiaircraft fire and missile launches were reportedly heavy at each target, the element of surprise, the darkness, jamming by the EA-6B/EF-111 force against the Tripoli defenses and by the EA-6Bs against Benghazi, and air defense suppression by the A-7 and F/A-18 support aircraft rendered the Libyan defenses ineffective."[113]

Third, coordinated planning between Navy and Air Force commands, dual service training exercises, and the exchange of liaison officers were instrumental in the flawless integration of a joint strike force in a radio silent, night attack against heavily defended targets. According to Lehman the success of Operation El Dorado Canyon "demonstrated the real cooperation, integration, and sharing of tactical training and know-how that is the real relationship between and among our armed forces."[114]

Finally, Kelso's insistence on a large strike force insured that all five targets would be attacked with devastating results. During the planning phase the Sixth Fleet commander and his subordinates acknowledged that some of the strike aircraft would probably suffer equipment failures prior to reaching their targets. Therefore they assembled a potent force with enough redundancy to accomplish the mission. "Without Pave Tack, TRAM, and guided weapons, the entire operation would have been impossible," stressed Daniel Bolger. "A few aborts did not detract from the advantages created by American technology."[115]

Many of the factors that accounted for the successful raid against Libya would be repeated five years later during the war to liberate Kuwait from the army of Saddam Hussein.

Task Force 60 and the Confrontation with Libya: An Operational Summary

The dispute between the United States and Libya in the 1980s demonstrated that the decisive application of military power could influence an adversary and facilitate the attainment of specific foreign policy goals without resorting to a war or a costly commitment of military forces. At the heart of American power arrayed against Libya was the U.S. Navy's formidable Battle Force Sixth Fleet—Task Force 60. The battle force contained one or more battle groups, each consisting of an aircraft carrier, an air wing of advanced tactical aircraft, and a shielding flotilla of modern cruisers, destroyers, and frigates. Owing to the overwhelming strength and flexibility of the battle force, U.S. ships and aircraft operated with impunity in the Libyan-claimed waters and airspace of the Gulf of Sidra and vigorously repulsed all attacks and threats of force by the Libyan military. In retaliation for Tripoli's sponsorship of a terrorist assault on American citizens, Task Force 60 and units of the U.S. Air Force based in Europe planned and executed a devastating air strike on terrorist headquarters and support facilities in Libya.

President Reagan's application of naval force against Libya was a modern example of "gunboat diplomacy." It was limited in scope, it supported specific national objectives, it was carried out with few political costs and no losses to personnel, it frustrated the enemy's ability to respond militarily, it secured favorable political outcomes in the dispute with a foreign power, and it was successful enough to forestall a large-scale military deployment to maintain those outcomes.[116]

In August 1981 Battle Force Sixth Fleet, commanded by Rear Adm. James E. Service and consisting of the *Nimitz* and *Forrestal* CVBGs, carried out a major FON exercise in and near the Gulf of Sidra. The goal of the naval maneuver was to reject Libyan leader Muammar al-Qaddafi's illegal claim of sovereignty over the waters of the Gulf of Sidra south of 32° 30' north latitude. When two Libyan Su-22 Fitter J aircraft attacked a pair of F-14 Tomcats over the gulf the Americans acted swiftly in self-defense and shot down the aggressors with Sidewinder air-to-air missiles in a dogfight lasting about a minute.

On three occasions during the first three months of 1986 Sixth Fleet commander Vice Adm. Frank B. Kelso dispatched Task Force 60 to the vicinity of Libya to defy once again Tripoli's claim of sovereignty over the gulf and confront Qaddafi over his practice of sponsoring, supporting, and encouraging acts of international terrorism. In January and February the *Saratoga* and the *Coral Sea* battle groups conducted Operations Attain Document I and Attain Document II. In each event the battle force, commanded by Rear Adm. David E. Jeremiah, promptly achieved naval and air superiority in the Tripoli FIR. Navy and Marine Corps aviators performed nearly 150 intercepts on a variety of Libyan aircraft, but not one Libyan pilot achieved a firing position on a U.S. fighter plane. In March, following the arrival in the Mediterranean of the *America* battle group, the huge battle force (totaling 26 warships and 250 carrier-based aircraft) carried out Operation Attain Document III, a large-scale freedom-of-navigation operation that involved extensive surface and air activity below 32° 30'—Qaddafi's "line of death." When Libya attacked American aircraft with long-range SA-5 surface-to-air missiles and threatened the force with missile patrol boats, the fleet defended itself with quick and deadly precision. A-7E Corsair IIs disabled the missile battery with HARMs, and A-6E Intruders sank two Libyan vessels with Harpoon antiship cruise missiles and Rockeye cluster bombs.

In a daring act of retaliation for Qaddafi's sponsorship of a terrorist bombing of a West Berlin nightclub that killed two American soldiers, A-6Es from the *Coral Sea* and the *America* and F-111F bombers based in England struck and severely damaged important terrorist facilities in the Libyan cities of Tripoli and Benghazi. In support of the joint strike Task Force 60 pilots skillfully performed several crucial missions. A-7Es, F/A-18s, and EA-6Bs suppressed enemy air defense systems; F-14s and F/A-18s protected the strike groups and the battle force from Libyan aircraft; E-2Cs performed long-range air and surface surveillance, strike coordination, and fighter control; and KA-6Ds and KA-7s provided invaluable tanking services.

Battle Force Sixth Fleet operations in the vicinity of Libya were conducted without suffering a single casualty. This remarkable achievement was the product of thorough preparation and a demanding training regime that achieved and maintained a high level of combat readiness. Of the many factors that contributed to the operational success of the battle force, a few are particularly noteworthy. First, flexible and unambiguous ROE were instrumental in neutralizing the Libyan armed forces. Frequent face-to-face discussions, timely approval of additions or modifications to the ROE, and the delegation of appropriate ROE ensured that commanders and aircrews knew what actions they could take in self-defense and under what circumstances. Second, employment of a multi-carrier battle force permitted around-the-clock air operations for fleet defense while maintaining short-notice strike capability. Third, a streamlined command, control, and communications structure facilitated quick crisis response and avoided many of the C3 problems frequently associated with the operation of multiple carrier battle groups in close proximity. Fourth, during later operations the superior sensors and C3 facilities of the Aegis cruisers significantly enhanced the capabilities of the battle force's antiair warfare and antisurface warfare commanders. Fifth, combat operations benefited from the superior performance of several modern U.S. weapons systems—most notably Aegis, the F-14 Tomcat, the F/A-18 Hornet, TRAM, Harpoon, HARM, and LAMPS

MK III. Finally, the exchange of liaison officers and coordinated planning by Navy and Air Force staffs insured the complete integration of the joint strike force in a high-speed, low-level night attack.[117]

The Reagan administration's employment of U.S. military forces in conjunction with strong political and economic measures sent a powerful message to Qaddafi and achieved important results. Libya's claim of sovereignty over the Gulf of Sidra was thoroughly discredited, and Qaddafi would wisely reduce his involvement in international terrorism. When tasked by national authority, Battle Force Sixth Fleet, unencumbered by the need to seek approval from foreign governments for its movements, established a powerful presence off the coast of Libya where it exerted a profound influence on Qaddafi's regime, exacted "swift and effective retribution" against any element of Libyan armed forces that meant it harm and, in one instance, projected decisive power ashore. After fulfilling each mission the battle force withdrew safely over the horizon.

7

The Aftermath of Operation
El Dorado Canyon

American Reaction to the Air Strike

Although two airmen were missing and nine missions were never carried out, Pentagon officials were immediately pleased with the performance of the Navy and Air Force under very challenging circumstances. On the night of the attack Secretary of Defense Weinberger told reporters that "the attack was carried out precisely as planned, and it was . . . evidence of very great skill . . . and done with great effectiveness."[1] In a report to Congress the following year Weinberger praised the forces that conducted or supported the Libyan air strike. He wrote: "The military operations conducted by U.S. forces in response to this act of aggression . . . were carried out with exceptional skill, daring, and effectiveness, in the best traditions of all our forces. The action demonstrated many things, one being that we are ready, on very short notice, for very long difficult actions involving the solution of particularly complex logistical problems."[2]

On the other hand, the first bomb damage assessment photographs taken by U.S. Air Force SR-71 reconnaissance aircraft flying out of RAF Mildenhall were disappointing to officials in Washington and to the officers who had planned and executed the strike. Large portions of the target areas were obscured by clouds, and the areas that were visible revealed very little damage.

Scorch marks indicated places where planes had been destroyed, but the Libyans apparently had removed the wreckage and filled bomb craters, leaving little evidence for the world to see.[3] "We had our head down a little bit in terms of the number of bombs hitting the target," commented one of 48 TFW's squadron commanders.[4] Colonel Venkus attempted to present the results of the mission in more realistic terms. He remarked, "There is no one . . . who can claim that the navy and air force fully met their pre-raid objectives, except to the extent that some visible damage was achieved at each of the five target complexes engaged."[5]

Eighteen F-111Fs flew from Lakenheath to Libya with the objective of delivering a total of seventy-two 500-pound bombs and forty-eight 2,000-pound bombs on three targets in and near Tripoli. If one measured the raid's success by the number of bombs that hit on or very near the DMPIs, then it was understandable that several F-111F crewmen were disappointed with the overall results. Approximately one-third of the total bomb load was never dropped. Six planes aborted their missions for a variety of reasons, such as equipment failure, human error, or strict adherence to the ROE. A seventh plane was lost before it could release its ordnance. Of the eleven planes that dropped their bombs only four put their bombs directly on or very near their aim points. Of the LGBs that were dropped only a third managed to hit their targets.[6] Particularly disappointing was the record of the nine F-111Fs sent to attack Bab al-Aziziyah. Only three planes dropped their bombs, and of these only two managed to hit the compound.

The Navy attack force fared better than its Air Force counterpart. Fewer bombers aborted, and only two bombs missed the target. The *America* and the *Coral Sea* planned to send out a strike force of fifteen A-6Es, but one Intruder aborted on the deck of the *America,* and two *Coral Sea* bombers aborted en route to the Benina Air Field. Of the six A-6Es that struck Benina, five planes scored sixty hits when they dropped sixty Mk-20 500-pound cluster bombs, while the sixth plane delivered twelve Mk-82 500-pound drag bombs and scored a dozen hits. Six planes attacked the Benghazi barracks with a total of seventy-two 500-pound drag bombs. Seventy Mk-82s hit the barracks complex; a pair of bombs slammed into a nearby neighborhood.[7]

Several Reagan administration officials, military officers, and defense analysts acknowledged that the ROE had directly affected the outcome of the raid. The rules demanded that the systems in each aircraft had to be fully operational for that aircraft to prosecute its mission. Weinberger admitted that the ROE was a major factor in minimizing the amount of damage generated by the air strike.[8] Admiral Crowe also criticized the ROE: "Any time you plan a raid when you're over the target [for only] fifteen seconds, and you have such a high political content to the raid—to reduce your casualties, to reduce peripheral damage, to reduce all these things that are not military but political—you're not going to have a lot of damage." A more relaxed ROE would have allowed more F-111Fs to carry out their attacks, but President Reagan never considered anything less than a very rigid ROE.

Other officers pointed out that the denial of overflight by the French stretched the F-111Fs and their crews to the limits of their endurance. The F-111F was not known to be the most dependable plane in the U.S. inventory, and maintenance records at Lakenheath revealed that for sorties of two-and-a-half hours or longer, 40 percent of the bombers would likely suffer a system failure serious enough to ground the plane until it was repaired. When this failure rate was combined with the extreme distances the F-111Fs were forced to fly, many experienced aviators felt that it was quite an accomplishment that any of the planes dropped their bombs at all.[9] "Successful bombing of three 'first-look' . . . targets at night was a significant achievement in itself," commented Venkus. "To do it . . . after a six-plus-hour flight was just short of incredible." In addition, the bomber crews had to contend with dense, hostile fire.[10] In the dark "every SAM looks like it's coming for you," noted Admiral Kelso. "Most of these kids had never seen a SAM fired in anger."[11] One statement in the American Defense Annual of 1987–1988 disabused the notion that precision bombing was easy to accomplish and put in perspective both the challenge and the results of the mission: "The raid against Tripoli was a clear military success, if not quite a textbook operation."[12]

Spirits were buoyed when General Gabriel returned from Lakenheath with videotapes taken by the Pave Tack infrared cameras mounted beneath the F-111Fs. The tapes provided little evidence of bomb damage, because each target was soon hidden in a huge cloud of smoke and debris, but they did give solid proof that the bomber crews were right on the target. Crowe remarked that the tapes were "much more descriptive, much more definitive" than the reconnaissance photographs.[13] The joint chiefs showed the tapes to Weinberger, who called them "the most dramatic evidence of our success."[14] Weinberger rushed the tapes to the White House and showed them to Reagan, who was delighted by the video replay of Puffy-11's bombing run over the Tripoli Military Airfield and another video sequence that showed Remit-31's four 2,000-pound bombs crashing into Muammar al-Qaddafi's headquarters at Bab al-Aziziyah. "The tapes were a public relations coup, turning a mediocre damage assessment into a dramatic strike against terrorism," wrote David Martin and John Walcott. "The raid was intended as a signal, a message, a warning, and its success would be measured not in material destroyed but by its effect on Qaddafi."[15] According to Secretary of the Navy Lehman, "The raid demonstrated that the United States can deal effectively with terrorism if it has the decisiveness and the wisdom to use the capacities at hand."[16] "The attack was eminently successful," Crowe remarked. "It had a major personal impact on Qaddafi and it achieved what we wanted—to make him reconsider his terrorism policy and impress him personally with Washington's determination not to be intimidated. Beyond that, it demonstrated our capabilities and the fact that we had an option to do the same, or worse, again."[17]

Aware that a few bombs had missed their targets and caused civilian casualties, Weinberger directed his staff to be as candid as security considerations would allow when publicly discussing the details of the raid. His goal was to refute forcefully Qaddafi's claim that the United States had deliberately attacked civilian targets.[18] To allow Qaddafi's allegations to go unchallenged would have invited a public relations disaster. According to W. Hays Parks, "Disinformation promoted by the enemy solidifies into irrefutable fact if not immediately rebutted."[19]

At a press briefing on 17 April Robert B. Sims, the assistant secretary of defense for public affairs, went out of his way to answer questions from members of the media. He provided a number of details on the planning and execution of the mission and readily acknowledged civilian casualties. He displayed aerial photos of the damage done to the Benghazi barracks and the Benina Airfield, showed videotapes of the F-111F attacks on Aziziyah and the Tripoli Military Airfield, and admitted that about 2 percent of the bombs had landed in civilian areas. Four 2,000-pound bombs stuck a civilian neighborhood near Aziziyah, and two 500-pound bombs flew wide of the Jamahiriyya barracks in Benghazi. Sims was quick to point out, however, that most of the civilian damage was caused by remnants of Libyan SAMs falling back to earth. He produced a photo which, according to the Libyans, displayed a large component from a downed American plane that crashed into a house. He correctly identified the part as the booster rocket of a Libyan SA-3 missile.

Sims was undoubtedly proud of the accomplishments of the combined naval and air forces, because he periodically lapsed into hyperbole to describe the success of the mission.[20] He called the operation "an absolutely flawless professional performance." Later he said: "This was a near-flawless professional operation under extremely difficult circumstances. I don't think there's been anything like it in U.S. military annals."[21] Sims was asked if dropping 2,000-pound bombs on Qaddafi's headquarters at Aziziyah constituted a deliberate attempt to assassinate the Libyan head of state. "We did not know where he was," Sims answered. "We did know where the nerve center for terrorist activity training was, and that's what we attacked. That was the target and not any individual."[22] Sims's briefing had been a success. The Libyan government's attempts to misrepresent the facts were discredited, and few reporters doubted that the United States had taken great care to minimize civilian casualties.

The American people overwhelmingly supported Reagan's decision to take military action against Libya. Their frustration and anger—powerful feelings that had been pent up since the bombing of the Marine Corps barracks in 1983 and had grown more intense with the spectacular terrorist incidents of 1985—were finally released. *Time* and *Newsweek* conducted polls that found 71 percent of the public in favor of the air strikes. In another *Time* poll 56 percent thought the raid would help curtail terrorist attacks on Americans. The raid also garnered favorable editorial comment in such staunchly liberal newspapers as the *New York Times* and the *Washington Post*.[23] Among those on Capitol Hill, Operation El Dorado Canyon enjoyed bipartisan support. Senate Majority Leader Robert Dole, Republican of Kansas, stated that "the president did what he had to do. . . . He met his responsibilities as commander in chief. . . . Now it is up to us to do our part . . . to stand together in doing whatever it takes to answer the challenge of international terrorism."[24] House Speaker Thomas P. O'Neill, Democrat of Massachusetts, declared that Qaddafi "has to be brought to his knees."

On the other hand, Senate Minority Leader Robert Byrd, Democrat of West Virginia, complained vigorously that the administration had not fully consulted with Congress before launching the attack. He maintained that the meeting called by Reagan on the afternoon of 14 April did not satisfy the consultation requirements of the War Powers Act, because it served "as 'notification' rather than consultation."[25] On Tuesday, 15 April, on the floor of the Senate he argued that "the purpose of consultation . . . is to seek the best possible advice so that the actions of this nation on the weighty matter of conducting hostile action is [sic] given the benefit of thoughtful consideration by responsible public officials in both branches of the Congress."[26] Senate Foreign Relations Committee Chairman Richard G. Lugar, Republican of Indiana, insisted that Congress had indeed been consulted in advance, because Reagan could have called off the attack had congressional leaders objected strongly at the meeting.[27]

European Reaction

In Great Britain Prime Minister Margaret Thatcher was sharply criticized and even ridiculed for her decision to support Reagan's action. Political rivals dubbed her "Reagan's poodle."[28] In the words of a member of the opposition Labor Party, "She has not only broken the confidence of the European Community and international law, but now has the blood of innocents on her hands."[29] The lead editorial in the 19 April issue of the *Economist* condemned the air raid: "In bombing Libya, the United States killed sleeping women and children and opened a dangerous new period in which terrorism against Americans and West Europeans may, for a time, get worse rather than better."[30] The *Observer* called the air strike "an act justified neither in law nor morality, designed to satisfy the simple appetites of the American public."[31]

The "Iron Lady" defended her decision with trademark determination before the House of Commons. "If Britain always refused to take risks because of the consequences then terrorist governments would win and one would only be able to cringe before them," she asserted. "To refuse to take action against terrorism would mean that Britain was supine and passive in the face of that terrorism."[32]

Mrs. Thatcher did have one very influential supporter: the *Sunday Times*. In an editorial titled "Alone but Right," the newspaper applauded the courage of the prime minister and President Reagan and excoriated their European partners. The editorial stated:

> There comes a time when a nation has to stand up for itself, whatever the fears . . . if it is to retain its self-respect. President Reagan decided the time had come last week, and the vast majority of the Americans agreed. The Europeans did not, and started the Americans wondering aloud just what sort of allies it has been defending for the past forty years. . . . They had every right to expect better of their European allies last week. Good allies should give each other the benefit of the doubt. . . . Mrs. Thatcher stood by Reagan . . . over-riding the doubts . . . about bombing being the best way to retaliate against terrorism. The rest of America's allies in Europe, however, seemed anxious to give everybody but America the benefit of the doubt: they even quibbled about the evidence proving Colonel Qaddafi's guilt.[33]

The editor of the *Sunday Telegraph* argued that if Mrs. Thatcher had refused to cooperate with the United States, her decision "would have put the Atlantic Alliance at risk." Therefore, by agreeing to let Reagan use bombers based in

Great Britain, Mrs. Thatcher prevented "such a backlash of anti-European resentment in the United States as could have undermined NATO." The editor described her actions as "the stuff of statesmanship."[34]

According to a *Newsweek* poll, 66 percent of the British public disapproved of the U.S. attack on Libya, 71 percent thought that the raid would probably lead to an increase in terrorist activity, and 56 percent believed that the government was too supportive of Reagan's Libya policy.[35] Undaunted by the lack of public support for her actions, Mrs. Thatcher told *Newsweek* that she did not pretend "that such decisions are easy or that there is not a price to be paid in the war against terrorism. But a stand has to be made. I believe that the British people, who have for so long supported our determination to confront terrorism in Northern Ireland and elsewhere, understand that perfectly well."[36]

The only allied leaders other than Mrs. Thatcher to express support for the U.S. raid were Prime Minister Brian Mulroney of Canada and Chancellor Helmut Kohl of West Germany.[37] In remarks delivered in the Bundestag—the West German parliament—Kohl disclosed that German government experts had obtained valid, independent evidence of Libyan involvement in the discothèque bombing by decoding cables sent to Tripoli from the people's bureau in East Berlin. Kohl also justified the military action, calling it "a preventive strike against the further escalation of terrorism." He poked a jab at Western leaders who did not support the United States: "It is easy to criticize the United States for resorting to measures we would not have chosen. . . . If we Europeans do not want to follow the Americans for reasons of our own, we must develop political initiatives. We will not eliminate international terrorism simply by wailing and lamenting."[38]

Two days after the raid, in a public appearance at the White House, Reagan praised supportive allies but did not mention any countries by name. As he remarked, "Our allies who cooperated with us in this action . . . proved that they stood for freedom and right, that as a free people they haven't let themselves be cowed by threats and violence. They have earned the lasting respect and friendship of the American people."[39]

Several European allies complained that the United States had discounted their concerns over the use of military force in the struggle against terrorism and purposely ignored the recent EC declaration that singled out Libya as a nation supporting terrorism. They sharply criticized Reagan's decision and doubted that the air strike would produce a desired change in Qaddafi's behavior. The allies also feared that it would disrupt their $12 billion commercial relationship with Libya, endanger the forty thousand Europeans working there, and spur a new wave of terrorist violence in Europe.[40] "Far from weakening terrorism, this military action risks provoking explosive reactions of fanaticism and criminal acts," declared Prime Minister Bettino Craxi of Italy.[41] President François Mitterand of France was more sharply critical of the United States. As he put it, "I don't believe that you can stop terrorism by killing 150 Libyans who have done nothing."[42]

Popular anti-American feeling was strongest in West Germany. Opinion polls found that three-quarters of the German citizenry opposed the air raid and only 7 percent agreed with Kohl's position. Four hundred protesters demonstrated in front of the American embassy in Bonn, and a march by several thousand demonstrators in West Berlin turned violent as protesters smashed the windows of several American-owned banks and businesses. Ironically, a *Newsweek* poll found that 61 percent of the French people approved of the U.S. military action, and 43 percent indicated that their government was not supportive enough of America's Libya policy.[43]

A majority of European leaders privately acknowledged that they bore some of the blame for the conflict between the United States and Libya, since they were unable to produce a Libya policy strong enough to dissuade Reagan from taking unilateral action. Reagan's decision to use force strengthened the credibility of his terrorism policy and challenged America's allies to take more resolute steps to deal with the problem and to demonstrate that further military action was unnecessary.[44] "Bombs alone cannot tame Colonel Qaddafi, nor bring down his regime," stated a *New York Times* editorial that ran one week after the air strike. "In the end, only ostracism and economic punishment can do that, while giving pause to other governments that sponsor and support terrorists."[45] In the immediate aftermath of the bombing of Libya, the European allies understood the risks posed to them by Libyan terrorism. They were nervous about the possibility of further hostilities between the United States and Libya, and they were ready to cooperate with the administration in the struggle against international terrorism. "We had finally gotten their attention," commented Secretary of State Shultz.[46]

Like an old married couple, the United States and its allies soon set aside their differences and enacted new political measures to deal with Qaddafi. On 21 April the EC foreign ministers met in Luxembourg and agreed to reduce the size of Libyan diplomatic missions in Europe to the "absolute minimum necessary" and to restrict the movement of Libyan diplomats to the vicinity of capital cities. The ministers approved a measure that placed nonofficial Libyans, such as students, teachers, and journalists, under closer scrutiny, and declared

that any Libyan citizen expelled from one EC country for involvement in terrorist activity would be banned from the other member countries as well.[47]
The day after the Luxembourg meeting Britain ordered the deportation of
twenty-one Libyan students for their membership in militant organizations
considered dangerous to national security.[48]

The Tokyo Summit

Two days after the raid Reagan called on the Europeans to join with the United
States in seeking a "collective solution" to international terrorism.[49] In early
May he had an opportunity to press his case when he and the other leaders of
the world's seven largest industrial democracies (or the "G-7," which included
Canada, France, Italy, Japan, the United Kingdom, the United States, and West
Germany) convened in Tokyo for the Western economic summit. At the sum-
mit Reagan proposed a number of measures to isolate Qaddafi, such as the
closure of all people's bureaus, the suspension of all trade with and credit for
Libya, a prohibition on the purchase of Libyan oil, the closure of ports to
Libyan-flagged vessels, the denial of landing rights to Libyan Arab Airlines, the
withdrawal of Western capital from Libyan-controlled banks, and the recall of
Western diplomats from Tripoli. Not surprisingly, Reagan and Shultz found a
potent ally at the G-7 meeting in the person of Prime Minister Thatcher, who
worked diligently with the Americans to hammer out a strong statement on
international terrorism.[50]

The final communiqué of the Tokyo summit contained a powerful uniform
declaration on terrorism, but it still avoided the controversial issue of economic
sanctions. The statement included the following important points:

> We, the heads of state or government of seven major democracies . . .
> strongly affirm our condemnation of international terrorism in all its forms,
> of its accomplices and of those, including governments, who sponsor or
> support it. We abhor the increase in the level of terrorism since our last
> meeting, and in particular its blatant and cynical use as an instrument of gov-
> ernment policy. Terrorism has no justification. It spreads only by the use of
> contemptible means, ignoring the values of human life, freedom, and dig-
> nity. It must be fought relentlessly and without compromise.
>
> Recognizing that the continuing fight against terrorism is a task, which the
> international community as a whole has to undertake, we pledge ourselves
> to fight against the scourge. Terrorism must be fought effectively through

determined, tenacious, discreet and patient action combining national measures with international cooperation.[51]

The communiqué reaffirmed several of the measures already taken by the EC against countries that support or sponsor terrorism. It limited the size of diplomatic missions of countries that engage in terrorist activities; it restricted the travel of diplomats assigned to those missions; it tightened immigration and visa requirements for the nationals of states that sponsor or support terrorism; it prohibited the entry of any person already expelled from another G-7 country for participating in terrorist activity; it banned arms sales to countries that advocate terrorism; and it condemned Libya by name for its involvement in international terrorism. The G-7 leaders also pledged to improve extradition procedures and achieve better cooperation between the law enforcement and intelligence agencies of member countries. The seven leaders agreed that law enforcement and diplomacy, not military force, should serve as the pillars of an effective international effort to contain terrorism.[52] When asked by a reporter what message the communiqué was sending to Qaddafi, Shultz responded unequivocally: "You've had it, pal! You are isolated! You are recognized as a terrorist!"[53]

The Tokyo summit was a major diplomatic victory for Ronald Reagan. Coming soon after Operation El Dorado Canyon, the communiqué provided a powerful follow-up punch in the fight against international terrorism. After the raid several European governments adopted measures aimed at curbing terrorism, and those measures were beginning to show results. For example, in the first three months following the strike the Europeans expelled over one hundred Libyan diplomats and businessmen; West Germany alone expelled twenty-five Libyans. A State Department official noted that by midsummer most of Libya's intelligence operatives in Europe had been sent home. By significantly reducing the number of Libyan diplomats in their countries the Europeans had effectively weakened Qaddafi's ability to conduct terrorist operations and had forced him to transfer components of his terror network from the people's bureaus to fronts that did not enjoy diplomatic immunity, such as Libyan Arab Airlines, businesses, and banks.[54]

Reaction from the Soviet Union

Immediately after the air raid the Soviet government registered diplomatic protests with both the United States and the United Kingdom. Soviet leader

Mikhail Gorbachev sharply denounced the American attack and suggested that he would assist Qaddafi in repairing Libya's defenses.[55] Gorbachev sent the following message to Qaddafi:

> I would like, on behalf of the leadership of the Soviet Union and all Soviet people, to express to you personally and to the friendly Libyan people feelings of solidarity in the face of the act of piracy committed by American imperialism. . . . While verbally declaring that they are acting as fighters against "international terrorism," in fact U.S. leaders have once more confirmed their allegiance to a policy of state terrorism . . . .
>
> In reaffirming our effective solidarity to you, Comrade Qaddafi, and to the entire Libyan people, I would like to assure you that the Soviet Union firmly intends to fulfill the commitments it has made with respect to the further strengthening of Libya's defense capability.[56]

The Soviets walked a narrow line after the air strike. They hoped to stir up international opposition to the American attack on Libya but did not want the incident to develop into a crisis between the United States and the Soviet Union. Gorbachev warned the United States that Reagan's aggressive behavior could have a negative effect on Soviet-American relations, and then promptly canceled the scheduled meeting between Soviet Foreign Minister Eduard Shevardnadze and Secretary of State Shultz to set the agenda for the next summit meeting between the leaders of the two superpowers. After a short interlude Gorbachev was satisfied that he had demonstrated sufficient "solidarity" with Qaddafi. He then agreed to reschedule the Shultz-Shevardnadze talks.[57]

To the Soviets Qaddafi was more of a liability than an asset. They carefully avoided making a commitment to defend Libya in the event of renewed hostilities, and advised Qaddafi to refrain from further terrorist attacks on American citizens. The Soviets had strong political and economic reasons for seeking improved relations with the United States and did not want their opportunistic relationship with Qaddafi to undermine their growing rapprochement with the United States.[58]

Reactions from the Middle East

Of the many states in the Middle East, only the Israeli government and press openly supported the U.S. attack on Libya. In an editorial titled "Warning to Syria," the Tel Aviv newspaper *Ma'ariv* made the following comment: "The

U.S. air attack . . . was truly revolutionary, in both political and global terms. It is hard to believe that Washington will return the sword to its sheath if the unholy alliance of Libya and its partners continues to disrupt the lives of Americans. Condemnation from hypocritically pious Western Europe (Britain excluded) probably will not influence those who shape American policy."[59]

Since no Arab leader could openly endorse a U.S. military attack against a brother Arab and expect to survive politically, several moderate, pro-Western Arab governments (namely Egypt, Jordan, Saudi Arabia, Kuwait, and the United Arab Emirates) publicly condemned the attack—Kuwait called it "an act of terrorism and flagrant aggression"[60]—but privately welcomed Reagan's use of force against one of the region's biggest troublemakers. The day after the air strike OPEC, which was dominated by moderate Arab states, refused Qaddafi's request to impose an oil embargo on the United States.[61] One of the noteworthy benefits of the air strike was the political boost it gave to moderate regimes in the Middle East. "The way to strengthen the Arab moderates is to show that radical policies fail," noted an administration official. "The way to hurt moderates is to let radicals like Qaddafi get away with murder."[62]

The most virulent denouncements of the United States came from Iran, Syria, radical Palestinian groups, and anti-Western factions in Lebanon. Iranian prime minister Hussein Musavi stated that "the USA will receive the due response for its stubborn attitude." A Lebanese group known as the Arab Armed Brigade threatened to "retaliate by kidnapping and killing all Americans, British, and French nationals in Lebanon."[63]

Despite the obligatory condemnation of the United States from a number of moderate Arab governments and vituperative support from radical quarters, Qaddafi's partners in the Third World did not follow up their rhetoric with action. After the raid moderate Arab and African leaders still distrusted and disliked Qaddafi and regarded him, in the words of political scientist Lisa Anderson, as "a meddlesome anachronism" who over the years had tried to subvert many of their regimes. Only Damascus and Tehran maintained cordial relations with Tripoli.[64]

A Terrorist Backlash

The American air strike unleashed a spasm of anti-Western violence in the Middle East and Europe in the days immediately following the raid. In Khartoum a U.S. embassy employee, William J. Calkins, was shot and critically wounded as he drove home. Ambassador Hume A. Horan subsequently ordered the evacuation of all but the most essential personnel from the post. In Lebanon the British ambassador's residence was hit with rocket shells, and a British television cameraman, John McCarthy, was abducted. In the Shuf Mountains near Beirut the bodies of three Western hostages, Britons Leigh Douglas and Philip Padfield and American Peter Kilburn, were discovered. They were executed by a terrorist group calling itself the Arab Revolutionary Cells, an organization with ties to Abu Nidal. A third Briton, Alec Collett, was hanged by a group also linked to Abu Nidal. Moreover, the CIA reported that a Libyan intelligence operative had bought Kilburn from his Lebanese captors and executed him. On 18 April Turkish authorities apprehended two Libyan men carrying a bag of explosives in the vicinity of the American officers' club in Ankara. Finally, alert security personnel at Heathrow Airport in London prevented a catastrophe when they discovered a bomb in the carry-on luggage of an Irish woman, Anne Marion Murphy, as she boarded El Al Flight 016 for Israel. She had been set up by her lover, a Jordanian-born Palestinian, Nizar Mansur Hindawi, who drove her to the airport, gave her a handbag containing ten pounds of plastic explosives, and then disappeared. He was arrested two days later by Scotland Yard. Hindawi told British authorities that he was operating on behalf of Syria and had obtained the explosives from the Syrian embassy in London.[65]

The terrorist attacks carried out in the wake of the Libya raid were largely the work of groups or individuals motivated by either hatred of the West or solidarity with Qaddafi. In the months that followed the United States and its Western allies hoped that their united stand against terrorism, along with the threat of renewed hostilities, would have a discernible effect on the behavior of Qaddafi and his murderous comrades-in-arms.

The Impact of El Dorado Canyon on Qaddafi

Only a few minutes after the Air Force and Navy bombers carried out their attacks on Tripoli and Benghazi, the Voice of America delivered the following message to the people of Libya: "The people of the United States bear Libya and its people no enmity or hatred. . . . However, Colonel Qaddafi is your head of state. So long as Libyans obey his orders, then they must accept the consequences. Colonel Qaddafi is your tragic burden. The Libyan people are responsible for Colonel Qaddafi and his actions. If you permit Colonel Qaddafi to continue with the present conflict, then you must also share some collective responsibility for his actions." The broadcast was nothing less than a call for the Libyan population to rise up and topple the Qaddafi regime.

The air strike was a devastating psychological and political defeat for Qaddafi. Two nights after the raid he briefly appeared on Libyan television. Wearing a white naval officer's uniform and sitting in front of a map of Libya, he spoke in a calm, steady tone. He declared that "we are ready to die for our country if attacked" and then implored his countrymen to "put back the lights in the streets." Within minutes of his brief address the lights of Libya's major cities were ablaze and the streets filled with people dancing, honking car horns, and chanting slogans.[66] Qaddafi accused Reagan of murdering children and destroying homes and pledged to continue "inciting revolution and establishing popular revolution everywhere in the world." He did not, however, call for reprisals as he had done before the air strike. "We have not issued any orders for murdering anybody," he said. "We can tell Reagan that he doesn't have to protect his children and citizens, because we do not bomb children like the United States does."[67]

After the speech Qaddafi left Tripoli and took refuge in the desert where he figured he would be safe from American LGBs and Libyan mutineers. For the next several weeks he maintained a low profile and remained out of public view for several days at a time. There were reports that he was depressed, shaken, and confused and, when he was seen, he seemed uncharacteristically subdued. Perhaps he wanted to elicit sympathy from the international community for his country's suffering at the hands of American imperialists. "Perhaps the very fact that someone had attacked and almost killed him had been a devastating blow to his pride and balance," commented Admiral Crowe. "Instead of making him fighting mad, it had shocked him profoundly."[68] CIA Director Casey confidently told a group of reporters that "this attack will scare the hell out of Qaddafi."[69] According to journalist David Ignatius, Operation El Dorado Canyon "broke the psychology that had allowed Qaddafi to intimidate much of the world and revealed that, far from being an international giant, Qaddafi was weak, isolated and vulnerable."[70]

While few air raids have changed the course of history, the removal of Qaddafi from power would have had a singular effect on international terrorism. In the days immediately following the air strike, U.S. intelligence received several reports of fighting between elements of the regular Libyan armed forces and Qaddafi's personal security forces. One incident was witnessed by members of the foreign press. On Wednesday afternoon, 16 April, a bus filled with reporters who had come to inspect the damage caused by American bombers arrived outside Bab al-Aziziyah. The moment the bus stopped the reporters observed a dozen soldiers with automatic weapons running from one of the gates of the compound, while the sound of machine gun fire rattled overhead. A few moments later they noticed a flash of bright light—probably the firing of a missile—behind the walls of Aziziyah. Once inside the reporters found the compound quiet but exhibiting signs of the U.S. bombing. A BBC report suggested that the gunfire around Aziziyah was evidence of a coup attempt. That same day ABC News reported that U.S. intelligence had information that a mutiny had occurred at the army base in Tarhunna, located fifty miles south of Tripoli, and that Qaddafi had ordered the Libyan air force to attack the mutineers. These incidents may have prompted Qaddafi to appear on television to demonstrate that he was still in control of the country.[71]

While Qaddafi was battling the threat from his own military, Shultz disclosed publicly that one of the purposes of the air strike was to encourage Qaddafi's opponents to remove him from power. At a news conference on 17 April Shultz pointed out "that there was . . . considerable dissidence in the armed forces of Libya with Qaddafi and what he is doing." He admitted that the targets were deliberately selected to send powerful messages to Qaddafi's military and his personal security detachments: "First . . . from the standpoint of equipment that the military [values] . . . the terrorist activities of Libya may cost them some of that equipment, and it . . . did. Second, that the Praetorian Guards that surround Qaddafi and intimidate people are not invulnerable." The secretary of state remarked that if a coup did take place it would be "all to the good," because those who would take over for Qaddafi would be more concerned with improving living conditions in Libya than with spreading revolution and supporting terrorism. "We know that there are lots of people in Libya who think Libya would be better off if Qaddafi was not there," he commented. "There are even more not in Libya who think that."[72]

Qaddafi took swift action to eliminate the threat posed by the regular armed forces. Convinced that the United States was attempting to foment a military rebellion, he scrutinized the loyalty of the officer corps and ruthlessly purged all "American agents" and malcontents.[73] According to intelligence reports Qaddafi executed, cashiered, or reassigned several senior officers in the weeks immediately following the raid.[74] By carrying out this action he weakened the one group in Libya that the Reagan administration hoped to embolden by carrying out the air strike.

The raid also weakened Qaddafi at home. Coming after a half-decade of declining oil revenues, shortfalls in consumer goods (including food), and a

reduced standard of living for the average Libyan, the U.S. attack did not produce a sustained outpouring of popular support but instead contributed to an
increase in political opposition and internal dissension.[75] In the spring and
summer of 1986 the "state of the masses" questioned the wisdom of its leader.
In particular many Libyans wondered why the country's huge arsenal had failed
to protect them from the United States. Fortunately for Qaddafi, the Libyan
people remembered the considerable increase in their material well-being after
the revolution and believed the slump in oil revenues was a temporary phenomenon. Furthermore, most Libyans remained quiet, confining their discontent to private complaining and discreet questioning of Qaddafi's motives and
policies.[76]

After almost two months of seclusion Qaddafi reemerged on 11 June when
he gave a lengthy, rambling speech on Libyan television. The performance was
quintessential Qaddafi and, at times, he seemed to be imitating his hero, Gamal
Abdul Nasser. Those who saw the speech knew that the Libyan leader was in
control of both himself and his country. He had been knocked down but not
out by the air raid. By the middle of the summer he was touring the country,
and on the first day of September—the seventeenth anniversary of the Libyan
revolution—he made his first major public appearance.[77] He reviewed a huge
military parade in Tripoli, rode proudly through the city in a red Cadillac con-
vertible, and delivered a blistering three hour speech before a huge crowd. In
the speech he described Reagan as a "madman"; called on Soviet leader Mikhail
Gorbachev to do more than just help defend Libya; declared that several European countries had apologized to him for imposing sanctions against Libya; and
ridiculed American officials who claimed that his power was declining. "They
don't know anything about Libya," he told the crowd, estimated at five thousand. "They said after the raid Qaddafi would give up authority. In Libya, the
people are the authority." Although the speech was full of powerful rhetoric,
Qaddafi clearly signaled that he wanted to prevent further U.S. military action.
He insisted that Libya had nothing to do with the terrorist attacks in Western
Europe that had prompted the U.S. air strike, and he challenged Reagan to produce evidence of Libyan involvement. Moreover, he told the crowd that while
he still supported national liberation movements, he never condoned terrorist
operations that might harm innocent civilians.[78]

Three days later Qaddafi took his first trip abroad after the air raid. At the
summit of the Nonaligned Movement in Harare, Zimbabwe, his irrational,
bombastic nature took center stage. He blasted the leaders of the movement
for not helping defend his country against attack from the United States. He

declared that they should have been ready to join him in a retaliatory attack against the United States or, at the very least, they should have severed relations with the United States and Great Britain.[79] Not surprisingly, he threatened to quit the movement: "I want to say goodbye, farewell to this funny movement, to this fallacy—farewell to this utter falsehood."[80]

Dealing with Qaddafi: Changing Realities, Disinformation, and a New Strategy

In the weeks following the air raid, disagreement persisted between Shultz and Weinberger over the use of force to combat terrorism. As before, Shultz seemed more willing to use military power than Weinberger. The secretary of state emphasized that the recent action ordered by Reagan demonstrated the willingness of the United States to use force to fight terrorism. On the other hand, the secretary of defense pointed out that the air strike was carried out "very reluctantly" and only as "a last resort" after the administration was unable to win allied support for stringent economic and political sanctions against Libya.

Despite his well-known advocacy of military force against states that sponsor or support terrorism, Shultz offered no clues as to what Reagan would do after the next terrorist incident. Administration officials continued to warn Qaddafi that if he did not modify his behavior, further attacks were possible, but Shultz and other senior policymakers privately acknowledged that Operation El Dorado Canyon was a single, extraordinary event. "We will judge every situation as it goes, and we're not going to get into a kind of automatic pilot on this," Shultz admitted to reporters.[81] According to one senior official, "If Qaddafi hits our forces or continues terrorist acts and we can prove it, the president will maintain and sustain military options on a case-by-case basis."[82]

Shultz and a number of other officials realized that the American public did not have the will to wage a protracted military campaign against terrorism, they recognized that there was widespread international concern about terrorist reprisals in wake of the attack, and they acknowledged that diplomatic support for a subsequent strike against a state that sponsored or supported terrorism would be difficult to obtain.[83] This tacit policy shift lifted tremendous pressure off Prime Minister Thatcher, who emphasized that in permitting the F-111Fs and their support aircraft to operate from British bases, her government was "not giving a blank check" for further attacks.[84]

As far as its Libya policy was concerned, by midsummer the Reagan White

House was not content to leave well enough alone. Qaddafi's prestige was badly tarnished and his authority had been challenged, but he had withstood a mighty blow and was still in charge in Tripoli. Nevertheless, Reagan and his senior aides (namely Shultz, CIA Director Casey, and National Security Adviser Poindexter) were determined to remove him from power.[85] In August the administration implemented an elaborate strategy of "closely coordinated events involving covert, diplomatic, military, and public actions" to exploit Qaddafi's insecurity and convince him that he was about to be attacked by the United States and might be ousted by a military coup.[86] The plan, which was developed under the direction of Poindexter, had ambitious objectives. It sought to "dissuade Qaddafi from engaging in terrorism, bring about a change in leadership, [and] minimize the possibility of Soviet gains in Libya." The plan contained an unusual element—"a disinformation program"—that combined "real and illusionary events . . . with the basic goal of making Qaddafi *think* that there is a high degree of internal opposition to him within Libya, that his key trusted aides are disloyal, [and] that the U.S. is about to move against him militarily." According to a key planning document, "Forces within Libya which desire his overthrow will be emboldened to take action . . . and energize those who would seek to replace him."[87] Reagan approved the secret strategy at a meeting of the NSPG on 14 August. Although the two-page NSDD contained few specifics, it called for increased pressure on Qaddafi, expanded covert action in support of dissident Libyan exiles, and overt military deployments to lend credibility to planted news reports that the United States was preparing to strike Libya.[88]

The components of the plan were outlined in a three-page memorandum that Poindexter sent to Reagan in early August in advance of the NSPG meeting. One month later an unidentified administration official leaked a copy of the memorandum to *Washington Post* reporter Bob Woodward.

While the architects of the newest anti-Qaddafi campaign intended to place the disinformation in foreign media outlets only, it inevitably spilled over into the American press. Thus, beginning with a 25 August article in the *Wall Street Journal*, American journalists conveyed as fact much of the disinformation fabricated by the new strategy. "The U.S. and Libya are on a collision course again," reported the *Journal*. "After a lull, Colonel Qaddafi has begun plotting new terrorist attacks, U.S. and European intelligence officials say. And the Reagan administration is preparing to teach the mercurial leader another lesson. Right now, the Pentagon is completing plans for a new and larger bombing of Libya in case the president orders it."[89] Poindexter embraced the *Journal* article, and Reagan's press secretary, Larry Speakes, called it "authoritative."[90] By August, however, U.S. intelligence had concluded that Qaddafi was "quiescent" with regard to terrorism and that the only "confrontation" was the one being orchestrated by the White House.[91]

The whole disinformation campaign exploded in the administration's face when Woodward's article, "Gadhafi Target of Secret U.S. Deception Plan," ran in the 2 October edition of the *Washington Post*. The article was based on Poindexter's memorandum, and with its publication the administration was suddenly caught pursuing a foreign policy initiative that the American public would find extremely difficult to support. Nevertheless, Reagan and a number of senior officials attempted to put the best face on a scheme that deliberately misled the American press and, ultimately, the American people. On the very day that Woodward's article hit the streets Reagan told reporters during a White House interview that he challenged "the veracity of that entire story" and that he did not recall attending any meeting where memoranda outlining a plan to mislead the American people had been discussed.[92] His comment about the memoranda was essentially correct. According to notes taken at the NSPG meeting on 14 August, the word "disinformation" was never mentioned. Moreover, it did not appear in the NSDD, which Reagan signed two days after the meeting. The president also made it clear to reporters that he had no regrets about making Qaddafi uncomfortable. "Our position has been one in which we would just as soon have Mr. Qaddafi go to bed every night wondering what we might do," he stated. "I think that's the best position for anyone like that to be in."[93] Shultz told reporters that he knew "of no decision to have people go out and tell lies to the media." He emphasized, however, "that if there are ways in which we can make Qaddafi nervous, why shouldn't we?"[94]

Disclosure of the deception campaign undermined the administration's credibility as it sought to curb Libyan involvement in terrorism and destabilize the Qaddafi regime. When caught red-handed the administration unwittingly deflected some of the world's attention away from Qaddafi and raised serious questions about its own integrity. One senior White House official acknowledged that the disinformation strategy "hurt the hell out of us" by raising doubts about the credibility of Reagan and his advisers. Poindexter became the principal lighting rod for criticism of the plan from sources both within and outside the administration. "It was naïve of John to believe that you could do something like this against Qaddafi and think that it wouldn't show up in the American press," said one administration official. Ironically, "it was the press stories, whether we intended them or not, that made the campaign effective."[95]

The disinformation campaign was neither well conceived nor well executed. Considering the harm it had done to the credibility of Reagan's national security team, the administration would have been better served letting the air raid and the achievements of the Tokyo summit attain full effect. Positive developments were already appearing: Qaddafi's involvement in terrorist operations was declining, and the European allies were actively involved in the U.S.-led effort to isolate the Libyan dictator.

In early 1987 Qaddafi suffered another crushing military defeat when Chadian government troops with considerable French support routed Libyan forces and captured the Libyan-held garrisons at Fada, Ouadi Doum, and Faya Largeau in northern Chad. During the three-month Chadian offensive, which culminated in late March, approximately three thousand Libyan soldiers were killed, were wounded, or deserted; nine hundred were captured; and a huge arsenal of fixed-wing aircraft, helicopters, tanks, armored personnel carriers, artillery, small arms, and ammunition fell into Chadian hands. In light of these developments a number of Western intelligence analysts reported that the Libyan officer corps was becoming increasingly restless and reluctant to suffer additional casualties in Chad, and that the rank and file troops were gripped by extremely low morale. The analysts speculated that Qaddafi was losing control of his military and predicted that his removal from power was only a matter of time.

Under pressure from the debacle in Chad, the impact of the American air strike, and increased diplomatic isolation, Qaddafi softened his rhetoric and even called for improved relations with the United States.[96] "They trained people to assassinate me and they failed," he told a *New York Times* reporter, referring to the U.S. air strike that had hit his headquarters and residence in Tripoli. "They have not succeeded in defeating us. They should look for other alternatives to have some kind of rapprochement." In the interview with the *Times* reporter, Qaddafi predicted a better relationship with the United States following the election of the next president. "We think . . . relations will probably improve after Reagan, regardless of who comes, Democrat or Republican," he stated. "Nobody is going to follow the Reagan American policy, because it is shameful."[97]

As the second anniversary of the air strike approached, the Reagan administration performed a thorough review of its Libya policy and a new strategy gradually emerged. Many senior policymakers realized that it would be difficult for the United States to remove Qaddafi through military or covert action and were convinced that the setbacks of the previous two years had weakened

Qaddafi to the extent that he no longer posed a threat to his neighbors in North Africa and the Middle East. Consequently, the administration developed a new policy that put less emphasis on confrontational measures designed to intimidate Qaddafi and more on isolating him in the region. Accordingly, the Sixth Fleet avoided the Gulf of Sidra, the CIA throttled back support for Libyan exile groups, and administration officials toned down their rhetoric against the Libyan dictator.

The new strategy sought to contain Qaddafi's power, influence, and ability to cause harm by isolating him diplomatically and economically in the region. "There's been a natural evolution of our policy," observed a member of the White House staff. "If one characterizes our earlier policy as one of active destabilization, one could say we're now trying to further isolate him." One State Department official believed that Qaddafi's credibility was irreparably damaged and that the United States could afford to wait him out. "Our policy is now geared to having him . . . in place for a long time, but in a weakened state," the official stated.

A number of foreign policy analysts such as Lisa Anderson characterized the administration's change in policy as a movement toward realism. "Clearly, a lot of enthusiasm for the anti-Libya campaign has abated, in part because the administration has run out of ideas," she said. "The United States is now according Libya the amount of attention it deserves." The departure of a number of hard-liners from key policy-making positions in the administration—most notably National Security Adviser Poindexter and CIA Director Casey—made it easier for advocates of the isolation policy to win their case. Poindexter resigned in November 1986 over his involvement in the Iran-Contra affair, which nearly wrecked Reagan's presidency. Casey, who had supported the secret transfer of arms to Iran, was hospitalized with a brain tumor in December 1986 and died five months later.[98]

As the administration embarked on a new strategy aimed at isolating Qaddafi, two North African leaders took just the opposite tack. President Chadli Benjedid of Algeria and President Zine al-Abidine Ben Ali of Tunisia actively courted the Libyan leader, hoping to put him in touch with the outside world. While Reagan and the two Arab presidents sought the same goal—stability in the region—Benjedid and Ben Ali feared that an isolated and friendless Qaddafi might upset regional stability by leading him to meddle in the internal affairs of other countries and by negotiating a deal with Moscow that would permit the Soviets greater use of military bases in Libya. In early 1988, at the behest of Benjedid, Qaddafi visited Algeria and Tunisia where flag-waving crowds greeted him enthusiastically. He conferred with both presidents and discussed several measures aimed at improving bilateral relations.[99] "After the U.S. bombing, Qaddafi realized that he was completely isolated, completely alone. It was a real shock," noted one Arab diplomat. "He was smart enough to realize he needed to make friends. . . . Now, through the good offices of Tunisia and Algeria, he wants to reach out."[100]

Building on the diplomatic opening engineered by Benjedid and Ben Ali, Qaddafi took several steps over the next five years to end Libya's regional isolation. He sought to mend relations with his Arab and African neighbors—most notably Egypt, Sudan, Chad, Morocco, Jordan, and the PLO—and to advance the respectability and prestige of his country. In 1988 Qaddafi and President Mubarak of Egypt held a face-to-face meeting, marking the start of a warm and durable rapprochement. In 1989 Qaddafi and the leaders of Algeria, Mauritania, Morocco, and Tunisia formed the Arab Maghreb Union, an association concerned primarily with regional economic and security issues. That same year Qaddafi decided to settle the long-running dispute with Chad over the Aouzou Strip by submitting the matter to the International Court of Justice in The Hague. During the early stages of the Gulf crisis of 1990–1991 Qaddafi condemned Iraq's invasion of Kuwait and proposed a settlement that called for the withdrawal of Iraqi troops from Kuwait and the removal of foreign troops from the region. Following the rejection of his peace plan Qaddafi retired to the sidelines and maintained Libya's neutrality while a huge international military coalition led by the United States drove the forces of Saddam Hussein from Kuwait.[101]

Qaddafi and Terrorism after El Dorado Canyon

Operation El Dorado Canyon—buttressed by the Tokyo Communiqué—yielded a perceptible change in Qaddafi's behavior regarding terrorism. Although he did not disavow its use, he moderated his public rhetoric in support of terrorist groups and acted with discernible restraint. Few Libyan-backed terrorist plots were uncovered in the months following the attack and, according to the State Department, the number of terrorist incidents linked to Libya dropped from nineteen in 1986 to six each in 1987 and 1988. To maintain terror as an instrument of state policy Qaddafi became more covert and disciplined about its use, enlisted more competent surrogates, and adopted stringent security measures to safeguard the secrecy of his terrorist network.[102]

Qaddafi had apparently received the West's message regarding terrorism. He understood that continuing to sponsor and support its practice would exact a terrible penalty. The United States demonstrated that it had both the means and the will to act in self-defense, and the specter of another strike haunted the Libyan dictator. Nevertheless, Qaddafi remained unapologetic and dedicated to the utility of terrorism. He may have become more cautious and circumspect, but he was unwavering in his justification of terrorism and the moral support he gave to murderers such as Abu Nidal.[103] In an interview with a *Washington Post* reporter, Qaddafi stated that Abu Nidal "has the right to fight and liberate his country. . . . This so-called terrorism . . . is not terrorism, it is a matter of [combatting] colonizations."[104] The State Department reported that it had "seen no evidence that Libya has abandoned support of international terrorism, subversion, and aggression," and that the United States would continue to keep Qaddafi isolated "diplomatically and economically, in order to limit his ability to cause harm."[105]

One Final Confrontation: The Air Battle off Tobruk and the Rabta Controversy

On New Year's Day 1989 the USS *John F. Kennedy* (CV 67) departed Cannes, France, and with the ships of her battle group commenced a transit to Haifa, Israel, where she planned to enjoy her last Mediterranean port visit before sailing for her home port in Norfolk, Virginia. On 4 January the "JFK" was conducting routine flight operations in international waters south of Greece. Shortly before noon an E-2C Hawkeye detected two Libyan MiG-23 Floggers as they took off from al-Bumbah airbase located west of Tobruk in eastern Libya. The Hawkeye vectored a pair of CAP F-14 Tomcats toward the MiGs. The Navy fighters were from VF-32, nicknamed the "Swordsmen." Comdr. Joseph B. Connelly, skipper of VF-32, piloted the lead Tomcat, call sign "Gypsy 207." His RIO was Comdr. Leo F. Enright, operations officer for CVW 3. Lt. Herman C. Cook and Lt. Comdr. Steven P. Collins were the pilot and RIO, respectively, in the second F-14, call sign "Gypsy 202." Both planes were armed with four medium-range, radar-homing Sparrow missiles and two short-range, heat-seeking Sidewinder missiles.[106]

The Tomcat crews immediately picked up the Libyan aircraft on their radars, seventy-two miles to the south. The MiGs were tracking north toward the carrier, which was steaming more than 120 miles from the Libyan coast.

Five times Connelly and Cook altered course to initiate a standard intercept of the MiG-23s, but the Libyans foiled each maneuver by pointing the noses of their aircraft at the American fighters. The Tomcats and Floggers were on a collision course at a combined speed of over one thousand knots. The Navy airmen interpreted the Libyan actions as hostile intent and, under the Peacetime ROE, they prepared to defend themselves. As a further precaution they assumed that the Libyans were armed with medium-range, radar-guided Apex missiles. Therefore, they would have to act before they came within the twelve-mile range of the Libyan missiles. When the Floggers closed within twenty miles the Swordsmen armed their missiles.

When the Floggers were approximately twelve miles out Enright initiated action by firing a Sparrow at the lead Flogger. A few seconds later he fired a second Sparrow from a range of about ten miles. Both missiles seemed to guide at first but, as they streaked toward the MiGs, both planes turned sharply to the left, breaking the radar lock. Neither Sparrow scored a hit. The Tomcats split in opposite directions. Gypsy 207 broke to the left; Gypsy 202 turned hard to the right. Both MiGs headed toward the wing F-14. Cook reversed his turn and banked left toward the Libyan fighters, which he now saw dead ahead at six miles. The MiGs were pointed directly at him but they did not launch a missile. Cook was not about to give them more of an opportunity. From a distance of roughly five miles he fired a third Sparrow. The missile struck the wing Flogger in its right intake duct. The fighter was immediately engulfed in a huge fireball. Cook pulled to the right to avoid the debris. At the same time Connelly put his plane in a hard right turn and wound up squarely behind the lead Flogger. Immediately he tried to fire a Sidewinder missile but could not acquire a tone alert. After a few frantic seconds Connelly heard a tone and at a range of one-and-a-half miles launched a Sidewinder that struck the MiG right behind its cockpit.

The Libyan pilots ejected from their aircraft and the American crewmen observed two parachutes. The Libyans launched a search and rescue effort to recover their downed pilots but it is not known whether the two men survived their ordeal. Immediately after the second kill Gypsy 207 and Gypsy 202 descended to the safety of a lower altitude and headed north at high speed. Once safely back on the JFK the four airmen received a stirring heroes' welcome. Two days later the *Kennedy* dropped anchor in Haifa. To no one's surprise, the Israelis gave her crew a very warm and grateful reception.[107]

The second air battle between American and Libyan aircraft took place about forty miles north of Tobruk. Like the contest in 1981, it lasted about a minute from first shot to last, and the results were the same. After two rounds of aerial combat the scorecard read: Libyan aircraft losses–four; U.S. Navy aircraft losses–zero.

An angry Qaddafi called for an emergency session of the United Nations to take up the incident, which he characterized as "official American terrorism . . . backed by brute force." Libya's UN ambassador, Ali Sunni Muntasser, accused the United States of carrying out a "premeditated attack" on two unarmed "reconnaissance airplanes, which were on a routine mission over international waters."[108] On 11 January the United States, Great Britain, and France vetoed a UN Security Council resolution that condemned the U.S. for downing the two Libyan planes.

As he had done in 1981, Ronald Reagan stood by the actions of his armed forces. "Our pilots acted in self-defense," he affirmed. "They did the right thing."[109] Secretary of Defense Frank C. Carlucci, who took over for Weinberger at the Pentagon in late 1987, reminded the press that the F-14 crews were not required to consult with higher authority before using deadly force to protect themselves and, ultimately, to defend the battle group. "Any time an [enemy] aircraft demonstrates hostile intent . . . our aircraft are entitled under the rules of engagement to defend themselves," he stated.[110] Two days after the battle the Pentagon released blurred photographs taken from a videotape of the dogfight. The photographs showed the lead MiG just seconds before it was hit by the Sidewinder fired by the lead F-14. Pentagon spokesman Dan Howard informed reporters that naval intelligence analysts reviewed the photographs and confirmed that the Flogger was armed with two Apex missiles and two short-range, heat-seeking Aphid missiles. He then stated very undiplomatically that the videotape and the photographs proved that "the Libyan ambassador to the United Nations is a liar. . . . We have the pictures now to prove that they were not unarmed aircraft. They were obviously armed aircraft, with hostile intent."[111]

The timing of the incident was uncanny. Although Reagan's term as president was nearly over, tension between Libya and the United States was extremely high. In the fall of 1988, the Reagan administration accused Qaddafi of constructing a large chemical weapons plant at Rabta, thirty-five miles south of Tripoli.[112] Qaddafi denied the charge, asserting instead that the plant was used for the manufacture of pharmaceuticals and that his government accepted international controls banning the use of chemical weapons. Unconvinced by Qaddafi's statements, Reagan was determined to keep chemical weapons out of the hands of the Libyan government—a regime unmistakably associated with international terrorism. He applied pressure on West Germany and other allied governments to halt the export of technology, materials, and expertise that Libya needed in order to bring the plant up to full production, he sought condemnation of Libya at an upcoming international conference on chemical weapons, and he refused to rule out a military operation to destroy the plant.

Since the chemical weapons controversy and the dogfight occurred coincidentally, many observers speculated that Qaddafi may have deliberately provoked the incident. If he believed that the United States was preparing to strike the Rabta facility, he may have ordered the Floggers simply to mount a preemptive attack on the *Kennedy* battle group. This explanation is highly unlikely owing to the lopsided combat record between Libyan and American forces, the weapons carried by the Floggers, and the fact that the battle group was six hundred miles from Rabta and steaming toward the eastern Mediterranean. He may have sent his fighters on what amounted to a suicide mission in order to win sympathy from the world community and undermine Reagan's efforts to isolate him on the issue of chemical weapons. Or he may have ordered the reckless operation in order to sabotage the recently initiated dialogue between the United States and the PLO.

Over the next several weeks the furor over Rabta and the air battle gradually subsided. At the Paris conference on chemical weapons 149 countries, including Libya, reaffirmed their commitment not to use the extremely lethal weapons. The West German government imposed strict export controls to prevent critical materials and technical expertise from reaching Libya. Lastly, Qaddafi suspended construction on the chemical weapons plant due to intense American and international pressure.

The inauguration of George Bush as the forty-first president of the United States on 20 January 1989 did not signal an improvement in U.S.-Libyan relations, but it effectively ended eight years of public animus between Ronald Reagan and Muammar al-Qaddafi.

Epilogue: Lockerbie and Beyond

Qaddafi and the Case of Pan Am Flight 103

Muammar al-Qaddafi had reduced his involvement in international terrorism and had altered his methods regarding its use, but soon there were horrible reminders that he had not abandoned the terror weapon completely. In November 1991 the United States and Great Britain charged two Libyan government employees with carrying out one of the worst terrorist attacks in history: the bombing of Pan Am Flight 103 over Lockerbie, Scotland, on 21 December 1988, an act that killed all 259 persons on board—189 of them American—and 11 people on the ground. Earlier that year a French magistrate had issued arrest warrants for four Libyan officials suspected of involvement in the bombing of Union de Transports Aeriens (UTA) Flight 772 over Niger on 11 September 1989, an incident that claimed the lives of all 171 people on board. Investigators in the United States, Great Britain, and France theorized that Libyan officials had ordered the bombing of Pan Am 103 to avenge Operation El Dorado Canyon and the attack on UTA 772 in response to the rout of Libyan forces by French-backed Chadian troops in 1987.[1]

Evidence pointed to official Libyan involvement in the destruction of Pan Am 103 and UTA 772, yet the American, British, and French governments elected not to retaliate with military force. A number of years had passed since the aircraft bombings so the allies settled on a more cautious response: they would treat the attacks as criminal cases rather than as acts of state terrorism and would pursue the perpetrators through diplomacy and the courts.

In January 1992 the UN Security Council passed Resolution 731, which directed Libya "to cooperate fully" with American, British, and French investigators "in establishing responsibility for the terrorist acts." The resolution did not expressly demand that the Libyan government hand over the suspects to American, British, and French authorities, although that was precisely what the Security Council had intended.[2] Two months later the Security Council approved Resolution 748, which imposed sanctions on Libya for Qaddafi's refusal to surrender to the United States or Great Britain the two men accused of masterminding the destruction of Pan Am 103 and for his failure to cooperate with French authorities in their investigation of the bombing of UTA 772. The sanctions prohibited the sale of weapons, aircraft, and aircraft parts to Libya, it banned air transportation into and out of the country, and it called on UN member states to reduce the number of Libyan diplomatic personnel serving in their countries. The resolution demanded that Tripoli compensate the families of the victims of Pan Am 103, cease all terrorist activities, and end its support for terrorist organizations. In November 1993 the Security Council tightened these sanctions by prohibiting the sale of oil industry equipment to Libya, freezing Libyan assets held in foreign banks, and closing all Libyan Arab Airline offices outside Libya.

Under the weight of UN sanctions and after several years of intense international pressure, Qaddafi eventually took steps to resolve the crisis over Pan Am 103 and UTA 772. He believed that ending the deadlock would benefit his country in a number of ways. For instance, compliance with the UN resolutions would reduce Libya's isolation and improve the country's chances for reconciliation with several Western nations, and lifting sanctions would stimulate foreign investment and help revive the long-slumping economy.[3]

In March 1999 a French court convicted in absentia six Libyans—including Abdallah as-Sanusi, Qaddafi's brother-in-law and former deputy director of the Libyan intelligence service—for conspiring to sabotage the French airliner. In July Qaddafi agreed to pay an estimated $40 million in damages to the victims' families, but the Libyan leader emphasized that paying damages did not constitute an admission of guilt.

Regarding the Lockerbie incident, the American and British governments demanded that Qaddafi comply with the UN resolutions and hand over the suspects for trial in either the United States or Great Britain. For seven years he refused to do so, believing that a criminal trial in either country would focus attention on his regime's involvement in international terrorism.[4] In March 1999 the two Western allies and Qaddafi accepted a compromise arrangement whereby the two suspects would stand trial in a Scottish court temporarily established in the Netherlands, a country acceptable to Qaddafi. The deal, which was brokered by UN Secretary General Kofi Annan with considerable help from President Nelson Mandela of South Africa, contained private assurances from Washington and London that the trial would deal exclusively with the actions of the two defendants, not those of the Qaddafi regime.[5] On 5 April 1999 Qaddafi surrendered Abd al-Basit Ali Muhammad al-Meghrahi and Al-Amin Khalifa Fahima—both former employees of Libyan Arab Airlines and alleged Libyan intelligence operatives—to Scottish authorities in the Netherlands. Following the surrender of the suspects the UN Security Council suspended—but did not terminate—the sanctions against Libya. The trial, in which both men pleaded not guilty, began in May 2000.

With Meghrahi and Fahima in custody, the Clinton administration announced that it would maintain the unilateral economic sanctions imposed by President Reagan in the 1980s and would neither support the permanent lifting of the UN sanctions nor consider a resumption of normal relations with Tripoli until the Libyan government satisfied the following conditions: full cooperation in the investigation of the destruction of Pan Am 103, admission of responsibility for the incident, payment of compensation to the victims' families, and an unambiguous statement renouncing terrorism. In July 1999 the administration blocked Libya's efforts at the United Nations to end the sanctions.

On 31 January 2001 the three-judge Scottish court found Meghrahi guilty of murdering 270 people and sentenced him to life in prison with the possibility of parole in twenty years. "Twenty years for 270 murders is less than a month per victim," commented the father of one young American victim. "It's just not right." The court acquitted Fahima, ruling that the prosecution failed to prove his guilt beyond a shadow of a doubt.[6] The judges concluded that Meghrahi was a member of the Libyan intelligence service, "occupying posts of fairly high rank," and that the Libyan government was involved in the planning and execution of the attack. "The clear inference which we draw from the evidence is that the conception, planning, and execution of the plot which led to the planting of the explosive device was of Libyan origin," the judges wrote in their opinion.[7]

President George W. Bush expressed his satisfaction with the Lockerbie

verdict but emphasized that the Libyan government had to accept full responsibility for the destruction of Pan Am 103 and pay damages to the families of
the victims before the United States would support a permanent lifting of the
UN sanctions. "Nothing can change the suffering and the loss of this terrible
act, but I hope the families do find some solace that a guilty verdict was rendered," Bush stated. "The United States government will continue to pressure
Libya to accept responsibility . . . and to compensate the families." The U.S.
Department of Justice issued a statement declaring that the United States would
continue its efforts to bring to justice all individuals involved in the destruction
of Pan Am 103.[8]

Qaddafi was forced to explain to his people how the legal arrangement
that he assented to resulted not in the acquittal of both defendants and a lifting
of international sanctions but in the conviction of one of their countrymen
and the casting of renewed suspicions on their government. At a welcoming
ceremony for Fahima, Qaddafi defiantly condemned the verdict and declared
that he would neither pay compensation to the victims' families nor acknowledge responsibility for the incident. A few days later he presented his own
analysis of the Lockerbie verdict. He described the Scottish government's case
against Meghrahi as "weak, laughable, a masquerade." He denounced "Christian justice" for convicting an innocent man, and alleged that the Scottish court
wanted to acquit Meghrahi but rendered a guilty verdict under intense pressure
from the American and British governments. He accused the judges of fabri-
cating a compromise verdict that acquitted Fahima to satisfy the Libyan people
and convicted Meghrahi so that the United States and Great Britain could save
face. Qaddafi referred to Meghrahi as "a hostage," who was "abducted in order
to terrorize the Libyan people," and urged the populace to fight the outrageous
verdict.[9] In a boisterous street demonstration several hundred Tripoli residents
angrily denounced the conviction of Meghrahi, calling it the latest attempt by
the West to cripple their country. They demanded immediate retribution against
the United States and its allies. The demonstrators urged Libya to quit the
United Nations, called for a boycott of Western goods and services, and
demanded monetary compensation for suffering under a decade of UN sanctions. "We have to band together to erase the shame caused by this political
verdict," one of the leaders of the demonstration told the crowd. "We declare
this verdict . . . a miserable document."[10]

The Pan Am 103 verdict reopened the debate between policymakers and
analysts who believed that effective sanctions and legal prosecution could
successfully punish states that practice or support terrorism and government

officials and experts who argued that a terrorist attack was an act of war that was best answered with appropriate military force. A number of State Department officials pointed out that the Lockerbie case demonstrated that determined international efforts and an unrelenting pursuit of the perpetrators could alter the behavior of a terrorist state. Diplomatic pressure and international isolation had compelled Qaddafi to surrender the suspects and distance himself from several terrorist organizations that he once supported. According to one senior official the verdict sent "a very forceful message" to terrorists "that you can't act against us with impunity and we will pursue guilty people as long as it takes."[11] On the other hand, some terrorism analysts asserted that terrorism could not be handled as a criminal justice matter like a murder or bank robbery. Rather, it should be considered a threat to a nation's peace and security and should be dealt with by military force once state support or sponsorship is established. Ian Lesser, an authority on terrorism, emphasized that it is extremely difficult to respond fully to state-sponsored or supported terrorism "without resorting to the use of force."[12] By handling the Pan Am bombing as a criminal case instead of a political act, the American and British governments effectively ruled out the use of force, thus assuring that those Libyan officials ultimately responsible for the tragedy would go unpunished.[13]

A New Qaddafi?

Fifteen years after Operation El Dorado Canyon, Qaddafi continued his efforts to rehabilitate his reputation and end Libya's isolation by resolving critical disputes with a number of Western countries, by pursuing positive relations with his African and Arab neighbors, and by convincing the world community that he no longer supports, sponsors, or advocates terrorism. In addition to initiating steps to resolve the Pan Am 103 and UTA 772 affairs, in July 1999 the Libyan government acknowledged responsibility for the death of a British policewoman outside the Libyan people's bureau in London in 1984. Tripoli agreed to cooperate in the investigation of the incident and offered to compensate the family of the slain officer. Great Britain and Libya resumed full diplomatic relations soon after.

As mentioned earlier, in the years immediately following the air strike Qaddafi sought to end his country's isolation by working toward better relations with several countries in Africa and the Middle East. In the late 1990s Qaddafi pursued a number of diplomatic initiatives intended to enhance his prestige among his fellow African and Arab leaders and to expand Libya's role in regional affairs. He shifted his focus away from the Arab world and toward Africa because he accused the former of deserting him over the issue of the UN sanctions. He was particularly angry that no Arab head of state dared to violate the air embargo as many African leaders had. In years past he would have retaliated against his brother Arabs with acts of subversion. Instead, he announced that he would reduce his contacts with the Arab world and expand his relations with African states. In early 1998 he hosted a summit of Saharan and Sahelian leaders during which he pledged Libyan funds for economic development and offered his landlocked neighbors access to the Mediterranean through Libyan ports. In 1999 Qaddafi attended the summit of the OAU for the first time since 1977; he hosted a summit of forty-three African leaders that coincided with the thirtieth anniversary of the Libyan revolution and during which he proposed a "United States of Africa" modeled on the European Union; he helped revive the Arab Maghreb Union, which had been moribund since 1992; and he committed Libya to several multinational peacekeeping operations in Africa. Concerning one issue of crucial importance to the Arabs, he gave tacit support to the Middle East peace process by recognizing the PLO as the sole representative of the Palestinian people and abandoning criticism of Arafat's acceptance of the 1993 Oslo Accords. In April 2000 Qaddafi attended a summit of African and European leaders in Cairo. He used the meeting to advance his image as a pragmatic leader and to mend relations with several Western countries. He stunned many participants and observers by inviting the leader of the Israeli Labor Party to visit Tripoli. The invitation was seen by many as a bold attempt to end his country's isolation and repair many years of strained relations with the West.

In December 1999 the prime minister of Italy, Massino D'Alema, became the first Western leader to visit Libya since Qaddafi had surrendered the Lockerbie suspects. During a public appearance with D'Alema, Qaddafi issued a strong denunciation of terrorism. He asserted that no state should provide support and protection to the practitioners of terrorist violence. He backed up his pronouncement by expelling the Abu Nidal organization and dismantling Libya's terrorist training facilities. "This is not the same Libya it was six years ago," remarked a senior State Department official in early 2000. "As far as we can tell, they have walked away from terrorism."[14] Nevertheless, the U.S. government was not ready to remove Libya from its list of states "that use terrorism as a means of political expression." "Qaddafi stated publicly that his government had adopted an antiterrorism stance," noted the State Department in its report

Patterns of Global Terrorism: 2000. "But it remains unclear whether his claims of distancing Libya from its terrorist past signifies a true change in policy. . . . Although Libya expelled the Abu Nidal organization and distanced itself from the Palestinian rejectionists in 1999, it continued to have contact with groups that use violence to oppose the Middle East Peace Process."[15]

Qaddafi and the Jamahiriyya Thirty Years after the Revolution

Today Qaddafi is in firm command of his country and his personality still pervades everyday life, yet in recent years the Leader of the Revolution has allowed Libyan society to become somewhat more open and the economy to become slightly less controlled. Western journalists, who have visited the country since the late 1990s, have documented many positive developments. For example, the government welcomes foreign business executives and their investment capital; European tourists are discovering the country in increasing numbers; ordinary Libyans readily strike up conversations with foreign visitors without worrying about the security services; journalists roam the country and are no longer dependent on government sources for their information; the *sūqs* (markets) are bustling and brimming with consumer goods as Libyans engage in small-scale free enterprise; a growing number of Libyans own satellite dishes, personal computers, and cellular phones; surfing the web at Internet cafes and listening to the latest American music are extremely popular pastimes for young Libyans; and many Libyans exude pride in the power they wield over their daily lives through the system of people's congresses.[16] Conversely, political scientist Dirk Vandewalle offered a realistic appraisal of the Libyan political system after several years of modest political and economic liberalization: "Important political directives in Libya are still made almost exclusively by Qaddafi and a small group of advisers. Libya remains a political system where no opposition is tolerated, where a high level of arbitrariness has usually been the rule of politics, and where the citizens have experienced great uncertainty. Despite changes made since 1987, the system is still not subject to institutional checks nor its leadership to accountability."[17]

Qaddafi's Libya was the subject of the lead article in the November 2000 issue of *National Geographic* magazine. The editor in chief of the magazine, William L. Allen, proudly stated that the article offered readers "the most thorough look inside Libya in many years and an objective glimpse of life in this closed society." The author, Andrew Cockburn, characterized Libya as a nation "long hidden behind the face and rhetoric of its leader" but struggling to end its seclusion and rejoin the community of nations.[18] The fact that Libya was the focus of a *National Geographic* cover story is nothing short of remarkable. It would have been unthinkable in the 1980s. The country has taken steps to reverse its reputation as a pariah state, but it will not be completely rehabilitated in the eyes of the international community until the latter is convinced beyond any doubt that the leopard—in this case Colonel Qaddafi—has indeed changed his spots and rejected terrorism.

The Legacy of Operation El Dorado Canyon

Operation El Dorado Canyon did not compel Muammar al-Qaddafi to renounce terrorism completely, but it achieved its principal objectives. The strike inflicted considerable damage to Qaddafi's terrorist apparatus, it deterred a number of terrorist operations targeting American citizens and interests, it forced Qaddafi to revamp his murderous methodology (which in turn reduced his involvement in terrorist activity), and it demonstrated that the United States has both the capability and the resolve to attack the supporters and sponsors of international terrorism. After five years of bold rhetoric and exhaustive policy debate but little action, President Ronald Reagan finally responded to a terrorist attack that targeted the United States. By bombing Libya he made it very clear that if Qaddafi or other practitioners of international terrorism were caught sponsoring or supporting their deadly craft, they would be held accountable for their actions and the United States would defend itself.

Military force is not the only viable weapon to use against terrorism. Other measures include timely intelligence, diplomatic action, economic sanctions, covert operations, and criminal prosecution. When measures short of military action fail to persuade states such as Libya to abandon their support or sponsorship of terrorist violence, however, a nation is left with no other choice but to use force. In the aftermath of El Dorado Canyon, any government or organization considering a terrorist act to advance its objectives would have to consider seriously the prospect of a military response.

On two occasions President Bill Clinton used force in response to international terrorism. In June 1993 he ordered a Tomahawk missile attack against the Iraqi intelligence headquarters in Baghdad after U.S. investigators uncovered a plot ordered by Saddam Hussein to assassinate former President George Bush during his visit to Kuwait two months earlier. In August 1998 massive terrorist truck bombs exploded at the U.S. embassies in Nairobi, Kenya, and Dar es Salaam, Tanzania. The attacks, which took place only minutes apart, killed more than 250 people, including 12 Americans. Clinton responded to the devastating bombings by launching scores of Tomahawks against terrorist facilities connected to the Saudi-born terrorist Usama bin Ladin, the mastermind of the attacks. Six months earlier bin Ladin had issued a *fatwa*, or religious decree, that called on every Muslim to kill Americans and their allies—whether military or civilian—in retaliation for any U.S. attack or demonstration of hostility against the Muslim world.[19] The cruise missiles struck bases operated by bin Ladin's *al-Qaida* terrorist network in Khost, Afghanistan, and a pharmaceutical plant near Khartoum which U.S. intelligence believed was manufacturing chemical-weapons components for bin Ladin.[20]

"With few exceptions, the world community by the late 1980s had had enough of exploding planes and assassinations in the middle of London," wrote the *Wall Street Journal* in an editorial that appeared the day after the Lockerbie verdict. "President Reagan's raid on Libya in April 1986 after the bombing of a discotheque in Berlin frequented by U.S. servicemen laid the groundwork for a get-tough policy."[21] After El Dorado Canyon terrorists and their supporters realized that they could no longer attack the United States with impunity. That idea changed forever when the LGBs slammed into Bab al-Aziziyah.

11 September 2001

The first chapter in America's long war against international terrorism—the one started by Ronald Reagan on 27 January 1981—with its powerful rhetoric, occasional action, and countless debates over how to defeat the enemy ended abruptly on the morning of 11 September 2001. On that clear, late summer day a band of radical Islamic terrorists belonging to bin Ladin's al-Qaida network carried out the most horrific terrorist operation in modern history. The terrorists hijacked four U.S. airliners and used the fuel-laden planes as guided missiles to attack prominent symbols of American economic and military power. Two planes were deliberately flown into the twin towers of the World Trade Center in lower Manhattan, completely destroying the magnificent financial complex. A third aircraft slammed into the Pentagon, causing major damage to the west face of the gigantic building. A group of heroic passengers on the fourth airliner overpowered the hijackers and thwarted their plans to crash the plane into yet another important landmark, possibly the White House or Capitol building. The aircraft never reached its intended target, instead plunging into a field in southwest Pennsylvania where it completely disintegrated.

More than three thousand innocent people—mostly Americans but also hundreds of citizens from more than eighty other countries—perished in the coordinated assaults. The horrendous events of that fateful day jolted the U.S. economy and shattered the once reassuring belief that major acts of international terrorism "can't happen here." Nevertheless, the attacks unified the American people to a degree not witnessed since the Second World War and girded their resolve to eradicate the menace of terrorism.

In an address before Congress nine days after the terrorist attacks President George W. Bush clearly and emphatically announced to the American people and the world a global war against international terrorism. "We are a country awakened to danger and called to defend freedom," he remarked. "Our grief has turned to anger and anger to resolution. Whether we bring our enemies to justice or bring justice to our enemies, justice will be done." He accused bin Ladin's al-Qaida network of carrying out the 11 September attacks and Afghanistan's repressive Islamic regime, the Taliban, of "aiding and abetting murder" by supporting and harboring the terrorists. He reminded his audience that al-Qaida had already carried out two major assaults on the United States: the bombings of the African embassies in 1998 and the suicide bombing of the guided-missile destroyer USS *Cole* (DDG 76) as she refueled in Aden, Yemen, in October 2000. The latter attack took the lives of seventeen sailors and caused extensive damage to the ship.

Bush delivered an unequivocal ultimatum to the Taliban. He demanded that they surrender to the United States all leaders of al-Qaida, close every terrorist training camp in the country, and turn over to appropriate authorities all terrorists and their support apparatus. "The Taliban must act and act immediately," he declared. "They will hand over the terrorists or they will share in their fate." Bush made it clear that the campaign against al-Qaida would mark only the starting point in the war against terrorism and that the conflict would not be limited to action in Afghanistan. "Our war on terror begins with al-Qaida, but it does not end there," he stated. "It will not end until every terrorist group of global reach has been found, stopped, and defeated."

He pledged that the United States would employ every instrument of diplomacy, intelligence, law enforcement, finance, and military force to defeat the international terror networks. "We will starve terrorists of funding, turn them one against another, drive them from place to place until there is no refuge or no rest," he remarked. "We will pursue nations that provide safe haven to terrorism. Every nation in every region now has a decision to make: Either you are with us or you are with the terrorists." This fight "is not . . . just America's fight. And what is at stake is not just America's freedom. This is the world's fight. This is civilization's fight. This is the fight of all who believe in . . . tolerance and freedom. We ask every nation to join us."

Bush warned the American public that the war to defeat terrorism would not end swiftly with a single battle and that victory would not be accomplished without combat losses. The conflict would be decided by "a lengthy campaign unlike any other we have ever seen." It may consist of "dramatic strikes visible on TV and covert operations secret even in success."

Near the end of his address the president reiterated that "great harm" had been inflicted on the United States and that the country had "suffered great loss," but he stressed that the American people had found their "mission" and their "moment" during a time of profound grief and anger. "Our nation, this generation, will lift the dark threat of violence from our people and our future," he stated. "We will rally the world to this cause by our efforts, by our courage. We will not tire, we will not falter, and we will not fail."[22]

The Taliban rejected Bush's demands. Consequently, on Sunday, 7 October 2001, U.S. and British forces launched air strikes against terrorist camps and military targets throughout Afghanistan. President Bush promised that the opening phase of "Operation Enduring Freedom" would "clear the way for sustained, comprehensive, and relentless operations" to root the terrorists responsible for the attacks on the World Trade Center and the Pentagon out of their hiding places and bring them to justice.[23] Operation Enduring Freedom marked the third occasion since Operation El Dorado Canyon that the United States responded to an act of terrorism with military force.

Finally, the 11 September 2001 terrorist attacks may influence a change in U.S.-Libyan relations. Within hours of the attacks Qaddafi reaffirmed his denunciation of terrorism and forcefully condemned the appalling violence that the American people had suffered. He also pledged humanitarian assistance for the families of the victims, regardless of his profound political differences with the United States. Furthermore, although he had once been the target of U.S. retribution for a terrorist act, he stated that the United States had the right to retaliate against those groups or individuals who carried out the attacks.

On 24 September President Bush ordered U.S. banks to freeze assets belonging to al-Qaida and twenty-six other individuals and organizations connected to bin Ladin and suspected of financing terrorist operations. One of the organizations affected by the presidential order is the Libyan Islamic Fighting Group (IFG), many of whose members served with bin Ladin in resisting the Soviet occupation of Afghanistan in the 1980s. The IFG is determined to replace the

Qaddafi regime with a strict Islamic government, and since the late 1990s it has carried out a series of attacks inside the country, including assassination attempts on Qaddafi. Recognizing that he and the United States have a common deadly enemy, Qaddafi directed his intelligence service to cooperate with its U.S. counterpart.[24] The Clinton and Bush administrations have made it absolutely clear what Qaddafi must do to end U.S. economic sanctions and reestablish diplomatic relations. Nevertheless, the Libyan dictator can hope that providing intelligence on bin Ladin and al-Qaida will produce a thaw in the bitter relationship between Tripoli and Washington.

List of Abbreviations

1MC	ship's general announcing circuit
4W Grid	"four whiskey" grid
AAA	antiaircraft artillery
AAWC	antiair warfare commander
ACM	air combat maneuvering
AE	ammunition ship
AF	air force
AFB	air force base
AGF	miscellaneous command ship
AO	oiler
AOE	fast combat support ship
APAM	antipersonnel-antimateriel
ARM	antiradiation Missile
ASU	Arab Socialist Union
Auto-TF	automatic terrain following
AWACS	airborne warning and control system
BDA	battle damage assessment
B/N	bombardier-navigator
BPC	Basic People's Congress
C3	command, control, and communications
CAP	combat air patrol
CG	guided missile cruiser
CGN	guided missile cruiser (nuclear)
CIA	Central Intelligence Agency
CIC	Combat Information Center
CINCEUR	commander in chief, Europe
CINCUSNAVEUR	commander in chief, U.S. Naval Forces Europe
CNO	chief of naval operations
CPPG	crisis preplanning group

CV	multipurpose aircraft carrier
CVA	attack aircraft carrier
CVBG	carrier battle group
CVN	multipurpose aircraft carrier (nuclear)
CVW	carrier air wing
DCNO	deputy chief of naval operations
DD	destroyer
DDG	guided missile destroyer
DIA	Defense Intelligence Agency
DMPI	desired mean point of impact
DSMAC	digital scene-matching area correlation
EC	European Community
ECM	electronic countermeasures
EMCON	emission control
EUCOM	European Command
FAA	Federal Aviation Administration
FAN	Armed Forces of the North
FAP	People's Armed Forces
FAR	Federation of Arab Republics
FBI	Federal Bureau of Investigation
FEMA	Federal Emergency Management Agency
FF	frigate
FFG	guided missile frigate
FIR	flight information region
FLIR	forward-looking infrared
FON	freedom of navigation
FRC	Fatah—the Revolutionary Council
G-7	Group of Seven—the World's Seven Largest Industrial Democracies
GCHQ	general communications headquarters
GCI	ground control intercept
GPC	General People's Congress
GUNT	transitional national unity government
HARM	high-speed antiradiation missile
HS	helicopter antisubmarine squadron
IFF	identification friend or foe

IFG	Libyan Islamic Fighting Group
IG/T	interdepartmental group on terrorism
INR	Bureau of Intelligence and Research
INS	inertial navigation system
JANA	Jamahiriyya Arab News Agency
JCS	Joint Chiefs of Staff
LAADC	Libyan Arab Air Defense Command
LAAF	Libyan Arab Air Force
LAMPS	light airborne multipurpose system
LGB	laser-guided bomb
MNF	multinational force
NATO	North American Treaty Organization
NFSL	National Front for the Salvation of Libya
NIE	national intelligence estimate
NOTAM	notices to airmen and mariners
NSA	National Security Agency
NSC	National Security Council
NSDD	national security decision directive
NSPG	National Security Planning Group
OAP	offset aim point
OAU	Organization of African Unity
OOMEX	open ocean missile exercise
OPEC	Organization of Petroleum Exporting Countries
OSG	operations subgroup
OTC	officer in tactical command
OVL	operations in the vicinity of Libya
PD	probability of damage
PFLP	Popular Front for the Liberation of Palestine
PLF	Palestine Liberation Front
PLO	Palestine Liberation Organization
PRG	policy review group
PROE	peacetime rules of engagement
RAF	Royal Air Force
RCC	Revolutionary Command Council
RHAW	radar homing and warning

RIO	radar intercept officer
ROE	rules of engagement
SAG	surface action group
SAM	surface-to-air missile
SAR	search and rescue
SEAD	suppression of enemy air defenses
SNIE	special national intelligence estimate
SOVA	Office of Soviet Analysis
SSG	special situation group
SSN	attack submarine (nuclear)
STWC	strike warfare commander
SUCAP	surface combat air patrol
TACAN	tactical air navigation
TF	task force
TFR	terrain following radar
TFS	tactical fighter squadron
TFW	tactical fighter wing
TIWG	terrorist incident working group
TOT	time over target
TRAM	target recognition and attack multisensor
UAA	United African Airlines
USAF	U.S. Air Force
USAFE	U.S. Air Forces Europe
UTA	Union de Transports Aeriens
VA	attack squadron
VAQ	tactical electronic warfare squadron
VAW	carrier airborne early-warning squadron
VF	fighter squadron
VFA	strike-fighter squadron
VMAQ	Marine electronic warfare squadron
VMFA	Marine fighter-attack squadron
VQ	fleet air reconnaissance squadron
VS	air antisubmarine squadron
WSO	weapon systems operator

Notes

Abbreviations Used in the Notes and Bibliography

AFPCD	Department of State, *American Foreign Policy Current Documents 1981* (Washington, D.C.: GPO, 1984)
AFT	*Air Force Times*
AVH	Aviation History Branch, Naval Historical Center, Washington, D.C.
Capital	*Annapolis (Md.) Capital*
CIA	Central Intelligence Agency
CNO/DCNO (LOG)	Records of CNO/DCNO (Logistics), Ship's Maintenance and Modernization Division (OP-43), "Libyan Operations" box, Operational Archives, Naval Historical Center, Washington, D.C. (henceforth shown as OA)
CNO/DCNO (NW)	Records of CNO/DCNO (Naval Warfare), Tactical Readiness Division (OP-73), Series VII, box 10 or 11, OA
COMSIXTHFLT	Commander U.S. Sixth Fleet
CSM	*Christian Science Monitor*
CTF	Commander Task Force
CTG	Commander Task Group
DOD	Department of Defense
DOS	Department of State
DTG	Date Time Group
GPO	Government Printing Office
King	Records of USS *King* (DDG-41), "Operational Messages in the Vicinity of Libya—December 1985–June 1986," box 1 or 2, OA
LAT	*Los Angeles Times*
NT	*Navy Times*
NWAC	Records of Naval Warfare Assessment Center, Corona, Calif., "1986 Operations against Libya" box, OA
NYT	*New York Times*
OA	Operational Archives, Naval Historical Center, Washington, D.C.
RRL	Ronald Reagan Library

ST	Sunday Times (London)
Times	Times (London)
WP	Washington Post
WSJ	Wall Street Journal

Prologue: The Air Battle Near Tobruk

1. A "bogey" is an unidentified air contact usually assumed to be hostile. To "jink" is to continually maneuver in the horizontal and vertical planes in order to present as unpredictable a target as possible. Robert K. Wilcox, *Scream of Eagles: The Creation of Top Gun—and the U.S. Air Victory in Vietnam* (New York: John Wiley and Sons, 1990), 293, 294.

2. The phrases "centering up on the T" and "centering the dot" describe the use of a cockpit steering cue that helps the pilot achieve the best position for firing a missile. "On Navy Tape, a Drama of Combat," *WP,* 6 January 1989, A22.

3. The code word "fox one" indicates that a medium-range, radar-guided Sparrow missile has been launched. Wilcox, *Scream of Eagles,* 294.

4. "Talley two" means that the pilot visually holds two planes. "Navy Tape, Drama of Combat."

5. "Fox two" indicates the firing of a short-range, heat-seeking Sidewinder missile. Wilcox, *Scream of Eagles,* 294.

6. Hearing a "tone" or "tone alert" on cockpit instruments informs the aircrew that the target aircraft is within effective range of a Sidewinder missile. "Navy Tape, Drama of Combat."

7. This transcript was compiled from the following sources: "Navy Tape, Drama of Combat"; "Seven Minutes," *Newsweek,* 16 January 1989, 18–21.

8. A CIA report published in 1981 defined terrorism as "the threat or use of violence for political purposes by individuals or groups, whether acting for or in opposition to established governmental authority, when such actions are intended to shock or intimidate or target groups wider than the immediate victims." The report also defined international terrorism as "terrorism conducted with the support of a foreign government or organization and/or directed against foreign nationals, institutions, or governments." CIA National Foreign Assessment Center, *Patterns of International Terrorism: 1980,* Research paper, June 1981, 9. Since 1983 the U.S. government has used the following definitions related to the phenomenon of terrorism: terrorism is "premeditated, politically motivated violence perpetrated against noncombatant targets (including military personnel who at the time of the incident are unarmed and/or not on duty) by subnational groups or clandestine agents, usually intended to influence an audience." International terrorism is "terrorism involving citizens or the territory of more than one country." A terrorist group is "any group practicing, or that has significant subgroups that practice, international terrorism." DOS Office of the Coordinator for Counterterrorism, *Patterns of Global Terrorism: 1997,* Annual Report, April 1998, vi.

Chapter 1. Muammar al-Qaddafi and the Libyan Jamahiriyya

1. Lillian Craig Harris, *Libya: Qadhafi's Revolution and the Modern State* (Boulder, Colo.: Westview, 1986), 1–2.

2. Ibid., 2–3; Helen Chapin Metz, ed., *Libya: A Country Study*, 4th ed. (Washington, D.C.: GPO, 1989), 8–10.

3. Harris, *Libya*, 3–4; Metz, *Country Study*, 11–13, 14–15.

4. Harris, *Libya*, 4; Metz, *Country Study*, 14–18.

5. Metz, *Country Study*, 18–19.

6. John K. Cooley, *Libyan Sandstorm* (New York: Holt, Rinehart, and Winston, 1982), 26–27; Jack Sweetman, *American Naval History: An Illustrated Chronology of the U.S. Navy and Marine Corps 1775–Present*, 2nd ed. (Annapolis, Md.: Naval Institute Press, 1991), 20.

7. E. B. Potter, ed., *Sea Power: A Naval History*, 2nd ed. (Annapolis, Md.: Naval Institute Press, 1981), 90–93; Lincoln P. Paine, "'War Is Better than Tribute,'" *Naval History* 15 (June 2001): 24, 25; Sweetman, *American Naval History*, 20–22, 24; Cooley, *Libyan Sandstorm*, 27 28.

8. Metz, *Country Study*, 20.

9. Harris, *Libya*, 4; Metz, *Country Study*, 20–21; Mansour O. El-Kikhia, *Libya's Qaddafi: The Politics of Contradiction* (Gainesville, Fla.: University Press of Florida, 1997), 15.

10. John Wright, *Libya: A Modern History* (Baltimore, Md.: Johns Hopkins University Press, 1982), 12–14; Cooley, *Libyan Sandstorm*, 28; El-Kikhia, *Libya's Qaddafi*, 16.

11. Wright, *Libya: Modern History*, 26–28; Cooley, *Libyan Sandstorm*, 31–32; Metz, *Country Study*, 23–24.

12. Wright, *Libya: Modern History*, 29–31; Cooley, *Libyan Sandstorm*, 32–33.

13. Harris, *Libya*, 6–7.

14. Wright, *Libya: Modern History*, 33–35; Metz, *Country Study*, 27–29; Cooley, *Libyan Sandstorm*, 35; El-Kikhia, *Libya's Qaddafi*, 21.

15. Wright, *Libya: Modern History*, 38–40; Harris, *Libya*, 8; Lisa Anderson, *The State and Social Transformation in Tunisia and Libya, 1830–1980* (Princeton, N.J.: Princeton University Press, 1986), 9.

16. Metz, *Country Study*, 32–33; Wright, *Libya: Modern History*, 45–47.

17. Harris, *Libya*, 9–10.

18. Metz, *Country Study*, 36–37; Lisa Anderson, "Qaddafi's Islam," in *Voices of Resurgent Islam*, ed. John L. Esposito (New York: Oxford University Press, 1983), 136; Wright, *Libya: Modern History*, 61, 66, 69, 73; Anderson, *State and Social Transformation*, 256.

19. Wright, *Libya: Modern History*, 82–83, 86–88; W. Hays Parks, "Crossing the Line," *United States Naval Institute Proceedings* 112 (November 1986): 41.

20. Wright, *Libya: Modern History*, 94, 96; Harris, *Libya*, 12; Metz, *Country Study*, 39–40; Lisa Anderson, "Assessing Libya's Qaddafi," *Current History* 84 (May 1985): 198.

21. Ray Takeyh, "Qadhafi's Libya and the Prospect of Islamic Succession," *Middle East Policy* 7 (February 2000): 155; Harris, *Libya*, 11–14; Metz, *Country Study*, 40–42; John K. Cooley, "The Libyan Menace," *Foreign Policy* 42 (spring 1981): 78.

22. "The Libyan Revolution in the Words of Its Leaders," *Middle East Journal* 24 (spring 1970): 203.

23. Cooley, *Libyan Sandstorm*, 13–14; Geoff Simons, *Libya: The Struggle for Survival* (New York: St. Martin's, 1993), 304.

24. Wright, *Libya: Modern History*, 132–35; Harris, *Libya*, 13–16, 37; Ronald B. St. John, *Qaddafi's World Design: Libyan Foreign Policy, 1969–1987* (Atlantic Highlands, N.J.: Saqi Books, 1987), 27; Marius K. Deeb and Mary Jane Deeb, *Libya since the Revolution: Aspects of Social and Political Development* (New York: Praeger, 1982), 98; Anderson, *State and Social Transformation*, 262; Claudia Wright, "Libya and the West: Headlong into Confrontation?" *International Affairs* 58 (winter 1981–82): 27.

25. Harris, *Libya*, 15–17, 43, 45–47; Wright, *Libya: Modern History*, 125–27, 135–36, 176–78; Metz, *Country Study*, 44–46; Ruth First, *Libya: The Elusive Revolution* (New York: Africana, 1975), 18; Lisa Anderson, "Qadhdhafi and His Opposition," *Middle East Journal* 40 (spring 1986): 229; Nathan Alexander, "Libya: The Continuous Revolution," *Middle Eastern Studies* 17 (April 1981): 215; Dirk Vandewalle, "The Libyan Jamahiriyya since 1969," in *Qadhafi's Libya, 1969–1994*, ed. Dirk Vandewalle (New York: St. Martin's, 1995), 9.

26. Harris, *Libya*, 12, 97; Metz, *Country Study*, 46, 274–75; Henry Kissinger, *Years of Upheaval* (Boston: Little, Brown, 1982), 860; St. John, *Qaddafi's World Design*, 87.

27. CIA Director of Central Intelligence, *Soviet Support for International Terrorism and Revolutionary Violence*, Special National Intelligence Estimate 11/2–81, 27 May 1981, 19; Nathan Alexander, "The Foreign Policy of Libya: Inflexibility amid Change," *Orbis* 24 (winter 1981): 830; U.S. Senate Committee on Foreign Relations, *Hearing on Libya's Role in Sub-Saharan Africa and the Near East*, 97th Cong., 1st sess., 8 July 1981, 4; El-Kikhia, *Libya's Qaddafi*, 131; CIA Foreign Broadcast Information Service, *Quotations from Qadhdhafi on Relations with the Soviet Union*, Special memorandum, 16 December 1981, ii.

28. Senate Committee, *Libya's Role in Sub-Saharan Africa*, 4.

29. Parks, "Crossing the Line," 41; P. Edward Haley, *Qaddafi and the United States since 1969* (New York: Praeger, 1984), 5; Cooley, "Libyan Menace," 84.

30. Metz, *Country Study*, 46, 209; Wright, *Libya: Modern History*, 183.

31. Wright, *Libya: Modern History*, 179.

32. Alexander, "Continuous Revolution," 216.

33. Muammar el-Qaddafi, "'Iranians Are Our Brothers,'" interview by Oriana Fallaci, *New York Times Magazine*, 16 December 1979, 40.

34. CIA Director of Central Intelligence, *Libya: Aims and Vulnerabilities*, Special National Intelligence Estimate 36.5–81, 30 January 1981, 3.

35. Vandewalle, "Libyan Jamahiriyya," 13.

36. Deeb and Deeb, *Libya since Revolution*, 120; Metz, *Country Study*, 47–48, 186–87; Cooley, *Libyan Sandstorm*, 142; Lisa Anderson, "Libya and American Foreign Policy," *Middle East Journal* 36 (autumn 1982): 521; Anderson, "Assessing Libya's Qaddafi," 200; Alexander, "Continuous Revolution," 219; Harris, *Libya*, 64.

37. Anderson, *State and Social Transformation*, 268.

38. Metz, *Country Study*, 49.

39. Cooley, *Libyan Sandstorm*, 145–46.

40. Wright, *Libya: Modern History*, 195–96, 264–65; Harris, *Libya*, 39; Metz, *Country Study*, 49; Deeb and Deeb, *Libya since Revolution*, 114, 119; Anderson, *State and Social Transformation*, 263.

41. David Blundy and Andrew Lycett, *Qaddafi and the Libyan Revolution* (Boston: Little, Brown, 1987), 26.

42. DOS Bureau of Public Affairs, *Libya under Qadhafi: A Pattern of Aggression*, Special Report No. 138, January 1986, 1; David C. Martin and John Walcott, *Best Laid Plans: The Inside Story of America's War against Terrorism* (New York: Harper & Row, 1988), 74.

43. DOS, "Libya: A Source of International Terrorism," by Kenneth Adelman, *Department of State Bulletin*, January 1982, 61.

44. Anderson, "Assessing Libya's Qaddafi," 199; Metz, *Country Study*, 50; El-Kikhia, *Libya's Qaddafi*, 133; Anderson, *State and Social Transformation*, 264; Bob Woodward, *Veil: The Secret Wars of the CIA 1981–1987* (New York: Simon and Schuster, 1987), 327.

45. Wright, *Libya: Modern History*, 158–59, 160–62, 163–64, 204–6; First, *Libya: Elusive Revolution*, 17; Alexander, "Foreign Policy," 838; Ronald B. St. John, "Terrorism and Libyan Foreign Policy, 1981–1986," *World Today* 42 (July 1986): 111; Cooley, *Libyan Sandstorm*, 101, 105, 118; Deeb and Deeb, *Libya since Revolution*, xi.

46. Harris, *Libya*, 61; Metz, *Country Study*, 50; Wright, *Libya: Modern History*, 237, 242, 248, 251.

47. DOS Public Affairs, *Libya under Qadhafi*, 1–3; Alexander, "Foreign Policy," 840.

48. El-Kikhia, *Libya's Qaddafi*, 120; Senate Committee, *Libya's Role in Sub-Saharan Africa*, 3, 5.

49. Wright, *Libya: Modern History*, 211; Blundy and Lycett, *Qaddafi and Libyan Revolution*, 188.

50. Senate Committee, *Libya's Role in Sub-Saharan Africa*, 5.

51. CIA Director of Central Intelligence, *Libya: Aims and Vulnerabilities*, 10; Senate Committee, *Libya's Role in Sub-Saharan Africa*, 4–5; William J. Foltz, "Libya's Military Power," in *The Green and the Black*, ed. René Lemarchand (Bloomington: Indiana University Press, 1988), 64.

52. Senate Committee, *Libya's Role in Sub-Saharan Africa*, 5.

53. Ibid., 2, 5; DOS, "Libya: Source of Terrorism," 61; Martin and Walcott, *Best Laid Plans*, 76.

54. DOS, "Libya: Source of Terrorism," 61.

55. Senate Committee, *Libya's Role in Sub-Saharan Africa*, 2.

56. Metz, *Country Study*, 56, 248; DOS, "Libya: Source of Terrorism," 61; Foltz, "Libya's Military Power," 62.

57. Senate Committee, *Libya's Role in Sub-Saharan Africa*, 5, 7; St. John, *Qaddafi's World Design*, 101.

58. CIA Assessment Center, *Patterns of International Terrorism*, 9.

59. Woodward, *Veil*, 166.

60. Parks, "Crossing the Line," 41; DOS Public Affairs, *Libya under Qadhafi*, 2; Claire Sterling, *The Terror Network: The Secret War of International Terrorism* (New York: Berkley Books, 1982), 142, 242, 247.

61. DOS, "Libya: Source of Terrorism," 60; DOS Public Affairs, *Libya under Qadhafi*, 1.

62. Among the countries where Qaddafi supported insurgent movements, opposition groups, and terrorist organizations are Italy, Portugal, Spain, Turkey, the United Kingdom, West Germany, Benin, Burundi, Cameroon, Chad, Djibouti, Egypt, Ethiopia, Ivory Coast, Mali, Mauritania, Morocco, Niger, Nigeria, Senegal, Somalia, South Africa, Sudan, Tunisia, Zaire, Iraq, Lebanon, North Yemen, Oman, Bangladesh, Pakistan, Indonesia, Japan, Malaysia, New Caledonia, the Philippines, Thailand, El Salvador, Guatemala, Nicaragua, Argentina, Chile, Colombia, Ecuador, Peru, and Uruguay. Qaddafi also aided disparate terrorist groups, dissident factions, and guerrilla organizations such as the Irish Republican Army; the Basque Euzkadi Ta Askatasuna; Portugal's FP-25; Italy's Red Brigades and the Fascist Avanguardia Nazionale; West Germany's Red Army Faction and Baader Meinhof Gang; Armenian anti-Turkish groups; the Polisario of the Western Sahara; the National Front for the Liberation of the Congo; the Congolese National Movement; the Palestinian Black September group; the Popular Front for the Liberation of Palestine (PFLP); the PFLP–General Command; Kurdish separatists in Iraq; the Union of Iraqi Democrats; the Yemeni National Democratic Front; Pakistan's al-Zulfiqar; the Japanese Red Army; the Moro National Liberation Front of the Philippines; the Free Papua Movement in Irian Jaya and the East Timor Liberation Movement of Indonesia; New Caledonia's Kanak Socialist National Liberation Front; Argentina's Montoneros; Colombia's M-19; Chile's Movement of the Revolution and the Manuel Rodrigues Patriotic Front; Ecuador's Alfaro Vive, Carajo; Peru's Shining Path; Uruguay's Tupamoros, and Nicaragua's Sandinistas.

Parks, "Crossing the Line," 41; Senate Committee, *Libya's Role in Sub-Saharan Africa*, 3; DOS Bureau of Public Affairs, *International Terrorism*, Selected Documents No. 24 (Washington, D.C.: GPO, 1986), 7; DOS, "Libya: Source of Terrorism," 61–62; DOS Public Affairs, *Libya under Qadhafi*, 3; Lillian Craig Harris, "Libya in the South Pacific: Wounded Innocence," *Middle East International* 301 (29 May 1987): 11.

63. Joseph Persico, *Casey: From the OSS to the CIA* (New York: Viking, 1990), 497.

64. Richard Stengel, John Borrell, and William Stewart, "Gaddafi: Obsessed by a Ruthless Messianic Vision," *Time*, 21 April 1986, 29; René Lemarchand, "Introduction: Beyond the Mad Dog Syndrome," in *The Green and the Black: Qadhafi's Policies in Africa*, ed. René Lemarchand (Bloomington: Indiana University Press, 1988), 3.

65. Stengel, Borrell, and Stewart, "Gaddafi: Obsessed," 29.

66. CIA Directorate of Intelligence, *Libya: Reviewing Terrorist Capabilities*, Research Paper, April 1989, 9.

67. DOS Public Affairs, *Libya under Qadhafi*, 1.

68. St. John, *Qaddafi's World Design*, 79.

Chapter 2. "Swift and Effective Retribution"

1. Kissinger, *Years of Upheaval*, 861; Wright, *Libya: Modern History*, 251; John F. Lehman, *Command of the Seas* (New York: Charles Scribner's Sons, 1988), 359; Martin and Walcott, *Best Laid Plans*, 76.

2. "The Military Balance 1985/86: Other Nations," *Air Force Magazine* 69 (February 1986): 108–9; John Moore, ed., *Jane's Fighting Ships, 1986–87* (New York: Jane's, 1986), 341; Blundy and Lycett, *Qaddafi and Libyan Revolution*, 3; Wright, *Libya: Modern History*, 201; DOS, "Libya: Source of Terrorism," 62.

3. Parks, "Crossing the Line," 41–42.

4. Dennis R. Neutze, "The Gulf of Sidra Incident: A Legal Perspective," *United States Naval Institute Proceedings* 108 (January 1982): 28.

5. Ibid., 27–28; Parks, "Crossing the Line," 42.

6. DOS Office of the Legal Adviser, *Digest of United States Practice in International Law* by Arthur W. Rovine (Washington, D.C.: GPO, 1975), 293–94.

7. Neutze, "Gulf of Sidra Incident," 29.

8. Parks, "Crossing the Line," 42; U.S. Sixth Fleet and Naval Striking and Support Forces Southern Europe, *Command History 1981*, declassified, Post-1974 Command File-Fleets: Sixth Fleet Histories, box 237, OA, encl. 2, p. 1.

9. John M. Goshko, "Scholars Say U.S. Action Seems Legal," *WP*, 25 March 1986, A12.

10. Parks, "Crossing the Line," 42; Robert W. Love, *History of the U.S. Navy Vol. 2: 1942–1991* (Harrisburg, Pa.: Stackpole, 1992), 730; Wright, "Libya and the West," 23; Jimmy Carter, *Keeping Faith: Memoirs of a President* (New York: Bantam Books, 1982), 458. Early in the Iran hostage crisis the Carter administration approached Qaddafi to assess his willingness to act as an intermediary between Washington and Tehran. Qaddafi expressed his profound concern for the hostages and hoped that his efforts on behalf of the United States would prompt the administration to adopt a "more evenhanded policy toward Libya" and "a more neutral posture" in the Arab-Israeli conflict. As it turned out, Qaddafi accomplished nothing, since he enjoyed very little influence with the Khomeini regime in Iran. Cooley, *Libyan Sandstorm*, 260–61.

11. Haley, *Qaddafi and United States*, 228–29.

12. Parks, "Crossing the Line," 42–43; George C. Wilson, "Libyan Fighters Suspected of Firing on U.S. Aircraft," *WP*, 18 September 1980, A17; George C. Wilson, "U.S. Fighters Chase Libyan Warplanes in Patrol Confrontation," *WP*, 26 September 1980, A8.

13. Muammar Qadhafi, "Message of Leader Brother Muammar Qadhafi to Mr. Carter and Mr. Reagan," advertisement in *WP*, 22 October 1980, A19.

14. Bernard Gwertzman, "U.S. Action: Sign to Libya," *NYT*, 21 August 1981, A1, A10; Lehman, *Command of Seas*, 362; Adam B. Siegel, *The Use of Naval Forces in the Post-War Era: U.S. Navy and U.S. Marine Corps Crisis Response Activity, 1946–1990*, Center for Naval Analysis Research Memorandum 90-246 (Alexandria, Va.: CNA, 1991), 36; Wilson, "Libyan Fighters Suspected"; "U.S. and Libya—Heading for a Showdown?" *U.S. News & World Report*, 31 August 1981, 17.

15. Ronald Reagan, *Reagan, in His Own Hand: The Writings of Ronald Reagan that Reveal His Revolutionary Vision for America*, ed. Kiron K. Skinner, Annelise Anderson, and Martin Anderson (New York: Free Press, 2001), 483.

16. Haley, *Qaddafi and United States*, 247; Alexander M. Haig, *Caveat: Realism, Reagan, and Foreign Policy* (New York: Macmillan, 1984), 77, 88; Anderson, "Libya and American Foreign Policy," 531.

17. Martin and Walcott, *Best Laid Plans,* 45–47; CIA Assessment Center, *Patterns of International Terrorism,* iii.

18. Martin and Walcott, *Best Laid Plans,* 43.

19. Ronald Reagan, *Public Papers of the Presidents of the United States: Ronald Reagan, 1981* (Washington, D.C.: GPO, 1982), 42.

20. Martin and Walcott, *Best Laid Plans,* 48.

21. DOS, "Secretary Haig's News Conference of 28 January," *Department of State Bulletin,* Special Section, February 1981, p. J.

22. Bernard Gwertzman, "Haig Says Teheran Will Not Get Arms; Asks Trade Caution," *NYT,* 29 January 1981, A1.

23. DOS, "Haig's News Conference," J.

24. Sterling, *Terror Network,* 10, 267, 274.

25. Woodward, *Veil,* 93; Robert M. Gates, *From the Shadows: The Ultimate Insider's Story of Five Presidents and How They Won the Cold War* (New York: Simon and Schuster, 1996), 203; Martin and Walcott, *Best Laid Plans,* 51–52.

26. Persico, *Casey,* 220, 286–87.

27. Gates, *From the Shadows,* 204–5.

28. CIA Director of Central Intelligence, *Soviet Support for Terrorism,* 10.

29. Ibid., 1–3.

30. Martin and Walcott, *Best Laid Plans,* 53, 55–56.

31. Ibid., 55–56.

32. Gates, *From the Shadows,* 206; Oliver North with William Novak, *Under Fire: An American Story* (New York: Harper Collins, 1992), 182n.

33. Lehman, *Command of Seas,* 361; CIA Assessment Center, *Patterns of International Terrorism,* 9.

34. Martin and Walcott, *Best Laid Plans,* 73; Sterling, *Terror Network,* 241–42.

35. "U.S. and Libya—Heading for a Showdown?" 17.

36. CIA Assessment Center, *Patterns of International Terrorism,* 9.

37. Haley, *Qaddafi and United States,* 247, 7; Don Oberdorfer, "U.S. Has Sought to Pressure Qaddafi," *WP,* 20 August 1981, A1.

38. Oberdorfer, "U.S. Sought Pressure," A1.

39. Haley, *Qaddafi and United States,* 7, 247; Oberdorfer, "U.S. Sought Pressure,"A1; Michael Getler, "Libya's Special Oil May Sweeten U.S. Distaste for Qaddafi Terrorism," *WP,* 21 March 1981, A3.

40. Haley, *Qaddafi and United States,* 248.

41. Don Oberdorfer, "Egypt Is Assured of U.S. Backing in Attack on Libya," *WP,* 8 November 1981, A4; Woodward, *Veil,* 94–96.

42. CIA Director of Central Intelligence, *Libya: Aims and Vulnerabilities,* 1, 4.

43. Ibid., 1, 9; Harris, *Libya,* 78; Bernard D. Nossiter, "Qaddafi Opposition Is Getting Stronger," *NYT,* 27 May 1981, A8; Woodward, *Veil,* 94.

44. CIA Director of Central Intelligence, *Libya: Aims and Vulnerabilities,* 2, 8.

45. Ibid., 1.

46. Martin and Walcott, *Best Laid Plans,* 76.

47. CIA Director of Central Intelligence, *Libya: Aims and Vulnerabilities,* 11, 12.

48. Woodward, *Veil*, 96–97, 157.

49. Martin and Walcott, *Best Laid Plans*, 75.

50. Ibid., 79; Michael Reese, John Walcott, and David C. Martin, "An Undeclared War," *Newsweek*, 31 August 1981, 17; Woodward, *Veil*, 302; Cooley, *Libyan Sandstorm*, 285.

51. Woodward, *Veil*, 157–58; "A Plan to Overthrow Kaddafi," *Newsweek*, 3 August 1981, 19.

52. Woodward, *Veil*, 366.

53. Ibid., 158, 160.

54. Parks, "Crossing the Line," 43; Gregory L. Vistica, *Fall from Glory: The Men Who Sank the U.S. Navy* (New York: Simon and Schuster, 1995), 107; Ronald Reagan, *An American Life* (New York: Simon and Schuster, 1990), 281; Gwertzman, "U.S. Action," A1, A10; William E. Smith, Bruce W. Nelan, and William Stewart, "Shootout over the Med," *Time*, 31 August 1981, 25; Oberdorfer, "Egypt Is Assured,"A4; Oberdorfer, "U.S. Sought Pressure,"A17; "The U.S. Challenges Libya's Kaddafi," *Newsweek*, 24 August 1981, 13.

55. Oberdorfer, "U.S. Sought Pressure,"A17.

56. Bernard D. Nossiter, "Qaddafi Tied to Shooting of Libyan in U.S.," *NYT*, 24 May 1981, A1; Martin and Walcott, *Best Laid Plans*, 74; Haley, *Qaddafi and United States*, 257.

57. Nossiter, "Qaddafi Tied to Shooting," A1.

58. DOS, "U.S. Asks Libyans to Close People's Bureau; Travel Advisory Issued: Department Statement 6 May 1981," *Department of State Bulletin*, July 1981, 45.

59. Haley, *Qaddafi and United States*, 255.

60. Bernard Gwertzman, "U.S. Pledges Aid to Countries in Africa that Resist Libyans," *NYT*, 3 June 1981, A1, A4; Haley, *Qaddafi and United States*, 293–95.

61. Haley, *Qaddafi and United States*, 247–48; CIA Director of Central Intelligence, *Libya: Aims and Vulnerabilities*, 6–7; Gates, *From the Shadows*, 255; Martin and Walcott, *Best Laid Plans*, 78, 82; Getler, "Libya's Special Oil"; Alan Cowell, "U.S. and Libya: Are the Views in Both Directions Distorted?" *NYT*, 28 November 1981, A6; Anderson, "Assessing Libya's Qaddafi," 226; Metz, *Country Study*, 226; St. John, *Qaddafi's World Design*, 89–90.

62. Haley, *Qaddafi and United States*, 273; Vistica, *Fall from Glory*, 107; Parks, "Crossing the Line," 43.

63. Parks, "Crossing the Line," 43.

64. Martin and Walcott, *Best Laid Plans*, 71.

65. Daniel P. Bolger, *Americans at War, 1975–1986: An Era of Violent Peace* (Novato, Calif.: Presidio, 1988), 172.

66. John Brecher et al., "To the Shores of Tripoli," *Newsweek*, 31 August 1981, 15.

67. Haig, *Caveat*, 109.

68. Brecher et al., "To Shores of Tripoli," 15.

69. Martin and Walcott, *Best Laid Plans*, 68–69; U.S. Sixth Fleet, *Command History 1981*, encl. 2, p.1.

70. Reagan, *American Life*, 289.

71. Brecher et al., "To Shores of Tripoli," 15; Smith, Nelan, and Stewart, "Shootout over the Med," 25; U.S. Sixth Fleet, *Command History 1981*, encl. 2, p.1; Martin and Walcott, *Best Laid Plans*, 68.

72. "Sixth Fleet F-14s Down Libyan Su-22s," *Aviation Week & Space Technology* 115 (24 August 1981): 20–21.

73. "U.S. Challenges Kaddafi," 13.

74. The following ships and squadrons participated in the Open Ocean Missile Exercise of 18–19 August 1981: *Nimitz* (CVN 68), CVW-8, VF-41, VF-84, VA-35, VA-82, VA-86, VAW-124, VMAQ-2 Detachment Y, VS-24, HS-9, *Forrestal* (CV 59), CVW-17, VF-74, VMFA-115, VA-81, VA-83, VA-85, VAW-125, VAQ-130, VS-30, HS-3, *Mississippi* (CGN 40), *Texas* (CGN 39), *Biddle* (CG 34), *Josephus Daniels* (CG 27), *William V. Pratt* (DDG 44), *Caron* (DD 970), *O'Bannon* (DD 987), *Thorn* (DD 988), *Talbot* (FFG 4), *Ainsworth* (FF 1090), *Connole* (FF 1056), *Paul* (FF 1080), and *Detroit* (AOE 4).

75. Bolger, *Americans at War,* 172–73; U.S. Sixth Fleet, *Command History 1981,* sect. III, pp. 6–7.

76. Woodward, *Veil,* 182–83; Bolger, *Americans at War,* 173; Oberdorfer, "U.S. Sought Pressure,"A1; Martin and Walcott, *Best Laid Plans,* 279; CIA National Foreign Assessment Center, *A Red Sea Security System: Political, Military, and Economic Issues,* Intelligence assessment, December 1981, 2.

77. Bolger, *Americans at War,* 173; U.S. Sixth Fleet, *Command History 1981,* encl. 2, p. 1; Larry Muczynski and James Anderson, "Black Aces Bag Two," interview by Barrett Tillman in *The Hook* 9 (fall 1981): 29; David A. Brown, "Libyan Incident Spurs Deployment Shift," *Aviation Week & Space Technology* 115 (31 August 1981): 19.

78. Martin and Walcott, *Best Laid Plans,* 69; "Libyan Pilots Demonstrate Varied Training," *Aviation Week & Space Technology* 115 (31 August 1981): 21.

79. Cooley, *Libyan Sandstorm,* 265; John K. Cooley, "Qadafi's Nervous Neighbors," *Middle East International* 157 (4 September 1981): 3.

80. Bolger, *Americans at War,* 179–81; Vistica, *Fall from Glory,* 120, 121; Brown, "Libyan Incident," 19.

81. Martin and Walcott, *Best Laid Plans,* 69; Muczynski and Anderson, "Black Aces Bag Two," 29; Brown, "Libyan Incident," 20; Parks, "Crossing the Line," 43; Robert K. Wilcox, *Wings of Fury: From Vietnam to the Gulf War—The Astonishing True Stories of America's Elite Fighter Pilots* (New York: Pocket Books, 1996), 21–24; Frank Marlowe and Robert R. Rini, "*Forrestal*/CVW-17—Another Successful Med Cruise," *The Hook* 9 (winter 1981): 34; Joseph T. Stanik, "Sudden Victory: The Gulf of Sidra Incident of August 1981," *Naval Aviation News* 78 (July–August 1996): 35.

82. U.S. Sixth Fleet, *Command History 1981,* encl. 2, p. 2; Brown, "Libyan Incident," 20; Martin and Walcott, *Best Laid Plans,* 69–70; Marlowe and Rini, "*Forrestal*/CVW-17," 33; Mac Flecnoe, comment on "Sharpening the Claws of the Tomcat," *United States Naval Institute Proceedings* 108 (August 1982): 86; Stanik, "Sudden Victory," 35.

83. Martin and Walcott, *Best Laid Plans,* 70; Muczynski and Anderson, "Black Aces Bag Two," 30; Wilcox, *Scream of Eagles,* 149; Bolger, *Americans at War,* 181.

84. Martin and Walcott, *Best Laid Plans,* 70.

85. Ibid.; Bolger, *Americans at War,* 181, 183; Muczynski and Anderson, "Black Aces Bag Two," 30.

86. Bolger, *Americans at War,* 181, 183.

87. Martin and Walcott, *Best Laid Plans*, 70, 71; Bolger, *Americans at War*, 183; Brown, "Libyan Incident," 20.

88. Vistica, *Fall from Glory*, 122.

89. Martin and Walcott, *Best Laid Plans*, 71; Bolger, *Americans at War*, 183; U.S. Sixth Fleet, *Command History 1981*, encl. 2, pp. 3, 12, 25; Muczynski and Anderson, "Black Aces Bag Two," 30.

90. Martin and Walcott, *Best Laid Plans*, 71.

91. U.S. Sixth Fleet, *Command History 1981*, encl. 2, p. 3.

92. Bolger, *Americans at War*, 183, 184; Brown, "Libyan Incident," 20.

93. U.S. Sixth Fleet, *Command History 1981*, encl. 2, pp. 3, 24.

94. Ibid., p. 3.

95. Martin and Walcott, *Best Laid Plans*, 71.

96. Brown, "Libyan Incident," 21; Muczynski and Anderson, "Black Aces Bag Two," 30.

97. Martin and Walcott, *Best Laid Plans*, 71–72.

98. Brown, "Libyan Incident," 21; Neutze, "Gulf of Sidra Incident," 27.

99. Muczynski and Anderson, "Black Aces Bag Two," 30.

100. Martin and Walcott, *Best Laid Plans*, 72.

101. Muczynski and Anderson, "Black Aces Bag Two," 30; Stanik, "Sudden Victory," 36; Martin and Walcott, *Best Laid Plans*, 72; Cooley, *Libyan Sandstorm*, 267; U.S. Sixth Fleet, *Command History 1981*, sect. III, p. 10, encl. 2, p. 4; USS *Nimitz* (CVN-68), *Command History 1981*, AVH, encl. 1, p. 2.

102. U.S. Sixth Fleet, *Command History 1981*, encl. 2, pp. 2, 11, 17.

103. Martin and Walcott, *Best Laid Plans*, 72.

104. Bolger, *Americans at War*, 185–86; Wilcox, *Wings of Fury*, 29–31; Ault, "Father of TOP GUN," *Shipmate* 62 (March 1999): 12; Wilcox, *Scream of Eagles*, v, 107; Richard P. Hallion, *Storm over Iraq: Air Power and the Gulf War* (Washington, D.C.: Smithsonian Institution, 1992), 30–31.

105. Muczynski and Anderson, "Black Aces Bag Two," 30–31.

106. Vistica, *Fall from Glory*, 128.

107. DOS, "U.S. Planes Attacked by Libyan Aircraft," *Department of State Bulletin*, October 1981, 57–58.

108. Gwertzman, "U.S. Action," A10.

109. DOS, "Department Statement 19 August 1981," *Department of State Bulletin*, October 1981, 60; Werner Wiskari, "Qaddafi Attacks U.S. 'Provocations,'" *NYT*, 21 August 1981, A11.

110. Vistica, *Fall from Glory*, 127.

111. Reagan, *Public Papers*, 1981, 721–24.

112. Reagan, *American Life*, 291.

113. Brecher et al., "To Shores of Tripoli," 17; Edwin Meese, *With Reagan: The Inside Story* (Washington, D.C.: Regnery Gateway, 1992), 204–5; Smith, Nelan, and Stewart, "Shootout over the Med," 25.

114. Reagan, *Public Papers*, 1981, 722, 729.

115. Howell Raines, "President Defends Libyan Encounter as 'Impressive' Act," *NYT*, 21 August 1981, A10. In his biography of Ronald Reagan, Lou Cannon wrote that Reagan thought that Edwin Meese had done the right thing, since no presidential decision was required. On the other hand, he reported that Mrs. Reagan, White House Chief of Staff James A. Baker III, and Deputy White House Chief of Staff Michael Deaver were furious over Meese's decision not to notify Reagan immediately. They believed that his handling of the matter reinforced the opinion held by many Reagan critics that the president did not have a strong grasp on what was going on in his own administration. Lou Cannon, *President Reagan: The Role of a Lifetime* (New York: Public Affairs, 2000), 158.

116. Brecher et al., "To Shores of Tripoli," 14.

117. Wiskari, "Qaddafi Attacks 'Provocations.'"

118. "Libya and Ethiopia Say U.S. Plots Killings," *WP*, 24 August 1981, A14.

119. Brecher et al., "To Shores of Tripoli," 14.

120. "Libyan Leader Threatens to Hit U.S. Nuclear Depots," *WP*, 2 September 1981, A20.

121. Smith, Nelan, and Stewart, "Shootout over the Med," 26.

122. Cooley, *Libyan Sandstorm*, 268.

123. Wiskari, "Qaddafi Attacks 'Provocations.'"

124. Reagan, *American Life*, 290.

125. Edmund Morris, *Dutch: A Memoir of Ronald Reagan* (New York: Random House, 1999), 444; Brecher et al., "To Shores of Tripoli," 18.

126. Smith, Nelan, and Stewart, "Shootout over the Med," 26.

127. Brecher et al., "To Shores of Tripoli," 18.

128. Steven Rattner, "Western Europeans Expressing Favor and Unease," *NYT*, 21 August 1981, A10.

129. Douglas Martin, "U.S. Oil Executives in Libya Discount Retaliation Threat," *NYT*, 21 August 1981, A11.

130. Wiskari, "Qaddafi Attacks 'Provocations.'"

131. Reagan, *American Life*, 292.

132. Haley, *Qaddafi and United States*, 277–78; Caspar W. Weinberger, *Fighting for Peace: Seven Critical Years in the Pentagon* (New York: Warner Books, 1990), 177–78.

133. Woodward, *Veil*, 167.

134. CIA Foreign Broadcast Information Service, *Quotations from Qadhdhafi on Terrorism*, Special memorandum, 9 December 1981, 3.

135. Haley, *Qaddafi and United States*, 260.

136. Christopher Simpson, *National Security Directives of the Reagan and Bush Administrations: The Declassified History of U.S. Political and Military Policy, 1981–1991* (Boulder, Colo.: Westview, 1995), 16, 51; George C. Wilson and Don Oberdorfer, "U.S. Plans Gulf War Game: Operation to Display Loyalty to Friends," *WP*, 13 October 1981, A1.

137. Haley, *Qaddafi and United States*, 262, 279, 286–87; Murrey Marder, "In Diplomacy, AWACS Replaces Gunboat," *WP*, 18 October 1981, A4; Wilson and Oberdorfer, "U.S. Plans War Game," A1.

Chapter 3. The Wave of Terror

1. Woodward, *Veil*, 181–82; "Kaddafi's Latest Plot," *Newsweek,* 9 November 1981, 29.
2. Woodward, *Veil*, 182.
3. Martin and Walcott, *Best Laid Plans,* 79; Woodward, *Veil,* 182; Philip Taubman, "U.S. Officials Say F.B.I. Is Hunting Terrorists Seeking to Kill President," *NYT,* 4 December 1981, A1; Blundy and Lycett, *Qaddafi and Libyan Revolution,* 6.
4. Taubman, "F.B.I. Hunting Terrorists," A1; David M. Alpern et al., "Coping with a Plot to Kill the President," *Newsweek,* 21 December 1981, 16.
5. Woodward, *Veil,* 183; Martin and Walcott, *Best Laid Plans,* 80; Seymour M. Hersh, "Target Qaddafi," *New York Times Magazine,* 22 February 1987, 24.
6. Haley, *Qaddafi and United States,* 248.
7. Martin and Walcott, *Best Laid Plans,* 76–77.
8. Simpson, *National Security Directives,* 17; Martin and Walcott, *Best Laid Plans,* 81; Haley, *Qaddafi and United States,* 287–88; Oberdorfer, "Egypt Is Assured," A4.
9. Woodward, *Veil,* 184.
10. Ibid.
11. Ibid.; Martin and Walcott, *Best Laid Plans,* 81.
12. Alpern et al., "Coping with a Plot," 19.
13. Woodward, *Veil,* 185.
14. Bernard Gwertzman, "Reagan Weighs Economic Steps against Libyans," *NYT,* 8 December 1981, A7.
15. Woodward, *Veil,* 185.
16. DOS, "Document 387: Presidential Request for U.S. Citizens to Leave Libya," *AFPCD,* 796.
17. James W. Nance, "Meeting with Chief Executive Officers of Companies that Deal with Libya," White House memorandum, 11 December 1981, Kemp Files, Folder "Libyan Crisis 1981 [1 of 2]," box 90219, RRL.
18. Martin and Walcott, *Best Laid Plans,* 81.
19. Haley, *Qaddafi and United States,* 267.
20. Woodward, *Veil,* 186.
21. Harris, *Libya,* 101.
22. Woodward, *Veil,* 186.
23. Ibid., 186–87.
24. Haley, *Qaddafi and United States,* 257, 269–70.
25. Ibid., 269–70.
26. Ibid., 289.
27. Simpson, *National Security Directives,* 60, 105.
28. DOS, "Libya: U.S. Economic Measures," *Department of State Bulletin,* June 1982, 68–69.
29. Martin and Walcott, *Best Laid Plans,* 82–83; Cooley, *Libyan Sandstorm,* 286.
30. Haley, *Qaddafi and United States,* 290.

31. Woodward, *Veil*, 215; Foltz, "Libya's Military Power," 64.

32. Haley, *Qaddafi and United States*, 305–6, 308.

33. "Sudan Claims Libyan Coup Plot," *Facts on File* 43 (25 February 1983): 124.

34. Martin and Walcott, *Best Laid Plans*, 259–60; Lou Cannon and George C. Wilson, "U.S. Says Libya Eyed Sudan Coup," *WP*, 19 February 1983, A1, A13; George C. Wilson, "Reagan Pulling U.S. Forces Back as Libya Episode Cools," *LAT*, 20 February 1983, I18; Richard K. Halloran, "Libyan Affair Over, U.S. Says AWACS Will Now Leave Egypt," *NYT*, 22 February 1983, A8; Siegel, *Use of Naval Forces*, 44.

35. Martin and Walcott, *Best Laid Plans*, 260.

36. "Libya Threatens 'Gulf of Blood'; Keep Carrier Out of Area, Kadafi Says," *LAT*, 18 February 1983, I1.

37. Cannon and Wilson, "Libya Eyed Coup," A13.

38. Martin and Walcott, *Best Laid Plans*, 261.

39. Bernard Gwertzman, "U.S. Officials Say Libyan Threat Led to AWACS Dispatch," *NYT*, 18 February 1983, A6.

40. Martin and Walcott, *Best Laid Plans*, 261.

41. Cannon and Wilson, "Libya Eyed Coup," A13.

42. Haley, *Qaddafi and United States*, 310.

43. George Skelton, "Libya Threatens 'Gulf of Blood'; U.S. Warns It's Ready to Aid Allies," *LAT*, 18 February 1983, I1, I10.

44. Ibid.

45. Gwertzman, "Libyan Threat Led to Dispatch," A6.

46. Wilson, "Reagan Pulling Forces Back," I18.

47. DOS, "The Secretary [Shultz]: Interview on *This Week with David Brinkley*," *Department of State Bulletin*, April 1983, 45.

48. Martin and Walcott, *Best Laid Plans*, 261.

49. Haley, *Qaddafi and United States*, 301, 305.

50. Ibid., 318–19; Gerald F. Seib, "U.S. Sends More AWACS in Growing Effort to Help Chad Resist Libya-Backed Rebels," *WSJ*, 8 August 1983, 3; Salet Gaba, "U.S. Aides, Arms Arrive in Chad," *WP*, 4 August 1983, A1; Bernard Gwertzman, "U.S. Is Withdrawing Aircraft It Sent to Help Chad," *NYT*, 24 August 1983, A9; J. Millard Burr and Robert O. Collins, *Africa's Thirty Years' War: Libya, Chad, and the Sudan, 1963–1993* (Boulder, Colo.: Westview, 1999), 165; Parks, "Crossing the Line," 44; "Libya MiGs Are Intercepted by Jets from a U.S. Carrier," *NYT*, 3 August 1983, A3; USS *Dwight D. Eisenhower, Command History 1983*, AVH, encl. 1, p. 5.

51. Haley, *Qaddafi and United States*, 318–20.

52. Alan Cowell, "Mobutu, On a Visit to Chad, Renews Zairian Support," *NYT*, 21 August 1983, A8.

53. William Echikson, "France Hopes Unused Strength Can Persuade Libya to Talk," *CSM*, 22 August 1983, 6; Alan Cowell, "French War Jets Are Sent to Chad," *NYT*, 22 August 1983, A1.

54. Woodward, *Veil*, 302–3.

55. Martin and Walcott, *Best Laid Plans*, 259; DOS Bureau of Public Affairs, *Background Notes: Libya* (Washington, D.C.: GPO, 1985), 6.

56. Brief, "Chronology of Libyan Support for Terrorism 1979–85," n.d., Fortier Files, Folder "Libya [3 of 4]," box 91673, RRL.

57. Martin and Walcott, *Best Laid Plans*, 261.

58. Brief, "Chronology of Libyan Support."

59. Ibid.; Burr and Collins, *Africa's Thirty Years' War*, 186n; DOS Bureau of Public Affairs, *Libya under Qadhafi*, 1–3; Martin and Walcott, *Best Laid Plans*, 261; "Qaddafi Revered at Home, Reviled in West," *WP*, 25 March 1986, A14.

60. Brief, "Libyan Involvement in Terrorism," n.d., Fortier Files, Folder "Terrorism and Libya [5 of 6]," box 91763, RRL; DOS Bureau of Public Affairs, *Libya under Qadhafi*, 1–2; Russell Watson et al., "Flake or Fox?" *Newsweek*, 20 January 1986, 19; Parks, "Crossing the Line," 44; Harris, *Libya*, 101.

61. CIA Director of Central Intelligence, *Libya: Aims and Vulnerabilities*, 4; DOS Bureau of Public Affairs, *Libya under Qadhafi*, 3; Woodward, *Veil*, 256.

62. Scott C. Truver, "Mines of August: An International Whodunit," *United States Naval Institute Proceedings* 111 (May 1985): 97, 111–12.

63. Martin and Walcott, *Best Laid Plans*, 261–62; Haig, *Caveat*, 137; DOS Bureau of Public Affairs, *Libya under Qadhafi*, 2, 3.

64. Parks, "Crossing the Line," 44; Harris, *Libya*, 70; Martin and Walcott, *Best Laid Plans*, 262; Woodward, *Veil*, 348; Jonathan Bearman, *Qadhafi's Libya* (Atlantic Highlands, N.J.: Zed Books, 1986), 247, 250.

65. Woodward, *Veil*, 348, 363–64.

66. Ibid., 364–65.

67. Martin and Walcott, *Best Laid Plans*, 262; Woodward, *Veil*, 365.

68. Woodward, *Veil*, 365–67.

69. Martin and Walcott, *Best Laid Plans*, 262; Woodward, *Veil*, 367.

70. Martin and Walcott, *Best Laid Plans*, 262.

71. Woodward, *Veil*, 367–68.

72. Martin and Walcott, *Best Laid Plans*, 262–63.

73. Ibid., 263–64.

74. Ibid., 264.

75. Constantine C. Menges, *Inside the National Security Council: The True Story of the Making and Unmaking of Reagan's Foreign Policy* (New York: Simon and Schuster, 1988), 252; Lehman, *Command of Seas*, 363.

76. Simpson, *National Security Directives*, 61, 113–14, 366. In early 1985 Casey acted in concert with a senior Saudi diplomat and the Lebanese intelligence service to plan and carry out a covert operation to eliminate Shaykh Muhammad Husayn Fadlallah, the leader of the militant Lebanese Shia organization *Hizballah* (Party of God). Fadlallah had been connected to the attacks on the U.S. embassy and Marine barracks in 1983 and to the bombing of the U.S. embassy annex in east Beirut the following year. In the Lebanese Shia community the outcome of this active measure was known as the "Bir al-Abed massacre." On 8 March 1985 Lebanese operatives detonated a massive car bomb only a few yards from Fadlallah's apartment building in south Beirut. Not far from the building was the Bir al-Abed mosque, where a large crowd had gathered for prayer. Fadlallah escaped unharmed, but the blast devastated the neighborhood, leveling several buildings, killing

eighty people, and injuring more than two hundred. In the wake of this horrendous operation the CIA eschewed further involvement in actions aimed at killing terrorist leaders. Martin and Walcott, *Best Laid Plans*, 219–21; Woodward, *Veil*, 396–98.

77. Woodward, *Veil*, 361–62; Simpson, *National Security Directives*, 365; George P. Shultz, *Turmoil and Triumph: My Years as Secretary of State* (New York: Charles Scribner's Sons, 1993), 645.

78. Martin and Walcott, *Best Laid Plans*, 156–57.

79. Woodward, *Veil*, 362.

80. Robert C. Toth, "Preemptive Anti-Terrorists Raids Allowed," *WP*, 16 April 1984, A19.

81. David Hoffman and Don Oberdorfer, "Secret Policy on Terrorism Given Airing," *WP*, 18 April 1984, A1.

82. Simpson, *National Security Directives*, 405–6.

83. Ibid., 366; Hoffman and Oberdorfer, "Secret Policy Given Airing," A1.

84. Shultz, *Turmoil and Triumph*, 646–48.

85. Weinberger, *Fighting for Peace*, 188.

86. Shultz, *Turmoil and Triumph*, 649–50.

87. Robert Timberg, *The Nightingale's Song* (New York: Simon and Schuster, 1995), 288–89.

88. Lehman, *Command of Seas*, 363.

89. Martin and Walcott, *Best Laid Plans*, 157.

90. James P. Terry, "An Appraisal of Lawful Military Response to State-Sponsored Terrorism," *Naval War College Review* 39 (May–June 1986): 59.

91. Ronald Reagan, "President's News Conference on Foreign and Domestic Issues," *NYT*, 19 June 1985, A18.

92. Cannon, *President Reagan*, 536.

93. Woodward, *Veil*, 409.

94. Martin and Walcott, *Best Laid Plans*, 264–65.

95. Bob Woodward, "U.S. Decided to Give Libya Firm Message," *WP*, 26 March 1986, A1.

96. Bernard Weinraub, "President Accuses 5 'Outlaw States' of World Terror," *NYT*, 9 July 1985, A1.

97. Ronald Reagan, "Excerpts from the President's Address Accusing Nations of 'Acts of War,'" 9 July 1985, A12.

98. Woodward, *Veil*, 409.

99. CIA Director of Central Intelligence, *Libya's Qadhafi: The Challenge to U.S. and Western Interests*, Special National Intelligence Estimate 36.5–85, March 1985, 3.

100. Ibid., 17.

101. Ibid., 2.

102. Woodward, *Veil*, 409–10; CIA Director of Central Intelligence, *Libya's Qadhafi*, 1.

103. Simpson, *National Security Directives*, 528.

104. Ibid., 448.

105. Woodward, *Veil*, 410.

106. Simpson, *National Security Directives*, 454, 476–77.

107. Woodward, *Veil*, 411–12; Woodward, "U.S. Decided to Give Message," A1.

108. Woodward, *Veil*, 411–12.

109. Ibid., 412; Gates, *From the Shadows*, 352.

110. Martin and Walcott, *Best Laid Plans*, 265; Woodward, *Veil*, 412. In response to a *Washington Post* article by Bob Woodward and Don Oberdorfer, which ran on 20 February 1987, Robert M. Gates, who became acting CIA director following the resignation of William Casey, issued the following public statement: "At no time has Acting Director Gates recommended an invasion of Libya. Moreover, any insinuation that Mr. Gates in July 1985 encouraged such action is unfounded." CIA, "Statement re. Acting Director Robert M. Gates," 20 February 1987.

111. Bob Woodward and Don Oberdorfer, "State Dept. Acted to Block U.S.-Egyptian Attack on Libya," *WP*, 20 February 1987, A27.

112. Martin and Walcott, *Best Laid Plans*, 265; Woodward, *Veil*, 414.

113. Weinberger, *Fighting for Peace*, 201.

114. Martin and Walcott, *Best Laid Plans*, 265.

115. Woodward and Oberdorfer, "State Dept. Acted," A1, A27.

116. Woodward, *Veil*, 414; Martin and Walcott, *Best Laid Plans*, 265–66.

117. Woodward and Oberdorfer, "State Dept. Acted," A27.

118. Woodward, *Veil*, 414.

119. Martin and Walcott, *Best Laid Plans*, 262, 266; Bob Woodward, "CIA Anti-Qaddafi Plan Backed," *WP*, 3 November 1985, A1; Woodward, *Veil*, 417–19.

120. Woodward, *Veil*, 419–20.

121. Martin and Walcott, *Best Laid Plans*, 266; DOS Bureau of Public Affairs, *Libya under Qadhafi*, 2; Gwendolyn J. Rich, "1985 Year in Review," *Naval Aviation News* 68 (July–August 1986): 29.

122. Ronald Reagan, "Transcript of White House News Conference on the Hijacking," *NYT*, 12 October 1985, A6.

123. Bolger, *Americans at War*, 384.

124. Martin and Walcott, *Best Laid Plans*, 266; DOS Bureau of Public Affairs, *Libya under Qadhafi*, 4.

125. Bolger, *Americans at War*, 385–86; Martin and Walcott, *Best Laid Plans*, 267; Harry Anderson et al., "Holiday of Terror," *Newsweek*, 6 January 1986, 26; Ed Magnuson, Walter Galling, and Gertraud Lessing, "Ten Minutes of Horror," *Time*, 6 January 1986, 74.

126. Magnuson, Galling, and Lessing, "Ten Minutes of Horror," 75.

127. Bolger, *Americans at War*, 386; Martin and Walcott, *Best Laid Plans*, 268; Loren Jenkins, "Airport Terrorists Reportedly Trained in Syrian-Controlled Area: European Probers Share Information," *WP*, 11 January 1986, A18.

128. Woodward, *Veil*, 431; Martin and Walcott, *Best Laid Plans*, 268. The United States later learned that the Rome and Vienna terrorists had used grenades drawn from Libyan Arab Army stocks. Grenades with the same ammunition manufacturing symbols and production lots turned up among Libyan materiel captured during combat in Chad in the spring of 1987. Bolger, *Americans at War*, 386.

129. Watson et al., "Flake or Fox?" 15.

130. Magnuson, Galling, and Lessing, "Ten Minutes of Horror," 76.

131. Anderson et al., "Holiday of Terror," 30.

132. Dan Fisher, "Rocket Attack from South Lebanon Poses Renewed Problem for Israel," *WP*, 3 January 1986, A14.

133. James M. Dorsey, "Qaddafi Warns against Retaliation for Attacks," *WP*, 2 January 1986, A17.

Chapter 4. Operation Prairie Fire

1. Bolger, *Americans at War*, 387. In the immediate aftermath of the Rome and Vienna airport attacks, Chief of Naval Operations Adm. James Watkins was the first senior Pentagon officer to propose a joint Air Force–Navy strike on Libya involving F-111Fs based in the United Kingdom in conjunction with carrier-based attack aircraft. Hallion, *Storm over Iraq*, 106.

2. George C. Wilson, "Reagan Denounces Warning by Qaddafi on Retaliation," *WP*, 3 January 1986, A1, A22.

3. Ronald Reagan, *Public Papers of the Presidents of the United States: Ronald Reagan, 1986* (Washington, D.C.: GPO, 1987), 1:17.

4. Woodward, *Veil*, 432; Harry Anderson et al., "Get Tough: The Reagan Plan," *Newsweek*, 20 January 1986, 17.

5. Woodward, *Veil*, 432.

6. Shultz, *Turmoil and Triumph*, 677.

7. Martin and Walcott, *Best Laid Plans*, 274; Bolger, *Americans at War*, 386–87; Watson et al., "Flake or Fox?" 15; David Hoffman and Lou Cannon, "Terrorism Provided Catalyst," *WP*, 25 March 1986, A12; Woodward, *Veil*, 432–33; Anderson et al., "Get Tough," 17; Weinberger, *Fighting for Peace*, 188, 200; Bernard Gwertzman, "Why Reagan Shuns Attack," *NYT*, 8 January 1986, A7.

8. Martin and Walcott, *Best Laid Plans*, 289; Melinda A. Beck et al., "A Syrian Connection," *Newsweek*, 12 May 1986, 54; Gates, *From the Shadows*, 351–52.

9. George J. Church et al., "Targeting Gaddafi," *Time*, 21 April 1986, 19–20.

10. Martin and Walcott, *Best Laid Plans*, 274–76; Bolger, *Americans at War*, 387; Barnaby J. Feder, "Libya Trade Was Low Before Ban," *New York Times*, 8 January 1986, A7.

11. Anderson et al., "Get Tough," 16; Weinberger, *Fighting for Peace*, 200; Cannon, *President Reagan*, 302; Woodward, "U.S. Decided to Give Message," 26; Bolger, *Americans at War*, 387–88.

12. Reagan, *Public Papers, 1986*, 1:14–16; Aric Press, Ann McDaniel, and Michael A. Lerner, "Getting Americans Out of Libya: Is It Legal?" *Newsweek*, 20 January 1986, 19; Martin and Walcott, *Best Laid Plans*, 276; Lisa Anderson, "Libya's Qaddafi: Still in Command?" *Current History* 86 (February 1987): 68; Unsigned article, "Libyan Oil Liftings Little Affected by Skirmish with United States," 31 March 1986, Fortier Files, Folder "Libya (Fortier File) [4 of 12]," box 91673, RRL.

13. Reagan, *Public Papers, 1986*, 1:17–18.

14. Reagan, *American Life*, 515.

15. Bernard Weinraub, "President Breaks All Economic Ties with the Libyans," *NYT*, 8 January 1986, A1.

16. Watson et al., "Flake or Fox?" 15.

17. Simpson, *National Security Directives*, 654–55.

18. Harold R. Teicher, "Memorandum for John M. Poindexter from Howard R. Teicher, Subject: NSDD on Libya" with attachments, 7 January 1986, Partially declassified, Teicher Files, Folder "Libya Sensitive 1986 [1 of 7]," box 91668, RRL.

19. Martin and Walcott, *Best Laid Plans*, 276.

20. Steven J. Dryden, "Europeans to Halt Arms Sales to Nations Backing Terrorists," *WP*, 28 January 1986, A10; DOS Bureau of Public Affairs, *International Terrorism*, 13; Martin and Walcott, *Best Laid Plans*, 276.

21. Loren Jenkins, "Rome Restricts Arms Sales to Libya, Says Italians Won't Fill U.S. Jobs There," *WP*, 10 January 1986, A25, A30.

22. Watson et al., "Flake or Fox?" 19.

23. DOS Bureau of Public Affairs, *International Terrorism*, 8.

24. John M. Goshko, "Armed Action against Libya Still Possible," *WP*, 28 January 1986, A10.

25. Martin and Walcott, *Best Laid Plans*, 276–77.

26. Anderson et al., "Get Tough," 16–17.

27. Watson et al., "Flake or Fox?" 15.

28. Brief, "El Dorado Canyon Observations: Joint Staff Introduction," Briefing for the Secretary of Defense, Partially declassified, Control no. 618–88, CNO/DCNO (NW), box 10; Robert E. Venkus, *Raid on Qaddafi* (New York: St. Martin's, 1993), 34; Peter E. Davies and Anthony M. Thornborough, *F-111 Aardvark* (Ramsbury, U.K.: Crowood, 1997), 118; Martin and Walcott, *Best Laid Plans*, 258–59. Rear Adm. Jerry C. Breast, commander of the *Coral Sea* CVBG, which was on deployment in the Mediterranean at the time of the Rome and Vienna airport attacks, stated that on the evening of 27 December 1985 he received orders to prepare contingency strike plans for targets in Libya. Jerry C. Breast, "The CV in Action . . . Battle Stations!" *Wings of Gold* 12 (summer 1987): S-27.

29. Martin and Walcott, *Best Laid Plans*, 268–69. Out of concern for the safety of the Navy and Air Force participants in Operation El Dorado Canyon and their families, only the names of those officers who have been identified in the open press will be used. Since the indictment of two Libyan intelligence operatives in 1991 for the bombing of Pan Am 103 over Lockerbie, Scotland, in 1988, Qaddafi has frequently demanded that the United States hand over for trial in Libya the American airmen who bombed Libya in 1986. So long as the Qaddafi regime remains in power, the welfare of the El Dorado Canyon airmen and their families cannot be taken for granted. Andrew North, "Lockerbie: Families' Change of Heart," *Middle East International* 561 (24 October 1997): 10.

30. Martin and Walcott, *Best Laid Plans*, 269.

31. Report, "Lessons Learned from Operations in the Vicinity of Libya," Report dated 6 October 1987, Partially declassified, Control no. 567–87, CNO/DCNO (NW), box 11, p. 15.

32. Venkus, *Raid on Qaddafi*, 37; Martin and Walcott, *Best Laid Plans*, 269.

33. Wilson, "Reagan Denounces Warning," A22.

34. Martin and Walcott, *Best Laid Plans*, 269–71; Venkus, *Raid on Qaddafi*, 38, 39.

35. Martin and Walcott, *Best Laid Plans*, 271–73.

36. Woodward, *Veil*, 435–36.

37. Simpson, *National Security Directives*, 656–57, 658.

38. Ben Bradlee, *Guts and Glory: The Rise and Fall of Oliver North* (New York: Donald I. Fine, 1988), 350–51.

39. Shultz, *Turmoil and Triumph*, 679.

40. Vice President's Task Force on Combatting Terrorism, *Public Report of the Vice President's Task Force on Combatting Terrorism, February 1986* (Washington, D.C.: GPO, 1986), 9, 13.

41. David Hoffman, "Terrorism Panel Still Divided on Use of Military Retaliation," *WP,* 7 March 1986, A28.

42. Martin and Walcott, *Best Laid Plans*, 277–78; Report, "Lessons Learned," 16; George C. Wilson, "U.S. Planes Retaliate for Libyan Attack," *WP,* 25 March 1986, A13; Joseph S. Bermudez, "Libyan SAMs and Air Defences," *Jane's Defence Weekly* 5 (17 May 1986): 880; Frank Elliot, "Shooting Match Provided Equipment Test," *NT,* 7 April 1986, 39.

43. Martin and Walcott, *Best Laid Plans*, 277.

44. "CVW-17/CV-60," *The Hook* 14 (summer 1986): 68. The *Saratoga* CVBG consisted of the following ships and squadrons: *Saratoga* (CV 60), CVW-17, VF-74, VF-103, VA-81, VA-83, VA-85, VAW-125, VAQ-137, VS-30, HS-3, VQ-2 Det, *Yorktown* (CG 48), *Richmond K. Turner* (CG 20), *Mahan* (DDG 42), *Scott* (DDG 995), *Caron* (DD 970), *Ainsworth* (FF 1090), *Donald B. Beary* (FF 1085), *Garcia* (FF 1040), *Paul* (FF 1080), and *Seattle* (AOE 3). The following ships and squadrons comprised the *Coral Sea* CVBG: *Coral Sea* (CV 43), CVW-13, VFA-131, VFA-132, VMFA-314, VMFA-323, VA-55, VAW-127, VAQ-135, HS-17, VQ-2 Det, *Biddle* (CG 34), *Dewert* (FFG 45), *Jack Williams* (FFG 24), *Capodanno* (FF 1093), *Jesse L. Brown* (FF 1089), *Mount Baker* (AE 34), and *Monongahela* (AO 178).

45. Bolger, *Americans at War,* 389; Martin and Walcott, *Best Laid Plans*, 278, 280.

46. Robert E. Stumpf, "Air War with Libya," *United States Naval Institute Proceedings* 112 (August 1986): 43–44; Commander VF-103, "Current F-14A Operations Lessons Learned," Letter dated 4 June 1986, Partially declassified, Control no. 671–88, CNO/DCNO (NW), box 11, encl. 2, p. 2.

47. Stumpf, "Air War with Libya," 44.

48. Michael Goldsmith, "Qaddafi Says His Forces Are on Alert after U.S. Exercises Announced," *WP,* 25 January 1986, A16.

49. Michael Goldsmith, "Qaddafi Sails Near U.S. Exercises," *WP,* 26 January 1986, A21; Moore, *Jane's Fighting Ships,* 344.

50. Goldsmith, "Qaddafi Sails."

51. Ibid.; Martin and Walcott, *Best Laid Plans*, 278–79.

52. Bolger, *Americans at War,* 389.

53. Stumpf, "Air War with Libya," 42, 44.

54. Ibid., 44–45; Bolger, *Americans at War,* 390–91.

55. Stumpf, "Air War with Libya," 45; Breast, "CV in Action," S-28.

56. Stumpf, "Air War with Libya," 44.

57. Martin and Walcott, *Best Laid Plans*, 279.

58. Stumpf, "Air War with Libya," 45; Report, "Lessons Learned," 18.

59. Stumpf, "Air War with Libya," 45.

60. Martin and Walcott, *Best Laid Plans*, 279.

61. Stumpf, "Air War with Libya," 45–46; Commander VF-103, "Current F-14A Operations," encl. 1, pp. 4, 6.

62. Stumpf, "Air War with Libya," 45.

63. "CVW-17/CV-60," 71.

64. Commander VF-103, "Current F-14A Operations," encl. 1, p. 7.

65. Stumpf, "Air War with Libya," 45–46.

66. Bolger, *Americans at War*, 392; Stumpf, "Air War with Libya," 45.

67. Weinberger, *Fighting for Peace*, 184; Bolger, *Americans at War*, 392; Simpson, *National Security Directives*, 638; William J. Crowe with David Chanoff, *The Line of Fire: From Washington to the Gulf, the Politics and Battles of the New Military* (New York: Simon and Schuster, 1993), 130.

68. Parks, "Crossing the Line," 44.

69. Martin and Walcott, *Best Laid Plans*, 281.

70. COMSIXTHFLT Message, DTG 241438ZMAR86, Declassified, *King*, box 2; Martin and Walcott, *Best Laid Plans*, 281; Brief, "Attain Document III," n.d., Partially declassified, CNO/DCNO (LOG).

71. Martin and Walcott, *Best Laid Plans*, 281.

72. Hoffman and Cannon, "Terrorism Provided Catalyst,"A12; Timberg, *Nightingale's Song*, 377–78; Woodward, *Veil*, 440; Geoffrey Parker and Larry J. Leturmy, "The Libya Raid: A Joint Response to State-Sponsored Terrorism," Case study (Maxwell AFB, Ala.: Air War College, 1987), 16.

73. Bolger, *Americans at War*, 342; Russell Watson et al., "Kaddafi's Crusade," *Newsweek*, 7 April 1986, 24; George C. Wilson and Fred Hiatt, "Navy Again Strikes Libyan Boats, Radar; Qaddafi Is Warned," *WP*, 26 March 1986, A1, A22; David Gelman, John Walcott, and Thomas M. DeFrank, "The Poindexter Doctrine," *Newsweek*, 21 April 1986, 24; Timberg, *Nightingale's Song*, 377.

74. Mark Whitaker et al., "Targeting a 'Mad Dog,'" *Newsweek*, 21 April 1986, 21.

75. Bolger, *Americans at War*, 393.

76. Wilson and Hiatt, "Navy Again Strikes," A1, A22; Larry Speakes with Robert Pack, *Speaking Out: The Reagan Presidency from Inside the White House* (New York: Charles Scribner's Sons, 1988), 183–84; Martin and Walcott, *Best Laid Plans*, 281.

77. Ed Magnuson, Johanna McGeary, and Bruce van Voorst, "To the Shores of Tripoli," *Time*, 31 March 1986, 26.

78. Lehman, *Command of Seas*, 370–71; Timberg, *Nightingale's Song*, 376–77.

79. Woodward, *Veil*, 441–42.

80. Martin and Walcott, *Best Laid Plans*, 280.

81. Ibid.; Woodward, *Veil*, 441.

82. Weinberger, *Fighting for Peace*, 184.

83. Lehman, *Command of Seas*, 368.

84. The *America* CVBG was comprised of the following ships and squadrons: *America* (CV 66), CVW-1, VF-33, VF-102, VA-34, VA-46, VA-72, VAW-123, VMAQ-2 Det Y, VS-32, HS-11, VQ-2 Det, *Ticonderoga* (CG 47), *Dale* (CG 19), *Farragut* (DDG 37), *King* (DDG 41), *Peterson* (DD 969), *Halyburton* (FFG 40), *Aylwin* (FF 1081), *Pharris* (FF 1094), *Vreeland* (FF 1068), and *Detroit* (AOE 4).

85. Breast, "CV in Action," S-28.

86. COMSIXTHFLT Message, DTG 271805ZMAR86, Declassified, *King*, box 2.

87. Frederick H. Hartmann, *Naval Renaissance: The U.S. Navy in the 1980s* (Annapolis, Md.: Naval Institute Press, 1990), 244.

88. Report, "Lessons Learned," 20; Stumpf, "Air War with Libya," 46; CTF Six Zero Message, DTG 210530ZMAR86, Partially declassified, *King*, box 1.

89. Breast, "CV in Action," S-28.

90. Report, "Lessons Learned," 18, 20; USS *Saratoga* Message, DTG 021332ZMAR86, Partially declassified, *King*, box 2.

91. CTF Six Zero Message, DTG 210810ZMAR86, Declassified, *King*, box 2.

92. Brief, "Attain Document III;" Parks, "Crossing the Line," 44–45; Martin and Walcott, *Best Laid Plans*, 281; Bolger, *Americans at War*, 395.

93. "The Gulf of Sidra" (Chronology), *WP*, 26 March 1986, A22; Report, "Lessons Learned," 20; "CVW-1/CV-66," *The Hook* 14 (summer 1986): 43; Bolger, *Americans at War*, 395; Martin and Walcott, *Best Laid Plans*, 281; Lehman, *Command of Seas*, 370.

94. Martin and Walcott, *Best Laid Plans*, 281–82.

95. Stumpf, "Air War with Libya," 47.

96. Parks, "Crossing the Line," 45; "CVW-17/CV-60," 71; Stumpf, "Air War with Libya," 47.

97. Hartmann, *Naval Renaissance*, 245.

98. Report, "Lessons Learned," 23; COMSIXTHFLT Message, DTG 241438ZMAR86.

99. Parks, "Crossing the Line," 45; Martin and Walcott, *Best Laid Plans*, 282.

100. Martin and Walcott, *Best Laid Plans*, 282. In the 4 December 1983 raid on Syrian SAM sites in Lebanon, two U.S. Navy attack aircraft were shot down and a third was damaged by Syrian air defense systems. An A-6E from VA-85, based on the *John F. Kennedy* (CV 67), was brought down by a SAM. The pilot, Lt. Mark A. Lange, was severely wounded when he ejected; he later died of his injuries. The bombardier-navigator, Lt. Robert O. Goodman, was captured by Syrian troops and was eventually repatriated through the efforts of the Rev. Jesse Jackson. An A-7E from VA-15, flown by Comdr. Edward Andrews, commander of CVW-6 based on the *Independence* (CV 62), was hit and damaged by anti-aircraft fire. Andrews guided his plane out over the water and then ejected. He was recovered and returned to the "Indy." Another VA-15 A-7E, piloted by Comdr. Les Kappel, was damaged by a SAM but was able to make it safely back to the carrier. Roy A. Grossnick, "1983 Year in Review," *Naval Aviation News* 66 (May–June 1984): 30–31.

101. "'Best Regards,'" *WP*, 26 March 1986, A22.

102. Report, "Lessons Learned," 22–23; "Gulf of Sidra (Chronology)"; Bolger, *Americans at War*, 395–96.

103. Report, "Lessons Learned," 27; Bolger, *Americans at War,* 396; Moore, *Jane's Fighting Ships,* 344.

104. Martin and Walcott, *Best Laid Plans,* 282.

105. Bolger, *Americans at War,* 396–97; Martin and Walcott, *Best Laid Plans,* 283; James Meacham, "Hits and Misses in Libyan Raid," *Defense Attaché* no. 2 (1986): 14.

106. Martin and Walcott, *Best Laid Plans,* 283.

107. Report, "Lessons Learned," 28; Bolger, *Americans at War,* 396–97; Elliot, "Shooting Match," 40; Timothy J. Christmann, "Harpoon Proves Its Tenacity: A-6Es Thump Libyan Combatants," *Naval Aviation News* 68 (July–August 1986): 12–14; Christopher Dickey, "Libya Silent on Casualties," *WP,* 28 March 1986, A1.

108. "The Year in Review 1986," *Naval Aviation News* 69 (July–August 1987): 8; Martin and Walcott, *Best Laid Plans,* 283.

109. Martin and Walcott, *Best Laid Plans,* 283; Elliot, "Shooting Match," 39; Bolger, *Americans at War,* 397.

110. Timothy J. Christmann, "The Navy Strikes Tripoli's Terrorist," *Naval Aviation News* 68 (July–August 1986): 16.

111. Martin and Walcott, *Best Laid Plans,* 283.

112. Bolger, *Americans at War,* 397–98; Christmann, "Harpoon Proves," 12; Report, "Lessons Learned," 28.

113. Report, "Lessons Learned," 29–30; COMSIXTHFLT Message, DTG 250547ZMAR86, Partially declassified, NWAC; Martin and Walcott, *Best Laid Plans,* 283–84; Bolger, *Americans at War,* 398; USS *Yorktown* Message, DTG 250149ZMAR86, Declassified, NWAC; Breast, "CV in Action," S-29; David M. North, "Merits of U.S., Soviet Weapons Explored in Libyan Conflict," *Aviation Week & Space Technology* 124 (31 March 1986): 21. A Pentagon official later admitted to the press that the contact engaged by the *Yorktown* had closed to within ten miles of Sixth Fleet ships. Michael R. Gordon, "U.S. Says One Vessel It Hit Had Come Within 10 Miles," *NYT,* 26 March 1986, A8.

114. Crowe with Chanoff, *Line of Fire,* 131–32; Breast, "CV in Action," S-29.

115. Elliot, "Shooting Match," 39.

116. Report, "Lessons Learned," 30.

117. Parks, "Crossing the Line," 45; "Libyan SA-5 Site Repaired after U.S. Strike," *Jane's Defence Weekly* 5 (5 April 1986): 595.

118. Bolger, *Americans at War,* 399; CTG Six Zero Point Five Message, DTG 301500ZMAR86, Declassified, *King,* box 1; Report, "Lessons Learned," 28.

119. Bolger, *Americans at War,* 399; Report, "Lessons Learned," 399.

120. Christmann, "Harpoon Proves," 13–14.

121. Bolger, *Americans at War,* 399–400; Christmann, "Harpoon Proves," 14; Martin and Walcott, *Best Laid Plans,* 284.

122. Martin and Walcott, *Best Laid Plans,* 284.

123. Parks, "Crossing the Line," 45; Stumpf, "Air War with Libya," 47.

124. Shultz, *Turmoil and Triumph,* 682.

125. Lehman, *Command of Seas,* 371.

126. Reagan, *Public Papers,* 1986, 1:407.

127. Bolger, *Americans at War*, 400; George C. Wilson, "Qaddafi Was a Target of U.S. Raid," *WP*, 18 April 1986, A1; Woodward, *Veil*, 443; John Burlage, "U.S. Asserts Right of Free Navigation," *NT*, 7 April 1986, 37; Parks, "Crossing the Line," 45; Breast, "CV in Action," S-29.

128. Burlage, "U.S. Asserts Right," 37.

129. Bolger, *Americans at War*, 399–401.

130. Martin and Walcott, *Best Laid Plans*, 284.

131. "Fearing Trouble: A *Newsweek* Poll," *Newsweek*, 7 April 1986, 23.

132. Helen Dewar and Milton Coleman, "Hill Gives Cautious Support," *WP*, 25 March 1986, A1, A12.

133. Burlage, "U.S. Asserts Right," 37.

134. Dewar and Coleman, "Hill Gives Cautious Support," A12.

135. Parks, "Crossing the Line," 45.

136. Ronald Reagan, "Transcript of President Reagan's News Conference," *WP*, 10 April 1986, A32.

137. Robert Fisk, "Arabs Urged to Hit US Embassies," *Times*, 26 March 1986, 1.

138. Dickey, "Libya Silent," A21.

139. Christopher Dickey, "Qaddafi Takes Militant Tone on Crisis in Gulf of Sidra," *WP*, 26 March 1986, A1.

140. CIA Foreign Broadcast Information Service, "Al-Qadhdhafi Addresses Rally," *Foreign Broadcast Information Service Daily Report—Middle East and Africa*, 31 March 1986, Q8.

141. Vox Militaris, "The U.S. Strike against Libya: Operation El Dorado Canyon," *Army Quarterly and Defence Journal* 116 (April 1986): 136.

142. Fisk, "Arabs Urged to Hit."

143. Wilson and Hiatt, "Navy Again Strikes," A1, A22.

144. "Europe Fearful as Arabs Back Gadaffi," *Times*, 26 March 1986, 16.

145. Bolger, *Americans at War*, 402; Martin and Walcott, *Best Laid Plans*, 284; Watson et al, "Kaddafi's Crusade," 21.

146. Vox Militaris, "U.S. Strike against Libya," 136.

147. Brief, "International Terrorism Escalates," 14 April 1986, Teicher Files, Folder "El Dorado Canyon April 14, 1986 [1 of 4]," box 91671, RRL; Felicity Barringer, "Soviet Rebuffs U.S. on Berlin Terror," *NYT*, 18 April 1986, A9. After the April 1986 U.S. air strike on Libya, which President Reagan ordered in response to the bombing of La Belle discothèque, the Soviet Foreign Ministry rejected as "cynical lies" the American claim that the Soviet government could have prevented the terrorist attack on the West Berlin nightclub.

148. Three of the four Americans killed on TWA Flight 840 were members of a close-knit Greek-American family from Annapolis, Maryland: Demetra Stylian, 52; her daughter Maria Klug, 25; and her nine-month-old granddaughter Demetra Klug. In the Parole section of Annapolis, about seven miles from the author's home, is the Greek Orthodox Cemetery of Saints Constantine and Helen. Within the cemetery is a large white marble tombstone in which the names of Demetra Stylian, Maria Klug, and Demetra Klug are chiseled. Lorraine Ahearn, "Terrorist Bomb Rips Jetliner, Killing 3 from Annapolis," *Capital*, 3 April 1986, 1.

149. Martin and Walcott, *Best Laid Plans*, 285; "Lebanese Woman Sought in TWA Bombing," *Capital*, 5 April 1986, 1, 10.

150. Martin and Walcott, *Best Laid Plans*, 285; Church et al., "Targeting Gaddafi," 20.

151. Martin and Walcott, *Best Laid Plans*, 285–86. During the trial of the five suspects accused of bombing La Belle discothèque, German prosecutors presented as evidence transcripts of intercepted cables sent from the Libyan people's bureau in East Berlin to Tripoli. Shortly before the bombing the people's bureau sent the following message: "Expect the result tomorrow morning—it is God's will." After the attack the people's bureau made the following report: "At 1:30 in the morning, one of the acts was carried out with success, without leaving behind a trace." Peter Finn, "4 Convicted in '86 Berlin Nightclub Bombing," *WP*, 14 November 2001, A30.

152. Stewart Powell and Robert A. Kittle, "Can Reagan Make Qadhafi Cry Uncle?" *U.S. News & World Report*, 21 April 1986, 6.

153. Woodward, *Veil*, 445; Venkus, *Raid on Qaddafi*, 67; William Drozdiak, "Murder Trial in Disco Bombing Opens in Berlin," *WP*, 19 November 1997, A23.

154. Woodward, *Veil*, 445.

155. CIA Foreign Broadcast Information Service, "Libya Deemed Responsible for Lockerbie Bombing," *FBIS Concatenated Daily Reports 1991*, 27 June 1991, 3; DOS Office of the Coordinator for Counterterrorism, *Patterns of Global Terrorism: 1991*, Annual report, April 1992, 78; Drozdiak, "Murder Trial Opens," A23, A27; "Five Go on Trial in Berlin over 1986 Bombing of Disco," *NYT*, 19 November 1997, A5.

156. Finn, "4 Convicted"; Steven Erlanger, "4 Guilty in 1986 Disco Bombing, Linked to Libya, in West Berlin," *NYT*, 14 November 2001, A5.

157. Erlanger, "4 Guilty in Disco Bombing." In the spring of 2001 a secret memorandum that detailed a conversation between Qaddafi and Michael Sterner, the principal foreign policy adviser to German Chancellor Gerhard Schroeder, was leaked by a source within the German Foreign Ministry to the press. According to the document, "Qaddafi admitted that Libya took part in terrorist actions (La Belle, Lockerbie)." The judge in the trial of the discothèque bombing sought the testimony of Mr. Sterner, but the German government refused to let him testify, citing national security concerns.

Chapter 5. Planning to Strike Qaddafi

1. Reagan, *American Life*, 517, 518; Martin and Walcott, *Best Laid Plans*, 286; Whitaker et al., "Targeting a 'Mad Dog,'" 22; Church et al., "Targeting Gaddafi," 21; Brief, "Questions and Answers for Press Spokesmen," 14 April 1986, Stark Files, Folder "Libya–El Dorado Canyon [9 of 10]," box 91747, RRL.

2. Martin and Walcott, *Best Laid Plans*, 313.

3. Church et al., "Targeting Gaddafi," 21.

4. Bolger, *Americans at War*, 405–06; "Reagan Ordered Air Strikes to Preempt Libyan Terrorists," *Aviation Week & Space Technology* 124 (21 April 1986): 22–23; Watson et al., "Kaddafi's Crusade," 21; Martin and Walcott, *Best Laid Plans*, 289–90; Gates, *From the Shad-*

ows, 353; Leslie H. Gelb, "U.S. Aides Deny Attack Is Start of an Escalation," *NYT,* 16 April 1986, A15.

5. Venkus, *Raid on Qaddafi,* 34; Breast, "CV in Action," S-27; Bolger, *Americans at War,* 407.

6. Parks, "Crossing the Line," 46.

7. Brief, "United States Navy Observations on El Dorado Canyon," Briefing for the Secretary of Defense, Partially declassified, Control no. 658–88 CNO/DCNO (NW), box 10; CTF Six Zero Message, DTG 131258ZAPR86, Partially declassified, CNO/DCNO (LOG); Stumpf, "Air War with Libya," 47–48; Breast, "CV in Action," S-29; "Med Forces Move; Security Tightens," *NT,* 21 April 1986, 4; Bolger, *Americans at War,* 418.

8. Breast, "CV in Action," S-29.

9. Bolger, *Americans at War,* 410; Parks, "Crossing the Line," 47.

10. Bolger, *Americans at War,* 407, 410; Gelb, "Aides Deny Attack Is Escalation"; Harris, *Libya,* 72, 73. Lillian Craig Harris mentioned "fifteen serious assassination attempts . . . on Qadhafi since 1976, almost all conducted by the military." Harris, *Libya,* 76.

11. Bolger, *Americans at War,* 407, 409.

12. Watson et al., "Kaddafi's Crusade," 23; Weinberger, *Fighting for Peace,* 192; Deborah Hart Strober and Gerald S. Strober, *Reagan: The Man and His Presidency* (New York: Houghton Mifflin, 1998), 382.

13. Shultz, *Turmoil and Triumph,* 683–84.

14. Crowe with Chanoff, *Line of Fire,* 133, 136.

15. Meese, *With Reagan,* 205; Shultz, *Turmoil and Triumph,* 684; Martin and Walcott, *Best Laid Plans,* 286–88; Reagan, *American Life,* 518.

16. Martin and Walcott, *Best Laid Plans,* 286–88; Bolger, *Americans at War,* 409–11.

17. Martin and Walcott, *Best Laid Plans,* 286–88.

18. Parks, "Crossing the Line," 47; Martin and Walcott, *Best Laid Plans,* 286–88.

19. Bernard Weinraub, "U.S. Calls Libya Raid a Success; 'Choice Is Theirs,' Reagan Says; Moscow Cancels Shultz Talks; Qaddafi Is Warned," *NYT,* 16 April 1986, A20.

20. Terry, "Appraisal of Response," 66; Martin and Walcott, *Best Laid Plans,* 286–88.

21. Martin and Walcott, *Best Laid Plans,* 287; Report, "Lessons Learned," 31.

22. Martin and Walcott, *Best Laid Plans,* 287–88.

23. North with Novak, *Under Fire,* 216.

24. Brief, "Questions and Answers for Press Spokesmen."

25. Bolger, *Americans at War,* 411, 414; Parks, "Crossing the Line," 48.

26. Parks, "Crossing the Line," 48–49.

27. Crowe with Chanoff, *Line of Fire,* 134; Anderson, "Libya's Qaddafi," 67; Venkus, *Raid on Qaddafi,* 7. There was a report that during the 15 April 1986 U.S. air strike outraged Libyan regular military personnel attacked members of revolutionary committees, who held the keys to lockers containing antiaircraft ammunition but were not available to distribute the ammunition in a timely fashion. Harris, *Libya,* 58.

28. Bolger, *Americans at War,* 411–13; "U.S. Demonstrates Advanced Weapons Technology in Libya," *Aviation Week & Space Technology* 124 (21 April 1986): 18, 21; Parks, "Crossing the Line," 49; Anthony H. Cordesman, "After the Raid: The Emerging Lessons

from the U.S. Attack on Libya," *Armed Forces* 5 (August 1986): 360; "Reagan Ordered Air Strikes," 22; Edgar Ulsamer, "Stealth in the Nick of Time," *Air Force Magazine* 69 (November 1986): 29.

29. Pat Towell, "After Raid on Libya, New Questions on Hill," *Congressional Quarterly Weekly Report* 44 (19 April 1986): 838; Crowe with Chanoff, *Line of Fire*, 137. Colonel Venkus argued that the raid would not have been carried out without the backing of at least one ally. Therefore the cooperation of the British government, not tactical planning, was the leading factor behind the use of U.K.–based F-111Fs. In Venkus's opinion, employing the F-111Fs had nothing to do with hitting a certain number of targets with a desired payload and had everything to do with securing allied involvement. On the other hand, on 21 April 1986 the *Wall Street Journal* reported that the Air Force had lobbied to take part in the air strike and that General Rogers had recommended the five targets to give the service an opportunity to demonstrate its long-range force projection capabilities. Venkus, *Raid on Qaddafi*, 159–60. Walter J. Boyne, the prolific Air Force historian, agrees with Admiral Crowe. In a 1999 article in *Air Force Magazine*, Boyne wrote: "When Washington decreed that there would be only one attack, it became absolutely necessary to mount a joint operation because only the inclusion of heavy USAF attack aircraft could provide the firepower needed to ensure that the operation would be more than a pinprick attack." Walter J. Boyne, "El Dorado Canyon," *Air Force Magazine* 82 (March 1999): 59–60.

30. "Planes Launch from 4 Bases," *AFT*, 28 April 1986, 18; Venkus, *Raid on Qaddafi*, 6, 8, 15–16.

31. Bolger, *Americans at War*, 413–14; Venkus, *Raid on Qaddafi*, 2; Hans Halberstadt, *F-111 Aardvark* (London: Windrow and Greene, 1992), 5; Jim Garamone, "F-111 'Most Capable Airplane' for Libya Raid," *AFT*, 28 April 1986, 4.

32. Garamone, "Most Capable Airplane"; Cordesman, "After the Raid," 360; Venkus, *Raid on Qaddafi*, 8.

33. Parks, "Crossing the Line," 49; Bolger, *Americans at War*, 414–15; J. D. Mayfield, "Bombs Away: High Tech in a Terrorist War," *Soldier of Fortune*, August 1986, 83; Venkus, *Raid on Qaddafi*, 10, 51.

34. Venkus, *Raid on Qaddafi*, 50.

35. Parks, "Crossing the Line," 49; Bolger, *Americans at War*, 414–15; Venkus, *Raid on Qaddafi*, 51; "U.S. Demonstrates," 21.

36. Margaret Thatcher, *The Downing Street Years* (New York: Harper Collins, 1993), 443, 445; Parks, "Crossing the Line," 50; "Basis for UK's Decision over Use of Air Bases," *Jane's Defence Weekly* 5 (26 April 1986): 740; Shultz, *Turmoil and Triumph*, 684; Vox Militaris, "U.S. Strike against Libya," 137–38; Strober and Strober, *Reagan*, 383–84.

37. DOS, "The President [Reagan]: News Conference of April 9 (Excerpts)," *Department of State Bulletin*, June 1986, 24–25.

38. Church et al., "Targeting Gaddafi," 21.

39. Bolger, *Americans at War*, 406; Parks, "Crossing the Line," 50; Stephen E. Anno and William E. Einspahr, "Command and Control and Communications Lessons Learned: Iranian Rescue, Falklands Conflict, Grenada Invasion, Libya Raid," Research report (Maxwell AFB, Ala.: Air War College, 1988), 55.

40. Venkus, *Raid on Qaddafi*, 85–86; Martin and Walcott, *Best Laid Plans*, 274.

41. Martin and Walcott, *Best Laid Plans*, 271.

42. Venkus, *Raid on Qaddafi*, 41–43, 55–56.

43. Ibid., 62, 64–66; Brief, "Operations in the Vicinity of Libya, January–April 1986," Part of Navy–Air Force Brief to the Secretary of Defense on Operations in the Vicinity of Libya from January to April 1986, 15–19 September 1986, Partially declassified, Control no. 658–88, CNO/DCNO (NW), box 10.

44. Brief, "United States Air Force Observations on El Dorado Canyon," Briefing for the Secretary of Defense, Partially declassified, Control no. 658–88, CNO/DCNO (NW), box 10.

45. Martin and Walcott, *Best Laid Plans*, 292.

46. Ibid., 292–93; Venkus, *Raid on Qaddafi*, 84–85.

47. Venkus, *Raid on Qaddafi*, 56, 86–87.

48. Ibid., 87; Martin and Walcott, *Best Laid Plans*, 293.

49. Bolger, *Americans at War*, 415; Venkus, *Raid on Qaddafi*, 69, 70.

50. Venkus, *Raid on Qaddafi*, 88–89.

51. Martin and Walcott, *Best Laid Plans*, 293; Venkus, *Raid on Qaddafi*, 91.

52. Venkus, *Raid on Qaddafi*, 88–89, 91–93.

53. Martin and Walcott, *Best Laid Plans*, 294–97.

54. Venkus, *Raid on Qaddafi*, 89, 91.

55. Ibid., 70–71.

56. Martin and Walcott, *Best Laid Plans*, 294–95.

57. Ibid., 295; Venkus, *Raid on Qaddafi*, 92.

58. Martin and Walcott, *Best Laid Plans*, 295.

59. Venkus, *Raid on Qaddafi*, 93, 98.

60. Ibid., 94–95.

61. Ibid., 95.

62. Ibid., 96.

63. Bolger, *Americans at War*, 415; Report, "Lessons Learned," 34.

64. Parks, "Crossing the Line," 49.

65. Bolger, *Americans at War*, 416; Report, "Lessons Learned," 50; "Planes Launch from 4 Bases," 18; "U.S. Demonstrates," 20; Frank Elliot and Len Famiglietti, "Training, Skill Used to Hilt in Raid on Libya," *NT*, 28 April 1986, 18; Brief, "United States Navy Observations."

66. Martin and Walcott, *Best Laid Plans*, 295; Venkus, *Raid on Qaddafi*, 99–100. The weather forecast for the Tripoli strike called for winds from the west-southwest. By the time the first bombs hit Aziziyah the winds over the compound had shifted dramatically to the east-southeast. Report, "Lessons Learned," 92.

67. Martin and Walcott, *Best Laid Plans*, 295–96.

68. Venkus, *Raid on Qaddafi*, 154.

69. Elliot and Famiglietti, "Training, Skill Used," 18; Bolger, *Americans at War*, 417–18; "Planes Launch from 4 Bases," 18; "U.S. Air Striking Power," *NT*, 28 April 1986, 40.

70. Venkus, *Raid on Qaddafi*, 13, 87, 176n; Martin and Walcott, *Best Laid Plans*, 302; Parks, "Crossing the Line," 51.

71. Venkus, *Raid on Qaddafi*, 97.

72. Martin and Walcott, *Best Laid Plans*, 298; Venkus, *Raid on Qaddafi*, 98–99; Brief, "United States Air Force Observations"; Richard K. Halloran, "The Tactics of Techno-warfare," *Regardies*, July 1986, 76.

73. Martin and Walcott, *Best Laid Plans*, 297.

74. Admiral Breast was senior in rank to Admiral Mauz but, since the *Coral Sea* battle group was preparing to depart the Mediterranean, Mauz retained command of Task Force 60, which he had inherited from Admiral Jeremiah following Operation Attain Document III. Breast served as battle force strike warfare commander for the Attain Document series of operations and for El Dorado Canyon. Hartmann, *Naval Renaissance*, 245.

75. Bolger, *Americans at War*, 418.

76. Stumpf, "Air War with Libya," 48.

77. Anno and Einspahr, "Command and Control and Communications," 34; Venkus, *Raid on Qaddafi*, 65.

78. Parks, "Crossing the Line," 50; Bolger, *Americans at War*, 418–19.

79. Martin and Walcott, *Best Laid Plans*, 291.

80. Bolger, *Americans at War*, 416; Anno and Einspahr, "Command and Control and Communications," 53.

81. Bernard Weinraub, "U.S. Sends Envoy to Elicit Support on Libya Response," *NYT*, 13 April 1986, A1, A15; James M. Markham, "Walters Lobbies Allies to Act against Qaddafi," *NYT*, 14 April 1986, A6.

82. George J. Church et al., "Hitting the Source," *Time*, 28 April 1986, 26; "The Bombs of April," *NYT*, 16 April 1986, A26; Parks, "Crossing the Line," 50–51.

83. Martin and Walcott, *Best Laid Plans*, 290.

84. "Why Britain Backed US Air Attack on Libya," *Times*, 16 April 1986, 4.

85. Fred Hiatt, "Use of Air Force Planes Raises Questions," *WP*, 20 April 1986, A24.

86. Thatcher, *Downing Street Years*, 446; "Basis for UK's Decision," 740; Shultz, *Turmoil and Triumph*, 685.

87. Church et al., "Hitting the Source," 26.

88. Weinberger, *Fighting for Peace*, 192.

89. Steve Eisenstadt, "Overflights Long a Thorn in International Relations," *NT*, 28 April 1986, 14.

90. Martin and Walcott, *Best Laid Plans*, 292; Venkus, *Raid on Qaddafi*, 86.

91. Reagan, *American Life*, 519.

92. Crowe with Chanoff, *Line of Fire*, 137; Weinberger, *Fighting for Peace*, 191–92; William R. Doerner, David Halevy, and Bruce van Voorst, "In the Dead of the Night," *Time*, 28 April 1986, 29; Martin and Walcott, *Best Laid Plans*, 290.

93. U.S. Embassy The Hague to Secretary of State, "EC Foreign Ministers' April 14 Statement on Terrorism," Cable, 15 April 1986, Stark Files, Folder "Libya–El Dorado Canyon [2 of 10]," box 91747, RRL.

94. Richard Owen, "EEC Imposes Diplomatic Sanctions Only," *Times*, 15 April 1986, 1.

95. Richard Owen, "EEC Caution Upsets US," *Times*, 15 April 1986, 7; Church et al., "Targeting Gaddafi," 24; "Raid Sparks European Protests, Special NATO and EEC Sessions," *Aviation Week & Space Technology* 124 (21 April 1986): 25.

96. Martin and Walcott, *Best Laid Plans*, 314.

97. Brief, "Questions and Answers for Press Spokesmen."

98. Martin and Walcott, *Best Laid Plans*, 299; Breast, "CV in Action," S-29.

99. Bolger, *Americans at War*, 417–19.

100. CTF Six Zero Message, DTG 141806ZAPR86, Partially declassified, *King*, box 2.

Chapter 6. Operation El Dorado Canyon

1. Martin and Walcott, *Best Laid Plans*, 300; Venkus, *Raid on Qaddafi*, 100.

2. Martin and Walcott, *Best Laid Plans*, 300; Venkus, *Raid on Qaddafi*, 101.

3. Martin and Walcott, *Best Laid Plans*, 300.

4. Halloran, "Tactics of Technowarfare," 76.

5. Martin and Walcott, *Best Laid Plans*, 300–301; Report, "Lessons Learned," 7.

6. Venkus, *Raid on Qaddafi*, 3–4.

7. Bolger, *Americans at War*, 419; Report, "Lessons Learned," 34.

8. Brief, "United States Air Force Observations"; Martin and Walcott, *Best Laid Plans*, 302.

9. Martin and Walcott, *Best Laid Plans*, 303; Venkus, *Raid on Qaddafi*, 2; Davies and Thornborough, *F-111 Aardvark*, 121.

10. Report, "Lessons Learned," 36; Martin and Walcott, *Best Laid Plans*, 303; Venkus, *Raid on Qaddafi*, 13, 32.

11. Fred Hiatt, "U.S. Attack on Libya: A Raid that Went Right," *WP*, 20 April 1986, A24; Halloran, "Tactics of Technowarfare," 75.

12. Venkus, *Raid on Qaddafi*, 22.

13. Hallion, *Storm over Iraq*, 106.

14. Venkus, *Raid on Qaddafi*, 49.

15. Martin and Walcott, *Best Laid Plans*, 303.

16. Brief, "United States Navy Observations"; Bolger, *Americans at War*, 419, 420; Martin and Walcott, *Best Laid Plans*, 301, 304; Hiatt, "U.S. Attack on Libya," 24; Report, "Lessons Learned," 31, 32, 33; CTF Six Zero, DTG 142220ZAPR86, Declassified, *King*, box 1; Dave Lee and Chris Holmes, "Operation El Dorado: The Men Behind the Headlines," *All Hands* 831 (June 1986): 27; David C. Isby, "Libyan Submarine Force Poses Limited Threat to Sixth Fleet," *Jane's Defence Weekly* 5 (17 May 1986): 882.

17. Parks, "Crossing the Line," 51.

18. Strober and Strober, *Reagan*, 381–82. Present at the meeting were President Reagan, Vice President Bush, Secretary of State Shultz, Secretary of Defense Weinberger, CIA Director Casey, Chairman of the JCS Admiral Crowe, and National Security Adviser Poindexter; Senators Robert Dole (R-Kans.), Robert Byrd (D-W.Va.), Richard Lugar (R-Ind.), and Barry Goldwater (R-Ariz.); and Representatives Thomas O'Neill (D-Mass.), Robert Michel (R-Ill.), James Wright (D-Tex.), Dante Fascell (D-Fla.), William Broomfield (R-Mich.), Les Aspin (D-Wis.), and William Dickinson (R-Ala.). Parks, "Crossing the Line," 51; Untitled note, n.d., Fortier Files, Folder "Libya (Fortier File) [12 of 12]," box 91673, RRL.

19. "Reagan Ordered Air Strikes," 23; Bolger, *Americans at War,* 420; Stumpf, "Air War with Libya," 48.

20. Stumpf, "Air War with Libya," 48.

21. Bolger, *Americans at War,* 417, 420–21. In the issues of *Newsweek* and *Time* that hit newsstands on Monday, 14 April, both magazines speculated that President Reagan might use F-111s based in the United Kingdom to attack Libya. They also reported that the British government had approved Reagan's request to use the planes. *Newsweek* reported that several tanker aircraft had deployed from the United States to bases in the United Kingdom. *Newsweek,* 21 April 1986, 23, 25; *Time,* 21 April 1986, 24.

22. Stumpf, "Air War with Libya," 48; Report, "Lessons Learned," 33–34, 37; "U.S. Demonstrates," 20; Bolger, *Americans at War,* 421; Cordesman, "After the Raid," 358; Halloran, "Tactics of Technowarfare," 72; Martin and Walcott, *Best Laid Plans,* 304.

23. Venkus, *Raid on Qaddafi,* 30–33.

24. Ibid., 24; Martin and Walcott, *Best Laid Plans,* 304.

25. Venkus, *Raid on Qaddafi,* 101–2.

26. Martin and Walcott, *Best Laid Plans,* 304.

27. Ibid., 304–5; Bolger, *Americans at War,* 421; Venkus, *Raid on Qaddafi,* 48–49.

28. Venkus, *Raid on Qaddafi,* 52–53, 71; Ulsamer, "Stealth in the Nick of Time," 29; Brief, "Joint Operation El Dorado Canyon: USAF Attack against Tripoli, Libya 14 April 1986," Part of Navy–Air Force Brief to the Secretary of Defense on Operations in the Vicinity of Libya from January to April 1986, 15–19 September, Partially declassified, Control no. 658–88, CNO/DCNO (NW), box 10; Report, "Lessons Learned," 50.

29. Hallion, *Storm over Iraq,* 107; Bolger, *Americans at War,* 417, 421.

30. Report, "Lessons Learned," 37; Lehman, *Command of Seas,* 373.

31. Bolger, *Americans at War,* 422; Cordesman, "After the Raid," 360. William J. Foltz, a political scientist at Yale University, estimated that full operational readiness of the Libyan air defense system required between fifteen thousand and eighteen thousand personnel. He further estimated that between six thousand and nine thousand Libyans and two thousand foreigners were available to man the system. Therefore, the air defense system operated under 60 percent of its equipment capacity. Foltz, "Libya's Military Power," 6. Secretary of the Navy Lehman stated that the Libyan air defense system operated under the supervision of three thousand Soviet technicians. Lehman, *Command of Seas,* 373. Air Force and Navy electronic monitoring of Libyan air defense activity revealed that radar operators at the SAM and AAA sites did not activate their equipment until four minutes before the first bombs struck Aziziyah. David M. North, "Air Force, Navy Brief Congress on Lessons from Libya Strikes," *Aviation Week & Space Technology* 124 (2 June 1986): 63.

32. Bolger, *Americans at War,* 422; Bermudez, "Libyan SAMs and Air Defences," 881.

33. Lee and Holmes, "Operation El Dorado," 27.

34. Martin and Walcott, *Best Laid Plans,* 305.

35. Russell Watson, John Barry, and John Walcott, "Reagan's Raiders," *Newsweek,* 28 April 1986, 28; Church et al., "Hitting the Source," 17; Stumpf, "Air War with Libya," 48.

36. Bermudez, "Libyan SAMs and Air Defences," 881; Stumpf, "Air War with Libya," 48.

37. Lee and Holmes, "Operation El Dorado," 28.

38. A U.S. Air Force Combat Pilot, "'How I Bombed Qaddafi': A Personal Account of an American Blow against Terrorism," *Popular Mechanics*, July 1987, 112; Andrew Cockburn, "Sixty Seconds over Tripoli," *Playboy*, May 1987, 146, 164.

39. U.S. Air Force Pilot, "'How I Bombed Qaddafi,'" 111.

40. Martin and Walcott, *Best Laid Plans*, 306.

41. Ibid.; Richard Stengel, Dean Fischer, and Roland Flamini, "So Close, Yet So Far," *Time*, 28 April 1986, 33.

42. Stengel, Fischer, and Flamini, "So Close," 33.

43. Crowe with Chanoff, *Line of Fire*, 142.

44. Martin and Walcott, *Best Laid Plans*, 306.

45. Venkus, *Raid on Qaddafi*, 72.

46. Martin and Walcott, *Best Laid Plans*, 306–07.

47. Davies and Thornborough, *F-111 Aardvark*, 121; Venkus, *Raid on Qaddafi*, 73.

48. Venkus, *Raid on Qaddafi*, 74; Martin and Walcott, *Best Laid Plans*, 307.

49. Martin and Walcott, *Best Laid Plans*, 310; Edward Schumacher, "Qaddafi, on TV, Condemns Attack," *NYT*, 17 April 1986, A22; Christopher Dickey, "Qaddafi Makes Appearance on TV," *WP*, 17 April 1986, A24.

50. Venkus, *Raid on Qaddafi*, 51–52, 76, 79–80, 109; Ruth Marshall, "A View from the Bull's-eye," *Newsweek*, 28 April 1986, 30; Meacham, "Hits and Misses," 14; Watson, Barry, and Walcott, "Reagan's Raiders," 31; "Libyan SAM Missiles Hit Civilian Areas, Says USA," *Jane's Defence Weekly* 5 (26 April 1986): 737.

51. Venkus, *Raid on Qaddafi*, 73, 75–79.

52. Ibid., 96; Martin and Walcott, *Best Laid Plans*, 309; Davies and Thornborough, *F-111 Aardvark*, 121. After the mission technicians discovered that the cooling lines in several Pave Tack pods were clogged, which caused the systems to overheat and resulted in a number of aborted attacks. Davies and Thornborough, *F-111 Aardvark*, 120.

53. Venkus, *Raid on Qaddafi*, 80–81.

54. Ibid., 81.

55. Martin and Walcott, *Best Laid Plans*, 308.

56. Ibid.; Venkus, *Raid on Qaddafi*, 81; Walt Morrissette, "DoD Details Civilian Damage in Libya Raid," *AFT*, 26 May 1986, 12.

57. Venkus, *Raid on Qaddafi*, 81–83; Report, "Lessons Learned," 36.

58. Halloran, "Tactics of Technowarfare," 76; Martin and Walcott, *Best Laid Plans*, 308.

59. Martin and Walcott, *Best Laid Plans*, 308.

60. Venkus, *Raid on Qaddafi*, 83–84; Martin and Walcott, *Best Laid Plans*, 309; Morrissette, "Civilian Damage."

61. Stumpf, "Air War with Libya," 48.

62. Bolger, *Americans at War*, 424; Parks, "Crossing the Line," 51.

63. Stumpf, "Air War with Libya," 48.

64. Parks, "Crossing the Line," 51.

65. "CVW-13/CV-43," 66.

66. Lee and Holmes, "Operation El Dorado," 28.

67. Report, "Lessons Learned," 41, 88; Hiatt, "U.S. Attack on Libya," A24; Morrissette, "Civilian Damage."

68. Stumpf, "Air War with Libya," 48.

69. Anderson, "Libya's Qaddafi," 86.

70. Crowe with Chanoff, *Line of Fire*, 142, 143.

71. Speakes with Pack, *Speaking Out*, 182.

72. DOS, "U.S. Exercises Right of Self-Defense against Libyan Terrorism," *Department of State Bulletin*, June 1986, 1–2.

73. Ronald Reagan, "Reagan's Remarks on Raid," *NYT*, 16 April 1986, A20.

74. DOS, "U.S. Exercises Right," 8.

75. Venkus, *Raid on Qaddafi*, 104–5.

76. "Countdown to Operation El Dorado Canyon," *Jane's Defence Weekly* 5 (26 April 1986): 736; Venkus, *Raid on Qaddafi*, 104.

77. Lee and Holmes, "Operation El Dorado," 28.

78. Stumpf, "Air War with Libya," 48; "Countdown to El Dorado Canyon," 736.

79. Lee and Holmes, "Operation El Dorado," 28.

80. Breast, "CV in Action," S-32.

81. Hiatt, "U.S. Attack on Libya," A24.

82. Stumpf, "Air War with Libya," 48; Report, "Lessons Learned," 41; Bolger, *Americans at War*, 424.

83. Venkus, *Raid on Qaddafi*, 105–6.

84. Ibid., 106–7.

85. U.S. Air Force Pilot, "'How I Bombed Qaddafi,'" 114, 153.

86. Martin and Walcott, *Best Laid Plans*, 309.

87. Venkus, *Raid on Qaddafi*, 107.

88. Ibid., 107–8.

89. Martin and Walcott, *Best Laid Plans*, 309–10.

90. Ibid., 310; Venkus, *Raid on Qaddafi*, 116–18.

91. "2 Listed as Killed in Raid," *AFT*, 28 April 1986, 4; "Countdown to El Dorado Canyon," 736.

92. Venkus, *Raid on Qaddafi*, 109, 112; U.S. Air Force Pilot, "'How I Bombed Qaddafi,'" 153; "Countdown to El Dorado Canyon," 736.

93. Venkus, *Raid on Qaddafi*, 113–14.

94. Ibid., 114.

95. "Countdown to El Dorado Canyon," 736; Brief, "United States Air Force Observations."

96. Venkus, *Raid on Qaddafi*, 129; "2 Listed as Killed."

97. Gerald M. Boyd, "U.S. Is Stepping Up Rebuke to Allies on World Terror," *NYT*, 17 April 1986, A22.

98. Venkus, *Raid on Qaddafi*, 129–30. On 16 January 1989 the arrival ceremony for the body of Captain Ribas-Dominicci was held at Dover AFB in Delaware. The Libyans announced earlier that they would be handing the body of one of the lost aviators to representatives of the Vatican. In their announcement the Libyans erroneously identified the

body as the remains of Captain Lorence. The mistaken identification was not discovered until after the body was in the custody of U.S. officials. On 14 January the body was positively identified by U.S. military forensic experts, and the two families had to struggle with this very emotional development. Qaddafi had held Ribas-Dominicci's body as a potential bargaining chip for over two years, hoping that it would help release Libyan assets held by the United States. Confronted with the possibility of renewed U.S. military action following the discovery of his chemical warfare capabilities, Qaddafi prudently released the body. Venkus, *Raid on Qaddafi*, 172–74.

99. "Libya Strike Details Revealed," *Flight International* 129 (26 April 1986): 13; "Station Attacked," *NT*, 28 April 1986, 18; "Missiles Shake Island," *Times*, 16 April 1986, 1; Judith Miller, "Italian Island, a Libyan Target, Escapes Unscathed," *NYT*, 16 April 1986, A15.

100. Parks, "Crossing the Line," 52; Watson, Barry, and Walcott, "Reagan's Raiders," 26; David Blundy, "Who Rules in Tripoli?" *ST*, 27 April 1986, 27; Blundy and Lycett, *Qaddafi and Libyan Revolution*, 11–12; Marshall, "View from Bull's-eye," 30; Martin and Walcott, *Best Laid Plans*, 310–1.

101. Martin and Walcott, *Best Laid Plans*, 310–1.

102. Venkus, *Raid on Qaddafi*, 166; Hallion, *Storm over Iraq*, 32.

103. Hallion, *Storm over Iraq*, 32.

104. Wilcox, *Wings of Fury*, 158; Davies and Thornborough, *F-111 Aardvark*, 85.

105. Bolger, *Americans at War*, 428.

106. Martin and Walcott, *Best Laid Plans*, 362.

107. Halloran, *Tactics of Technowarfare*, 78.

108. Bolger, *Americans at War*, 428–29; Martin and Walcott, *Best Laid Plans*, 362; Barrett Tillman, "Strike U," *United States Naval Institute Proceedings* 113 (January 1987): 83–84; Lehman, *Command of Seas*, 348.

109. Lehman, *Command of Seas*, 349; Bolger, *Americans at War*, 429.

110. Bolger, *Americans at War*, 429.

111. North, "Air Force, Navy Brief Congress," 63.

112. Report, "Lessons Learned," 40; Parks, "Crossing the Line," 51; Hiatt, "U.S. Attack on Libya," A24.

113. Parks, "Crossing the Line," 51.

114. Report, "Lessons Learned," 5; Lehman, *Command of Seas*, 376.

115. Bolger, *Americans at War*, 430.

116. James Cable, "Gunboat Diplomacy's Future," *United States Naval Institute Proceedings* 112 (August 1986): 38, 40.

117. Report, "Lessons Learned," 4–5.

Chapter 7. The Aftermath of Operation El Dorado Canyon

1. DOS, "U.S. Exercises Right," 4.

2. DOD, *Report of the Secretary of Defense Caspar W. Weinberger to the Congress on the FY 1988/FY 1989 Budget and FY 1988–92 Defense Programs, January 12, 1987* (Washington, D.C.: GPO, 1987), 61.

3. Meacham, "Hits and Misses," 14; Martin and Walcott, *Best Laid Plans*, 311–12.

4. Martin and Walcott, *Best Laid Plans*, 311.

5. Venkus, *Raid on Qaddafi*, 149.

6. Ibid., 144–45.

7. Bolger, *Americans at War*, 423.

8. Venkus, *Raid on Qaddafi*, 144–45.

9. Martin and Walcott, *Best Laid Plans*, 311–12. The length of flight in Operation El Dorado Canyon was five times that of a normal EF-111A sortie and six times that of a normal F-111F sortie. Brief, "Joint Operation El Dorado Canyon: USAF Attack against Tripoli, Libya 14 April 1986."

10. Venkus, *Raid on Qaddafi*, 148.

11. Martin and Walcott, *Best Laid Plans*, 312.

12. Venkus, *Raid on Qaddafi*, 149.

13. Martin and Walcott, *Best Laid Plans*, 312.

14. Weinberger, *Fighting for Peace*, 198.

15. Martin and Walcott, *Best Laid Plans*, 312.

16. Lehman, *Command of Seas*, 375–76.

17. Crowe with Chanoff, *Line of Fire*, 145.

18. Bolger, *Americans at War*, 431.

19. Parks, "Crossing the Line," 52.

20. Ibid.; Bolger, *Americans at War*, 431–32; Richard K. Halloran, "Hyperbole and Grins," *NYT*, 18 April 1986, A16.

21. Michael R. Gordon, "7 American Planes Aborted Mission," *NYT*, 18 April 1986, A1.

22. Wilson, "Qaddafi Was Target," A1.

23. Parks, "Crossing the Line," 52; Church et al., "Hitting the Source," 26; "Reagan Decides It Had to Be Done," *Economist* 299 (19 April 1986): 17; "A Poll: Europe vs. the U.S.," *Newsweek*, 28 April 1986, 22.

24. Rick Maze, "Hill for Air Strike," *NT*, 28 April 1986, 14.

25. Towell, "After Raid on Libya," 839.

26. U.S. Senate, Senator Byrd of West Virginia Speaking on the Military Operation against Libya, 99th Cong., 2nd sess. *Congressional Record* (15 April 1986), vol. 132, pt. 46, S4316.

27. Towell, "After Raid on Libya," 839.

28. Henry Trewhitt, "A New War—And New Risks," *U.S. News & World Report*, 28 April 1986, 20.

29. "Britain Cannot Be Supine or Passive towards Terrorism," *Times*, 16 April 1986, 4.

30. "Appointment in Tripoli," *Economist* 299 (19 April 1986): 11.

31. Vox Militaris, "U.S. Strike against Libya," 148.

32. "Britain Cannot Be Supine or Passive."

33. "Alone but Right," *ST*, 20 April 1986, 26.

34. Vox Militaris, "U.S. Strike against Libya," 148.

35. "Poll: Europe vs. U.S," 22.

36. Margaret Thatcher, "Thatcher: A Friend in Need," interview in *Newsweek*, 28 April 1986, 35.

37. Trewhitt, "New War," 21; William Drozdiak, "Bonn Cites Own Proof of Libyan Bomb at Disco," *WP*, 17 April 1986, A22.

38. Drozdiak, "Bonn Cites Proof," A22.

39. Boyd, "U.S. Stepping Up Rebuke," A22.

40. Scott Sullivan, "Why Europe Is Angry," *Newsweek*, 28 April 1986, 34.

41. Robert A. Manning, "In Western Europe, Strains among Friends," *U.S. News & World Report*, 28 April 1986, 24.

42. Burr and Collins, *Africa's Thirty Years' War*, 203.

43. Drozdiak, "Bonn Cites Proof," A21; "Raid Sparks European Protests,"25; "Poll: Europe vs. U.S.," 22.

44. Loren Jenkins, "Europeans Criticize U.S. Stand on Terror," *WP*, 20 April 1986, A25; Brian Jenkins, "What Have We Learned? How Can We Fight Back?" interview by Michael Reese, *Newsweek*, 15 September 1986, 27.

45. "The Bombs Bestir the Allies," *NYT*, 24 April 1986, A22.

46. Shultz, *Turmoil and Triumph*, 687.

47. Sullivan, "Why Europe Is Angry," 36; Richard Owen, "EEC Toughens Sanctions Against Libya," *Times*, 22 April 1986, 1.

48. Karen DeYoung, "Britain Deports 21 Libyans," *WP*, 23 April 1986, A1.

49. Boyd, "U.S. Stepping Up Rebuke," A22.

50. Beck et al., "Syrian Connection," 54; Note, "Actions against Terrorism" (Given to Allies at Summit), n.d., Stark Files, Folder "Next Steps [2 of 2]," box 91747, RRL.

51. "Texts of Statements Adopted by Leaders of 7 Industrial Democracies," *NYT*, 6 May 1986, A12.

52. "Texts of Statements"; Shultz, *Turmoil and Triumph*, 688; Martin and Walcott, *Best Laid Plans*, 366; Jacob V. Lamar, David Beckwith, and Jay Branegan, "A Summit of Substance," *Time*, 19 May 1986, 15–16.

53. Lamar, Beckwith, and Branegan, "Summit of Substance," 16.

54. David Ignatius, "Bombing Gadhafi Worked," *WP*, 13 July 1986, B5; Martin and Walcott, *Best Laid Plans*, 314, 366; DOS, "Terrorism: Its Evolving Nature," by L. Paul Bremer, *Department of State Bulletin*, May 1989, 75.

55. Celestine Bohlen, "Soviet Leader Reaffirms Support for Libya," *WP*, 17 April 1986, A25.

56. Mikhail Gorbachev, "Gorbachev Voices Solidarity to Qaddafi, Recounts 'Unheeded Warnings' to U.S.; Moscow Will 'Fulfill Commitments to Strengthen Libya's Defense Capability,'" *Current Digest of the Soviet Press* 38 (14 May 1986): 4.

57. CIA, "Moscow Balances Warnings to U.S., Commitment to Dialogue; USSR Voices Outrage, Gives Cautious Support to Libya," News analysis, 23 April 1986; Nicholas Daniloff and Maureen Santini, "From the Kremlin, a New Chill toward the U.S.," *U.S. News & World Report*, 28 April 1986, 25; Parker and Leturmy, "Libya Raid," 40.

58. Burr and Collins, *Africa's Thirty Years' War*, 203; Anderson, "Libya's Qaddafi," 87; Mark Whitaker, John Walcott, and Anne Underwood, "Getting Rid of Kaddafi," *Newsweek*, 28 April 1986, 25; George D. Moffett, "Libya Quiet after U.S. Raid—But How Long?" *CSM*, 25 June 1986, 32.

59. "Gaddafi and Terrorism: Sampling Global Opinion on the U.S. Raid and the Future," *World Press Review* 33 (June 1986): 23–24.

60. "Arabs Denounce US Action," *Jane's Defence Weekly* 5 (26 April 1986): 742.

61. Whitaker, Walcott, and Underwood, "Getting Rid of Kaddafi," 25; James Wallace and Steven Emerson, "Revenge and Anger Resound in Arab World," *U.S. News & World Report,* 28 April 1986, 27.

62. Ignatius, "Bombing Gadhafi Worked."

63. "Arabs Denounce US Action," 742.

64. Barry Rubin, "The Reagan Administration and the Middle East," in *Eagle Resurgent?: The Reagan Era in American Foreign Policy,* ed. Kenneth A. Oye, Robert J. Leiber, and Donald Rothchild (Boston: Little, Brown, 1987), 453; Anderson, "Libya's Qaddafi," 65.

65. Martin and Walcott, *Best Laid Plans,* 313–14; Tom Morganthau and Rod Nordland, "A Terrorist Jihad," *Newsweek,* 28 April 1986, 31–33; Church et al., "Hitting the Source," 19; Russell Watson, John Barry, and Milan J. Kubic, "A Syrian Smoking Gun?" *Newsweek,* 19 May 1986, 40; William Drozdiak, "Police Cooperation Led to Palestinians' Arrest," *WP,* 23 April 1986, A27. During his interrogation at Scotland Yard Hindawi revealed that one of the men involved in the bombing of the La Belle discothèque was his brother, Ahmed Mansur Hasi. Soon after, the West German police arrested Hasi and held him on suspicion of involvement in the discothèque attack. Ultimately Hasi was not charged. Drozdiak, "Murder Trial Opens," A27.

66. Dickey, "Qaddafi Makes Appearance," A1.

67. Schumacher, "Qaddafi Condemns Attack," A22.

68. Crowe with Chanoff, *Line of Fire,* 145.

69. Persico, *Casey,* 499.

70. Ignatius, "Bombing Gadhafi Worked."

71. Schumacher, "Qaddafi Condemns Attack"; Bernard Gwertzman, "Shultz Expresses Hope for a Coup to Oust Qaddafi," *NYT,* 18 April 1986, A1.

72. Gwertzman, "Shultz Expresses Hope," A1, A10.

73. Anderson, "Libya's Qaddafi," 87.

74. John Walcott and Gerald F. Seib, "Collision Course: New Signs that Libya Is Plotting Terrorism Bring Quick Response," *WSJ,* 25 August 1986, 16.

75. Anderson, "Libya's Qaddafi," 65; Ignatius, "Bombing Gadhafi Worked."

76. Harris, *Libya,* 121.

77. Martin and Walcott, *Best Laid Plans,* 316; Anderson, "Libya's Qaddafi," 86–87.

78. Gerald F. Seib, "Gadhafi Returns to Limelight in Libya, Reasserting Grip on Nation's Leadership," *WSJ,* 2 September 1986, 31.

79. Sheila Rule, "Qaddafi Calls Third World Helpless," *NYT,* 5 September 1986, A3; Allister Sparks, "Gadhafi Denounces Nonaligned; Vows to Lead Anti-Imperialist Army," *WP,* 5 September 1986, A32.

80. Rule, "Qaddafi Calls Third World Helpless."

81. Bernard Gwertzman, "U.S. Aides Divided on Further Attacks," *NYT,* 27 April 1986, A14.

82. Gelb, "Aides Deny Attack Is Escalation."

83. Martin and Walcott, *Best Laid Plans*, 312; Venkus, *Raid on Qaddafi*, 149.

84. Martin and Walcott, *Best Laid Plans*, 312.

85. Woodward, *Veil*, 471, 473; Bob Woodward, "Gadhafi Target of Secret U.S. Deception Plan," *WP*, 2 October 1986, A12.

86. Woodward, "Gadhafi Target of Plan," A12.

87. Woodward, *Veil*, 474, 475.

88. Martin and Walcott, *Best Laid Plans*, 321. In August a number of U.S. military developments took place that might have convinced Qaddafi that the United States was indeed preparing to attack his country. In mid-August Gen. Richard Lawson, deputy commander of EUCOM, visited Chad and offered U.S. support to President Habré in his ongoing struggle against Libya and Libyan-backed rebels. In late August the U.S. Sixth Fleet conducted "Operation Sea Wind" in waters off Libya. During Sea Wind carrier-based aircraft flew directly toward the Libyan coast in an attempt to elicit a response from Libyan radars. Also, in late August the U.S. Air Force transferred eighteen F-111 bombers to bases in the United Kingdom. George Tremlett, *Gadaffi: The Desert Mystic* (New York: Carroll and Graf, 1993), 259, 260.

89. Walcott and Seib, "Collision Course," A1. David Martin and John Walcott, the latter the co-author of the 25 August 1986 *Journal* article, wrote in the "Source Notes" section of their book *Best Laid Plans* that "the *Journal* story was factually accurate but seriously flawed in claiming that the United States and Libya were on a 'collision course,' suggesting that military action against Libya was imminent while failing to note that psychological warfare had been a major element of the administration's Libya policy since the beginning of 1986." Martin and Walcott, *Best Laid Plans*, 380.

90. Woodward, *Veil*, 475.

91. Woodward, "Gadhafi Target of Plan," A1.

92. David Hoffman, "President Says He Intends to Keep Gadhafi Off Balance," *WP*, 3 October 1986, A20; Martin and Walcott, *Best Laid Plans*, 321.

93. Ronald Reagan, "Reagan: Gadhafi Should 'Go to Bed . . . Wondering What We Might Do,'" interview in *WP*, 3 October 1986, A20.

94. George P. Shultz, "Shultz Defends Administration Efforts to 'Make Gadhafi Nervous,'" interview in *WP*, 4 October 1986, A12.

95. Lou Cannon, "Administration 'Hurt,'" *WP*, 4 October 1986, A1, A12.

96. Patrick E. Tyler, "Gadhafi Rule Seen in Peril Following Military Setbacks," *WP*, 27 March 1987, A1, A32; Jane Perlez, "Qaddafi, Taking Softer Tone, Urges U.S. 'Meet Us Halfway,'" *NYT*, 12 April 1987, A1, A14.

97. Perlez, "Meet Us Halfway."

98. Elaine Sciolino, "U.S. Sees Qaddafi as Being Weaker," *NYT*, 10 January 1988, A9.

99. Christopher Dickey, "A Kaddafi Comeback?" *Newsweek*, 22 February 1988, 30.

100. Jennifer Parmelee, "Libya, Despite Animus, Looks toward U.S. Ties," *WP*, 29 September 1988, A34.

101. Vandewalle, "Libyan Jamahiriyya," 36; Dirk Vandewalle, ed., *Qadhafi's Libya, 1969–1994* (New York: St. Martin's, 1995), xxxi; Omar Fayeq, "Libya's Gains and Losses from the Gulf Crisis," *Middle East International* 402 (14 June 1991): 17. In February 1993 the

International Court of Justice awarded the Aouzou Strip to Chad. Vandewalle, *Qadhafi's Libya*, xxxi.

102. DOS, "Terrorism: Its Evolving Nature," 75; Noel Koch, "The Hostage Labyrinth . . . Our 'No Negotiations' Policy May Not Have Helped," *WP*, 18 March 1990, B4.

103. Harris, *Libya*, 130.

104. Jennifer Parmelee, "Gadhafi Sees Election Aiding U.S.-Libya Ties," *WP*, 6 September 1988, A23.

105. David B. Ottaway, "U.S. Still Certain that Libya Was behind Nightclub Attack," *WP*, 12 January 1988, A18.

106. USS *John F. Kennedy* (CV 67), *Command History 1989*, AVH, encl. 3, p. 1; Fighter Squadron 32, *Command History 1989*, AVH, encl. 10, p. 3; Jon Lake, ed., *Grumman F-14 Tomcat: Shipborne Superfighter* (London, U.K.: Aerospace Publishing, 1998), 97; Roy Grossnick et al., *United States Naval Aviation, 1910–1995* (Washington, D.C.: GPO, 1997), 771.

107. Lake, *Grumman F-14 Tomcat*, 97, 98; *Kennedy, Command History 1989*, encl. 3, p. 1; George C. Wilson, "Despite New Details, Libyan MiG Incident Still Puzzling," *WP*, 26 March 1989, A16; Brendan M. Greeley, "U.S. F-14s Down Libyan MiG-23s in Dogfight over Mediterranean," *Aviation Week & Space Technology* 130 (9 January 1989): 20, 21; William Matthews, "MiGs Seemingly Goaded F-14s into Shootdown," *NT*, 16 January 1989, 6.

108. Jennifer Parmelee, "U.S. Navy Jets Shoot Down 2 Libyan Fighters; Gadhafi Seeks UN Meeting," *WP*, 5 January 1989, A1, A32.

109. George C. Wilson, "U.S. Releases Photos of Libyan Jets; Videotape Shows MiG Fighter Was Armed, Pentagon Says," *WP*, 6 January 1989, A22.

110. Molly Moore and George C. Wilson, "U.S. Navy Jets Shoot Down 2 Libyan Fighters; 'Hostile Intent' of MiGs Is Cited," *WP*, 5 January 1989, A29.

111. Richard Halloran, "U.S. Says Tape Shows Missiles on a Libyan Jet," *NYT*, 6 January 1989, A1.

112. CIA Directorate of Intelligence, *Chemical and Biological Weapons: The Poor Man's Atomic Bomb*, Intelligence assessment, December 1988, 11.

Epilogue: Lockerbie and Beyond

1. George Lardner, "French Link Libyans to Bombings," *WP*, 27 June 1991, A16.

2. Jules Kagian, "UN and Libya: A Step towards Sanctions," *Middle East International* 418 (7 February 1992) 12.

3. Takeyh, "Qadhafi's Libya," 159–60.

4. Stephen Hubbell, "Libya: Content with the Status Quo," *Middle East International* 437 (6 November 1992): 13.

5. On 25 August 2000 a letter to Qaddafi from UN Secretary General Kofi Annan was made public at the behest of the defense team at the Lockerbie trial. The letter, dated 17 February 1999 and written with the concurrence of the American and British governments, outlined the U.S.-U.K.-Libyan "understanding," which spelled out how the two Libyan suspects would be treated while in Scottish custody, and promised Qaddafi that

the two men would "not be used to undermine the Libyan regime." To many families of Lockerbie victims Annan's letter was nothing less than a grant of immunity to the Libyan leader. In their view neither Qaddafi nor his regime would be placed at risk by the outcome of the trial. On the other hand, several Clinton administration officials argued that nothing in the letter would prevent prosecutors from indicting Qaddafi in the future if there was sufficient evidence. John R. Bolton, "Appraising Qaddafi," *WP*, 29 August 2000, A17; John Lancaster, "Compromising Positions," *Washington Post Magazine*, 9 July 2000, 23, 25.

6. Donald G. McNeil, "Libyan Convicted by Scottish Court in '88 Pan Am Blast," *NYT*, 1 February 2001, A8.

7. Peter Finn, "Libyan Convicted of Lockerbie Bombing," *WP*, 1 February 2001, A1, A16.

8. Deborah Charles (Reuters), "Bush Applauds Lockerbie Verdict, Sanctions Still On," AT&T WorldNet Service, 31 January 2001.

9. Howard Schneider, "Gaddafi Dissects Lockerbie Decision," *WP*, 6 February 2001, A14; Howard Schneider, "Lockerbie Defendant Embraced by Gaddafi," *WP*, 2 February 2001, A1; Heba Saleh, "Libya: After the Trial," *Middle East International* 643 (9 February 2001): 16.

10. Howard Schneider, "Libyans Condemn Conviction by Court Gaddafi Sanctioned," *WP*, 4 February 2001, A24.

11. Daniel Benjamin and Steven Simon, "Pan Am 103: Keep Up the Fight," *WP*, 1 February 2001, A21.

12. David Johnston, "Courts a Limited Anti-Terror Weapon," *NYT*, 1 February 2001, A8; John Lancaster and Alan Sipress, "A Muted Victory against Terrorism," *WP*, 1 February 2001, A16.

13. Benjamin and Simon, "Pan Am 103."

14. Colum Lynch and John Lancaster, "U.S. Considers Easing Restrictions on Libya," *WP*, 27 February 2000, A29.

15. DOS, *Patterns of Global Terrorism: 2000*, Annual report, April 2001.

16. Andrew Cockburn, "Libya: An End to Isolation?" *National Geographic*, November 2000, 14, 16–17, 27; Heba Saleh, "Letter from Tripoli," *Middle East International* 640 (22 December 2000): 24; Howard Schneider, "The Softer Side of Libya," *WP*, 12 September 1999, A27; Barbara Slavin, "Analysis: Qadhafi's Libya," *Middle East Insight* 15 (July–August 2000): 52–53; Milton Viorst, "The Colonel in His Labyrinth," *Foreign Affairs* 78 (March–April 1999): 69; Adel Darwish, "Has the Leopard Changed Its Spots?" *Middle East* 298 (February 2000): 6.

17. Vandewalle, "Libyan Jamahiriyya," 37.

18. William L. Allen, "From the Editor," *National Geographic*, November 2000, ii; Cockburn, "End to Isolation," 3.

19. Yossef Bodansky, *Bin Laden: The Man Who Declared War on America* (Rocklin, Calif.: Forum, 1999), 225–27.

20. Al-Qaida is translated as "the Base."

21. "A Lockerbie Verdict," *WSJ*, 1 February 2001, A22.

22. George W. Bush, "Transcript of President Bush's Address," *WP*, 21 September 2001, A24.

23. George W. Bush, "Bush's Address to the Nation," *WP*, 8 October 2001, A6.

24. Mike Allen and Paul Blustein, "Bush Moves to Cut Terrorists' Support; Foreign Banks Urged to Help Freeze Assets of 27 Entities," *WP*, 25 September 2001, A1, A8; Nick Pelham, "Libya: Sea Change," *Middle East International* 660 (12 October 2001): 19–20; John K. Cooley, *Unholy Wars: Afghanistan, America, and International Terrorism* (Sterling, Va.: Pluto, 2000), 7. In a secret German government document that detailed a March 2001 conversation between Qaddafi and Michael Sterner, the chief foreign policy adviser to German Chancellor Gerhard Schroeder, Qaddafi admitted Libya's involvement in earlier terrorist actions, namely the bombings of La Belle discothèque and Pan Am Flight 103, but, "he clarified that he had abandoned terrorism and seeks the opportunity to make Libya's new position known." A source within the German Foreign Ministry leaked the document to the press later that spring. Erlanger, "4 Guilty in Disco Bombing."

Bibliography

Archival Collections

Marine Corps Historical Center, Washington, D.C.

Archives Section. Command Chronologies

Naval Historical Center, Washington, D.C.

Aviation History Branch. Command Histories
Operational Archives Branch
    Command Histories
    Records of CNO/DCNO (LOG)
    Records of CNO/DCNO (NW)
    Records of NWAC
    Records of USS *King*
Ships' History Branch. Command Histories

Ronald Reagan Library, Simi Valley, Calif.

Burns, William J., Files
Fortier, Donald, Files
Kemp, Geoffrey, Files
NSC, Executive Secretariat, Files
NSC, Near East and South Asia Directorate, Records
Stark, James, Files
Teicher, Howard, Files

U.S. Air Forces in Europe

20th Tactical Fighter Wing. *Historical Narrative.* 1 January–30 June 1986. Partially declassified.
"Joint Operation El Dorado Canyon: USAF Attack Against Tripoli, Libya 14 April 1986." Part of Navy–Air Force Brief to the Secretary of Defense (15–19 September 1986) on Operations in the Vicinity of Libya from January–April 1986. Partially declassified.

U.S. Government Documents

Executive Office Documents

Reagan, Ronald. *Public Papers of the Presidents of the United States: Ronald Reagan, 1981.* Washington, D.C.: GPO, 1982.

———. *Public Papers of the Presidents of the United States: Ronald Reagan, 1986.* Vol. 1. Washington, D.C.: GPO, 1987.

Vice President's Task Force on Combatting Terrorism. *Public Report of the Vice President's Task Force on Combatting Terrorism, February 1986.* Washington, D.C.: GPO, 1986.

Executive Department Documents

CIA. "Moscow Balances Warnings to U.S., Commitment to Dialogue; USSR Voices Outrage, Give Cautious Support to Libya." News Analysis. Document No. 126599. 23 April 1986.

———. "Statement re. Acting Director Robert M. Gates." Document ID No. 7265. 20 February 1987.

CIA Directorate of Intelligence. *Chemical and Biological Weapons: The Poor Man's Atomic Bomb.* Intelligence Assessment. Document ID No. 126929. December 1988. Partially declassified.

———. *Libya: Reviewing Terrorist Capabilities.* Research Paper. Document ID No. 124186. April 1989. Partially declassified.

CIA Director of Central Intelligence. *Libya: Aims and Vulnerabilities.* Special National Intelligence Estimate 36.5-81. 30 January 1981. Partially declassified.

———. *Libya's Qadhafi: The Challenge to U.S. and Western Interests.* Special National Intelligence Estimate 36.5-85. March 1985. Partially declassified.

———. *Soviet Support for International Terrorism and Revolutionary Violence.* Special National Intelligence Estimate 11/2-81. 27 May 1981. Partially declassified.

CIA Foreign Broadcast Information Service. "Libya Deemed Responsible for Lockerbie Bombing." *FBIS Concatenated Daily Reports 1991.* Document ID No. 139140. 27 June 1991.

———. "Al-Qadhdhafi Addresses Rally." *Foreign Broadcast Information Service Daily Report—Middle East and Africa,* 31 March 1986, Q2-9.

———. *Quotations from Qadhdhafi on Relations with the Soviet Union.* Special Memorandum. Document ID No. 36242. 16 December 1981. Declassified.

———. *Quotations from Qadhdhafi on Terrorism.* Special Memorandum. Document ID No. 28028. 9 December 1981. Declassified.

CIA National Foreign Assessment Center. *Patterns of International Terrorism: 1980.* Research Paper. June 1981.

———. *A Red Sea Security System: Political, Military, and Economic Issues.* Intelligence Assessment. Document ID No. 98721. December 1981. Partially declassified.

DOD. *Report of the Secretary of Defense Caspar W. Weinberger to the Congress on the FY 1988/FY 1989 Budget and FY 1988–92 Defense Programs, January 12, 1987: This Report Reflects the FY 1988/FY 1989 Budget as of January 1, 1987*. Washington, D.C.: GPO, 1987.

DOS. *AFPCD 1981*. Washington, D.C.: GPO, 1984.

———. "Department Statement, Aug. 19, 1981." *Department of State Bulletin*, October 1981, 60.

———. "Libya: A Source of International Terrorism," by Kenneth Adelman. *Department of State Bulletin*, January 1982, 60–62.

———. "Libya: U.S. Economic Measures." *Department of State Bulletin*, June 1982, 68–69.

———. "The President [Reagan]: News Conference of April 9 (Excerpts)." *Department of State Bulletin*, June 1986, 24–27.

———. "Secretary Haig's News Conference of January 28." *Department of State Bulletin*, February 1981, Special Section, pp. G–K.

———. "The Secretary [Shultz]: Interview on *This Week with David Brinkley*." *Department of State Bulletin*, April 1983, 44–45.

———. "Terrorism: Its Evolving Nature," by L. Paul Bremer. *Department of State Bulletin*, May 1989, /4–78.

———. "U.S. Asks Libyans to Close People's Bureau; Travel Advisory Issued: Department Statement 6 May 1981." *Department of State Bulletin*, July 1981, 45.

———. "U.S. Exercises Right of Self-Defense against Libyan Terrorism." *Department of State Bulletin*, June 1986, 1–18.

———. "U.S. Planes Attacked by Libyan Aircraft." *Department of State Bulletin*, October 1981, 57–60.

DOS Bureau of Public Affairs. *Background Notes: Libya*. Washington, D.C.: GPO, 1985.

———. *International Terrorism*. Selected Documents No. 24. Washington, D.C.: GPO, 1986.

———. *Libya under Qadhafi: A Pattern of Aggression*. Special Report No. 138. January 1986.

DOS Office of the Coordinator for Counterterrorism. *Patterns of Global Terrorism: 1991*. Annual Report. April 1992.

———. *Patterns of Global Terrorism: 1997*. Annual Report. April 1998.

———. *Patterns of Global Terrorism: 2000*. Annual Report. April 2001.

DOS Office of the Legal Adviser. *Digest of United States Practice in International Law*, by Arthur W. Rovine. Washington, D.C.: GPO, 1975.

Congressional Documents

U.S. Congress, Senate. Committee on Foreign Relations. Subcommittee on African Affairs and Subcommittee on Near Eastern and South Asian Affairs. *Hearing on Libya's Role in Sub-Saharan Africa and the Near East*, 97th Cong., 1st sess., 8 July 1981.

———. Senator Byrd of West Virginia Speaking on the Military Operation against Libya. 99th Cong., 2nd sess. *Congressional Record* (15 April 1986), vol. 132, pt. 46.

Books, Periodicals, and Papers

"2 Listed as Killed in Raid." *AFT,* 28 April 1986, 4.

Ahearn, Lorraine. "Terrorist Bomb Rips Jetliner, Killing 3 from Annapolis." *Capital,* 3 April 1986, 1, 8.

Alexander, Nathan. "The Foreign Policy of Libya: Inflexibility amid Change." *Orbis* 24 (winter 1981): 819–46.

———. "Libya: The Continuous Revolution." *Middle Eastern Studies* 17 (April 1981): 210–27.

Allen, Mike, and Paul Blustein. "Bush Moves to Cut Terrorists' Support; Foreign Banks Urged to Help Freeze Assets of 27 Entities." *WP,* 25 September 2001, sec. A, pp. 1, 8.

Allen, William L. "From the Editor." *National Geographic,* November 2000, ii.

"Alone but Right." *ST,* 20 April 1986, 26.

Alpern, David M., et al. "Coping with a Plot to Kill the President." *Newsweek,* 21 December 1981, 16–17, 19.

Anderson, Harry, et al. "Get Tough: The Reagan Plan." *Newsweek,* 20 January 1986, 16–17.

———. "Holiday of Terror." *Newsweek,* 6 January 1986, 26–28, 30.

Anderson, Lisa. "Assessing Libya's Qaddafi." *Current History* 84 (May 1985): 197–200, 226–27.

———. "Libya and American Foreign Policy." *Middle East Journal* 36 (autumn 1982): 516–34.

———. "Libya's Qaddafi: Still in Command?" *Current History* 86 (February 1987): 65–68, 86–87.

———. "Qaddafi's Islam." In *Voices of Resurgent Islam,* edited by John L. Esposito, 134–49. New York: Oxford University Press, 1983.

———. "Qadhdhafi and His Opposition." *Middle East Journal* 40 (spring 1986): 225–37.

———. *The State and Social Transformation in Tunisia and Libya, 1830–1980.* Princeton, N.J.: Princeton University Press, 1986.

Anno, Stephen E., and William E. Einspahr. "Command and Control and Communications Lessons Learned: Iranian Rescue, Falklands Conflict, Grenada Invasion, Libya Raid." Research Report. Maxwell Air Force Base, Ala.: Air War College, 1988.

"Appointment in Tripoli." *Economist* 299 (19 April 1986): 11–12.

"Arabs Denounce US Action." *Jane's Defence Weekly* 5 (26 April 1986): 742.

Ault, Frank. "The Father of TOP GUN [*sic*]." *Shipmate* 62 (March 1999): 12.

Barringer, Felicity. "Soviet Rebuffs U.S. on Berlin Terror." *NYT,* 18 April 1986, sec. A, p. 9.

"Basis for UK's Decision over Use of Air Bases." *Jane's Defence Weekly* 5 (26 April 1986): 740.

Bearman, Jonathan. *Qadhafi's Libya.* Atlantic Highlands, N.J.: Zed Books, 1986.

Beck, Melinda A., et al. "A Syrian Connection." *Newsweek,* 12 May 1986, 54.

Benjamin, Daniel, and Steven Simon, "Pan Am 103: Keep up the Fight." *WP,* 1 February 2001, sec. A, p. 21.

Bermudez, Joseph S. "Libyan SAMs and Air Defences." *Jane's Defence Weekly* 5 (17 May 1986): 880–81.

"'Best Regards'." *WP,* 26 March 1986, sec. A, p. 22.

Blundy, David. "Who Rules in Tripoli?" *ST,* 27 April 1986, 27.

Blundy, David, and Andrew Lycett. *Qaddafi and the Libyan Revolution.* Boston: Little, Brown, 1987.

Bodansky, Yossef. *Bin Ladin: The Man Who Declared War on America.* Rocklin, Calif.: Forum, 1999.

Bohlen, Celestine. "Soviet Leader Reaffirms Support for Libya." *WP,* 17 April 1986, sec. A, pp. 21, 25.

Bolger, Daniel P. *Americans at War, 1975–1986: An Era of Violent Peace.* Novato, Calif.: Presidio, 1988.

Bolton, John R. "Appeasing Gadhafi." *WP,* 29 August 2000, sec. A, p. 17.

"The Bombs Bestir the Allies." *NYT,* 24 April 1986, sec. A, p. 22.

"The Bombs of April." *NYT,* 16 April 1986, sec. A, p. 26.

Boyd, Gerald M. "U.S. Is Stepping Up Rebuke to Allies on World Terror." *NYT,* 17 April 1986, sec. A, pp. 1, 22.

Boyne, Walter J. *Beyond the Wild Blue: A History of the United States Air Force, 1947–1997.* New York: St. Martin's, 1997.

———. "El Dorado Canyon." *Air Force Magazine* 82 (March 1999): 56–62.

Bradlee, Ben. *Guts and Glory: The Rise and Fall of Oliver North.* New York: Donald I. Fine, 1988.

Breast, Jerry C. "The CV in Action . . . Battle Stations!" *Wings of Gold* 12 (summer 1987): S26-29, 32.

Brecher, John, et al. "To the Shores of Tripoli." *Newsweek,* 31 August 1981, 14–18.

"Britain Cannot Be Supine or Passive towards Terrorism." *Times,* 16 April 1986, 4.

Brown, David A. "Libyan Incident Spurs Deployment Shift." *Aviation Week & Space Technology* 115 (31 August 1981): 19–21.

Burlage, John. "U. S. Asserts Right of Free Navigation." *NT,* 7 April 1986, 37, 40.

Burr, J. Millard, and Robert O. Collins. *Africa's Thirty Years' War: Libya, Chad, and the Sudan, 1963–1993.* Boulder, Colo.: Westview, 1999.

Bush, George W. "Bush's Address to the Nation." *WP,* 8 October 2001, sec. A, p. 6.

———. "Transcript of President Bush's Address." *WP,* 21 September 2001, sec. A, p. 24.

Cable, James. "Gunboat Diplomacy's Future." *United States Naval Institute Proceedings* 112 (August 1986): 36–41.

Cannon, Lou. "Administration 'Hurt.'" *WP,* 4 October 1986, sec. A, pp. 1, 12.

————. *President Reagan: The Role of a Lifetime.* New York: Public Affairs, 2000.

Cannon, Lou, and George C. Wilson. "U.S. Says Libya Eyed Sudan Coup." *WP,* 19 February 1983, sec. A, pp. 1, 13.

Carter, Jimmy. *Keeping Faith: Memoirs of a President.* New York: Bantam, 1982.

Charles, Deborah (Reuters). "Bush Applauds Lockerbie Verdict, Sanctions Still On," AT&T Worldnet Service, 31 January 2001.

Christmann, Timothy J. "Harpoon Proves Its Tenacity: A-6Es Thump Libyan Combatants." *Naval Aviation News* 68 (July–August 1986): 12–14.

————. "The Navy Strikes Tripoli's Terrorist." *Naval Aviation News* 68 (July–August 1986): 15–17.

Church, George J., et al. "Hitting the Source." *Time,* 28 April 1986, 16–20, 23–24, 26–27.

————. "Targeting Gaddafi." *Time,* 21 April 1986, 18–22, 24, 27.

Cockburn, Andrew. "Libya: An End to Isolation?" *National Geographic,* November 2000, 2–31.

————. "Sixty Seconds over Tripoli." *Playboy,* May 1987, 130, 132, 144, 146, 164–65.

Cooley, John K. "The Libyan Menace." *Foreign Policy* 42 (spring 1981): 74–93.

————. *Libyan Sandstorm.* New York: Holt, Rinehart, and Winston, 1982.

————. "Qadafi's Nervous Neighbors." *Middle East International* no. 157 (4 September 1981): 2–3.

————. *Unholy Wars: Afghanistan, America, and International Terrorism.* Sterling, Va.: Pluto, 2000.

Cordesman, Anthony H. "After the Raid: The Emerging Lessons from the U.S. Attack on Libya." *Armed Forces* 5 (August 1986): 355–60.

"Countdown to Operation El Dorado Canyon." *Jane's Defence Weekly* 5 (26 April 1986): 736.

Cowell, Alan. "French War Jets Are Sent to Chad." *NYT,* 22 August 1983, sec. A, pp. 1, 10.

————. "Mobutu, on a Visit to Chad, Renews Zairian Support." *NYT,* 21 August 1983, sec. A, pp. 1, 8.

————. "U.S. and Libya: Are the Views in Both Directions Distorted?" *NYT,* 28 November 1981, sec. A, pp. 1, 6.

Crowe, William J., with David Chanoff. *The Line of Fire: From Washington to the Gulf, the Politics and Battles of the New Military.* New York: Simon and Schuster, 1993.

"CVW-1/CV-66." *The Hook* 14 (summer 1986): 40–44.

"CVW-13/CV-43." *The Hook* 14 (summer 1986): 58–66.

"CVW-17/CV-60." *The Hook* 14 (summer 1986): 68, 71.

Daniloff, Nicholas, and Maureen Santini. "From the Kremlin, a New Chill toward the U.S." *U.S. News & World Report,* 28 April 1986, 25.

Darwish, Adel. "Has the Leopard Changed Its Spots?" *Middle East* no. 298 (February 2000): 4–6.

Davies, Peter E., and Anthony M. Thornborough. *F-111 Aardvark.* Ramsbury, U.K.: Crowood, 1997.

Davis, Brian L. *Qaddafi, Terrorism, and the Origins of the U.S. Attack on Libya.* New York: Preager, 1990.

Deeb, Marius K., and Mary Jane Deeb. *Libya since the Revolution: Aspects of Social and Political Development.* New York: Praeger, 1982.

Dewar, Helen, and Milton Coleman. "Hill Gives Cautious Support." *WP,* 25 March 1986, sec. A, pp. 1, 12.

DeYoung, Karen. "Britain Deports 21 Libyans." *WP,* 23 April 1986, sec. A, pp. 1, 27.

Dickey, Christopher. "A Kaddafi Comeback?" *Newsweek,* 22 February 1988, 30, 33.

———. "Libya Silent on Casualties." *WP,* 28 March 1986, sec. A, pp. 1, 21.

———. "Qaddafi Makes Appearance on TV." *WP,* 17 April 1986, sec. A, pp. 1, 24.

———. "Qaddafi Takes Militant Tone on Crisis in Gulf of Sidra." *WP,* 26 March 1986, sec. A, pp. 1, 24.

Doerner, William R., David Halevy, and Bruce van Voorst. "In the Dead of the Night." *Time,* 28 April 1986, 28–31.

Dorsey, James M. "Qaddafi Warns against Retaliation for Attacks." *WP,* 2 January 1986, sec. A, p. 17.

Drozdiak, William. "Bonn Cites Own Proof of Libyan Bomb at Disco." *WP,* 17 April 1986, sec. A, pp. 21–22.

———. "Murder Trial in Disco Bombing Opens in Berlin." *WP,* 19 November 1997, sec. A, pp. 23, 27.

———. "Police Cooperation Led to Palestinians' Arrest." *WP,* 23 April 1986, sec. A, p. 27.

Dryden, Steven J. "Europeans to Halt Arms Sales to Nations Backing Terrorists." *WP,* 28 January 1986, sec. A, p. 10.

Echikson, William. "France Hopes Unused Strength Can Persuade Libya to Talk." *CSM,* 22 August 1983, 6.

Eisenstadt, Steve. "Overflights Long a Thorn in International Relations." *NT,* 28 April 1986, 14.

El-Kikhia, Mansour O. *Libya's Qaddafi: The Politics of Contradiction.* Gainesville, Fla.: University Press of Florida, 1997.

Elliot, Frank. "Shooting Match Provided Equipment Test." *NT,* 7 April 1986, 39–40.

Elliot, Frank, and Len Famiglietti. "Training, Skill Used to Hilt in Raid on Libya." *NT,* 28 April 1986, 4, 18.

Erlanger, Steven. "4 Guilty in 1986 Disco Bombing, Linked to Libya, in West Berlin." *NYT,* 14 November 2001, sec. A, p. 5.

"Europe Fearful as Arabs Back Gadaffi." *Times,* 26 March 1986, 16.

Fayeq, Omar. "Libya's Gains and Losses from the Gulf Crisis." *Middle East International* no. 402 (14 June 1991): 17–18.

"Fearing Trouble: A *Newsweek* Poll." *Newsweek,* 7 April 1986, 23.

Feder, Barnaby J. "Libya Trade Was Low Before Ban." *NYT,* 8 January 1986, sec. A, p. 7.

Finn, Peter. "4 Convicted in '86 Berlin Nightclub Bombing." *WP*, 14 November 2001, sec. A, p. 30.

———. "Libyan Convicted of Lockerbie Bombing." *WP*, 1 February 2001, sec. A, pp. 1, 16.

First, Ruth. *Libya: The Elusive Revolution.* New York: Africana Publishing, 1975.

Fisher, Dan. "Rocket Attack from South Lebanon Poses Renewed Problem for Israel." *WP*, 3 January 1986, sec. A, p. 14.

Fisk, Robert. "Arabs Urged to Hit US Embassies." *Times*, 26 March 1986, 1.

"Five Go on Trial in Berlin over 1986 Bombing of Disco." *NYT*, 19 November 1997, sec. A, p. 5.

Flecnoe, Mac. Comment on "Sharpening the Claws of the Tomcat." *United States Naval Institute Proceedings* 108 (August 1982): 86.

Foltz, William J. "Libya's Military Power." In *The Green and the Black: Qaddafi's Policies in Africa,* edited by René Lemarchand, 52–69. Bloomington, Ind.: Indiana University Press, 1988.

Gaba, Salet. "U.S. Aides, Arms Arrive in Chad." *WP*, 4 August 1983, sec. A, pp. 1, 17.

"Gaddafi and Terrorism: Sampling Global Opinion on the U.S. Raid and the Future." *World Press Review* 33 (June 1986): 21–26.

Garamone, Jim. "F-111 'Most Capable Airplane' for Libya Raid." *AFT*, 28 April 1986, 4.

Gates, Robert M. *From the Shadows: The Ultimate Insider's Story of Five Presidents and How They Won the Cold War.* New York: Simon and Schuster, 1996.

Gelb, Leslie H. "U.S. Aides Deny Attack Is Start of an Escalation." *NYT*, 16 April 1986, sec. A, p. 15.

Gelman, David, John Walcott, and Thomas M. DeFrank. "The Poindexter Doctrine." *Newsweek*, 21 April 1986, 24.

Getler, Michael. "Libya's Special Oil May Sweeten U.S. Distaste for Qaddafi Terrorism." *WP*, 21 March 1981, sec. A, p. 3.

Goldsmith, Michael. "Qaddafi Sails Near U.S. Exercises." *WP*, 26 January 1986, sec. A, p. 21.

———. "Qaddafi Says His Forces Are on Alert After U.S. Exercises Announced." *WP*, 25 January 1986, sec. A, p. 16.

Gorbachev, Mikhail. "Gorbachev Voices Solidarity to Qaddafi, Recounts 'Unheeded Warnings' to U.S.; Moscow Will 'Fulfill Commitments to Strengthen Libya's Defense Capability.'" *Current Digest of the Soviet Press* 38 (14 May 1986): 4.

Gordon, Michael R. "7 American Planes Aborted Mission." *NYT*, 18 April 1986, sec. A, pp. 1, 11.

———. "U.S. Says One Vessel It Hit Had Come Within 10 Miles." *NYT*, 26 March 1986, sec. A. p. 8.

Goshko, John M. "Armed Action against Libya Still Possible." *WP*, 28 January 1986, sec. A, p. 10.

————. "Scholars Say U.S. Action Seemed Legal." *WP,* 25 March 1986, sec. A, p. 12.

Greeley, Brendan M. "U.S. F-14s Down Libyan MiG-23s in Dogfight over Mediterranean." *Aviation Week & Space Technology* 130 (9 January 1989): 20–21.

Grossnick, Roy A. "1983 Year in Review." *Naval Aviation News* 66 (May–June 1984): 26–35.

Grossnick, Roy A., et al. *United States Naval Aviation, 1910–1995.* Washington, D.C.: GPO, 1997.

"The Gulf of Sidra" (Chronology). *WP,* 26 March 1986, sec. A, p. 22.

Gwertzman, Bernard. "Haig Says Teheran Will Not Get Arms; Asks Trade Caution." *NYT,* 29 January 1981, sec. A, pp. 1, 11.

————. "Reagan Weighs Economic Steps against Libyans." *NYT,* 8 December 1981, sec. A, pp. 1, 7.

————. "Shultz Expresses Hopes for a Coup to Oust Qaddafi." *NYT,* 18 April 1986, sec. A., pp. 1, 10.

————. "U.S. Action: Sign to Libya." *NYT,* 21 August 1981, sec. A, pp. 1, 10.

————. "U.S. Aides Divided on Further Attacks." *NYT,* 27 April 1986, sec. A, pp. 1, 14.

————. "U.S. Is Withdrawing Aircraft It Sent to Help Chad." *NYT,* 24 August 1983, sec. A, p. 9.

————. "U.S. Officials Say Libyan Threat Led to AWACS Dispatch." *NYT,* 18 February 1983, sec. A, pp. 1, 6.

————. "U.S. Pledges to Aid Countries in Africa that Resist Libyans." *NYT,* 3 June 1981, sec. A, pp. 1, 4.

————. "Why Reagan Shuns Attack." *NYT,* 8 January 1986, sec. A, pp. 1, 7.

Haig, Alexander M. *Caveat: Realism, Reagan, and Foreign Policy.* New York: Macmillan, 1984.

Halberstadt, Hans. *F-111 Aardvark.* London, U.K.: Windrow and Greene, 1992.

Haley, P. Edward. *Qaddafi and the United States since 1969.* New York: Praeger, 1984.

Hallion, Richard P. *Storm over Iraq: Air Power and the Gulf War.* Washington, D.C.:Smithsonian Institution, 1992.

Halloran, Richard K. "Hyperbole and Grins." *NYT,* 18 April 1986, sec. A, p. 16.

————. "Libyan Affair Over, U.S. Says AWACS Will Now Leave Egypt." *NYT,* 22 February 1983, sec. A, p. 8.

————. "The Tactics of Technowarfare." *Regardies,* July 1986, 69–79.

————. "U.S. Says Tape Shows Missiles on a Libyan Jet." *NYT,* 6 January 1989, sec. A, pp. 1, 10.

Harris, Lillian Craig. "Libya in the South Pacific: Wounded Innocence." *Middle East International* no. 301 (29 May 1987): 11.

————. *Libya: Qadhafi's Revolution and the Modern State.* Boulder, Colo.: Westview, 1986.

Hartmann, Frederick H. *Naval Renaissance: The U.S. Navy in the 1980s.* Annapolis, Md.: Naval Institute Press, 1990.

Hersh, Seymour M. "Target Qaddafi." *New York Times Magazine,* 22 February 1987, 16–22, 24, 26, 48, 71, 74, 84.

Hiatt, Fred. "U.S. Attack on Libya: A Raid that Went Right." *WP,* 20 April 1986, sec. A, pp. 1, 24.

———. "Use of Air Force Planes Raises Questions." *WP,* 20 April 1986, sec. A, p. 24.

Hoffman, David. "President Says He Intends to Keep Gadhafi Off Balance." *WP,* 3 October 1986, sec. A, pp. 1, 20.

———. "Terrorism Panel Still Divided on Use of Military Retaliation." *WP,* 7 March 1986, sec. A, p. 28.

Hoffman, David, and Lou Cannon. "Terrorism Provided Catalyst." *WP,* 25 March 1986, sec. A, pp. 1, 12.

Hoffman, David, and Don Oberdorfer. "Secret Policy on Terrorism Given Airing." *WP,* 18 April 1984, sec. A, pp. 1, 18.

Hubbell, Stephen. "Libya: Content with the Status Quo." *Middle East International* no. 437 (6 November 1992): 12–13.

Ignatius, David. "Bombing Gadhafi Worked." *WP,* 13 July 1986, sec. B, p. 5.

Isby, David C. "Libyan Submarine Force Poses Limited Threat to Sixth Fleet." *Jane's Defence Weekly* 5 (17 May 1986): 882.

Jenkins, Brian. "What Have We Learned? How Can We Fight Back?" Interview by Michael Reese. *Newsweek,* 15 September 1986, 27.

Jenkins, Loren. "Airport Terrorists Reportedly Trained in Syrian-Controlled Area: European Probers Share Information." *WP,* 11 January 1986, sec. A, pp. 1, 18.

———. "Europeans Criticize U.S. Stand on Terror." *WP,* 20 April 1986, sec. A, pp. 21, 25.

———. "Rome Restricts Arms Sales to Libya, Says Italians Won't Fill U.S. Jobs There." *WP,* 10 January 1986, sec. A, pp. 25, 30.

Johnston, David. "Courts a Limited Anti-Terror Weapon." *NYT,* 1 February 2001, sec. A, p. 8.

"Kaddafi's Latest Plot." *Newsweek,* 9 November 1981, 29.

Kagian, Jules. "UN and Libya: A Step towards Sanctions." *Middle East International* no. 418 (7 February 1992): 12.

Kissinger, Henry. *Years of Upheaval.* Boston: Little, Brown, 1982.

Koch, Noel. "The Hostage Labyrinth . . . Our 'No Negotiations' Policy May Not Have Helped." *WP,* 18 March 1990, sec. B, pp. 1, 4.

Lake, Jon, ed. *Grumman F-14 Tomcat: Shipborne Superfighter.* London, U.K.: Aerospace Publishing, 1998.

Lamar, Jacob V., David Beckwith, and Jay Branegan. "A Summit of Substance." *Time,* 19 May 1986, 15–16.

Lancaster, John. "Compromising Positions." *Washington Post Magazine,* 9 July 2000, 10–15, 22–26.

Lancaster, John, and Alan Sipress. "A Muted Victory against Terror." *WP,* 1 February 2001, sec. A, pp. 1, 16.

Lardner, George. "French Link Libyans to Bombings." *WP,* 27 June 1991, sec. A, pp. 1, 16.

"Lebanese Woman Sought in TWA Bombing." *Capital,* 5 April 1986, 1, 10.

Lee, Dave, and Chris Holmes. "Operation El Dorado [*sic*]: The Men Behind the Headlines." *All Hands* no. 831 (June 1986): 24–29.

Lehman, John F. *Command of the Seas.* New York: Charles Scribner's Sons, 1988.

Lemarchand, René. "Introduction: Beyond the Mad Dog Syndrome." In *The Green and the Black: Qadhafi's Policies in Africa,* edited by René Lemarchand, 1–15. Bloomington: Indiana University Press, 1988.

"Libya and Ethiopia Say U.S. Plots Killings." *WP,* 24 August 1981, sec. A, p. 14.

"Libya MiGs Are Intercepted by Jets from a U.S. Carrier." *NYT,* 3 August 1983, sec. A, p. 3.

"Libya: Reagan Decides It Had to Be Done." *Economist* 299 (19 April 1986): 17–18, 23.

"Libya Strike Details Revealed." *Flight International* 129 (26 April 1986): 12–14.

"Libya Threatens 'Gulf of Blood'; Keep Carrier Out of Area, Kadafi Says." *LAT,* 18 February 1983, sec. I, pp. 1, 10.

"Libyan Leader Threatens to Hit U.S. Nuclear Depots." *WP,* 2 September 1981, sec. A, p. 20.

"Libyan Pilots Demonstrate Varied Training." *Aviation Week & Space Technology* 115 (31 August 1981): 21.

"The Libyan Revolution in the Words of Its Leaders." *Middle East Journal* 24 (spring 1970): 203–19.

"Libyan SA-5 Site Repaired after U.S. Strike." *Jane's Defence Weekly* 5 (5 April 1986): 595.

"Libyan SAM Missiles Hit Civilian Areas, Says USA." *Jane's Defence Weekly* 5 (26 April 1986): 737.

"A Lockerbie Verdict." *WSJ,* 1 February 2001, sec. A, p. 22.

Love, Robert W. *History of the U.S. Navy, Vol. 2, 1942–1991.* Harrisburg, Pa.: Stackpole, 1992.

Lynch, Colum, and John Lancaster. "U.S. Considers Easing Restrictions on Libya." *WP,* 27 February 2000, sec. A, p. 29.

Magnuson, Ed, Walter Galling, and Gertraud Lessing. "Ten Minutes of Horror." *Time,* 6 January 1986, 74–76.

Magnuson, Ed, Johanna McGeary, and Bruce van Voorst. "To the Shores of Tripoli." *Time,* 31 March 1986, 26.

Manning, Robert A. "In Western Europe, Strains among Friends." *U.S. News & World Report,* 28 April 1986, 24.

Marder, Murrey. "In Diplomacy, AWACS Replaces Gunboat." *WP,* 18 October 1981, sec. A, p. 4.

Markham, James M. "Walters Lobbies Allies to Act against Qaddafi." *NYT,* 14 April 1986, sec. A, p. 6.

Marlowe, Frank, and Robert R. Rini. "*Forrestal*/CVW-17—Another Successful Med Cruise." *The Hook* 9 (winter 1981): 33–38.

Marshall, Ruth. "A View from the Bull's-eye." *Newsweek,* 28 April 1986, 30.

Martin, David C., and John Walcott. *Best Laid Plans: The Inside Story of America's War against Terrorism.* New York: Harper and Row, 1988.

Martin, Douglas. "U.S. Oil Executives in Libya Discount Retaliation Threat." *NYT,* 21 August 1981, sec. A, p. 11.

Matthews, William. "MiGs Seemingly Goaded F-14s into Shootdown." *NT,* 16 January 1989, 6, 16.

Mayfield, J. D. "Bombs Away: High Tech in a Terrorist War." *Soldier of Fortune,* August 1986, 82–89.

Maze, Rick. "Hill for Air Strike." *NT,* 28 April 1986, 14.

McNeil, Donald G. "Libyan Convicted by Scottish Court in '88 Pan Am Blast." *NYT,* 1 February 2001, sec. A, pp. 1, 8.

Meacham, James. "Hits and Misses in Libyan Raid." *Defence Attaché* no. 2 (1986): 11–12, 14.

"Med Forces Move; Security Tightens." *NT,* 21 April 1986, 4.

Meese, Edwin. *With Reagan: The Inside Story.* Washington, D.C.: Regnery Gateway, 1992.

Menges, Constantine C. *Inside the National Security Council: The True Story of the Making and Unmaking of Reagan's Foreign Policy.* New York: Simon and Schuster, 1988.

Metz, Helen Chapin, ed. *Libya: A Country Study.* 4th ed. Washington, D.C.: GPO, 1989.

"The Military Balance 1985/86: Other Nations." *Air Force Magazine* 69 (February 1986): 92–118, 121–26.

Miller, Judith. "Italian Island, a Libyan Target, Escapes Unscathed." *NYT,* 16 April 1986, sec. A, p. 15.

"Missiles Shake Island." *Times,* 16 April 1986, 1.

Moffett, George D. "Libya Quiet after U.S. Raid—But How Long?" *CSM,* 25 June 1986, 1, 32.

Moore, John, ed. *Jane's Fighting Ships, 1986–87.* New York: Jane's, 1986.

Moore, Molly, and George C. Wilson. "U.S. Navy Jets Shoot Down 2 Libyan Fighters; 'Hostile Intent' of MiGs Is Cited." *WP,* 5 January 1989, sec. A, pp. 1, 29.

Morganthau, Tom, and Rod Nordland. "A Terrorist Jihad." *Newsweek,* 28 April 1986, 31–33.

Morris, Edmund. *Dutch: A Memoir of Ronald Reagan.* New York: Random House, 1999.

Morrissette, Walt. "DoD Details Civilian Damage in Libya Raid." *AFT,* 26 May 1986, 12.

Muczynski, Larry, and James Anderson. "Black Aces Bag Two." Interview by Barrett Tillman. *The Hook* 9 (fall 1981): 29–30.

Neutze, Dennis R. "The Gulf of Sidra Incident: A Legal Perspective." *United States Naval Institute Proceedings* 108 (January 1982): 26–31.

North, Andrew. "Lockerbie: Families' Change of Heart." *Middle East International* no. 561 (24 October 1997): 10.

North, David M. "Air Force, Navy Brief Congress on Lessons from Libya Strikes." *Aviation Week & Space Technology* 124 (2 June 1986): 63.

———. "Merits of U. S., Soviet Weapons Explored in Libyan Conflict." *Aviation Week & Space Technology* 124 (31 March 1986): 20–21.

North, Oliver, with William Novak. *Under Fire: An American Story*. New York: Harper Collins, 1992.

Nossiter, Bernard D. "Qaddafi Opposition Is Getting Stronger." *NYT*, 27 May 1981, sec. A, pp. 1, 8.

———. "Qaddafi Tied to Shooting of Libyan in U.S." *NYT*, 24 May 1981, sec. A, pp. 1, 16.

Oberdorfer, Don. "Egypt Is Assured of U.S. Backing in Attack on Libya." *WP*, 8 November 1981, sec. A, pp. 1, 4.

———. "U.S. Has Sought to Pressure Qaddafi." *WP*, 20 August 1981, sec. A, pp. 1, 17.

"On Navy Tape, a Drama of Combat." *WP*, 6 January 1989, sec. A, p. 22.

Ottaway, David B. "U.S. Still Certain that Libya Was Behind Nightclub Attack." *WP*, 12 January 1988, sec. A, pp. 16, 18.

Owen, Richard. "EEC Caution Upsets U.S." *Times*, 15 April 1986, 7.

———. "EEC Imposes Diplomatic Sanctions Only." *Times*, 15 April 1986, 1.

———. "EEC Toughens Sanctions against Libya." *Times*, 22 April 1986, 1.

Paine, Lincoln P. "'War Is Better than Tribute.'" *Naval History* 15 (June 2001): 20–25.

Parker, Geoffrey, and Larry J. Leturmy. "The Libya Raid: A Joint Response to State-Sponsored Terrorism." Research Case Study. Maxwell Air Force Base, Ala.: Air War College, 1987.

Parks, W. Hays. "Crossing the Line." *United States Naval Institute Proceedings* 112 (November 1986): 40–52.

Parmelee, Jennifer. "Gadhafi Sees Election Aiding U.S.-Libya Ties." *WP*, 6 September 1988, sec. A, pp. 23, 27.

———. "Libya, Despite Animus, Looks toward U.S. Ties." *WP*, 29 September 1988, sec. A, p. 34.

———. "U.S. Navy Jets Shoot Down 2 Libyan Fighters; Gadhafi Seeks UN Meeting." *WP*, 5 January 1989, sec. A, pp. 1, 32.

Pelham, Nick. "Libya: Sea Change." *Middle East International* no. 660 (12 October 2001): 19–20.

Perlez, Jane. "Qaddafi, Taking Softer Tone, Urges U.S. 'Meet Us Halfway.'" *NYT*, 12 April 1987, sec. A, pp. 1, 14.

Persico, Joseph. *Casey: From the OSS to the CIA*. New York: Viking, 1990.

"A Plan to Overthrow Kaddafi." *Newsweek*, 3 August 1981, 19.

"Planes Launch from 4 Bases." *AFT*, 28 April 1986, 4, 18.

"A Poll: Europe vs. the U.S." *Newsweek*, 28 April 1986, 22.

Potter, E. B., ed. *Sea Power: A Naval History*. 2nd ed. Annapolis, Md.: Naval Institute Press, 1981.

Powell, Stewart, and Robert A. Kittle. "Can Reagan Make Qadhafi Cry Uncle?" *U.S. News & World Report*, 21 April 1986, 6.

Press, Aric, Ann McDaniel, and Michael A. Lerner. "Getting Americans Out of Libya: Is It Legal?" *Newsweek,* 20 January 1986, 19.

Qaddafi, Muammar. "'Iranians Are Our Brothers.'" Interview by Oriana Fallaci. *New York Times Magazine,* 16 December 1979, 40, 116, 118–21, 123, 125, 127–28.

"Qaddafi Revered at Home, Reviled in West." *WP,* 25 March 1986, sec. A, p. 14.

Qadhafi, Muammar. "Message of Leader Brother Muammar Qadhafi to Mr. Carter and Mr. Reagan." Advertisement in *WP,* 22 October 1980, sec. A, p. 19.

"Raid Sparks European Protests, Special NATO and EEC Sessions." *Aviation Week & Space Technology* 124 (21 April 1986): 25.

Raines, Howell. "President Defends Libyan Encounter as 'Impressive' Act." *NYT,* 21 August 1981, sec. A, pp. 1, 10.

Rattner, Steven. "Western Europeans Expressing Favor and Unease." *NYT,* 21 August 1981, sec. A, p. 10.

"Reagan Ordered Air Strikes to Preempt Libyan Terrorists." *Aviation Week & Space Technology* 124 (21 April 1986): 22–23.

Reagan, Ronald. *An American Life.* New York: Simon and Schuster, 1990.

————. "Excerpts from the President's Address Accusing Nations of 'Acts of War.'" *NYT,* 9 July 1985, sec. A, p. 12.

————. "President's News Conference on Foreign and Domestic Issues," *NYT,* 19 June 1985, sec. A. p. 18.

————. "Reagan: Gadhafi Should 'Go to Bed . . . Wondering What We Might Do.'" Interview in *WP,* 3 October 1986, sec. A, p. 20.

————. *Reagan, in His Own Hand: The Writings of Ronald Reagan that Reveal His Revolutionary Vision for America.* Edited by Kiron K. Skinner, Annelise Anderson, and Martin Anderson. New York: Free Press, 2001.

————. "Reagan's Remarks on Raid." *NYT,* 16 April 1986, sec. A, p. 20.

————. "Transcript of President Reagan's News Conference." *WP,* 10 April 1986, sec. A, pp. 32–33.

————. "Transcript of White House News Conference on Hijacking." *NYT,* 12 October 1985, sec. A, p. 6.

Reese, Michael, John Walcott, and David C. Martin. "An Undeclared War." *Newsweek,* 31 August 1981, 16–17.

Rich, Gwendolyn J. "1985 Year in Review." *Naval Aviation News* 68 (July–August 1986): 22–29.

Rubin, Barry. "The Reagan Administration and the Middle East." In *Eagle Resurgent?: The Reagan Era in American Foreign Policy,* edited by Kenneth A. Oye, Robert J. Leiber, and Donald Rothchild, 431–57. Boston: Little, Brown, 1987.

Rule, Sheila. "Qaddafi Calls Third World Helpless." *NYT,* 5 September 1986, sec. A, p. 3.

Saleh, Heba. "Letter from Tripoli." *Middle East International* no. 640 (22 December 2000): 24.

————. "Libya: After the Trial." *Middle East International* no. 643 (9 February 2001): 16–18.

Schneider, Howard. "Gaddafi Dissects Lockerbie Decision." *WP,* 6 February 2001, sec. A, p. 14.

————. "Libyans Condemn Conviction by Court Gaddafi Sanctioned." *WP,* 4 February 2001, sec. A, p. 24.

————. "Lockerbie Defendant Embraced by Gaddafi," *WP,* 2 February 2001, sec. A, pp. 1, 19.

————. "The Softer Side of Libya." *WP,* 12 September 1999, sec. A, pp. 27, 31.

Schumacher, Edward. "Qaddafi, on TV, Condemns Attack." *NYT,* 17 April 1986, sec. A, pp. 1, 22.

Sciolino, Elaine. "U.S. Sees Qaddafi as Being Weaker." *NYT,* 10 January 1988, sec. A, p. 9.

Seib, Gerald F. "Gadhafi Returns to Limelight in Libya, Reasserting Grip on Nation's Leadership." *WSJ,* 2 September 1986, 31.

————. "U.S. Sends More AWACS in Growing Effort to Help Chad Resist Libya-Backed Rebels." *WSJ,* 8 August 1983, 3.

"Seven Minutes." *Newsweek,* 16 January 1989, 18–21.

Shultz, George P. "Shultz Defends Administration Efforts to 'Make Gadhafi Nervous.'" Interview in *WP,* 4 October 1986, sec. A, p. 12.

————. *Turmoil and Triumph: My Years as Secretary of State.* New York: Charles Scribner's Sons, 1993.

Siegel, Adam B. *The Use of Naval Forces in the Post-War Era: U.S. Navy and U.S. Marine Corps Crisis Response Activity, 1946–1990.* Center for Naval Analysis Research Memorandum 90-246, February 1991. Alexandria, Va.: CNA, 1991.

Simons, Geoff. *Libya: The Struggle for Survival.* New York: St. Martin's, 1993.

Simpson, Christopher. *National Security Directives of the Reagan and Bush Administrations: The Declassified History of U.S. Political and Military Policy, 1981–1991.* Boulder, Colo.: Westview, 1995.

"Sixth Fleet F-14s Down Libyan Su-22s." *Aviation Week & Space Technology* 115 (24 August 1981): 20–21.

Skelton, George. "Libya Threatens 'Gulf of Blood'; U.S. Warns It's Ready to Aid Allies." *LAT,* 18 February 1983, sec. I, pp. 1, 10.

Slavin, Barbara. "Analysis: Qadhafi's Libya." *Middle East Insight* 15 (July–August 2000): 51–53.

Smith, William E., Bruce W. Nelan, and William Stewart. "Shootout over the Med." *Time,* 31 August 1981, 24–26.

Sparks, Allister. "Gadhafi Denounces Nonaligned; Vows to Lead Anti-Imperialist Army." *WP,* 5 September 1986, sec. A, pp. 1, 32.

Speakes, Larry, with Robert Pack. *Speaking Out: The Reagan Presidency from inside the White House.* New York: Charles Scribner's Sons, 1988.

Stanik, Joseph T. "Sudden Victory: The Gulf of Sidra Incident of August 1981." *Naval Aviation News* 78 (July–August 1996): 32–36.

―――. "Swift and Effective Retribution:" The U.S. Sixth Fleet and the Confrontation with Qaddafi. Washington, D.C.: GPO, 1996.

―――. "Welcome to El Dorado Canyon." United States Naval Institute Proceedings 122 (April 1996): 57–62.

"Station Attacked." NT, 28 April 1986, 18.

Stengel, Richard, John Borrell, and William Stewart. "Gaddafi: Obsessed by a Ruthless, Messianic Vision." Time, 21 April 1986, 28–29.

Stengel, Richard, Dean Fischer, and Roland Flamini. "So Close, Yet So Far." Time, 28 April 1986, 33.

Sterling, Claire. The Terror Network: The Secret War of International Terrorism. New York: Berkley Books, 1982.

St. John, Ronald B. Qaddafi's World Design: Libyan Foreign Policy, 1969–1987. Atlantic Highlands, N.J.: Saqi Books, 1987.

―――. "Terrorism and Libyan Foreign Policy, 1981–1986." World Today 42 (July 1986): 111–16.

Strober, Deborah Hart, and Gerald S. Strober. Reagan: The Man and His Presidency. New York: Houghton Mifflin, 1998.

Stumpf, Robert E. "Air War with Libya." United States Naval Institute Proceedings 112 (August 1986): 42–48.

"Sudan Claims Libyan Coup Plot." Facts on File 43 (25 February 1983): 123–24.

Sullivan, Scott. "Why Europe Is Angry." Newsweek, 28 April 1986, 34, 36.

Sweetman, Jack. American Naval History: An Illustrated Chronology of the U.S. Navy and Marine Corps 1775–Present. 2nd ed. Annapolis, Md.: Naval Institute Press, 1991.

Takeyh, Ray. "Qadhafi's Libya and the Prospect of Islamic Succession." Middle East Policy 7 (February 2000): 154–64.

Taubman, Philip. "U.S. Officials Say F.B.I. Is Hunting Terrorists Seeking to Kill President." NYT, 4 December 1981, sec. A, pp. 1, 27.

Terry, James P. "An Appraisal of Lawful Military Response to State-Sponsored Terrorism." Naval War College Review 39 (May–June 1986): 59–68.

"Texts of the Statements Adopted by Leaders of 7 Industrial Democracies." NYT, 6 May 1986, sec. A, p. 12.

Thatcher, Margaret. The Downing Street Years. New York: Harper Collins, 1993.

―――. "Thatcher: A Friend in Need." Interview in Newsweek, 28 April 1986, 35.

Tillman, Barrett. "Strike U." United States Naval Institute Proceedings 113 (January 1987): 81–85.

Timberg, Robert. The Nightingale's Song. New York: Simon and Schuster, 1995.

Toth, Robert C. "Preemptive Anti-Terrorist Raids Allowed." WP, 16 April 1984, sec. A, p. 19.

Towell, Pat. "After Raid on Libya, New Questions on Hill." Congressional Quarterly Weekly Report 44 (19 April 1986): 838–39.

Tremlett, George. *Gadaffi: The Desert Mystic.* New York: Carroll and Graf, 1993.

Trewhitt, Henry. "A New War—And New Risks." *U.S. News & World Report,* 28 April 1986, 20–23.

Truver, Scott C. "Mines of August: An International Whodunit." *United States Naval Institute Proceedings* 111 (May 1985): 94–117.

Tyler, Patrick E. "Gadhafi Rule Seen in Peril Following Military Setbacks." *WP,* 27 March 1987, sec. A, pp. 1, 32.

Ulsamer, Edgar. "Stealth in the Nick of Time." *Air Force Magazine* 69 (November 1986), 25–26, 29.

U.S. Air Force Combat Pilot. "'How I Bombed Qaddafi': A Personal Account of an American Blow against Terrorism." *Popular Mechanics,* July 1987, 111–14, 153.

"U.S. Air Striking Power." *NT,* 28 April 1986, 40.

"U.S. and Libya—Heading for a Showdown?" *U.S. News & World Report,* 31 August 1981, 16–17.

"The U.S. Challenges Libya's Kaddafi." *Newsweek,* 24 August 1981, 13.

"U.S. Demonstrates Advanced Weapons Technology in Libya." *Aviation Week & Space Technology* 124 (21 April 1986): 18–21.

Vandewalle, Dirk. "The Libyan Jamahiriyya since 1969." In *Qadhafi's Libya, 1969–1994,* edited by Dirk Vandewalle, 3–46. New York: St. Martin's, 1995.

———, ed. *Qadhafi's Libya, 1969–1994.* New York: St. Martin's, 1995.

Venkus, Robert E. *Raid on Qaddafi.* New York: St. Martin's, 1993.

Viorst, Milton. "The Colonel in His Labyrinth." *Foreign Affairs* 78 (March–April 1999): 60–75.

Vistica, Gregory L. *Fall from Glory: The Men Who Sank the U.S. Navy.* New York: Simon and Schuster, 1995.

Vox Militaris. "The U.S. Strike against Libya: Operation El Dorado Canyon." *Army Quarterly and Defence Journal* 116 (April 1986): 134–48.

Walcott, John, and Gerald F. Seib. "Collision Course: New Signs that Libya Is Plotting Terrorism Bring Quick Response." *WSJ,* 25 August 1986, 1, 16.

Wallace, James, and Steven Emerson. "Revenge and Anger Resound in Arab World." *U.S. News & World Report,* 28 April 1986, 27–28.

Watson, Russell, et al. "Flake or Fox?" *Newsweek,* 20 January 1986, 14–20.

———. "Kaddafi's Crusade." *Newsweek,* 7 April 1986, 20–24.

Watson, Russell, John Barry, and Milan J. Kubic. "A Syrian Smoking Gun?" *Newsweek,* 19 May 1986, 40.

Watson, Russell, John Barry, and John Walcott. "Reagan's Raiders." *Newsweek,* 28 April 1986, 26–28, 31.

Weinberger, Caspar W. *Fighting for Peace: Seven Critical Years in the Pentagon.* New York: Warner Books, 1990.

Weinraub, Bernard. "President Accuses 5 'Outlaw States' of World Terror." *NYT*, 9 July 1985, sec. A, pp. 1, 12.

———. "President Breaks All Economic Ties with the Libyans." *NYT*, 8 January 1986, sec. A, pp. 1, 7.

———. "U.S. Calls Libya Raid a Success; 'Choice Is Theirs,' Reagan Says; Moscow Cancels Shultz Talks." *NYT*, 16 April 1986, sec. A, pp. 1, 20.

———. "U.S. Sends Envoy to Elicit Support on Libya Response." *NYT*, 13 April 1986, sec. A. pp. 1, 15.

Whitaker, Mark, et al. "Targeting a 'Mad Dog.'" *Newsweek*, 21 April 1986, 20–23, 25.

Whitaker, Mark, John Walcott, and Anne Underwood. "Getting Rid of Kaddafi." *Newsweek*, 28 April 1986, 18–22, 25.

"Why Britain Backed US Air Attack on Libya." *Times*, 16 April 1986, 4.

Wilcox, Robert K. *Scream of Eagles: The Creation of Top Gun—And the U.S. Air Victory in Vietnam*. New York: John Wiley and Sons, 1990.

———. *Wings of Fury: From Vietnam to the Gulf War—The Astonishing True Stories of America's Elite Fighter Pilots*. New York: Pocket Books, 1996.

Wilson, George C. "Despite New Details, Libyan MiG Incident Still Puzzling." *WP*, 26 March 1989, sec. A, p. 16.

———. "Libyan Fighters Suspected of Firing on U.S. Aircraft." *WP*, 18 September 1980, sec. A, p. 17.

———. "Qaddafi Was a Target of U.S. Raid." *WP*, 18 April 1986, sec. A, pp. 1, 24.

———. "Reagan Denounces Warning by Qaddafi on Retaliation." *WP*, 3 January 1986, sec. A, pp. 1, 22.

———. "Reagan Pulling U.S. Forces Back as Libya Episode Cools." *LAT*, 20 February 1983, sec. I, pp. 1, 18.

———. "U.S. Fighters Chase Libyan Warplanes in Patrol Confrontation." *WP*, 26 September 1980, sec. A, p. 8.

———. "U.S. Planes Retaliate for Libyan Attack." *WP*, 25 March 1986, sec. A, pp. 1, 13.

———. "U.S. Releases Photos of Libyan Jets; Videotape Shows MiG Fighter Was Armed, Pentagon Says." *WP*, 6 January 1989, sec. A, pp. 1, 22.

Wilson, George C., and Fred Hiatt. "Navy Again Strikes Libyan Boats, Radar; Qaddafi is Warned." *WP*, 26 March 1986, sec. A, pp. 1, 22.

Wilson, George C., and Don Oberdorfer. "U.S. Plans Gulf War Game: Operation to Display Loyalty to Friends." *WP*, 13 October 1981, sec. A, pp. 1, 17.

Winnefeld, James A., and Dana J. Johnson. *Joint Air Operations: Pursuit of Unity in Command and Control, 1942–1991*. Annapolis, Md.: Naval Institute Press, 1993.

Wiskari, Werner. "Qaddafi Attacks U.S. 'Provocations.'" *NYT*, 21 August 1981, sec. A, p. 11.

Woodward, Bob. "CIA Anti-Qaddafi Plan Backed." *WP*, 3 November 1985, sec. A, pp. 1, 19.

———. "Gadhafi Target of Secret U.S. Deception Plan." *WP*, 2 October 1986, sec. A, pp. 1, 12–13.

e Libya Firm Message." *WP*, 26 N.

the CIA 1981–1987. New York: Simo.

rdorfer. "State Dept. Acted to Block ι

87, sec. A, pp. 1, 27.

ie West: Headlong into Confrontation?

13–41.

nistory. Baltimore, Md.: Johns Hopkins University

ie Year in Review 1986." *Naval Aviation News* 69 (July–August 1987): 4–13.

Index

ing by Qaddafi, 16–18; early history of, 3–5; economic reforms under Qaddafi, 17–18; increased dissension following El Dorado Canyon, 220–21; independence, 9–11; industrial facilities as targets of U.S. strike, 148; intervention in Chad, 73, 78–81, 225; Islamic Legion, 149; Italian colonization, 7–9; Libyan Revolution, 11–13; military facilities as targets of U.S. strike, 148–49; Popular Resistance Forces, 148, 149, 153; reaction to Gulf of Sidra incident, 61, 62–63; society and culture in 2002, 238–39; and Soviet support, 15, 26–27, 84, 215–16; targets in, for retaliatory strikes, 116–18, 148–52; UN sanctions imposed over Pan Am 103 and UTA 772, 233–34; U.S. mission in, 30; in World War II, 9–10

Libya: Aims and Vulnerabilities, 39

Libyan Arab Air Defense Command (LAADC), 139, 153

Libyan Arab Air Force (LAAF), 50, 74, 78, 123–26, 133, 134, 139, 153, 195

Libyan Arab Force, 9

Libyan exiles: assessment of possible activity of, 86–87; CIA recruits and trains, 41; death penalty imposed upon, 81; Qaddafi's liquidation campaign against, 43–44, 82; Tulip operation, 101, 103–4

Libyan targets, for retaliatory strikes, 116–18, 148–52

Lockerbie, Scotland, 232–36

Lorence, Paul, 190, 197, 199

Lugar, Richard G., 210

Lujac-21, 178

Mali, 22

Mandela, Nelson, 234

Mansur, May Elias, 143

Marine Fighter-Attack Squadrons: VMFA 115 "Fighting Silver Eagles," 49

Martin, David, 140

Mauz, Henry H. Jr., 130, 170, 175

McCarthy, John, 218

McFarlane, Robert C., 93, 100

McInerney, Thomas G., 161, 164, 165–66, 175, 183, 198

McMahon, John, 87

McWerthy, John, 75

media, U.S.: and disinformation campaign against Qaddafi, 224; on-site reports of El Dorado Canyon, 186, 188; and Oper-

ation Rose, 118; Reagan administration's manipulation of, 71–72; reports by, disrupt Operation Early Call, 75–76; reports by, of "Prime Pump" strike plans, 116; speculation about El Dorado Canyon, 180–81

Meese, Edwin, 60

al-Meghrahi, Abd al-Basit Muhammad, 234–35

MiG-21 Fishbed, 57

MiG-23 Flogger, 2, 27, 52, 124, 192, 193, 228–30

MiG-25 Foxtrot, 27, 52, 124, 125, 133

Mississippi (CGN 40), 49

Mitterand, François, 80, 173

Montgomery, Bernard L., 9

Moore, George C., 24

Morocco, 44

Morris, Richard V., 5

Morton, Elaine, 110

Moynihan, Daniel P., 69

Mubarak, Husni, 65, 82, 102–3, 227

Muczynski, Lawrence M. "Music," 51–56, 57–58

al-Mukhtar, Shaykh Umar, 8

Mulroney, Brian, 212

Muntasser, Sunni, 230

al-Muqaryaf, Muhammad Yusuf, 41, 81

Murat Sidi Bilal Training Camp, 150, 162, 190–91

Mussolini, Benito, 8

Nafi, Uqba ibn, 4

Nanuchka II, 136

Nasser, Gamal Abdul, 10–11, 13, 19

National Front for the Salvation of Libya (NFSL), 41, 81, 85

National Security Council (NSC): Operation Flower, 101–4; Policy Review Group (PRG), 88

National Security Decision Directives (NSDDs): NSDD 14, 64; NSDD 16, 68; NSDD 27, 72; NSDD 30, 91–92, 101, 119; NSDD 138, 93, 94, 97, 101; NSDD 168, 100; NSDD 179, 100–101; NSDD 205, 113; NSDD 207, 118–19

National Security Planning Group (NSPG) meetings: approves FON exercise in Gulf of Sidra, 42–43; approves oil embargo and export restrictions, 72; discusses strategy following Rome and Vienna attacks, 109; military response plans in event of assassination, 69

About the Author

Joseph T. Stanik, a native of California, graduated with distinction from the U.S. Naval Academy in 1978. He subsequently earned a master of arts in national security affairs from the Naval Postgraduate School and an MA in secondary education from the University of Maryland, Baltimore County. He also completed the course in Modern Standard Arabic at the Defense Language Institute. During his career as a U.S. Navy surface warfare officer, he served in the *John Young* (DD 973), *Ticonderoga* (CG 47), and *Fairfax County* (LST 1193), and on the staff of the Commander, U.S. Naval Forces, Central Command (now the U.S. Fifth Fleet).

From 1989 to 1992, Stanik taught several history courses, including the history of the Middle East, and served as the associate chair of the history department at the Naval Academy, attaining the rank of master instructor and earning the Navy distinction of proven subspecialist in history. Prior to his retirement from the Navy with the rank of lieutenant commander in 1994, he worked as a historian in the Naval Historian Center and authored the monograph *"Swift and Effective Retribution": The U.S. Sixth Fleet and the Confrontation with Qaddafi.*

Since leaving active duty, Stanik has served as the social studies instructor at the Walbrook Maritime Academy in Baltimore. He resides in Arnold, Maryland, with his wife and two sons.